OK

MARRIAGE: *Human Reality and Saving Mystery*

MARRIAGE
Human Reality and Saving Mystery

E. SCHILLEBEECKX, O.P.
*Professor of Dogmatic Theology and the History
of Theology at the Catholic University of Nijmegan*

TRANSLATED BY N. D. SMITH

Volume I: Marriage in the Old and New Testaments

Volume II: Marriage in the History of the Church

SHEED AND WARD : NEW YORK

Originally published as *Het Huwelijk: aardse werke-lijkheid en heilsmysterie,* Uitgeverij H. Nelissen, Bilt-hoven (1963). Published in two separate volumes in Great Britain under the title, *Marriage: Secular Reality and Saving Mystery, Vols. 1 & 2.*

Nihil obstat:
   Lionel Swain, S.T.L., L.S.S.
   Censor deputatus
Imprimatur:
   Patritius Casey, Vic. Gen.
   Westmonasterii, die 18a Octobris 1965

The *Nihil obstat* and *Imprimatur* are a declaration that a book or pamphlet is considered to be free from doc-trinal or moral error. It is not implied that those who have granted the *Nihil obstat* and *Imprimatur* agree with the contents, opinions, or statements expressed.

Library of Congress Catalog Card Number 66-12263

Manufactured in the United States of America

Foreword

Marriage has become, especially since the last war, the object of a great deal of lively discussion, which has concerned itself both with the experience of marriage and with our thinking about it. In the past, partly because he had still not attained a truly adult status and partly because of his obedience in faith to the word of God, the Christian layman turned to his priest or minister for guidance in all marriage questions. The priest or minister in his turn tended to fall back on the theology he had been taught as a student at the seminary or theological college. Our present time has, however, witnessed a complete breakthrough in this monopoly of clerical and theological authority. Experts in many fields—among them psychologists, sociologists, psychiatrists, medical practitioners, historians, philosophers, and even novelists —now have an authoritative contribution to make on the subject, and rightly so.

In the past, the theologian had traditionally little regard for the various levels of meaning and experience in human life, tending to approach the question from an exclusively theological point of view. His experience as a confessor may well have helped to correct and amplify his theological background. The considerable amount of knowledge concerning human behaviour which, in the course of the church's history, has accumulated in theological manuals may also have influenced him. Nevertheless, his approach was always fundamentally theological. Now, however, he frequently finds his theses challenged or even flatly contradicted by experts in psychology, sociology, philosophy, and kindred subjects. There is a constant clash of views which surrounds and necessarily affects married people. Frequently this is occasioned by the fact that the theologian or expert in some particular field tends to overstep the limits of his own special sphere of knowledge. Theologians, for example, would like to regulate human psychology according to their own theological views, while psychologists are often inclined to think that what they have to say completely invalidates the *dicta* of the theologians. In the meantime married Christians, whose circumstances of life confront them with all kinds of problems and difficulties, become more and more uncertain, confused as they are by the many different statements they hear on the subject of marriage.

Along with all those who study human behaviour, the theologian shares the duty of clearing away the uncertainties which stem from ignorance, misconception, or confusion due to an inadequate synthesis of apparently contradictory views. If he is successful in this task, the believer ought to be able to live a better life with and within that uncertainty which is inherent in the mystery in which man finds himself, and to which he is called to surrender himself.

The theologian has a modest function here, but for the believer what he has to say is of fundamental importance. For this reason I am fully conscious of my responsibility as a theologian here, and at the same time of my inability to provide a completely satisfactory synthesis. The theologian should never keep silent merely in order to play safe. On the other hand he should never speak out merely in order to pay court to fashion. He must be cautious in faith, but this same faith also constrains him to be bold. His is not a "free" calling or profession, for he is always subject to the authority of the church, though subject in Christian freedom.

Theology lives by man's experience of his own existence and by patiently listening to the Word of God. God's word was addressed to the world and his deeds were performed for the world. In revealing himself to man, the word of God at the same time revealed man to himself. A systematic theology of marriage, such as the one attempted in outline in this book, stands a reasonable chance of success only if it manages to clarify both the word of God concerning man, and man's experience of his own existence in the light of the demands made by the situation in which he finds himself living today. A complete and finished theology of marriage is, however, out of the question. Marriage is confronted by numerous problems, and it is these which occupy the centre of interest in this study.

Among these contemporary problems may be included the psychological and social aspects of marriage, the question of "mixed marriages," the secular dimension of marriage and (linked to this) the question of civil marriage, celibacy (considered both on its own and in connection with the secular priesthood), and marital difficulties and the allied problem of responsible parenthood. These are all problems which cannot be solved neatly, and which in any case can be properly understood only when seen within a total vision which embraces the whole anthropological reality of human sexuality, and at the same time within a mature submission to faith. Seen in isolation these problems are almost devoid of meaning, and no valid or lasting solution to them is possible, since the very thing which helps to determine the answer to these questions is in this way by-passed.

In this work, which is to appear in several volumes, the aim will be to try to combine an anthropological understanding of human sexuality and marriage with a total Christian vision of marriage. With this aim in mind, then, it will be the author's constant endeavour to throw light upon man's experience of his own existence. First and foremost, however, an attempt will be made to establish what it is that the Bible has to tell us about man's experience of marriage—in the Old Testament, from the point of view of Israel's faith in Yahweh, and, in the New Testament, from the point of view of man's experience of the redemptive mystery of Christ.

Moving on in history, the author will trace the church's attempts to give concrete form to the fundamental biblical vision of man and marriage in circumstances which have always been changing and which are constantly posing new problems. After all, it is obvious that no solution can ever be reached simply by quoting at random from the Bible, the writings of the church Fathers, the medieval schoolmen, or here and there an isolated pronouncement of the church.

Although the subject of marriage is examined in this book on a broad basis of positive theology, I feel strongly that this basis is still too narrow and insufficient. But there must, I suppose, be limits, for the writer as well as for the reader. I have carefully avoided introducing topics or individual matters simply because they are interesting in themselves, and have confined myself to those things in Scripture and in the tradition of the church which are really relevant to the subject of the human reality of marriage, its constant state of development, its value and importance for those of us who believe, and its significance for our faith. This, then, forms the substance of the first two volumes of this work. Later on, guided by what has been learnt from an examination of Scripture and tradition, I shall consider the whole vital problem as it faces us today and as it is reflected in the positive treatment accorded to the subject in these earlier volumes.

To trace the development of man's, and believing man's, idea of marriage in a spirit of impartial detachment can in itself have a liberating effect. It can help us to see that man never holds a "lease" on truth, but must discover it again and again for himself in situations which are constantly new, and thereby learn to see it more clearly. On the other hand, the inner continuity which can be discerned within the apparent vagaries of life does show that this awareness of the truth—our relative, partial comprehension of it—is nonetheless regulated by the absolute reality which is always beyond our reach but which we know continuously nourishes and refreshes us.

Until recently I had no intention of allowing the various parts of this work, which are so intimately connected, to be published separately. The scope of the entire work has, however, become greatly extended, and it will undoubtedly be some time before the next part is completed. For these reasons, I have decided to allow these earlier parts to be published separately before the rest. My decision to do this has been reached also out of a sense of obligation towards my publisher, who has been patient for so long and who has now, quite reasonably, begun to press me. The next volume should, if all goes well, appear quite soon after these first two volumes.

E. Schillebeeckx, O.P.

Nijmegen, 6 September 1963

Contents

Foreword   v

General Introduction: The Modern Pattern of Marriage as
an Opportunity for Grace   xv

Introduction to Volumes I and II: A Secular Reality Enters
Salvation   xxxi

VOLUME I: MARRIAGE IN THE OLD AND NEW
TESTAMENTS   1

PART 1: MARRIAGE IN THE DIVINE
REVELATION OF THE OLD TESTAMENT   5

INTRODUCTION   7

1 THE OLD TESTAMENT TEACHING ON MARRIAGE   11
   Secular Marriage as a Gift of Creation   11
      The Theology of Marriage in the Account of Creation   11
      Human Sexuality and Eroticism in the Song of
      Solomon   27
   Marriage as Revealing the Community between Yahweh
   and Israel   31
      Preliminary Theological Observations   31
      The Covenant of Grace Proclaimed by the Prophets
      in the Image of Marriage   34
      The Day-to-Day Experience of Marriage and the
      Prophetic Marriage Image; the Wisdom Literature   52

Secular Marriage Seen Through the Prism of the
Covenant of Grace   63
The Perspective of Salvation History: Marriage and
Belief in the Creation   68
"I will make of you a great nation": Marriage and the
Christ Who Was to Come   71
Conclusion: Salvation History as a Marriage Drama and
Marriage as a Prophetic Figure   76

2 THE OLD TESTAMENT ETHOS OF MARRIAGE   82
    Married Love and Founding a Family   84
    Monogamy as the Ideal to Which Israel Aspired   89
    The Husband's Right to Divorce   91
    Mixed Marriages in the Old Testament   94

3 THE OLD TESTAMENT SOLEMNISATION OF MARRIAGE   97

PART 2: MARRIAGE IN THE MESSAGE OF THE
NEW TESTAMENT   103

    INTRODUCTION   105

4 THE NEW TESTAMENT TEACHING ON MARRIAGE   107
    Marriage and Christ's Covenant of Grace with the
    Church   107
        The Covenant with the Heavenly Bridegroom at the
        Second Coming   107
        Christ's Bridal Relationship with the Church on Earth   110
        "This is a great mystery" (Eph v. 32)   111
        "Love, as Christ loved the church" (Eph v. 25)   113
    The Primacy of the Bridal Relationship with Christ,
    Even in Marriage Itself   119
        "Unmarried for the kingdom of God"   119
        "Marriage in the Lord": the Christian Secular Life of
        Marriage   133

5 THE NEW TESTAMENT MORAL TEACHING ON MARRIAGE   141
    The Absolute Indissolubility of Marriage   141
        Jesus' Statement   142

Contents

The Becoming One of Man and Wife and the
Community of Faith 155
Paul's Opposition to Mixed Marriage 170
Patterns of Behaviour 171
"The husband is the head of the wife": Biblical
Assertion, or Simply Social Pattern? 171
The Condemnation of Porneia 201

CONCLUSION TO PART 2 206

Bibliography 209
Index of Biblical References 213

VOLUME II: MARRIAGE IN THE HISTORY OF
THE CHURCH 225

INTRODUCTION 231

1 THE FORMATION OF CHURCH MARRIAGE 233
The Environment of the First Four Centuries 233
Christian Marriage in the Early Centuries 244
Christian Marriage from the Fourth to the Eleventh
Centuries 256
Secular Marriage, Contracted Civilly and in the Family 256
The Formation of a Non-Obligatory Ecclesiastical
Liturgy of Marriage 260
The priestly marriage blessing or veiling 260
Tendencies within the church to make marriage an
ecclesiastical affair: the Pseudo-Isidorian Decretals 266
The Movement Towards an Exclusively Ecclesiastical
Contract of Marriage 272
The Sacramental Nature of Marriage: the Eleventh to
the Thirteenth Centuries 280
Spiritual Communion and Sexual Intercourse: The
Indissolubility of Consummated Marriage 287
Marriage as a Sacrament 302
The Marriage liturgy of the church as a point of
departure 303

Marriage as a sacramentum *or sacral symbol*   312
Marriage as a sacrament in the technical sense: one
of the seven sacraments   327
Marriage as an effective saving sign   332
Marriage: Secular Reality and Saving Mystery   338

2 THE CONCEPTION OF MARRIAGE IN THE EASTERN CHURCHES   344

3 THE POST-TRIDENTINE PERIOD   357
The Tridentine Form of the Marriage Contract   357
Post-Tridentine Speculation about Marriage as Contract
and as Sacrament   370
Modern Secularisation and the Reactions of the Church   373

CONCLUSION: THE RELATION OF MARRIAGE TO THE CHURCH   378

Epilogue: Conclusion to Volumes I and II   381
Bibliography   398
Index of Patristic, Theological and Dogmatic Sources   405

General Introduction

The modern pattern of marriage as an opportunity for grace

It is commonplace nowadays to hear the modern pattern of marriage referred to with scorn, even from the pulpit. This black-and-white judgment certainly lacks subtlety, and I very much doubt whether it is at all just. There have been enormous structural changes in our society during the last hundred and fifty years, and these changes show no signs of ceasing. If we look impartially at present-day married life against this background of social change, we can come to only one conclusion: that never before in the history of man has married life been led back in such a remarkable way to its original, authentic shape and form as it has today.

Before the nineteenth century, the inner stability of marriage and the family was for a great part derived from objective situations and factors which lay outside marriage itself.[1] The family and the extended family of parents, grandparents, children, grand-

[1] A great deal has been written in the last decade, especially concerning the influence of social changes on marriage. See Bibliography (N.B.—Bibliographical references in the footnotes appear mainly in an abbreviated form. The full references will be found in the bibliography at the end of the book. Only in certain cases, such as where detailed reference is made to the book in the text, does the footnote, and not the bibliography, contain the full reference).

children, married children, and even of resident employees, sometimes embracing the entire locality and the village itself—these formed, as it were, a single economic unit of a patriarchal and authoritarian kind. The smaller family community and the larger community merged into one another. There was constant interchange and movement between the one and the other. No doorbell kept the two communities apart. Marriage meant entry into a prearranged social entity, a working community which more or less coincided with the extended "family" outlined above.

The economic and social life of the people was carried by marriage and the family, but married life and the family were also supported by society. This does not mean that the personal and subjective aspect of marriage was entirely lacking. It was there, but as a silent background, and it was taboo. It was precisely because this personal and subjective side of marriage was present, though silent and inconspicuous, that public, social, and economic life was to some extent permeated by the family spirit. People worked with those with whom they lived. What preserved marriage was not so much the married partners as the entire structure of this working community and of the whole of society. The superior power of objective social relationships predominated over personal life. The extended family was held together by communally shared work.

In the same way, though love was not precluded, the choice of partners in marriage was determined far more by objective factors and the prevailing situation. Marriage set a seal on the status of a young couple within the working community of the extended family. There is an old German proverb, going back to the peasant family communities, which says that "love ends when marriage begins." This should be taken with a grain of salt, of course, but it does neatly sum up the situation. There was clearly a great difference between the enjoyable game of love before marriage and marital love itself. Married love seemed to be of a totally different order.

The structural changes which have taken place in society, especially since the rise of industrialization and the urban communities, have profoundly affected the position of marriage and family life. The family has suffered a functional loss. A wide variety of functions previously performed by the larger family community have been taken over by units outside the family. This process has continued unabated, eventually reaching the present-day situation, in which the State machinery—in its economic, social and political aspect—has assumed almost all of the functions of the older family unit. Society is divided into various specialised sectors, which form a single entity confronting the family. Living and working have become separated from each other.

One important consequence of all this functional loss is that marriage and the family have been, so to speak, thrown back upon themselves. Marriage no longer means that the partners are automatically incorporated into the objective and fixed social pattern of the extended family community. This firm foundation for stable married life is lacking, and the newly married couple of today has to start at the very beginning and, what is more, it must start alone, or rather as two people alone. The objective social situation into which the married couple was previously introduced as a matter of course no longer exists.

But the decline of this objective social situation has led to a greater freedom and scope in the personal and subjective aspect of married life. Marriage and the family, thrown back on their own resources, are compelled to think about their own essential nature. I would go so far as to say that there is only one function left to marriage and the family—that of being marriage and being family. All that remains to the family and to marriage is this personal and subjective aspect, this intimate, inner life, since all the other functional aspects of marriage and family life have been assumed by the various specialised departments of modern society.

Within an increasingly functionalised and technical social pattern which undoubtedly challenges the family to a very great extent, marriage and family life have become an oasis, a refuge, an island of safety and a place of security. Modern society itself has forced marriage into this position. Married couples of today realise that they are faced with the task of building up their marriage into a place of security. This security is no longer given to them when they marry. The task of creating it is something which they have to do themselves. This task is all the more urgent by reason of the fact that the home is no longer the place of work. Work today does not serve to unite the family. On the contrary, it tends to divide the father and the mother, both of whom frequently work in different places. At the end of their working day, however, both fall back on marriage and on their family life together.

This functional loss in married and family life has resulted in married couples being faced with an unknown future which they have to build up for themselves. But this functional loss has also been accompanied by a change in the structure of the family itself. As a result of this internal change, the greatest emphasis is now placed upon the so-called "primary relationships," that is, the relationships existing between the married partners themselves and between the parents and their children. (This shift of emphasis is clearly reflected in the extent of modern legislation concerning the rights of married women and children.) Married life has been thrown back on itself, and its stability and fidelity can no longer rely upon the extrinsic organization of society for support. Married stability and faithfulness are now supported from within, by the marriage itself—by the mutual dependence of the married couple upon each other. This does not mean that society is indifferent to marriage and the family, or that it no longer exercises any form of control over them. The standards by which society judges the family—the husband, the wife, and the children—have changed considerably, however, and are now in tune with the primary relationships within the family referred to above.

Newly married couples of today have no firm exterior support to rely on. They find themselves in an isolated position in which they have only each other to depend on. This situation has, however, opened our eyes to the interpersonal relationship of the married state, and this personal relationship between the partners has now become the mainstay of married and family life. The patriarchal and authoritarian pattern of family relationships has gone, and a more friendly relationship of companionship and comradeship has taken its place in marriage. Now that the authority of the father in the patriarchal system is no longer necessary even to provide leadership in the family's communal working life, more and more importance is placed upon the existence—between the husband and wife, and between the parents and children—of an inner unity and affection, a mutual trust and a close interdependence, whereby each member of the family can find support in the other members when the need arises. Modern marriage is, in a word, democratic.

The functional loss which has made itself felt within the family increasingly over the course of the last century and a half has in particular affected the wife and mother at home. She above all has more and more to rely upon herself. The increase in the number and application of household aids has given her greater freedom and scope. This has been accompanied by a gradual emancipation of women, whose personal qualities and potentialities have become the object of considerable attention.

If, in the sixteenth century, it was possible to write: "I love you, because you are my wife," there is no doubt that modern man would express this the other way round: "You are my wife, because I love you." It would be wrong to draw such a sharp contrast between the two types of marriage, of course, but this sharp delineation does at least show how much man's attitude to marriage has changed, and that there is a noticeable difference between the pattern of marriage and family life now and in the older form of human society.

The loss of the functional aspect of the family brought about by the changes in the structure of society, and the dissociation of marriage from the older forms of human communal life, have stripped marriage of all its outer coverings. As a result we are now able to see what, in all its naked reality, marriage really is. This gives us an enormous opportunity to work for the deepening and intensifying of married life. It is possible to see it as a new offer of grace, a new and splendid opportunity for modern marriage to play a leading part in man's salvation. Despite the fact that modern family life is in a vulnerable situation, very many—indeed most—marriages do not break up. We have no cause to despair of mankind, but rather every reason to be optimistic.

The relaxation of the older social ties, and the resultant dependence of marriage on its personal intersubjective side has, it has been claimed, also brought another, more casual type of modern marriage into being. In my opinion, this is merely the darker side of an otherwise shining coin. Then there is the question whether these easy-come, easy-go marriages, so often short-lived, mark a decline from the married life of the past. Statisticians assure us that extramarital and premarital relationships are on the increase, even among religious people. The question that comes to mind here is not so much whether such relationships are more frequent, as whether they do not perhaps follow a different course. It should hardly be necessary to add that prostitution is a mere drop in the ocean of our contemporary society compared to what it was up to the beginning of the present century. At that time it was practically impossible to walk along the quaysides of Amsterdam or the alleyways of Antwerp without being accosted a dozen times. Today these places are as quiet as the by-ways of a small provincial town. In many middle-class families, it was regarded as "normal" to visit prostitutes in those days.

Have we really declined so much in our standards? In my opinion, it is our manner of behaving that is different; it is very difficult to say for certain whether morality in general, taken in

conjunction with our sexual life, has in fact declined or im-
proved. We have no clear analysis on which to base any positive
statement. I am not in any way amazed at the figures given in
the Kinsey Report on the sexual life of the Americans—everything would seem to indicate that these high numbers could
easily be rivalled by what happened under the *ancien régime* in
the dim and distant past. No, it is the interpretation of these
figures which disturbs me—that these high figures should state
the norm of human behaviour. Leaving out of account for the
present the fact that man's sense of the Absolute is less strong
than it was and is still diminishing, but taking every other factor
into consideration, I would, on the contrary, see the modern
marriage-type in an extremely hopeful light. Moreover, I would
retain this optimism in spite of all the new dangers with which
marriage is today associated, and despite all the blunders committed on all sides in marriage.

This new marriage-type does, however, present more difficult
problems for children of today, and we are not always sufficiently
alert to these. In the past, of course, the children's future presented no serious problem. It was invariably mapped out in advance—it was assumed, from a very early age, that they would
take their place in the working community of the extended
family into which they had been born. What the adults in this
family did now, the children would carry on doing later. All the
child's experience had, as it were, been lived out for him in advance, and his future was all around him for him to see. In this
way there was no real future. Children of our time, however, are
in a very real sense faced by a future—an unknown, uncertain
future—as a result of the divorce which has taken place between
the home and the place of work, and between the family unit
and modern society as a whole. For our children the future of
necessity implies a personal choice, a decision between many possibilities. For them there is a diminishing sense of security.

A certain incompatibility will continue to exist between the
new society and the new family pattern, and the children of such

families will find it difficult to adjust themselves to society, until the modern type of marriage and family finds suitable ways and means of preparing its children to take their place in the new, large, and "alien" society. This element of inadaptability is bound to be felt all the more keenly so long as the new marriage-type still contains—as it frequently does—residual traces of the older patriarchal and authoritarian pattern of family life, an inevitable cause of conflict—either open or unspoken—between parents and children.

On the other hand, it is frequently asserted that the introduction into marriage of what those who make this claim call "romantic love"—the discovery, in other words, of the personal aspect of marriage—is a phenomenon peculiar to this period of human history and one which will soon pass. In my opinion, history—past history—proves them wrong. It is no new phenomenon which faces us today, but the re-emergence of something which is as old as man himself. There has always been romantic love. It has always been present in every racial group, differing according to the temperament of the people. In the past, however, it was seldom the subject of discussion. When it was discussed, it was always as the love which was experienced outside marriage. It is only recently that love in this sense has come to be regarded as a structural principle of married life.

Even for the great philosophers of ancient Greece, Plato included, the wife's function was to bring up the children. The art of love was practised with paramours or with boys, not with a man's own wife. The loved one was seldom the partner in marriage. In the Middle Ages this became a leading theme in literature, especially in Provence and Brittany. There was unquestionably something of a reaction in this phenomenon. De Rougemont has written that the story of Tristram and Iseult would be unthinkable if they had been married;[2] and a French court chaplain,

---

[2] His book, *Passion and Society* is a clear, though not always reliable, illustration of this view. See also: C. S. Lewis, *The Allegory of Love*, New York, Oxford, 1938; J. Langdon-Davies, *Sex, Sin and Sanctity*, London,

one Andreas, clearly defined the medieval morality in this respect: "Love cannot exist between man and woman in marriage."[3] Nothing was in fact said about married love in the theology of marriage of those times, which was strictly canonical in its orientation.

When the theme of married love was praised or celebrated in the Middle Ages—as, for example, by Hugh of St. Victor—this love was treated independently, in such a way that the loving relationship was not connected intrinsically with sexual intercourse in marriage, but rather—for reasons extrinsic to this marital love—associated from outside by God with the living marital relationship.[4] Hugh's idea of married life was, however, too much derived from the marriage of the virgin Mary, and his attitude towards sexual relationships was strongly marked by the characteristic pessimism of the Middle Ages.[5] Were this not so, the essence of his synthesis might well be regarded as representative of, and as foreshadowing the modern view of, marriage. This must also be seen, however, against the background of the fact that the concept of "marital rights" (*debitum coniugale*: the mutual right of partners in marriage to each other's bodies) was developed within the spiritual environment of the canonists and within a historical situation in which the marriage of love was out of favour.[6] Indeed, Albert the Great was one of the few at

---

1954; D. de Rougemont, "The Crisis of the Modern Couple," in R. Anshen, *The Family*, pp. 325 ff. Also relevant to the study of the medieval view of love is G. Paré, *Le roman de la rose et la scolastique courtoise*, Paris and Ottawa (1941).

3 *De amore*, published by Trajel, Hafnia, 1892, p. 172.

4 W. Göszmann, "Die Bedeutung der Liebe in der Eheauffassung Hugos von St. Viktor und Wolframs von Eschenbach," *MTZ*, 5 (1954), pp. 205–13. We are not, however, able fully to support Göszmann's interpretation; see Volume 2 of this book.

5 M. Müller, *Die Lehre des hl. Augustinus von der Paradiesehe und ihre Auswirkung in der Sexualethik des 12. und 13. Jahrhunderts bis Thomas von Aquin*, Regensburg (1954).

6 See, among others, P. Delhaye, *Permanence du droit naturel* (Analecta Mediaevalia Namurcensia, no. 10), Louvain and Lille (1961), p. 87. But this writer's view needs to be approached with circumspection. Even St. Paul

that time who tried to find some measure of reconciliation, within marriage itself, between marital love and sexual relationships, and to establish the need for a loving relationship between the partners in marriage on the basis that it is marital love which makes sexual intercourse human.[7]

I am well aware of the fact that life is more powerful than theory. In the actual practice and experience of marriage, love has doubtless always been known. And the fact that the literature of that period was to some extent a reaction is also an indication of the presence of romantic love, though this was in particular a theme for extramarital relationships. It is hardly surprising, then, that James of Vitry should have written in 1240 (for this as well as for other reasons) that "the married state is more difficult than the rule of many monastic orders."[8]

But such a one-sided view of the situation in the Middle Ages, although contrasting favourably with the patristic view of marriage, would be fundamentally unjust. Asked why she was so concerned with infidelity and the tragic aspect of married life in her books, Sigrid Undset said: "Good is inexpressible; only evil has a history." If in a hundred years' time men were to judge the twentieth-century morality of marriage from the films that have been produced in our time, they might be able to understand one aspect of marriage in this century, but the other aspect—the unspeaking love and the silent loyalty of so many marriages—they would miss completely. It is possible that certain periods have left no record of marital love because this was simply accepted as a matter of course and not deemed worthy of special theological analysis. It is not very surprising, therefore,

---

referred to a "debitum" (1 Cor vii. 3) and the Romans to "honos matrimonii"; see A. Steinwenter, *Corpus Iuris*, 7, *RAC*, 2 (1959), pp. 459-60.

[7] A fine study of Albert's view of marriage has been written by L. Brandl, *Die Sexualethik des hl. Albertus*, Regensburg (1955).

[8] Quoted by D. Lindner, *Der "usus matrimonii." Eine Untersuchung über seine sittliche Bewertung in der Moraltheologie alter und neuer Zeit*, Munich (1929), no. 161.

that there have been many objections to de Rougemont's view of the extramarital character of romantic love in the West.

Furthermore, historians often lose sight of the fact that—as our analysis will in due course show—the medieval attitude to marriage was not directly aimed at the reality of marriage itself, but was rather the result of approaching marriage from a "formalised" juridical standpoint. That is to say, marriage was seen purely in the light of its juridical structure, which had to be known for the proper administration of justice in matrimonial lawsuits. This is a fundamentally one-sided way of looking at marriage, of course. We must, however, grasp the consequences of this view. By definition, it is bound to preserve silence on the subject of married love, which—while certainly taken for granted—is scarcely able to act as the starting point for a canonically-orientated theology of marriage. The reproach levelled at the human experience of marriage in the past by certain writers is, therefore, less a criticism of that experience of marriage itself, considered as an existential reality, than of this "formalised" theology of marriage.

The fact that present-day theology and philosophy are constantly posing new problems in connection with marriage cannot be traced back to the abstract book-learning of a handful of out-of-touch scholars. There are also sociological reasons for it. Thrown back on its own resources, contemporary married life is itself asking about the personal interior aspect of marriage. The actual situation has forced the theologian and the philosopher to overstep the frontiers of juridical abstraction, to go straight to the reality itself, and to consider the whole subject afresh in the light of the traditional view. It is not the theologians and the philosophers who have posed the problem. It is life itself. Nothing that is completely new or unheard-of has been discovered, of course. But a start has been made on a "thematic" treatment of married love and interpersonal relationship, and the conclusion has already been reached that this is the true structural principle of marriage and the family, the factor which binds the marriage and the family together.

Going even further in this direction, efforts have also been made, as yet perhaps tentative and fumbling, to locate the fundamental, ethical principle of the morality of marriage in its interpersonal relationship. Seen in this perspective, the traditional theses may be more clearly justified. New aspects and shades of meaning inherent in them may be brought to light. In exceptional cases it may even be necessary to make a complete revision of the traditional view; and here and there, perhaps, the result may be simply an open question. In view of the fact that stability in marriage can no longer be provided from outside, everything possible is being done to give married and family life stability and unity from within, having recourse to all the aspects of marriage which are inherent in it, through the fidelity of fully human, marital intersubjectivity. For the religious person, this means that conjugal fidelity is only possible in our society if our belief in God is so strong that we can also believe in the depth of our fellow human beings despite everything.

But the modern marriage-type does at the same time need to be geared to social services of every kind. The new situation in which marriage is placed can lead to the family being isolated. One of the consequences of the extremely functionalised character of modern society is that personal problems —sorrow as well as joy—remain within the family circle. It is precisely in these personal elements that society leaves the members of the family alone. That is why there is such need for a comprehensive spiritual "national health service" to provide spiritual, psychological, psychiatric and other kinds of assistance at all levels for families which, in modern society, have been thrown back on their own resources. The task which partners in marriage and parents have to undertake within the family has become so delicate that outside help is more urgently required than ever before.

It is not so much that a new pattern of married and family life has been created, but rather that every married person and each family realises that there is a task to be accomplished. What each marriage has to do is to establish its own pattern of married life, building this up on a foundation of the inspirational force of an inner conviction and an inner plan of life. This can no longer be a question of settling into a traditional way of family life, a pattern previously provided by the parents and grandparents and the generations preceding them. It must now take the form of a new, personal creation *ab ovo*, and each family has to achieve this in its own way. Anyone who has recently observed married couples engaged in this activity is bound to realise that their successful attempts to establish new values are not simply the result of fine words originating in the speculative minds of thinkers who have no practical experience of marriage. It is clearly a living and very wonderful reality, though often a hard one, in the struggle of two young people to make something of their marriage. The fact that the efforts of so many are obviously crowned with success makes it possible and safe for us to claim that, in comparison with marriages in previous ages, present-day married and family life has made great progress in inner values and religious depth.

We should indeed be wasting our time if we were to stand still, rapt in envious admiration of the past. We can feel nothing but respect and admiration when we look around and see how the modern family, despite the isolation and vulnerability to which it is subject, is able to achieve such depth in interpersonal relationships—practically the only buttress left to support the entire building. I do not believe those preachers who see nothing but materialism and egoism in the life of families today. Materialism is there, but certainly no more—and no less—than in the past. Or is it, perhaps, more materialistic now to long for a radio or a television set than it was in the past to long for a new easy chair for the drawing room in which no one ever set foot.

But let us not forget that in previous generations there were families whose pattern of life was already the same as that of the modern type of family, in that they were similarly thrown back on themselves, but which were obliged to manage without the social benefits of modern state welfare. The respect and admira-

tion that we feel for these families is even greater. Utterly dependent upon their own resources, such families struggled on
with the business of living because they were borne up by their
disarming trust in God. But our age recognises that the passing
of this "order"—which was not in fact an order—was inevitable.
Human values were violated, but other values—quieter and
deeper values—flourished out of sight of profane eyes. Only
heaven can pay a fitting tribute to these values. Our view of them
is often one-sided and unjust.

Against the background of this historical situation, in which the
inner and interpersonal aspect of married life has gained a measure
of scope and freedom, it should be helpful to throw some theological light on the interior sources of marriage in its worldly and
religious dimensions. In this context our attention is especially
directed towards certain actual problems. For this reason I have
decided to avoid as far as possible a technical analysis, but at the
same time not to yield to the temptation to edify. What follows
is strictly a theological examination of the secular reality which
is marriage, and which moreover—precisely in its secular aspect
—is a sacrament of a religious reality. The distinctive quality of
this particular sacrament is to be found less in some secular, earthbound form of a supernatural reality than in a reality secular by
origin which has acquired a deeper meaning in the order of salvation in which we live and which, for this reason, points to
something higher.

Whenever we say that the marriage of two Christians is a
sacrament, what we are implying is that God himself *does* something, and gives us tangible proof of his divine action. It is a
sacred sign that God's activity becomes visible to us all in faith.
It is, of course, true that even before the marriage is contracted,
the love existing between two people who are engaged is not
outside God's influence. For they do not come to the altar in
order to strip their human love for each other of its human
quality. *Ubi caritas et amor, Deus ibi est*—where two people
have found each other in true love, God is already in their midst,

and this love is sacred. By permitting these two to find each other in love, God has already begun in them what he will finally accomplish in the sacrament of marriage. God indeed had a share in this love from the very beginning. A sacrament is always the culminating point of an event set in motion in us by God. But the living God aims to bring about something more profound in the love of a boy for a girl and of a girl for a boy in and through the sacrament of marriage. It is his personal love, going out to the bride and bridegroom as a bridal couple, that becomes visible and tangible in the sacramental sign of the marriage.

Christ is present when the marriage is contracted, and he is there in order to do and to say something. In a striking gesture he makes it known to the bride and bridegroom, and to all those who are present at the event, that he himself is giving these two people, who already love each other so much, to each other for life. In these two who love each other, God himself arouses a new and greater love—a love like that which he himself has for his people, the church. The bride and bridegroom have nothing more to do here than simply to let God take his own course. All that they have to do is to say: "I will"—I will let God's activity break through in this holy sign of our mutual consent and our future life together in marriage. The exchange of marriage vows is, therefore, first and foremost a concurrence with the holy will of Christ. But it is because Christ's holy will in this case means that Christ himself wishes to give these two to each other for life, so that their human love may be able to rise above its natural limitations and become—precisely as a *human* institution—a sacred sign of a greater and deeper love, that the bride and bridegroom say "I will" unconditionally *to each other*.

This outline of the sacrament of marriage may, in its simplicity, seem attractive, but it is also disconcertingly vague. In the course of the theological examination of the subject, upon which we now propose to enter, we shall leave this attractive image far behind. But, after putting down our somewhat frightening dissecting knife at the end of the examination, and looking back without prejudice at the artless, unstudied image given here, we may well find it even more attractive than before and think of what the Bible calls one of the three things which must give the greatest joy to God and man: "a wife and husband who live in harmony" (Sir xxv. 2).

Introduction to Volumes I and II
A secular reality enters salvation

IN SEARCH OF GOD'S SAVING PURPOSE

If we are to approach the institution of marriage with the mind of faith, we must above all try to listen attentively to what God himself has said about it. It is not so much marriage itself as the significance of marriage in the life of the people of God within the history of salvation that is a fact of revelation. Theology is indeed concerned with the saving significance of a secular reality set in the framework of all the other secular realities. Because of this, it is open to comment from the biologist, the psychologist and the philosopher. The full, concrete significance of this reality can, however, be perceived only by those who listen in faith to what God himself has communicated to man on the subject. Only those who attempt to interpret the impressions left behind on this secular reality we call marriage by the presence in this world of a God-Man can hope to understand its meaning at this level. The theologian must therefore try to discover, in the life of religious mankind, how marriage was conceived by one who knew himself to have been addressed by the living God, and who himself experienced the saving acts of God in history.

We can certainly catch a glimmer of the religious significance of marriage in those aspects of marriage that appeal to us directly as religious in the life of all races and peoples. Yet this universal divine revelation, still unspoken and thus anonymous, which is apparent in the life of all peoples, leaves the real aspect of marriage in obscurity. There is only one way in which we can become fully aware of the saving mystery of marriage, and that is when God's saving acts emerge from behind the veil of anonymity. This happened, of course, when God became personally concerned with the history of one people—a people which could make no claim to deserve this election. In particular, it happened when he showed himself to be exceptionally concerned with one man in history, a man who proved to be the Son of God. The mystery accomplished by this man, the Son of God, in marriage becomes further apparent to us when we see how the community which he established still continues to try to experience marriage, supported by the ecclesiastical office which acknowledges its subjection to the one unassailable standard—its apostolic witness concerning Jesus, the historical man who was raised up as Lord.

We have to look for God's saving purpose with marriage in the divine revelation of the Old Testament. We must look for this purpose too in the good news brought to us by Christ in his new covenant. Finally, we must seek it in the life of the church which, faithful to Christ's word and deed and guided by God's Spirit, has throughout the course of history constantly striven to become more clearly aware of its significance.

VOLUME I

Marriage in the Old and New Testaments

Abbreviations

BBB	*Bonner Biblische Beiträge*
Bbl	*Biblica*
BHT	Beiträge zur historischen Theologie
BJ	*Bible de Jérusalem*, Paris (1949)
BJRL	*Bulletin of the John Rylands Library*
BKAT	*Biblische Kommentar, Altes Testament*
BL	*Bibel und Liturgie*
BOT	*De boeken van het Oude Testament*, Roermond and Maaseik
BW	*Bijbels Woordenboek*
BZAW	*Beihefte zur Zeitschrift für die alttestamentliche Wissenschaft*
CBQ	*Catholic Biblical Quarterly*
CG	*Collationes Gandavenses*
CS	*Current Sociology*
DB	H. Denzinger, *Enchiridion Symbolorum, Definitionum, et Declarationum de Rebus Fidei et Morum*, ed. C. Bannwart, SJ (1908–13[10-12]) and others (1913–60[13-30])
DBS	*Dictionnaire de la Bible, Supplément*, ed. L. Pirot and others, Paris (1928–)
DS	H. Denzinger, *Enchiridion Symbolorum*, ed. A. Schönmetzer, SJ (1962[32-])
ETL	*Ephemerides Theologicae Lovanienses*
HUCA	*Hebrew Union College Annual*
Ist	*Istina*
JQR	*Jewish Quarterly Review*

JTS	*Journal of Theological Studies*
LD	Series "Lectio Divina"
LV	*Lumière et Vie*
MD	*La Maison-Dieu*
MTZ	*Münchener Theologische Zeitschrift*
Mus	*Le Muséon*
NKS	*Nederlandse Katholiecke Stemmen*
NRT	*Nouvelle Revue théologique*
NV	*Nova et Vetera*
NvT	*Novum Testamentum*
PG	*Patrologia Graeca*, ed. J. P. Migne, Paris (1857–66)
PL	*Patrologia Latina*, ed. J. P. Migne, Paris (1844–64)
RA	*Revue anthropologique*
RAC	*Reallexikon für Antike und Christentum*
RB	*Revue biblique*
RGG	*Religion in Geschichte und Gegenwart*, Tübingen, 3rd edn, ed. K. Galling (1956–)
RHPR	*Revue d'Histoire et de Philosophie religieuses*
RSPT	*Revue des Sciences philosophiques et théologiques*
RSR	*Recherches de Science religieuse*
RSV	Revised Standard Version
RTP	*Revue de Théologie et de Philosophie*
SB	H. L. Strack and P. Billerbeck, *Kommentar zum Neuen Testament aus Talmud und Midrash*, Munich (1922–8)
SC	*Studia Catholica*
SF	*Social Forces*
ST	*Studia Theologica*
TL	*Tijdschrift voor Liturgie*
TT	*Tijdschrift voor Theologie*
TV	*Theologia Viatorum*
TWNT	*Theologisches Worterbuch zum Neuen Testament*, ed. G. Kittel, Stuttgart (1930–)
TZ	*Theologische Zeitschrift*
VD	*Verbum Domini*
VP	*Vivre et Penser*
ZAW	*Zeitschrift für die alttestamentliche Wissenschaft*
ZEE	*Zeitschrift für evangelische Ethik*
ZST	*Zeitschrift für systematische Theologie*

Part 1

MARRIAGE IN THE DIVINE
REVELATION OF
THE OLD TESTAMENT

Introduction

1. The Old Testament merits a place of special honour in any consideration of the saving reality of marriage. Of course, it is true that it is only when seen from the point of view of the complete revelation of Christ that marriage can be perceived in its full light. Nonetheless, one of the most important elements which Christianity has inherited from Israel is the Old Testament's living, almost passionate, and certainly joyous confession of everyday secular values, understood not as self-contained, but as dynamic and proceeding directly from God. The vision which we derive from the Old Testament comes as an intense relief, especially in an age of closed secularisation in marriage as well as in most other spheres. It is in the Old Testament more than anywhere else that we can come into immediate contact with the concrete experience of the goodness of secular values and realities. These are never allowed to evaporate—to become insubstantial, supernatural, and falsely mystical qualities. Nor are they ever held in contempt. In the Old Testament they are always recognised and lived as something matter-of-fact and belonging to this world. Yet this very "worldliness" was for Israel a divine miracle—the "work of his hands" and a source of grace for man.

Since marriage is first and foremost a secular value, and since it entered salvation history as a secular reality, we may reasonably expect Israel to have a great deal to impart to us as Christians, perhaps of a cautionary nature. It may well be that Israel, as the people of God, can help us not only to avoid placing too much emphasis on the sacramental aspect of this secular, anthropological reality, but also to avoid the error of underestimating this aspect of marriage. It is precisely this vision of the people of God which Christianity should strive to preserve and illuminate in the light of Christ.

2. This study of the biblical conception of marriage is theological. Our exposition of the subject will always have to rely on scientific biblical exegesis, and the all-too-easy temptation to bypass serious biblical scholarship and express lofty sentiments which have little or nothing to do with the authentic interpretation of the Bible must be firmly resisted. Our study is essentially one of dogmatic theology. Our search is for the word of God concerning marriage, the word which has been heard with a gradually increasing clarity throughout salvation history and which, at this moment of time, claims our attention with particular authority. In the first place this means that we must seek to answer the question: How did Israel, as the people of God, experience the reality of marriage?

I stress, *Israel as the people of God,* since it is frequently forgotten that everything that is "biblical"—that is to say, everything that is to be found in the Bible—is not necessarily the word of revelation, even though it is inspired. Expressions such as "biblical anthropology" or the "biblical relationship between man and woman" have a double meaning. They may just denote, quite straightforwardly, the ancient oriental, and more particularly the Semitic, view of man or of marriage; in which case, the dogmatic question as to what is "biblical" in the Old Testament in the theological sense of the word—that is, as the expression of God's word which is binding on Christians—remains unanswered. Sometimes it is simply a matter of the concrete framework, determined by the historical period and the social environment in which it is set, within which the word of God comes to us. To overlook this important dis-

tinction, especially in connection with marriage, may well result
in letting loose the forces of reaction—with regard, for example,
to modern views on marriage and the family which are set in a
different social and historical framework, but which are nonetheless reconcilable with God's word.

On the other hand, the fact remains that it pleased God to
reveal himself within a Semitic society and in the course of a
Semitic history, and from the dogmatic point of view this must
always be seen as a caution to us. We can ignore this history and
civilisation only at our peril, for it is impossible to grasp the
word of God as a pure, divine reality somehow divorced from
its human expression. It is precisely in Israelite man that the Old
Testament revelation comes to us. For this reason the Israelite
expression of God's word is not in itself determined by the historical and social setting, but is rather formed by its being at
the service of God's revelation. The form of expression and what
is expressed are, of course, different, but they cannot be separated
like the pieces of two puzzles and then put together to build up
two distinct pictures. Many aspects of Israel's social and historical
setting bear the imprint of divine revelation or of her association
with the living God. Many voices, not always in harmony with
each other, have warned against the danger of divorcing God's
word from Israel, since, by so doing, we cannot guarantee that
we shall in fact hear God's meaning more clearly.

On the other hand, "biblicism" is also pernicious. It can so
easily give the impression that theology of the so-called "speculative" kind does not appear on the stage until the first and second
acts—the exegesis of the Old and the New Testaments—are over.
But speculative theology has a distinctive and important part to
play even in these opening acts. Exegetes cannot and ought not
to take exception to the appearance of speculative theology at
this stage in the drama, unless the theologians are unscientific in
their treatment of the principles of critical exegesis or simply
neglect them altogether. If speculative theology plays its rightful
part in the first two acts, it will be able to develop organically

out of these biblical acts and then come into its own in an integral third act, without initiating a completely new play.

This is all the more important because it is remarkable how Christians of today, living, as they believe, in an age of biblical renewal, seem to listen less seriously and less obediently than in "unbiblical" times to God's Word concerning marriage. Indeed, they appear to confine their interest solely to man's experience of his own existence. But in my opinion this self-interpretation, this examination of our own human experience, only deserves to be called truly biblical and Christian when it is conducted in the light of the revelation of God's Word. It is only when we repeatedly measure our own experience of our human existence —which always contains, albeit anonymously, the element of factual revelation—against God's word concerning man and at the same time concerning himself that we really begin to practise authentic theology. Outside this sphere the threat of danger is always present, either from biblicism or from some kind of self-interpretation which is not faith, but self-justification.

1

The Old Testament Teaching on Marriage

It is possible to approach marriage in Israel from many different sides. There is first of all the experienced reality of marriage itself, as an implication of human existence. But this reality was not only seen and experienced in Israel from the vantage-point of Israel's community of grace with God; the revelation of God's Word also sheds light upon it. Israel's belief that everything was created by the God of Israel, Yahweh, and the fact that the prophetic message of the covenant of grace existing between God and his people was interpreted in terms of human marital love, together reveal the essence of marriage in the form in which it was pleasing to God.

SECULAR MARRIAGE AS A GIFT OF CREATION

The Theology of Marriage in the Account of the Creation

1. Although the universal human idea of creation is present in ancient Israel, it was not until much later that real belief in God's creation developed—through revelation in the cult of Yahweh and through the saving acts of God with his people—into a characteristically Israelite belief in creation. This belief reached its culminating point in Ezekiel and the prophets who followed

him, but especially in Deutero-Isaiah and in the Wisdom literature. The final editing of the account of the creation in the book
of Genesis is closely connected with this view of the creation.

So God created man in his own image, in the image of God he created him; male and female he created them. And God blessed them,
and God said to them, "Be fruitful and multiply, and fill the earth and
subdue it." [Gen i. 27–8, in the Priestly account of the creation.]

Then Yahweh said, "It is not good that the man should be alone; I
will make him a helper fit for him." . . . So Yahweh caused a deep
sleep to fall upon the man, and while he slept took one of his ribs and
closed up its place with flesh; and the rib which Yahweh had taken
from the man he made into a woman and brought her to the man.
Then the man said, "This at last is bone of my bones and flesh of my
flesh; she shall be called Woman [From the Man], because she was
taken out of Man." Therefore a man leaves his father and his mother
and cleaves to his wife, and they become one flesh. [Gen ii. 18–24, in
the older, Yahwist account of the creation.]

When God created man [the Adam], he made *him* in the likeness of
God. Male and female he created *them*, and he blessed *them* and
named *them* Man [Adam]. [Gen v. 1–2; this is followed by the genealogy of Adam; it is either a Priestly account, or a later editing incor-
porating elements deriving from the Priestly tradition.]

If we examine these Old Testament texts on marriage and the
relationship between man and wife—they were, of course, the
outcome of a long process of development which we will not
follow here chronologically—against the background of the views
on marriage in the ancient Near East, and in particular against
those prevalent in Canaan with its Phoenician civilisation, then
it becomes immediately apparent that faith in Yahweh in effect
"desacralised," or secularised, marriage—took it out of a purely
religious sphere and set it squarely in the human, secular sphere.
Looked at from the social point of view, there was no very
great difference between the married life of the ancient Near

East and that of Israel in Canaan,[1] but—measured against its significance within the cult of Yahweh—the difference between the two is basic.

It is important to estimate this secularisation of marriage at its true value. Worship of the fertility gods was especially rife in Canaan, where Israel had settled. (Num xxv. 3–8; Ex xxiv. 15–16; Jer ii. 20; iii. 1–2; xiii. 27; Hos *passim*.) Sexuality and procreation were seen as something mysterious belonging to the sphere of the divine. The fertility gods were deities of the forces of nature and of the cycle of fertility in man and the natural world. They were both male and female and their intercourse was regarded as the prototype of everything that happened on earth. Those who worshipped them endeavoured to ensure by means of magic rites that both their land and their wives were fertile. It was upon these gods that all fertility and the entire force of life was believed to depend, and this led to orgies of prostitution in the temples in which the deities were worshipped.

The Israelites were not always able to remain undefiled (1 Kings xiv. 24; see also Num xxv. 3–8), and again and again vigorous protests were heard in Israel against this form of ritual prostitution and associated rites. The view of marriage expressed in the book of Genesis, in contrast to the ideas prevalent among Israel's neighbours, was thus instrumental in carrying out a thorough demythologization. However, we must be careful to assess what Israel did in this respect—that is, depriving her pagan neighbours' ideas of their power—at its precise value. For both Canaan and Israel, sexuality and everything that it involved was a mysterious gift of God. The new element was not that Israel conceived sexuality as something that was not religious, or that she regarded the fruits of virility in man and of fertility in woman as being of less value as divine gifts. What was totally new was Israel's view of God. For Israel it was a question of a "new god."

The first words of the Decalogue, or Ten Commandments,

---

[1] The bibliography relevant to this chapter is given at the end of this volume. See Bibliography, Part I.

are: "I am Yahweh, your God" (Ex xx. 2)—a god who is not and was not restricted to nature or to the cycle of fertility in nature and in woman. By the association of a marriage with Yahweh and with no other god, this human event was brought directly under the protection of the free and sovereign God, the God of the covenant and of human history. In Israel, then, fertility was something which might be expected only from Yahweh's gracious, elective loving-kindness, and this was not open to force or persuasion by magic rites. It was because Israel had a totally new god that marriage in Israel was dissociated from these pagan fertility rites.

The "secularisation" of pagan marriage was the result of Israel's demythologizing of God; but at the same time marriage was placed in a different religious sphere, that of the creation by Yahweh's free and sovereign love. It is in this way that we can best understand how God's word to Israel was linked to a particular situation. Israel was, as a people, placed in a given, actual situation and had ethical views and ideas which had developed out of this situation and were closely related to those of her neighbours. In short, Israel was a people situated in a definite civilisation, a people which had gained a new god, the authentic God, Yahweh.

Israel's faith in the free and sovereign God who was able to bestow fertility upon the barren was also to lead gradually to a totally different experience of marriage. It is here that the source of all Israel's demythologizing of marriage is to be found. This "secularization," this removal of sexuality from the religious sphere of the fertility cults, which was in fact a transference of sexuality into the sphere of the worship of Yahweh, or a "Yahwehisation" of the theological themes of Canaan, can be regarded as the first-fruit of the revelation made to Israel in connection with marriage. It was through her association with the God Yahweh that Israel's conception of the creation was purified, becoming a faith in a Creator who was in no way restricted and who was generous and free, elective and loving in the sharing of his abundant riches. That is precisely why marriage was first and foremost a secular reality which could not be allowed to evaporate, to become an insubstantial representation of something that might previously have been enacted in the divine sphere. In Israel there existed no divine prototype of marriage which could then be directly associated with marriage at the human level by means of religious rites. Marriage in Israel did not recognise the liturgical mediation of priests or Levites or any kind of religious ritual. It was, for Israel, a secular reality.

This "desacralised" marriage, this simple, secular, and thoroughly human reality, was "worldly" in the Israelite sense of that word. Israel's world was in no way either a Greek "cosmos" or "nature" in the modern sense. It was a "work of God," a "divine miracle" or—in the biblical phrase—a "work of his hands." It was God's world, and God had given it to man to inhabit. Man was to enjoy this world, work in it, and praise God for the miracle of its existence (Ps cxxxix. 14). But, as God's minister or deputy on earth and as God's image, acting in subordination and obedience to the will of his Lord, man was to be holy as Yahweh was holy.[2] Seen in the context of this belief in God's creation, secular demythologized marriage acquired a deeply religious significance in Israel. For Israel, it was a good gift of the creation, coming from Yahweh, the God of the covenant. What was called into existence by God's creation was sanctified by the fact of creation itself and subject to God's holy laws. It was not the sacred rites which surrounded marriage that made it a holy thing. The great rite which sanctified marriage was God's act of creation itself. The blessing promised to married couples in the oriental world was seen by Israel as Yahweh's blessing. It was Yahweh and none other who, as the founder of marriage, blessed the union of man and wife. This blessing was the very blessing of God's act of creation. This divine blessing made the first marriage of history the prototype of all married life.

[2] Lev xi. 44; xix. 2; xx. 26; see also Deut vii. 6; xiv. 2. These texts are also located in the context of the covenant.

It is important to see this, in the light of the Old Testament manner of writing history, as a proclamatory presentation, in the literal sense of a making present of the past. In the Old Testament form of historiography, there was always a strong tendency to shift a fundamental vision of Israel's faith—or an institution which was regarded by Israel as important—to the beginning or to one or other of the central turning-points of Israel's history of salvation. What was true in principle was true from the beginning. Principle and beginning were of course derived from the same root in Hebrew (*rē'šîth* and *rô'š*, cf. Latin *principium*, meaning both principle and beginning). To the Semitic mind the deepest meaning and being of anything was to be found in its origin—that is why, in the biblical sense, the creation is a "creation from the beginning of time." And so Genesis is presenting the fundamental creation structure of the relationship in marriage between man and woman. It is remarkable that chapter vii of the Greek text of the Book of Sirach, which provides a kind of commentary on the Genesis account of creation, refers to Adam in the plural. What is said in Sir vii is applicable to all men. It was something which constituted mankind, and for this reason it was applicable from the very beginning. It was in the first Adam that God himself constituted the essential structure of marriage between man and woman—the structure which we should expect to encounter in every marriage.

This first tendency—the tendency to seek the deepest meaning of a thing in its origins—was at the same time accompanied by a tendency to expound God's actions, to make them visible, sometimes even by introducing the miraculous, or at least by bringing the miraculous into sharper relief. Yahweh himself was brought onto the stage. The point at issue was that it should be clearly realised that God took a hand in earthly events.

Israel's belief in the divine institution of marriage is expressed in Genesis. It was God himself who, in this first marriage, and thus in every marriage in Israel, gave the woman to the man—

"he . . . brought her to the man [Adam]" (ii. 22). Marriage was thus a good and holy undertaking, bearing God's blessing in the structure that God intended it to have. That children leave their parents and home, with their father's blessing, to join together in marriage, is a fact verifiable in everyday experience, and one which forms part of the good and divinely instituted plan of creation.

Man's companion, woman, is a gift made to man by the living God. The Genesis text (ii. 18) reads literally: "I shall make a helper for man, as an *opposite to him.*" In Lagrange's phrase, woman is man's *vis-à-vis.* She is a partner over against man, turned in his direction and fit for him to encounter. Genesis here aims to show that animals are not of the same race as man, and that no animal is a worthy partner for him. Man was called *'iš*, and this word contained the idea of strength (the "stronger sex"),[3] in contrast to the general designation for man, *'ādhām*, which stressed his lowly origin from the earth and his weakness. Yet—according to some scholars—*'iš* may also refer to a "being capable of choice," in contrast to animals which have no power of choice.[4] Adam, as a man (*'iš*), a being with the power of choice, chose woman (*'iššāh*) for himself. There is a good deal of subtle linguistic hairsplitting at this point, not all of it philologically sound. What the sacred writer is really emphasizing here is that, after all kinds of beings had been brought before him, and shown to him, man took woman as his chosen one. In this way, *'iššāh*, woman, was the one chosen by man, his beloved. The pure etymology (*'iš*, man as the stronger sex, and *'iššāh*, the feminine of man or the "weaker sex") was thus distorted by popular etymology into a kind of spirituality of marriage. The glorification of animals is also strongly attacked in this account.

Only woman is man's equal. She is a human being as he is, a partner at the same level of life. That is why the sacred writer

---

[3] *'iš* can also mean a "male animal" (see Köhler and Baumgartner).
[4] See, for example, E. Jacob, *The Theology of the Old Testament*, New York (Harper, 1958).

described her as having been taken out of man as "one of his
ribs." What he wanted to show was that she was of the same race
as man, that there was a blood-relationship involved here. A
statement of this kind was not simply biological. It was also anthropological, and therefore referred to the whole of man. In a
society with a clan and family structure "blood-relationship" was
an expression of that unity which made peace (*šālôm*). Belonging to a definite group, belonging together, solidarity—this was
blood-relationship, even when the relationship was not by blood,
and even in the case of legal adoption or of purely fictitious
consanguinity, so long as the person in question belonged to the
"clan." Man and woman belonged to each other. They were the
principle, the beginning, of the family, the group, and the clan.
They were therefore related by blood and "flesh of each other's
flesh." The statement: "this . . . is bone of my bones and flesh of
my flesh" (Gen ii. 23) occurs again and again in the Bible as an
expression of blood-relationship, and implies a fully human unity
and an attitude of peace which is characteristic of the pattern of
life of the clan.

The relationship was, in the Semitic view, never purely spiritual. Because it was always authentically human in the full sense
of the word it was expressed as a *physical blood-relationship*.[5]
In this expression—as in the expression *bāśār 'eḥādh* (one flesh)—
three elements are fused together. The first is the idea of blood-
relationship, seen as an extension of the idea of peace (*šālôm*) in
the life of the clan and the solidarity of the family, the extended
family, the clan, and the tribe. The second is the idea of woman
as complementary to man, woman as man's life companion—man
was not complete without woman, and both complemented each
other in their humanity. This complementary aspect was seen as
the work of God. Thirdly, there was the idea of physical, marital
union—man and woman forming one person. "Flesh" denoted

[5] Gen xxix. 14; Judg ix. 2; 2 Sam v. 1; xix. 12–13. One's "own flesh" sometimes means one's fellow-man who was to be loved (Is lviii. 7). Joseph's
brothers said of him: "He is our brother, our own flesh" (Gen xxxvii. 27).

here the whole person, the *ego* in physical form. This idea was expressed mythically as being "taken out of the rib of the man." It is said that the Arabs still refer to a bosom friend or a relative as their "rib," and our word "sweetheart" still to some extent conveys this idea.[6] God made man and woman for each other. It is fundamentally a question of a partnership at the human level; a man's wife is his *alter ego*.

The fact that man's "equal" was called a "help" for man did not mean that a wife was a help only in the day-to-day management of the home. "Help" or "helper" had a distinctly personal meaning in the Old Testament. This is clear from the texts in which the word is used in relation to God. For example, "help" in the phrase "God is our help" (Ps xxxiii. 20; xlvi. 5) means refuge or support—the staff on which I can lean, someone in whom I can trust and in whom I can find security. With reference to human relationships in general, and to married relationships in particular, the Wisdom literature—echoing Genesis—calls the wife "a helper fit for him and a pillar of support" (Sir xxxvi. 24–6).

A servile submission of the wife to her husband, of the kind that existed at the time that religious thought had the form encountered in Genesis ii, was seen, even in Genesis, as a sinful situation, a consequence of and a punishment for the sin in Paradise (Gen iii. 16).

The essentially *dialogic* nature of an equal partnership between man and wife is clearly stated in Genesis. Man and woman together were truly Adam, mankind. In the third text quoted in this chapter (Gen v. 1–2), both man and woman are promised the name "Adam" and thus human dignity. For this reason they were able to become "one flesh" in marriage. There was no ques-

[6] H. van den Bussche, *De godsdienstige boodschap van de oergeschiedenis*, Ghent and Tielt (1959), p. 269; J. de Fraine, *De bijbel en het ontstaan van de mens*, Antwerp (1953), pp. 39–45. The Hebrew word for "rib" may also be connected with a Sumerian word meaning both "rib" and "life." (Sumerian was the language spoken in the land before the Semitic conquest.)

tion here of a purely physical union; the expression was anthropological. Man and wife became "one life" in marriage. The
Genesis text is further developed in Malachi: "Has he [God] not
made them one flesh and one life?"[7] And, looking forward to St.
Paul ("Even so husbands should love their wives as their own
bodies," Eph v. 28), Malachi adds, "So take heed to *your life*
[yourselves]"—that is, for your wife.[8] The "one flesh" clearly
points to the incarnate dialogic form of existence of peace between
man and woman, although we should not see in this the full,
modern content of personal relationship in marriage.

The idea of "one flesh" provides an answer to the question:
How can the division of the old clans and the foundation of new
clans be justified? "A man leaves his father and his mother"
(Gen ii. 24) in order to found a new clan, a "new house," or a
new "one flesh." Intimate spiritual and intellectual intercourse
between man and wife was not, of course, known in the Old
Covenant. And is the concrete social subordination of the woman
not also reflected in the second account of the creation, in
which woman was "taken out of man" and—as it were—created
according to the man, in contrast to the first account, in which
"mankind" was created immediately in both male and female
forms? This must, of course, be examined in connection with St.
Paul's appeal to Genesis in his statement that "the husband is the
head of the wife" (Eph v. 23).

What cannot be justified from the texts is that Genesis as a
whole refers merely to the creation of woman and man, and not
directly to marriage. The intention of the whole text was to re-
store the social fact of marriage to a divine institution. With a
deliberately pointed reference to monogamous marriage, that is,
to marriage between one man and one woman, the Samaritan

---

[7] This phrase is translated directly from the Dutch, and differs in several
respects from the RSV reading. [Translator's note.]

[8] Mal ii. 14-16. It is possible that I am concluding more from this text
than can, from the purely philological point of view, be justified. In
the original, there is no reference to "one flesh." The Hebrew is, in any
case, very puzzling.

Pentateuch and the Septuagint translated the Hebrew "and they become one flesh" interpretatively as "and *these two* become one flesh" (Gen ii. 24). This ideal of marriage, based on a belief in God's creation, was not stated by the sacred writer without a certain element of conscious polemic against the ancient oriental views concerning marriage which had tainted the Israelites. Polygamy was certainly rife among the upper circles in Israelitic society at the time of the Judges and Kings. The possession of a harem was a sign of wealth and power. Although this was accepted as a fact, there was a noticeable reaction against it in Deuteronomy, in the Priestly tradition, and in the Wisdom literature.[9] Although polygamy was officially tolerated by the Law, it was in no sense an expression of the deepest experience of the Israelite ethic. The purest expression of this ethic of married life is to be found in Genesis and in the commentary of the Book of Sirach upon it.

The author of Genesis ii. makes man's need of woman and woman's longing for man clear, by seeing in this human institution a mysterious plan on the part of the Creator. His presentation is, of course, very primitive, in that he states that the woman was made out of man, "while he slept" (ii. 21). The meaning of this passage is much disputed. Possibly it had a necessary place within the account as a whole, in which case it would be senseless to look for a theological meaning in it—as if, for example, the writer was here trying to say that man received his life-companion as a gift from heaven, and indeed as a surprising gift, making him rejoice that this was "flesh of my flesh." But it is certainly possible to claim that the mythical remnant in this idea —the man's "magic sleep"—points to the fact that the sacred writer experienced the woman's longing for the man as a mystery[10]—a mystery with its origin in God, who had not revealed its secret.

[9] This reaction was, incidentally, not directed against polygamy as such, but against the taking of foreign wives, who were felt to be a danger to the pure cult of Yahweh. See Deut xvii. 17: "He [the king] shall not multiply wives for himself, lest his heart turn away" (i.e., from Yahweh).

[10] See also Prov xxx. 18-19; Song viii. 6-7.

The inner meaning of marriage is to be found in the authentic personal community, the "one flesh" (Gen ii. 24) which those who share in this community become. The specific task involved in this community was expressed in terms of the clan, however. As God ruled over the world, so man—the image, the governor or sheik, of God—was master in the whole of the larger family unit. The blessing of creation pronounced over the union of man and woman clearly recalls the blessing pronounced by the patriarchs over their eldest sons who would assume control of the whole of the family (Gen xxvii. 27–9; xlix. 3–4, 8; also xxiv. 6a). The eldest son eventually became the sheik of the clan, and as such was God's "envoy" on earth. The first man did not transmit the "image of God" so much as his own governorship or power over the whole clan. The son was the hereditary successor of the leader of the clan, and this position of power came from God (Gen v. 3).

The two elements which were always expressed in the patriarchal blessing were the position of leadership in the clan and fertility. Needless to say, no clan existed at the time of the creation of the first man, and the marriage blessing was therefore one of fertility and overlordship over the earth ("dominion" over the fish of the sea, etc.). It would therefore seem to be unjustified, from the biblical point of view, to regard the foundation of the family according to Genesis as a social task. The passage referring to the "image of God" and "dominion over the earth" is, moreover, alien to the preceding and the subsequent text, in which there is a similar reference to man's position of leadership.[11] In this passage, a different Hebrew word is used for "subdue" than the one used in the preceding and the subsequent text. Genesis, therefore, does not say that man and woman were together to subdue the earth, but rather that what the man initially did alone in respect of things he was now to do in respect of the woman and his offspring—he was to be the leader of the whole clan, including the woman.

[11] Compare Gen i. 26 with i. 28.

It is thus once more apparent that divine revelation did not at once create a *new* people, but that it did give a "new God"—the authentic God, Yahweh—to a people living according to the ethics of the clan system. The new people was, of course, gradually brought into being through this faith in Yahweh, though this was fully realized only through Christ. Furthermore, in the final editing, the two passages were eventually combined to form a single whole, and in view of this we can say—in apparent contradiction to the original conception—that the text as it now stands involves the woman far more intimately in the man's position of power. As a mother, the woman is *ḥawwāh*, Eve. As a bride and a companion in marriage, as the one chosen, she is *'iššāh*.

That a child was the divine blessing on marriage cannot be regarded as an attitude characteristic of Israel. Here, too, what is distinctively Israelite is faith in the true God, Yahweh, who was not restricted to the laws of nature and biological cycles, but who was able to act in free and sovereign power in giving a child to parents—even to infertile parents. Children in Israel were therefore Yahweh's (Gen iv. 1; xxiv. 60; Ruth iv. 11; Ps cxiii. 9) and not Baal's. They were Yahweh's inheritance (Ps cxxvii. 3; Ezek xvi. 20–21). The birth of Seth was therefore seen as the fulfilment of God's blessing on the first two human beings (Gen. v. 1–3). Malachi said: "Has not he made them one flesh and one life? And what does he desire? Godly offspring." (Mal ii. 14–16).[12] The child was the fruit of the "one flesh," or the loving communion of marriage as a gift of God, so that it must of necessity belong to Yahweh.

The duty to bring the children up to have faith in Yahweh was based upon this. The children were not simply Yahweh's gift to the parents; they were Yahweh's inheritance, and the parents were bound to treat them as such, and give them to God.[13] What was expressed in birth was an act of Yahweh's creation (Is xliii.

[12] See note 7. [Translator's note.]
[13] See, for example, Ezek xiv. 20–21.

7; Jer i. 5; Job xxxi. 15), and it was on this that the need for
obedience and submission to Yahweh was based. Man was able to
name the things of the earth (Gen ii. 20), but it was God himself
who gave a name to man (v. 2)—that is to say, man had, in
God's name, lordship over the world, but God had lordship over
man. To be created by God, or to be named by him, implied a
commission to serve him. The whole of the Old Testament ethic
of marriage and the family was based on this. The things of the
earth and man received their *ḥōq* or *ḥûqqāh* with their creation:
each received, on creation, its intrinsic conditions of existence,
its defined limits.[14] This intrinsic legality was none other than
God's creative will which called an order, a system, into existence.

Thus, on the day when he created mankind, Yahweh gave a
particular meaning and a task to married life. This was, for man,
a commission. "(Hear, O Israel), what does Yahweh require of
you, but to fear Yahweh, to walk in all his ways, to love him, to
serve Yahweh with all your heart and with all your soul, and to
keep the commandments and statutes of Yahweh."[15] The covenant
which Yahweh concluded with his people had, so to speak, to be
made actual again and again at every new birth—every birth of a
boy—by circumcision[16] and upbringing in faith in Yahweh.

In Israel, then, the secular reality of marriage was experienced
fundamentally in the light of Israel's belief in the creation. What
God had brought about was not subject to human criticism. Marriage was a good and glorious undertaking and God's blessing
was upon it. Israel did not desire any kind of "mystique" of
marriage, but was satisfied with the sober realism of creation.

---

[14] Gen i. 14 ff. See also Jer v. 24; xxxi. 35–6; xxxiii. 25 (*ḥōq* or *ḥûqqāh*, in
the plural *ḥûqqîm* or *ḥûqqôth*, mean firm law(s), the expression of God's
will).

[15] Deut x. 12–16. This text is of course not concerned with an ordinance
of creation, but with a law of the covenant. There is no clear distinction
between the two levels—creation itself can be seen in the light of the idea
of the covenant.

[16] See, among other texts, Gen xvii. 10–11.

Moreover, this creation was a wonderful thing, demanding respect for the entire order of creation.

2. Nonetheless, Israel was equally well acquainted with the tragic aspect of marriage. In Israel, too, sin was a fundamental fact of everyday human existence. The actual, disastrous situation in which marriage was placed penetrated so deeply into Israel's consciousness that it was able to change faith in the goodness of God's creation into doubt. Here too we find that, for Israel, what was true in principle had been true from the beginning. To express this idea in another way, what was factually and unavoidably true—that is, what belonged, not to the essential, but to the actual, existential "constitution" of a human fact or reality—obtained "from the very beginning," and had its origin in an ancient initial fact, a primordial datum of history. The radical, deep-seated impotence experienced in achieving a happy and successful married life was explained in the Old Testament by transferring the "constitution" of this impotence to the beginning of the fact of marriage, to the life of the first man and woman in history. The man had sinned together with his help—with his wife. From being his wife's leader (Gen ii. 18), the man had, through sin, become her tyrant (Gen iii. 16). In the same way, the wife who had been assigned to him as a help became a help in evil, a temptress. This is encountered again and again in the Old Testament.[17]

In describing the temptation and the fall the authors of Genesis had in mind the idea of God prevalent among Israel's neighbours, who made God dependent upon nature and the natural cycles and therefore associated fertility with magic rites. The woman was naturally considered first in these rites, but they took place with the full knowledge and the approval of the husband. When Jeremiah protested against these practices, the women pleaded that their husbands had consented to them: "Was

[17] In addition to the main passage, Gen iii. 6 and 12, see also xix. 30–38; xxxix. 1–23; Judg xvi. 4–22; and the Wisdom literature.

it without our husbands' approval?"—that is, without their husbands' knowledge and consent (Jer xliv. 19). The serpent, which was intimately connected with the fertility rites of the ancient world, addressed the woman, who in turn persuaded Adam. Instead of trusting in God's blessing on marriage, Eve, the wife and mother, turned, with Adam's consent, to magic fertility rites. In this way man dissociated marriage from the *ḥûqqôth*, the divinely appointed limits of creation.

What happened here, in the case of the first man and woman, was repeated again and again throughout the history of mankind, in new and different situations. Trust in God was lost, and man and woman both entered on a history of sin. This had its effect upon all their relationships. Their "community" was impaired, so that the husband came to dominate the wife, to treat her as a slave, and woman became man's temptress.[18] Marriage remained a good gift of creation, but it was affected by sin. The pure, undefiled state of trust in God and familiar association with him was lost in married life too. As the "image of God," man was God's representative for all that was in the world. In the world he was God's minister and "ambassador." When he broke off relations with God, whose envoy he was, his mission in the world inevitably took its own stubborn and high-handed course, the consequences of which man himself has had to bear.

Far more than the tragedy of one single married life was involved in the disability shown up in marriage. The whole of human existence was affected. Here too "principle" and "beginning" can be seen to coincide. What happened in the beginning both expounds and at the same time elucidates what we can see happening all around us every day—the tragedy of marriage. The description of this beginning shows that what has been happening in married life throughout the centuries crosses the frontiers of each individual marriage. The powerlessness of marriage due to the entry of sin into God's good creation is withdrawn from

18 See J. Coppens, "La soumission de la femme à l'homme d'après Genèse 3. 16b," *ETL*, 14 (1937), pp. 634–41.

each new intervention made by a particular married couple. Man himself became powerless.

In contrast to the image of marriage which those who were living at the time of the Book of Genesis could see all around them, an image of faithfulness to Yahweh which had been defaced, the original ideal of marriage was set up—marriage as it had come into the world from God's hands, untouched by human sinfulness. Indeed, it is possible to say that the Genesis text contains no more than this, but, seen against the sombre backcloth of marriage as it was experienced in those times, it is certainly more than enough. Genesis stated, in contrast to the broken and tarnished image of marriage, that "in the beginning it was not like this." The divine institution of marriage was not to be put aside for purely human considerations. Only later did it become apparent that it was not enough simply to go back beyond mankind's initiative in sin and point to the perfect beginning of creation, but that a re-creation would be necessary. Only the provision from above of a completely new beginning could change the actual situation. What was necessary, in other words, was the redeeming power of God, who could provide this new beginning in the history of mankind in Christ.

Human Sexuality and Eroticism in the Song of Solomon

The Song of Solomon stands out in bold relief against the background of Israel's faith in Yahweh which took marriage and sexuality outside the purely religious sphere, and did this in an environment which was permeated with a religious, mythical view, amounting almost to a deification, of sexuality.

The Song, which was accepted into the Palestinian canon of the Bible, conveys a view of erotic love and sexuality as a purely human reality, spiritualised but profane. We shall see that another and deeper meaning was discovered in the Song as a result of a later Jewish revision of it. However, it is important to keep the first and primary meaning of the Song firmly in mind.[19] On the basis of textual criticism and comparative analysis, exegetes have come more and more to accept the view that the Song is a very early Israelite composition inspired by the Egyptian love-lyric; and that it was not popular poetry, but rather verses which derived from the Solomonic humanism of the days of the Kings. The arguments put forward in support of this view (by G. Gerleman especially; see bibliography) would seem to be absolutely convincing. What is more, the Song belonged to the Palestinian canon of the Bible before there was any reference in the Jewish tradition to an allegorical interpretation of it as an expression of Yahweh's love for his bride, Israel. There is, in any case, less reference in the Song to marital love than to the physical beauty and erotic love of two young people, although it is quite possible that this love is set in the context of a bridal feast. The environment in which it originated—the royal court of ancient Israel during the age of the Kings—rules out the possibility of any influence from the later prophetic tradition, which depicted the covenant in the form of a marriage.

As literature, and as a portrayal of erotic love, the Song of Solomon is somewhat isolated from the rest of the Old Testament. If it has anything at all in common with other books of the Old Testament, it is most closely related to the Books of Samuel and Kings which describe the time of David and his successors,

[19] Bibliography on the Song of Solomon (with varying interpretations): G. Gerleman, "Das Hohelied," *BKAT*, XVIII-2 (1963); A. Robert, *Le Cantique des Cantiques* (La Sainte Bible), Paris (1951); A. Dubarle, "L'amour humain dans le Cantique des Cantiques," *RB*, 61 (1954), pp. 67-86, and "Le Cantique des Cantiques," *RSPT*, 38 (1954), pp. 92-102; A. Feuillet, "Le Cantique des Cantiques et la tradition biblique," *NRT*, 83 (1952), pp. 706-33, and *Le Cantique des Cantiques*, Paris (1953); G. Geslin, "L'allégorie matrimoniale de Jahvé et d'Israël et le Cantique des Cantiques," *VP*, (1945), pp. 77-90; J. Audet, "Le sens du Cantique des Cantiques," *RB*, 62 (1955), pp. 197-221, and "Love and Marriage in the Old Testament," *Scr*, 10 (1958), pp. 65-83. See also: A. Jepson, "Zur Kanongeschichte des Alten Testaments," *ZAW*, 71 (1959), pp. 114-36; W. Rudolph, "Das Hohe Lied im Kanon," *ZAW*, 18 (1942-3), pp. 189-99; M. A. van den Oudenrijn, "Het Hooglied," *BOT*, VIII-3 (1962).

and to the Yahwist tradition of the Pentateuch. These are the only Old Testament books in which love and lovemaking (in marriage) are frankly mentioned, but even then they are referred to only in passing.[20] In the later Wisdom literature, on the other hand, physical beauty is spoken of with a certain reserve, and the moralising tendency of these books inevitably results in physical beauty being incorporated into the higher beauty of virtue and loyalty in married love. Some scholars believe that Sir ix. 8 is directed polemically against the purely erotic humanism of the Song of Solomon.

The fact that the Song had been included in the Hebrew canon of the Bible even before there was any mention of an allegorical interpretation is a powerful argument for believing that Israel's faith did not see its profane nature as an impediment to its acceptance as "biblical literature," though factual recognition of the Song as canonical, in itself indicating its theological significance in the history of salvation, can only have been based formally on its great antiquity and its "Solomonic origin." At all events, the theological import of the Song as a book incorporated into the Palestinian canon of the Bible, and as Word of God in this sense, can therefore in the first place be found in the fact that, although Israel's environment was quite different, it testified to a complete break with the deification of sexuality. Eroticism in Israel was something profane, something that was completely removed from the sphere of the religious and from all myth. It should emerge, in the exposition of the prophet Hosea which follows, that in such an environment the human and profane nature of the Song is only conceivable in the light of Israel's belief in Yahweh.

Ancient Israel preferred to experience sex and sexuality in a spiritualised, human, and profane environment. It is here that the

[20] These texts will be met with later in this book in Chapter 2, "The Old Testament Ethos of Marriage," Section I, "Married Love and Founding a Family," pp. 130 ff. In the Yahwist tradition: Gen xxiv. 16, 67; xxvi. 8–9: xxix. 20. In Samuel: 1 Sam xviii. 20 (this is the only place in the Old Testament in which we are told that the woman loves the man); 2 Sam xiii. 2–15.

primary theological importance of the Song is to be found. Negatively, it was a frank protest against the mythical and religious rites of Canaan's worship of Baal and against the religious sexuality which pervaded the whole of the ancient Near East. Positively, it was an affirmation of the creaturely goodness of the relationship between man and woman—a relationship which ended in a bridal feast. This would be all the more compelling if Song vii. 11 were an allusion to the most ancient account of the creation (Gen iii. 16), as many exegetes claim (Dubarle, Robert, Rudolph, and others). The fact that Yahweh is not named in the Song was undoubtedly dictated by motives of awe—of a reluctance to associate Yahweh with religious sexual myths. This awe was overcome in the case of Genesis by that book's assertion of the idea of creation. The assumption made in the Song, which in itself makes no explicit reference to religious or moral aspects, is nonetheless the unerring feeling that belief in Yahweh was incompatible with any deification of human sexuality. Hosea was the first to use marriage as an image of Yahweh's activity with Israel under the covenant, and this was indeed a bold innovation. At the same time, however, he took care to strike hard at mythical religious sexuality.

The Song describes the creaturely splendour of human love and the refreshing playfulness which testifies to this gift, and places it all in the natural setting of a beautiful countryside. On the other hand, there is no suggestion of frivolity in the Song. Great value is placed upon the virgin state of the beloved (iv. 12; viii. 8–10), and true love is expressed as unshakable fidelity (viii. 6–7): "for love is strong as death." In this way, the Song forms a healthy counterpart to the other Old Testament tendency to see the function of marriage almost exclusively as the perpetuation of the clan and the nation. It extols not fertility (this may also be a reaction against the fertility rites), but human love. It thus forms an idyllic commentary, taken from life, on what the oldest creation account in Genesis—which must have originated more or less at the same period—had to say concerning the relationship between man and woman.

MARRIAGE AS REVEALING THE COMMUNITY BETWEEN YAHWEH AND ISRAEL

Preliminary Theological Observations

We know from the first chapters of the Book of Genesis that marriage—especially marriage seen in the light of the prophets' concern for a pure and undefiled faith in Yahweh, their insistent preaching of Yahweh as the only, the jealous, God of Israel— was valued as a fact and reality of this world, a secular reality which was borne up by the sovereign, free, and creator God. The relationship in marriage between man and woman was good, very good even—a pre-eminently good gift of creation. The belief in creation by Yahweh "demythologized" marriage and exempted sexuality and marriage from all mystical obscurity.

In addition to this idea of marriage, another grew up in Israel, namely that marriage was the means of revealing the community existing between Yahweh and his people. It cannot be claimed without reserve that Israel regarded marriage between human beings both as a representation of and a reference to the covenant of grace between Yahweh and his people. Whenever the connection between human marriage and the covenant is established in texts of the Old Testament, what is at issue is not marriage but this saving covenant itself. In other words, the saving covenant of Yahweh and Israel was—like every other reality of revelation —expressed in human terms. Because it is essentially a dialogue in which God addresses man who, hearing his words, reacts to them, revelation is essentially something heard in human form. God's self-disclosure, as mankind's salvation, is expressed in the form of a human knowledge of what is revealed, and thus essentially contains a reference to man's experience of his own existence. This experience was the source of the material with which Israel, in her encounter with her God Yahweh, sought to express—in concept and in image—this revelation: a revelation which actually came about in the course of that encounter. In other words, it was by way of actual human experience that God's saving actions and his Word in the preaching of the prophets were expressed in humanly intelligible terms, and that divine revelation became a revelation that was listened to by man. And so the facts of human existence became the means of revealing the fact of salvation.

It is in this light that the Old Testament affirmation concerning marriage must be seen. The loving, intimate relationship between God and his chosen people—a relationship full of grace and mystery and far transcending all human comprehension—was expressed, in Israel, in the message of her prophets, in words and concepts—in things intelligible in human terms, drawn from an everyday, human experience, married love. The married life of human beings, with all its ups and downs, its certainties about the past and its uncertainties about the future, with the recollective pleasures of happiness enjoyed and the more bitter memories of hard times, infidelity, and the deprivation of love—all this formed the prism through which the prophets saw the saving covenant of God with his people, and enabled the people to comprehend the covenant. Human marriage became the means of revealing the covenant of salvation.

The prophets, then, were not here directly concerned with marriage, or with a revealed insight into marriage itself, but with the revelation of the covenant between God and his people. In other words, it was not their intention to provide a theology of marriage of the kind given in Genesis. What they aimed to do was to give a theology of the community of grace existing between God and his people, a theology of salvation.

On the other hand, however, this theology, or meaningful proclamation of man's saving community with God, was still presented in terms derived from human married life. This means that those who were intent upon providing this theology made use of facts of human experience which were already well known. But it is only possible to appeal to these well-known, natural, and clearly recognisable facts for the purpose of expressing a religious, transcendent datum in one of two situations. The first is that marriage itself, as a human institution, includes an intrinsic objective reference to the saving mystery of the covenant of grace, or at least is inwardly receptive and open to a reference of this kind. Alternatively marriage must—on a basis of this open receptivity—gain the inner reference from revelation itself. If neither of these situations obtained, it would not be possible to express the covenant meaningfully by appealing to this particular natural, human institution.

Theologically speaking, it will be clear that the reality of creation contains—as a fact of nature—an objective reference to God, the basis of our natural knowledge of God—to God as a mystery. But we cannot form any idea of the real features of the mystery of God from these created realities. It is only from revelation that we can get a sight of those features. Thus it was that, through the human awareness of the prophets and of the man Jesus, his Son, God himself made use, in his self-revelation, of precisely this receptivity and openness of secular realities; and, revealing himself through human awareness (of the prophets, of Jesus), he gave an objective referential power to certain concepts relating to human existence—those, for example, of father, son, marriage, and so on. He did this in order to make a supernatural mystery truly recognisable and capable of being experienced by the men who believed in him in a real and human, albeit inadequate, manner. But this also means that marriage, as the means—or as one of the means—of revealing the covenant between God and Israel, gained this referential power in revelation from God, though certainly on a basis of human receptivity—"basis-symbolism."

The consequence of this was what we might call a "reciprocal illumination." Revealing his covenant through the medium of human marriage, God simultaneously revealed to men a meaning of marriage which they had not hitherto suspected. He did not do this by means of a separate revelation, but by revealing himself in marriage and thus setting it in a "luminous circle" so that it became transparent and was sanctified by the God of salvation. In this way, marriage itself entered salvation. The covenant of salvation was not revealed to us by means of some abstract concept, but through a fact of human existence, though this fact nonetheless contains a marginal trace of the conceptual. What was revealed, although a transcendental grace, thus became capable of being experienced and assimilated by human beings. Conversely the transcendental, "sacramental" value of the secular reality of marriage became capable of penetration by us men. However, this did not become fully possible until divine revelation was fulfilled in Christ, and at the present stage we must continue to confine our attention to God's revelation in the Old Testament.

What we have been saying can be seen to be even more significant in the Semitic mode of thought, in which an image was, far more than to the modern Western mind, not simply an "image" —the image and what was symbolized in the image were almost identical. In symbolic action, Jeremiah carried a yoke on his neck; but this yoke was *in fact* Israel's bondage.[21] Thus marriage was in fact also a representation of God's community of grace with Israel.

The Covenant of Grace Proclaimed by the Prophets in the Image of Marriage

1. The prophet *Hosea* was the first to express the community of grace existing between Yahweh and Israel by appealing to the secular reality of marriage (see especially chapters i–iii). If we are fully to understand the vision of Hosea, we must remember that his prophetic activity took place between the years 752 and

---

[21] Jer xxviii. 10; xxvii. 2. See G. Fohrer, *Die symbolische Handlungen der Propheten*, Abhandlungen zur Theologie des Alten u. Neuen Testaments, 25, Basel and Zürich (1953).

(about) 724 B.C., first of all in the last years of the reign of Jeroboam II, then especially during the state of emergency caused by the wars against Syria and Ephraim (v. 8–11) and the conquest of even more of Israel's territories by Tiglath-pileser III, and finally during the period of calm immediately preceding and following the accession of Shalmanezer V.[22] Following the example of the priests, the people of God had gone over to the practice of Canaanite fertility rites in the promised land of Canaan. The cult of Yahweh had become deeply influenced by the religion of Baal. The consequence of this was a syncretism between the worship of Baal and the ancient faith of Yahweh. Baal was a god associated with the soil and the land, with "high places," and with the rhythm of fertility both of the earth and of woman. In the Baal-cult the myth of the marriage between the land—the goddess—and the heavenly god prevailed, and it was believed that the people was a result of this marriage between the goddess and the god. Religious prostitution was practised in the worship of the temple. Israelite girls gave themselves to men whom they did not know for sugared cakes, and "religious marriage" was imitated in worship, the girls imploring Baal to make them fertile.

In the context of the Book of Hosea, certain biographical data are to some extent involved; we are confronted with the question of Hosea's personal married life. But this actual, particular marriage does not stand on its own in the Book of Hosea; it stands out clearly only as a prophetic figure, since it is in itself a message which Hosea had to bring to the people, not in words alone, but also—as frequently in the prophets—by means of an action. The prophetic symbolic action which God required of Hosea

[22] Important works on the subject of Hosea include H. W. Wolff, "Dodekapropheton, I Hosea," *BKAT*, XIV–1 (1961); J. Coppens, "L'histoire matrimoniale d'Osée," *BBB*, 1 (1950), pp. 38–45; H. H. Rowley, "The Marriage of Hosea," *BJRL*, 39 (1956), pp. 200–33; H. Schmidt, "Die Ehe des Hosea," *ZAW*, 42 (1924), pp. 245–72; L. Batten, "Hosea's Message and Marriage," *HUCA*, 25 (1954), pp. 9–35.

was his married life. There are two principal elements in this "message-by-action."

The first is that Yahweh told Hosea to marry Gomer, a "harlot," that is, an Israelite girl who had been initiated into the fertility rites of the Canaanite worship of Baal. Yahweh may have wanted to show by this that he still loved Israel despite her faithlessness. On the other hand, it is possible that all that is said here is that Israel had become so faithless that only initiated girls could be found in Israel. Hosea had three children by this marriage, two sons and a daughter. Their names, and especially the names of the two youngest children, show clearly that the curse of the worship of Baal was upon them. The second child was called "Not pitied" and the third "Not my people" (i. 1-9). After a little while, Gomer left her husband and, committing adultery, came "legally" into the possession of another (ii. 4-17).

The second prophetic action which Hosea was called upon to perform is even more remarkable, if it is correct that the commandment of Deut xxiv. 1 ff. (see also Lev xxi. 7) was already in force in Israelite society at the time of Hosea—namely, that a woman who was legally divorced and married to another man was not permitted to return to her first husband. Nonetheless, at Yahweh's command Hosea had to take Gomer back after she had left him and fallen into the hands of another man, and look after her with loving care in lasting union (iii. 1-5, taken in conjunction with ii. 18-25).

These first three chapters of Hosea are concerned with the marriage relationship between Yahweh and Israel, his faithless people, but this relationship is expressed in and by a "biographical" symbolic action, the life of the prophet himself. The secular reality of marriage—in this case of one particular, concrete marriage—here becomes the image of God's saving action with his people. First in Israel to make use of marriage as a comparison with the relationship between Yahweh and his people within the covenant, Hosea clearly borrowed the image from the religion of Baal against which he directed his polemic, and did this to the benefit of the pure cult of Yahweh. The reason why this image was taken over is to be found in Israel's "whoredom," that is, in the people's faithlessness, adultery, and divorce, with regard to Yahweh. But this image of adultery is quite new as compared with the myths and rites of Canaan, and so the mythical element is brought down to the level of an analogy which is used polemically precisely against this mythology. Israel betrayed her "first husband," Yahweh (ii. 7, 16), and followed Baal. The image of marriage was taken over precisely in order to emphasize the exclusiveness of the religion of Yahweh. Yahweh is the "living God" (i. 10); it is he who is God (xii. 9; viii. 4). The fundamental theme of Hosea is "Yahweh, your God" (xii. 9; xiii. 4; xiv. 1). Hosea took over these mythical themes, but did so in order to assign them to the one, true God.

The image of marriage is not new as seen in relation to the religion of Canaan, but the image of God is new—the image of the sovereign Yahweh, the God of salvation history, the God of free, sovereign election who was not tied down to the natural, biological rhythm of the land and the womb, but bestowed fertility freely and in sovereign power. The Israelites were to expect everything from Yahweh, their God. Fertility and prosperity came not from Baal, but from Yahweh, and were not connected with rites and cultic actions. Israel owed her fertility and welfare entirely to the transcendent freedom of God's generous love.

The fact that Israel, with whom Yahweh concluded his covenant of grace, was not faithful to Yahweh sanctioned Hosea's use of the marriage image. That is to say, Hosea made reference to the image which he had taken over, not from the perspective of Yahweh, but from the perspective of faithless Israel: "for the land commits great harlotry by forsaking Yahweh" (i. 2). The marriage image, in its positive elements, says no more than what is implied by the divine covenant—the *berîth*—in its juridical, salvation-history aspect. The relationship within the covenant between Yahweh and Israel is called a marriage relationship, and is seen from the point of view of Israel's faithless betrayal of this covenant, the betrayal being made concrete in the cultic participation of Israel's girls in "religious" marriage between Baal and the goddess in the temple, during which they allowed themselves to be made fertile. Hosea effected a demythologizing of the marriage image by calling these sexual motives and the religious cult itself "harlotry" when he took marriage over as an image of the relationship within the covenant.

From then on it was possible for Hosea to elaborate the idea of God's marital love for his people without fear that any sexual connotations would continue to be associated with the image. The relationship between Hosea's own marriage and God's covenant can be clearly seen against this background. Yahweh himself took the initiative and Hosea, in his capacity as prophet, had to marry Gomer, a marriageable Israelite girl who had taken part in the initiation rite practised in Canaan at the time and who visibly bore the marks of this initiation (ii. 4: amulets or wounds?). This woman was an image of Israel in her apostasy from Yahweh, and as God's envoy Hosea took her to himself. Gomer was an image of Israel, but at the same time she was the living type of the Israelite women of that time. Hosea saw her fault to be not that she had expected fertility from God, but that she had expected it to come from a strange god, Baal. It was a matter of prostitution *in respect of Yahweh*.

Hosea's marriage with Gomer was no more than an initial preparation for God's saving actions. His children were to bear God's judgment over faithless Israel: "you are not my people." Because the Israelites had sought help and protection from others than Yahweh (ii. 5, 8, 13), Yahweh would deny them his help, and in this way they would learn how worthless Baal really was (ii. 6, 7, 13, 16–17).

Israel was divorced from Yahweh. The text reads literally: "she is not my *'iššāh* (woman), I am not her *'iš* (man)" (ii. 2). The reality of the "one flesh" referred to in the older, Yahwist account of the creation in Genesis was destroyed. Hosea writes of this in terms derived from the legal divorce proceedings of Israel (ii. 2–13). It was Israel and not Yahweh who took the initiative in this divorce. Even though the woman was, in these circumstances, liable at law to be punished by death, Yahweh was content merely to deny her his positive help. This deprivation had serious implications, for (according to Ex. xxi. 10) the husband was obliged to provide his wife with clothing; in other words, he had to remain with her and care for her. Now Israel was "stripped naked" (ii. 3) and became, without the care of her husband, a barren "forest" (ii. 12). Thus Israel became afflicted by extreme distress; becoming infertile, her harvests ceased and she celebrated no more feasts.

It was precisely while she was suffering under this judgment that Yahweh visited her, to ask her whether she would come back to him. Yahweh was personally affected by the separation. His thoughts returned again and again to the early days of their marriage in the wilderness, and he was unable permanently to accept the divorce brought about by his wife, Israel. Once more he set out to win her heart (ii. 14–15), to win her back to their "first love" (ii. 7–15). The day of the New Covenant was at last in sight—the day when Israel would no longer call Yahweh "my Baal," expressing the syncretism which had taken place between the true cult of Yahweh and the religion of Canaan, but "my husband" (ii. 16). Reunited with Israel, Yahweh would once again bestow fertility upon the land, its animals, and its inhabitants, and there would be peace and security once more (ii. 16–23). A new, and this time lasting, marriage would take place (ii. 19–20). Yahweh would pay the bridal price for this wedding, and this and the wedding gifts would comprise fidelity, goodness and affection, mercy and the husband's presence and care, and the settled state of a permanent life-relationship (ii. 19–20).

For her part, Israel would "know" Yahweh. She would be grateful to Yahweh for his wedding gifts in her experience of this perfect union of love. "Not my people" would then become "my people" (ii. 23). Israel would thus accept the new confession of faith: "Yahweh, my God" (ii. 23). She would be for ever the bride of Yahweh. This love which Yahweh had for his people was brought to Israel as a message by Hosea's prophetic life:

And Yahweh said to me, "Go again, love a woman who is beloved of a paramour and is an adulteress; *even as Yahweh* loves the people of Israel, though they turn to other gods and love cakes of raisins." So I bought her for fifteen shekels of silver and a homer and a lecheth of barley. And I said to her, "You must dwell as mine for many days; you shall not play the harlot, or belong to another man; so will I also be to you." For the children of Israel shall dwell many days without king or prince, without sacrifice or pillar, without ephod or teraphim. Afterward the children of Israel shall return and seek Yahweh their God . . . and they shall come in fear to Yahweh and to his goodness in the latter days. [iii. 1–5.]

Hosea's act of taking back Gomer, the wife who had been unfaithful to him, was the public message of Yahweh's love for Israel: "As Yahweh loved the people of Israel." (It should be noted here that chapter iii in all probability refers back, not to chapter i, but to chapter ii, although exegetes hold divergent opinions about this.) Hosea's loving his unfaithful wife again, in spite of everything, was a prophetic action, a message coming from Yahweh which was delivered, not in mere words alone, but through the actual circumstances of Hosea's own married life. "As Yahweh"—it was through his discovery of God's love for faithless Israel that Hosea learned what he had to do in respect of his own unfaithful wife, who was also faithless in the religious sense. God's activity within the covenant provided the model for his own married life, as a prophetic message to be passed on to God's people. A lasting divorce was out of the question for this prophet, who had knowledge of the nature of God's love for Israel. It is above all God's sovereign, unmerited love which was expressed in this prophetic action—a prophetic action which was made tangible in that Hosea took his unfaithful wife back again.

Yahweh remained "in love" with a woman who followed strangers for the "cakes of raisins" (iii. 1) and was ready to buy her for a high price. (It should be noted that Hosea's wife had also incurred obligations towards a third party, and had thus to be bought back in due legal form.) Hosea also imposed certain restrictions upon himself and upon the wife whom he had taken back, in order to perfect Gomer's repentance (iii. 2–4). Thus Yahweh's love did not merely provide the model for Hosea's love, it also provided a sharp contrast to the love of Gomer's alien friends, the friends of Baal. For Yahweh it was as impossible to bid farewell to his love for Israel as it was for him to renounce his claim to divinity. (See xi. 1–11.) Yet this love was sovereign and free: "I will love them freely" (xiv. 4).

This vision grew out of Hosea's polemic against the Canaanite and Phoenician fertility rites and mythology and from the experience of Israel's infidelity to God's activity within the covenant, and was not directly concerned with marriage as such. It was a theology of the covenant in the form of a demythologized "sacral marriage." The demythologizing emerges all the more clearly because the form of this saving reality is the actual, secular married life of Hosea himself, seen as a prophetic message. Hosea did not claim that human marriage in general was a symbolization of the divine covenant, but rather that this particular marriage—Hosea's own marriage—was certainly called on to be a tangible message from God to Israel, to symbolize Yahweh's covenant activity prophetically. However, it was here that the seed was sown from which, over the centuries, insight into the meaning of marriage as such within the cult of Yahweh was gradually to grow. Marriage in this sense was what was experienced in the spirit of Yahweh's unshakable love, even for the unfaithful partner.

What emerges from the particular, vocational form of the historical marriage of Hosea is that marriage is able, by virtue of a divine vocation, to gain a deeper meaning—a saving significance within the history of salvation—as the expression of the love existing between God and his people in the covenant. In the case of Hosea's marriage with Gomer, this deeper meaning was actually present. But the fact of Hosea's marriage implies that what is involved is a prophetic form of marriage, which marriage does not possess on its own account, but only by virtue of its being the object of a call from the God of salvation. From this it will be clear that the special, saving form which secular marriage is open to receive within salvation history not only has a saving significance for the partners of a particular marriage, but also contains a message for the world. Moreover, this message can be real and efficacious only so long as love remains constant and unshakable even for the unfaithful partner—even if this love demands great sacrifices from the faithful partner. For such was the love of Yahweh for his people.

Hosea was faithful to his marriage to the very end and, even for pious Israelites, this must have been an unprecedented and therefore very striking action. It must also have been a challenge to a nation which had made permanent separation on account of adultery almost a legal obligation. The prophetic character of Hosea's conduct could not have been expressed more clearly— the message for the people contained in it comes through with crystal clarity.

But this message must not cause us to lose sight of the fact that the essence of Hosea's action is to be found in a call to a practical and actual confession of faith in the one, true God, Yahweh, a God who was not tied to the rhythm of nature and the laws of biological fertility but who was free and sovereign in the disposal of his gifts. The immediate concern of this message was an unreserved confidence in the true and living God, but, as appears from the whole historical connection with the mythical fertility rites, a confidence placed in God in the context of married life. Marriage was to be experienced from the standpoint of an unconditional faith and confidence in Yahweh, since this was the very core of the covenant of grace and it was in this way that man was to express his response to Yahweh's love. The symbolic action of Hosea's marriage was not simply the message of God's covenant with and love for Israel. It had a more profound implication. It was the message of "God so loved the world": Yahweh had such love for Israel that it could be both exemplified and accomplished—in a way disconcerting to the Israelites—in the marriage of Hosea, who remained faithful to his wife despite her infidelity and adultery, and agreed to certain conditions in order to win her back again. The acquisition of this prophetic message by human marriage—or, at least, by the actual marriage of this one man, and seen from the standpoint of his existential religious experience of what Yahweh signified for Israel—may well be called a veiled breakthrough of the New Testament idea of marriage.

2. The book of *Jeremiah* constantly refers back to the image of marriage as used by Hosea. But here too Israel's unchastity, that is, her infidelity to Yahweh in worshipping the Baals, was the immediate cause of Jeremiah's expression of the covenant of grace with Yahweh in terms of marriage. The image of marital infidelity can all the more readily be understood if it is remembered that Israel's marital infidelity to Yahweh was concretely situated in the worship of the Baals or alien gods, and that this worship was accompanied by all kinds of sexual debauchery in connection with the cult of the fertility gods. (See Hos i–iv; iv. 13 f.; ix. 1; Jer ii. 20 and iii.) The after-effects of this fact are very pronounced in Jeremiah. He alludes to the sacrifice of children (ii. 34) which was closely connected with this cult— the woman who had taken part in a religious fertility rite and had conceived her first child by Baal had to consecrate and sacrifice this child to Baal. At the same time, however, Jeremiah was also voicing a reaction against Judah's attempts to secure the political support of Egypt and Assyria (ii. 18), which constituted a lack of trust in Yahweh and thus also unchastity and adultery. Although Judah had witnessed Yahweh's punishment of her sister Israel, the Northern Kingdom, for adultery—Yahweh had

given Israel a bill of divorce and had legally repudiated her (iii. 7–8)—Judah still carried on with her unchastity. As a threat to the people, Jeremiah appealed to the Law: "If a man divorces his wife, and she goes from him and becomes another man's wife, will he return to her?" (iii. 1). But, in the tradition of Hosea, Jeremiah's prophecy ultimately results in an affirmation of Yahweh's eternal love: "Yahweh appeared to him from afar. I have loved you with an everlasting love; therefore I have continued my faithfulness to you. Again I will build you" (xxxi. 3 f.). But here too the desert-phase is once more necessary: "The people . . . found grace in the wilderness" (xxxi. 2). The infidelity of the people—"As a faithless wife leaves her husband, so have you been faithless to me, O house of Israel, says Yahweh" (iii. 20)— was ultimately to change into lasting fidelity because of Yahweh's powerful mercy: "For Yahweh has created a new thing on the earth: a woman protects a man (= the wife shall return to her husband)" (xxxi. 22). If Israel acknowledged her sin, Yahweh would not remain angry for ever (iii. 12–13).

The image of marriage had become thoroughly established in the case of Jeremiah. Influenced by Hosea, he took it directly from man's existential experience of marriage and so not, or at least not directly, from the Canaanite mythology of marriage. But this Israelite experience of marriage still implied certain limitations affecting human marriage and remarriage. A woman's second marriage after legal divorce meant the end of her first marriage. Menacingly Jeremiah pointed this out, in the event of Israel's infidelity to Yahweh's love of his bride. But Yahweh was not like this. Even though man's experience of marriage incorporated the idea of faithfulness, and even though marriage was— for precisely this reason—a suitable means of expressing God's covenant of grace, it was not man's experience of marriage, but his experience of Yahweh's activity within the covenant, which caused the idea of the possibility of faithfulness in spite of everything to develop so fully. The reality, which was symbolically portrayed in marriage, transcended Israel's experience of the secular reality itself.

3. The marriage image of Hosea and Jeremiah is given a striking characteristic in the Book of *Ezekiel*,[23] and this is especially noticeable in chapters xvi and xxiii. Chapter xvi deals with Jerusalem's marriage with Yahweh and her adultery. The image of infidelity, of the "harlot" and the "adulteress," is once again prominent. Aiming publicly to expose Jerusalem's historical unfaithfulness, Ezekiel uses the device of a matrimonial lawsuit and sets the scene at the gates of the city. He too is reminded of the time in the desert when Yahweh and Israel first loved each other and the wedding was celebrated. Israel was not unfaithful until the people entered the Promised Land. But, unlike Hosea, who was directly concerned with Israel, a people whose origins were outside Canaan, Ezekiel points to the fact that the City of Jerusalem had its first beginnings in the pagan land of Canaan. In Ezekiel, then, the early and innocent youth of Jerusalem is not a historical reality, but is present only as the intention of Yahweh's saving activity (Ezek xv.).

Jerusalem's origins were pagan, and this acts as an inherited burden on Yahweh's chosen city. The two culminating points in Ezekiel's account occur when Yahweh "passes by" Jerusalem. On the first encounter Yahweh finds an abandoned infant, a foundling on whom he takes pity (xvi. 4–5). The second time he meets her, he marries her (xvi. 6–7). Choosing her as his wife, Yahweh bestows marriage gifts upon her (xvi. 8–14). This marriage is a covenant, confirmed by an oath (xvi. 8). The birth of sons and daughters (xvi. 20) is evidence that the marriage was fully consummated. Thus Ezekiel too emphasizes that there was a perfect marriage, legally contracted and made in love, between Yahweh and Israel, a covenant relationship which would permit no infidelity and which was indissoluble. Divorce was in this case an

[23] See especially W. Zimmerli's commentary on Ezekiel, *BKAT*, xiii, pp. 1–10.

outrage against the covenant of God; yet Israel was guilty of it.

Ezekiel's account of this love is blunt and straightforward, and includes the stages which we noted in the case of Hosea: the birth of Yahweh's bride (xvi. 4), her puberty or marriageable age (xvi. 7), their betrothal, wedding, and marriage ("living together," xvi. 8), the infidelity and adultery of the beloved (xvi. 15–34), and Yahweh's punishment of this infidelity (xvi. 40). Jerusalem's parents were pagan, and this, for Israel, meant that she was born of "godless parents." From the moment of her birth she was unsightly, poor, and wretched, and no one cared for her except Yahweh. He took pity on the abandoned child and looked after her until she reached a marriageable age. Then he entered into a covenant with her, a marriage covenant of grace. He washed and cleansed her and dressed her in the finest clothes and ornaments so that she became the most beautiful of women—"without spot or wrinkle," as Paul was to say at a later stage (Eph v. 27).

But Israel was unfaithful to Yahweh and committed one act of adultery after another. Whereas it was the normal practice of prostitutes to take money from their lovers, Israel in her adultery gave Yahweh's gifts and ornaments to those who sinned with her. Yahweh, however, remained faithful. It is true that he was to bring her to repentance by punishing her and putting her to the test, but he would not forget his covenant with her in the days of her youth, and would establish with her an everlasting covenant (xvi. 60). This lasting marriage alliance, made in mutual trust, constitutes an eschatological perspective of the covenant of grace—reveals a perspective of marriage in the "eschatological" period, that is, in the time when Christ, the *Eschaton*, was to appear. But in Israel this particular perspective of marriage remained unconscious and implicit.

Chapter xxiii deals with Yahweh's marriage with two sisters, Oholah and Oholibah, that is, with the Northern Kingdom, which had its own forms of worship ("Oholah" = "she who has her own tent"), and with Judah, the Southern Kingdom with its

legitimate temple of Yahweh ("Oholibah" = "my tent is in her").
Yahweh's marriage with two wives caused no surprise here, since
Israel and Judah formed the single, though disunited, people of
God. Moreover, a marriage with one wife and a concubine was
accepted as normal and good in the society of the time; and this
also indicates that marriage, as a revelation of the divine covenant,
was thoroughly in accordance with marriage as evidenced in
everyday experience. It is also possible that a Canaanite image of
a marriage between a god and two women is present in this idea,
but, if this is so, the Canaanite image had been completely demythologized. In any case, it is probable that the prophetic message
was aimed exclusively at Judah (Jerusalem), which at that time
was the only free, unoccupied part of Yahweh's domain. Moreover, the double alliance is due entirely to the division of the one
chosen people into two states, so that the pure image of Hosea
is in the last analysis preserved—the image of Yahweh's married
love for the one people of God.

According to the historical situation which chapter xxiii had
in mind—the time of Manasseh, when child sacrifice was practised, under the influence of Assyria, in connection with the
initiation rites (see xvi. 20–21)—the adultery consisted of Judah's,
and previously also Israel's, abandonment of faith in Yahweh and
reliance on foreign political powers (Egypt, Assyria, and Babylon) for help. In this way, Judah's marital love for Yahweh was
destroyed. The point of Ezekiel's application of the marriage
image to the covenant of grace was still the same as that of
Hosea's: this covenant demanded from Israel an unreserved trust
and confidence in Yahweh's solicitous presence with Israel, a
complete faith in Yahweh. But Ezekiel goes further than Hosea
and elaborates an idea which Jeremiah did no more than intro-
duce. Even in her infidelity Israel continued to pride herself upon
the fact that she was God's "chosen people." Ezekiel wished to
eliminate this self-assurance, based on the covenant—to stress
that Israel had no legal title to God under the covenant, but
rather that it was a matter of a gratuitous gift. Egypt was the

enticer—the man to whom Israel, in her unfaithfulness to Yahweh, now turned for help and support, and the name Egypt
should have recalled the redemption from Egypt and God's
mercy and help. So Israel was in fact punished by her lovers—
by Egypt, Assyria, and Babylon.

In this great prophecy—this interpretation of history in the
form of an image of marriage—given in chapter xxiii of the Book
of Ezekiel we find a moral conclusion in the shape of the sentence
passed on Judah after a matrimonial lawsuit. This conclusion contains an admonition to "all women" and all men and gives an
example for their married lives and social relationships (xxiii.
48-9). The prophecy of the people of God that is punished for
its infidelity to married love implies a moral lesson for the married life of men and women. In this chapter of Ezekiel we can
see the already classic marriage-symbolism of Hosea and Jeremiah having its effect on the everyday married life of the men
and women of God's chosen people. Seen as a dynamic course
of events in the stormy love affair between Yahweh and his people, salvation history had a great deal to teach the Israelites in
their married and family life. This is the concluding thought of
Ezek xxiii. 48-9. It is only expressed in passing, but it provides
a point of departure.

The theology of the history of salvation contains a *kerygma*
and a *parainesis*—a message and a moral admonition addressed to
the relationship between man and woman in marriage. It was
only when the final stage of the history of man's salvation was
begun in Christ that it was to become apparent that the inner
essence of marriage within the order of salvation could not be
determined exclusively by the Genesis blessing on marriage, although this was certainly of fundamental and lasting importance.
It had also to be seen in its essential relationship with Christ's exclusive love for his church, so that the inner boundaries of secular
marriage, consecrated by Christ, were apparent in confrontation
with the kingdom of heaven.

4. The prophetic marriage image occurs once more in the Book of *Isaiah*, chapters xl–lv, but it is noticeable here that there is an immediate prospect of the solemn return of the abandoned partner to Yahweh's house. Cyrus had already struck his first blows against the Babylonian empire, and the return of the Jews to their own country was imminent. The prophecies of Hosea, Jeremiah, and Ezekiel that the divorce was not permanent were about to be fulfilled.

Thus says Yahweh: "Where is your mother's bill of divorce, with which I put her away? Or which of my creditors is it to whom I have sold you? Behold, for your iniquities you were sold, and for your transgressions your mother was put away." [Is l. 1.]

Jeremiah had already referred to a bill of divorce (Jer iii. 1, 7–8), but at the same time had made it clear that the divorce was not to be permanent. Pursuing this point, but incidentally somewhat blurring the sharpness of Jeremiah's and Ezekiel's image, Isaiah says that Zion in exile did not receive a bill of divorce and the separation was not permanent. In Is liv, the abandoned bride is taken back into her husband's house and the permanent marriage which Yahweh contracts with his people is celebrated in joyful song.

For Yahweh has called you like a wife forsaken and grieved in spirit, like a wife of youth when she is cast off, says your God. For a brief moment I forsook you, but with great compassion I will gather you. In overflowing wrath for a moment I hid my face from you, but with everlasting love I will have compassion on you, says Yahweh, your Redeemer. [liv. 6–8.]

It is not absolutely clear whether the text alludes to an entirely new marriage or to the resumption—in a completely new way— of previous marital relationships. The interpretation of the text depends partly on the vocalization of the Hebrew word which, with different vowels, can mean either "the one who is marrying you now" or simply "your partner in marriage" or "your possessor." Thus the passage (liv. 5) may mean "For your Maker shall become your husband," "For your partner in marriage, he will be the Creator," or "The one who is marrying you now is the Creator." What chapter liv wishes to make clear, in contrast to the shameful situation of the wife (liv. 4) who has left her husband, is that Israel's husband is the Creator. This idea is elaborated by Deutero-Isaiah in the context of salvation history— Yahweh is the God of the absolutely new beginning, the God who makes all things new. Precisely as Israel's husband he is also the Creator who can effect a complete renewal of the marriage, however disrupted it was. "The Holy One of Israel is your Redeemer" (liv. 5).

The new marriage was the continuation of the covenant concluded once and for all; but, on the other hand, it was also an absolutely new beginning. All purely juridical considerations as to whether the covenant was really annulled by a legal act of adultery break down here. The covenant was annulled by the human partner, but not on God's part. Consequently, what was absolutely new for the human partner was for God only the eternal newness of his love, which is never old, but permanent and consistent. "I have given you no bill of divorce," said God, in effect, "but by your sins you have forsaken me" (l. 1).

Here, of course, creation should be seen as God's saving activity, the activity which is peculiar to him and which results in constant and absolute renewal. This is the surprising consequence of God's restoration of this marriage by creation thus understood:

Sing, O barren one, who did not bear; break forth into singing and cry aloud, you who have not been in travail! For the children of the desolate one will be more than the children of her that is married, says Yahweh . . . For you will spread abroad to the right and to the left, and your descendants will possess the nations and will people the desolate cities. [liv. 1–3.]

In contrast to the previous situation in which the wife found herself—she had been unfaithful but, despite the exile, she had not been repudiated—life under the renewed covenant was to be immeasurably more fruitful. Yahweh, Israel's protector, emerges more clearly now as the Creator of the universe and of all nations. Thus the realization that the "Creator of heaven and earth" was Israel's husband was to give world-wide dimensions to the spread of the children of Israel (liv. 3).

In the context of marriage, chapter liv of the Book of Isaiah is most significant. Not only is the already familiar prophetic idea preserved; it also gains "eschatological" dimensions. (In Gal iv. 27 Paul was to apply the passage to the heavenly church.) But Deutero-Isaiah's idea of creation goes further than this, rejecting despair over even the most disrupted and disjointed circumstances. Should he, who had created the sun, the moon, and the stars, and who holds the world together, not be able to rejoin a broken marriage? This is the main idea of Is liv. A more solid foundation is given to the already basic idea of trust in Yahweh, who had been described by the prophets as—seen from the point of view of man—the very soul of the covenant of grace: the absolute creative power of God, capable of renewing all things, in the service of salvation, that is, in the service of the marriage relationship between Yahweh and Israel.

With Isaiah the prophetic image of marriage as a means of revealing God's covenant activity was, so to speak, exhausted. No more new elements occur in connection with this theme in the Old Testament. All that was to be said about the image had already been said, and all that remained was for it to be made historically concrete in the human appearance of Christ; for here God's creative power, capable of renewing all things, would really purify the church and attire her as the permanent bride of Christ. But, before we turn to a consideration of this definitive realisation in Christ, we must attempt to synthesize the various elements which were presupposed in this image of marriage and which went to make up married life, and to trace the experience of human marriage in the post-exilic period. The question we must ask is this: Did the prophetic theme of marriage really have any noticeable influence on everyday married life in Jewish society?

The Day-to-Day Experience of Marriage and the Prophetic Marriage Image; the Wisdom Literature

The "beloved" of Israel as an expression for Yahweh himself, and the religious idea of adultery in respect of Yahweh, occur after the major prophets in various books of the Old Testament.[24] This prophetic vision had without more ado become one of Israel's acquisitions. Nonetheless, it is remarkable that although marriage—despite certain distinctly anti-feminist elements—was presented in the post-exilic Wisdom literature as a profoundly human experience, there are no allusions, except in a few of the Psalms, to the prophetic vision of God's marriage covenant with his people. In contrast to the older Song of Solomon, the Wisdom literature shows more concern for the moral and religious soundness of marriage, though without neglecting to make frank affirmation of man's love for his own wife. But in the texts no trace can be found of any explicit effect of Hosea's prophetic symbolic action, or of Ezekiel's final admonition to Israel's men and women to allow themselves to be inspired—in their everyday married lives—by Yahweh's disconcerting marital fidelity to Israel. The moral and religious humanised married life of the time must therefore have developed as the result of a combination of human experience and various social factors.[25]

---

[24] For example, Is v. 1; i. 21–6; l. 1; liv. 6–7; lxii. 5; Ps xlvii. 4. Texts in which there is reference to such expressions as the "daughter of Israel," the "daughter of Zion," etc., have another meaning. In the ancient world cities were called "virgin" or "daughter." The Old Testament also speaks in this way of the "daughter of Egypt."

[25] Before the exile the pattern of family life was patriarchal. After the exile, however, this covenant was broken and the family was thrown back much more on its own resources, with the result that the personal relationships of marriage became more pronounced. In this way social factors had a share in the "humanisation" of married life.

Even more remarkable is the fact that the Septuagint translation of the Song of Solomon, which was made at about this time, shows equally few traces of an allegorical interpretation of the original Song in the sense of a hymn to the covenant of grace. The earliest allegorical Jewish exegesis of the Song that we possess is that of the Rabbi Akiba, written a century after Christ.[26] This exegesis was soon taken over by Christians like Hippolytus of Rome, who was the first to mention it,[27] and Origen, who systematically worked out the allegory.[28] As we have already seen, the Song had been taken into the Palestinian canon of the Bible even before there was any question of an allegorical exegesis of it. Even if it is not possible to account for the acceptance of the Song into the canon of the Bible on a basis of its interpretation as a hymn to the covenant of grace, this does not mean that such an exegesis is unbiblical or that it goes back to a purely interpolated or "pious" interpretation without any biblical foundation. While retaining its original meaning, the Song could be read again against the background of the prophetic vision of Yahweh's marriage covenant which had in the meantime made itself felt in Israel, and thereby—within the dynamism of a revelation which was still taking place—gain a further dimension.

This was all the more possible because the ancient setting of the Song had become less distinct and theologically less relevant by the time of the Jews, for sexuality and eroticism had long since been stripped of their earlier mythological connotations. The contents of the original Song, now accepted as canonical, almost as a matter of course called for a new interpretation, and this was readily available from the perspective of the prophetic vision. This was also to be expected since we do find here and there in the Song—perhaps because of a similar general religious and social background—certain ideas which called the book of Isaiah to mind, and because the Song was read aloud in the

[26] See *SB*, pt. 4, pp. 432–3, and P. Benoit, RB, 54 (1947), p. 68.
[27] *Hom. in Cantica Canticorum* (PG, 10, 627–30).
[28] *Hom. in Cant. Cant.* (PG, 13, 37–216).

liturgy of the synagogue during the feast of the Passover. The
Rabbi Akiba, who was the first to defend the exclusively allegorical meaning of the Song, also remarks on the fact that this problem did trouble some exegetes of his own time. The writings of
the church Fathers also show clearly that the meaning of allegorical interpretations of this kind soon loses its force and becomes
debased when the historical, literal meaning of the biblical texts
in their original setting is left out of account. A direct application of the Song to the covenant of grace was all the more
difficult since sexual and erotic themes would thereby be accorded
a place in the very expression of the image, and this would have
been considered an abomination by the prophets and indeed by
all pious Israelites. Although Israel did speak in very human terms
about God, this anthropomorphism always stopped short at
certain limits, especially if God's transcendence was in any way
threatened by an element of sex.

Furthermore, awareness of the "deeper meaning" of the Song
developed during the rabbinical period, when a decidedly stricter,
more prudish attitude was prevalent, in contrast to the earlier,
more open-minded affirmation of sexuality and eroticism. For the
Jews of this period the presence of the Song in the canon of
the Bible could in the long run only be explained by its "spiritual"
significance. Nevertheless, the Song was eventually interpreted,
both by Jewish and by Christian exegetes, as an image of the
covenant of grace, that is, as a moving account in image form
describing Yahweh's reunion with his bride Israel after the separation of the exile. This certainly indicates that the prophetic
vision continued to have an effect on human experience even
though, with the exception of a few references in the Psalms, it
was no longer put forward as a theme after the exile. On the
other hand, this in no way invalidates the claim that it was experience of the covenant of grace which contributed to the moral
and religious soundness of married life as described in the Wisdom literature, although this was not expressed in terms derived

from the language of marital love. How, then, was everyday married life seen in the Wisdom books?

A notable characteristic of the post-exilic vision of marriage is that it continues the line of thought begun in the second account of the creation and the (in spirit not dissimilar) Song of Solomon—the idea that marriage is good for the man who fears Yahweh. The nucleus of the Wisdom literature was the wisdom of the ancient Near East drawn into the orbit of religious faith in Yahweh. Among three things which are too wonderful even for the sage to fathom is listed "the way of a man with a maiden" (Prov xxx. 18–19). A wife is regarded as a treasure, the priceless value of which is frankly extolled in the Wisdom literature. "He who finds a wife finds a good thing, and obtains favour from Yahweh" (Prov xviii. 22). One of the three things which delight the sage is "a wife and husband who live in harmony" (Sir xxv. 1). But this is accorded only to the man who fears God: "Happy is the husband of a good wife. . . . A good wife is a great blessing; she will be granted among the blessings of the man who fears Yahweh" (Sir xxvi. 1, 3). "He who acquires a wife gets his best possession, a helper fit for him and a pillar of support" (Sir xxxvi. 24), for "where there is no wife, a man will wander about and sigh" (Sir xxxvi. 25), as helpless and insecure as if he had no home. "She is far more precious than jewels" (Prov xxxi. 10). A happy marriage is therefore a blessing from God (Prov xviii. 22; xix. 14; Sir xxvi. 3, 14).

Although "a wife's charm delights her husband" (Sir xxvi. 13) and "a woman's beauty gladdens the countenance, and surpasses every human desire" (Sir xxxvi. 22), the Wisdom books are very careful not to extol physical beauty in isolation. The believer may enjoy this beauty only in faithful love and virtue: "Like the sun rising in the heights of Yahweh, so is the beauty of a good wife in her well-ordered home" (Sir xxvi. 16), and "no balance can weigh the value of a chaste soul" (Sir xxvi. 15). The emphasis is always on the "wise," the "prudent" woman (Prov xix. 14; xxxi. 10–31; Sir vii. 19; xxv. 8). Praise of the "beautiful

woman" is permissible only within marriage. Man's eyes must be
turned away from the beautiful woman who is not his wife, for
"many have been misled by a woman's beauty" (Sir ix. 8; see
also the whole passage ix. 3–9). "Do not be ensnared by a
woman's beauty, and do not desire a woman for her beauty"
(Sir xxv. 28).[29]

The Wisdom books contain repeated warnings against adultery
and infidelity (Sir xxiii. 18–27; Prov v), and insist on caution
with regard to other men's wives (Prov v. 2–14; vii. 4–27; Sir ix.
3–9): "Let your fountain be blessed, and rejoice in the wife of
your youth" (Prov v. 18). A man should not be infatuated "with
a loose woman and embrace the bosom of an adventuress" (Prov
v. 20), but should "drink water from [his] own cistern" (Prov
v. 15). In connection with adultery, it is said that seeking after
wisdom should protect a man "from the loose woman" who
"forsakes the companion of her youth," that is, her first husband,
and "forgets the covenant of her God" (Prov ii. 16–17). Marriage is certainly called "covenant of God," but it is probable that
here "covenant of God" only means that the adulterous wife has,
by her action, trodden the "law of God" underfoot.

The Wisdom books, therefore, praise the happiness of the husband of a wife who is beautiful as well as good, prudent, and
virtuous. The alphabetical hymn to this "worthy woman and
wife" in Prov xxxi. 10–31, although set within the framework of
the civilization of the time, is a fine summary of the timeless
spirituality of marriage which the *Bible de Jérusalem* calls "un
humanisme dévot" (p. 597). This passage in Proverbs should also
be compared with Sir xxvi. 1–4.

> A good wife who can find?
>   she is far more precious than jewels.
> The heart of her husband trusts in her,
>   and he will have no lack of gain.

[29] The RSV text reads "for her possessions," but cites "for her beauty"
as an alternative reading. [Translator's note.]

She does him good, and not harm,
   all the days of her life.
She seeks wool and flax,
   and works with willing hands.

She is like the ships of the merchant,
   she brings her food from afar.
She rises while it is yet night
   and provides food for her household and
     tasks for her maidens.

She considers a field and buys it;
   with the fruit of her hands she plants a vineyard.
She girds her loins with strength
   and makes her arms strong.

She perceives that her merchandise is profitable.
   Her lamp does not go out at night.
She puts her hands to the distaff,
   and her hands hold the spindle.

She opens her hand to the poor,
   and reaches out her hands to the needy.
She is not afraid of snow for her household,
   for all her household are clothed in scarlet.

She makes herself coverings;
   her clothing is fine linen and purple.
Her husband is known in the gates,
   when he sits among the elders of the land.

She makes linen garments and sells them;
   she delivers girdles to the merchant.
Strength and dignity are her clothing,
   and she laughs at the time to come.

She opens her mouth with wisdom,
   and the teaching of kindness is on her tongue.

She looks well to the ways of her household,
  and does not eat the bread of idleness.

Her children rise up and call her blessed;
  her husband also, and he praises her:
"Many women have done excellently,
  but you surpass them all."

Charm is deceitful, and beauty is vain,
  but a woman who fears Yahweh is to be praised.
Give her of the fruit of her hands,
  and let her works praise her in the gates.
                                                    [Prov xxxi. 10–31.]

On the other hand, however, the Wisdom literature is also full
of anti-feminist references, similar to those found in the sayings
of all peoples. These sayings in the Wisdom books allude to the
"evil woman": "I would rather dwell with a lion and a dragon
than dwell with an evil wife" (Sir xxv. 16; cf. xxv. 13); "any
iniquity is insignificant compared to a wife's iniquity" (Sir xxv.
19); and "there is grief of heart and sorrow when a wife is envious of a rival" (Sir xxvi. 6). And, although these remarks are
undoubtedly prompted by the high expectations which man has
of woman, the Wisdom literature is not entirely free from bitterness where woman is concerned: "Better is the wickedness of
a man than a woman who does good; and it is a woman
who brings shame and disgrace" (Sir xlii. 14); and "from garments comes the moth, and from a woman comes woman's
wickedness" (Sir xlii. 13). She is the eternal Eve: "From a
woman sin had its beginning, and because of her we all die" (Sir
xxv. 24).

The Wisdom literature is well aware of the universal problems
of family life and of parents' worries for their daughters:

A daughter keeps her father secretly wakeful, and worry over her
robs him of sleep; when she is young, lest she do not marry, or if

married, lest she should be hated; while a virgin, lest she be defiled or become pregnant in her father's house . . . [Sir xlii. 9 f.]

Finally, several new themes are to be found in the Wisdom of Solomon. The marriage image is used here not—as in the prophets—for the covenant of grace, but for the love of wisdom: "I desired to take her for my bride, and I became enamoured of her beauty . . . I determined to take her to live with me . . . Companionship with her has no bitterness, and life with her has no pain, but gladness and joy" (Wis viii. 1, 9, 16). The work of a hellenized Jew probably living in Egypt, this book was intended for Jewish readers in Egypt who would undoubtedly have come across large, prosperous families among the "pagans." This fact must have confronted the Jews with a problem, since they regarded a large family as a blessing from Yahweh. And so the writer of the Book of Wisdom consoled his readers with the strength of the religion of faith in Yahweh, and in so doing achieved a degree of demythologization of the large family as such. The theme of Wis iii. 10 to iv. 6 is "a large family is not a blessing for the ungodly." "The prolific brood of the ungodly will be of no use" (iv. 3), for the children of those who worship false gods will follow the same path as their parents. This was the germ of a new idea which emerged in post-exilic Israel: "Blessed is the barren woman who is undefiled . . . [and] the eunuch whose hands have done no lawless deed" (iii. 13 f.). A large number of children was, in itself, no blessing; it was better to have no children at all, if this childless state went together with virtue (iv. 1). In this deutero-canonical writing, then, the large family was characterized, not as something of intrinsic value in itself, but as a value within the context of the moral and religious life. It is clear, too, that it was a polemic against the prosperity of the "ungodly Egyptians" which gave the first impetus to this new idea.

We may therefore conclude that the Wisdom literature testifies

to the Israelite and Jewish faith in the goodness of marriage based
on a firm foundation of religion and morals. It is this which distin-
guishes it from the much earlier Song of Solomon, which certainly
had some influence on these Jewish writings.[30] A living echo of this
essentially healthy conception of marriage can be detected in the
experience of marriage of an average pious family living in the
diaspora. Within the same body of Wisdom literature the Bible
presents us with a concrete example of the Jewish ideal of marriage—that of Tobit and his wife Anna and the young Tobias
and his wife Sarah. From the very first, the young Tobias and
Sarah lived their married life in a serenely religious atmosphere,
although they had many difficulties. "Thou hast taken pity upon
two only children. Make them, O Lord, bless thee more fully:
and to offer up to thee a sacrifice of thy praise, and of their
health" (Tobit viii. 19).[31] The explicit model for this marriage is
Gen ii. 18 (Tobit viii. 6).[32] Tobias and Sarah did not marry
"for lust" (Tobit viii. 7)[33] but "with an upright heart."[34] They
set a high value on sexual intercourse, but for religious reasons
they were able to live in continence. Indeed, they began their
married life with three nights of continence, hence the "three

[30] Compare, for example, Prov vii. 17 with Song iv. 14; Prov v. 3 with
Song iv. 11; Prov v. 19 with Song ii. 9; iv. 5; viii. 14; Prov v. 15–18 with .
Song iv. 12, 15; Prov vi, 31 with Song viii. 7.

[31] Vulgate—Douai.

[32] Greek—RSV.

[33] Greek—RSV.

[34] According to one version, which is also followed by *BJ*. The original
text of the book of Tobit is not known, but several versions are extant.
The Vulgate translation goes back to an original Semitic fragment. The
older translations show all kinds of divergences. Other translations of
viii. 7, for example, read: "not for lust . . . but only because of a longing
for offspring." It is undeniable that many different ascetic tendencies grew
up in connection with marriage after the exile. One of these was the
practice of having intercourse only when it was necessary for the continuation of the family. According to J. van der Ploeg, this is what marriage
meant to part at least of the Essene community, not all the members of
which lived strictly celibate lives. See *Vondsten in de woestijn van Juda*,
Utrecht (1957), pp. 131 ff.

nights of Tobias" which have played an important part in the history of the church and in the liturgy.[35]

The motivation for this practice is provided in the following way in the book of Tobit. Tobias tells his bride: "We are the children of saints: and we must not be joined together in marriage like heathens that know not God" (Tobit viii. 5).[36] This leads Tobias to decide: "Sarah, . . . let us pray to God today, and tomorrow, and the next day: because for these three nights we are joined to God. And when the third night is over, we will be in our own wedlock" (viii. 4; vi. 16–22).[37] Their prayer was not alien to marriage, however, because the words of their prayer were precisely those of Gen ii. 18 (this is especially clear in the Greek version).

Even now newly married couples exercise self-restraint for similar religious reasons, although in their case the reasons are implicit in mutual respect. The husband leads his bride very gradually towards full sexual intercourse, not because he is prudish, but because he is anxious not to offend her natural feminine modesty. He does this because he is aware of the danger of sowing the seed for the future failure of the entire married relationship on the wedding night. If he is too hasty, "unpsychological" in his approach to his bride, or simply selfish, he may be the cause of an unspoken resentment in his wife which could endanger the whole marriage at a later stage. The "nights of Tobias" may thus still have a salutary message for our own times.

The "civil," or rather family, wedding ceremony of the Jews was celebrated in the family circle of Tobit and his son Tobias. The father of the house conducted the service.

[35] See M. Schumpp, *Das Buch des Tobias,* Münster i.W. (1933), pp. 144 ff.; P. Saint-Yves, "Les trois nuits de Tobie ou la continence durant la première ou les premières nuits du mariage," *RA,* 44 (1934), pp. 266–9.

[36] Vulg.–Douai.

[37] Vulg.–Douai. The account of the "nights of Tobias" is lacking in other versions.

And taking the right hand of his daughter, he gave it into the right hand of Tobias, saying: "The God of Abraham, and the God of Isaac, and the God of Jacob be with you. And may he join you together, and fulfil his blessing in you." And taking paper they made a writing of the marriage. [vii. 15–16.]³⁸

The book of Tobit depicts the religious climax of Old Testament married and family life, in which the partners placed themselves completely under the protection of divine providence and the *Torah* and conformed, in faithful obedience, to the saving will of the God of creation. Moreover it is precisely in the Wisdom literature, in which marriage reaches a climax, that the tradition of the Genesis account of the creation and the prophetic message of God's covenant of grace as a marriage come together. In the family life of Tobias we have a particularly clear example of the experience of secular human values lived in the light of God, with whom the married couple are on intimate terms. Living with God in this way impresses a mark upon the experience of marriage itself, so that—in some respects, at least—it is experienced differently by those who live their marriage in God's light than by those "who know not God." In the case of the Jews, religion had a concrete effect upon marriage, as on every natural human value. When accompanied by thanksgiving to— or rather praise of—God, it was for the Jews an experience that was good, glorious, and pleasing to God.³⁹ We may therefore conclude that in Israel, thanks to faith in God's creation and in the covenant of grace, together with a combination of many dif-

³⁸ According to one version, which was followed by the Vulgate; see also in connection with the solemnisation of marriage, which is treated later in this book.

³⁹ The *berākhāh*, blessing, praise, was pronounced by the Jews when something secular and human was involved—over food and drink, and sometimes even over very commonplace things. See, for example, R. Aron, *Les années obscures de Jésus*, Paris (1960). Aron is himself a Jew, and he describes in his book the Jewish life of the young Jesus during the hidden years of his life, from the perspective of a Jewish boy of those days. For "blessing" see also pp. 72 ff. below.

ferent social factors, the sober, but nonetheless real, religious dimension to marriage was gradually revealed, although the forms in which its practical experience were apparent were conditioned by its historical and social context.

SECULAR MARRIAGE SEEN THROUGH THE PRISM OF THE COVENANT OF GRACE

If we are to synthesize the content of the marriage relationship, insofar as it is presupposed in the human interpretation of the covenant of grace in the image of marriage, and insofar as the covenant itself is expressed in that interpretation, we must take the following ideas into account.

The marriage concepts most commonly used in connection with Yahweh's relationship with Israel under the covenant are those of *ḥesedh*, *'emûnāh*, and *qinᵉʾāh*. By *ḥesedh* is meant love, goodness, and an inward feeling of tenderness and mercy (Is lxiii. 7; Joel ii. 13; Mic vii. 18; Ps v. 7; xxxvi. 5; xlviii. 9; Jer iii. 12). *'Emûnāh* is loving faithfulness or firmness, constancy in love, in which the lovers continue to say "amen" to each other. (Deut vii. 9; Is xlix. 7; Jer xlii. 5; Hos xi. 12.) By *qinᵉʾāh* is meant jealousy of a possible rival, for this love is exclusive and forbids rivals. (Ezek xvi. 38–42; xxiii. 25.)[40] The concept *ḥesedh* is particularly important in the context of marriage as *bᵉrîth*—a covenant between man and woman. (Mal ii. 14; Ezek xvi. 8; Prov ii. 17.)[41]

It is, of course, true that in the later books the concept *ḥesedh* came to denote Yahweh's one-sided love for Israel, a love which

[40] It is clear from B. Renaud's study, "Je suis un Dieu jaloux," LD, 36 (1963), that the idea of the "jealous God" was derived from Deuteronomic circles and does not relate to the marriage image. Ezekiel alone associates jealousy with Yahweh's marital love for Israel. *Qinᵉʾah* or jealousy here indicates the anger of betrayed love intent on the punishment of the faithless partner. (Ezek xvi. 35–43; xxiii. 24–5.)

[41] See also Hos ii. 18 ff. It should be remembered that the Old Testament has no technical term for "marriage."

remained constant even though it evoked no response. (Ex xxxiv.
7; Is lxiii. 7; Jer xxxii. 18; Ps v. 7; lxxxvi. 5; cvi. 7–45; cxlv. 8.)
First and foremost, however, and especially in the case of the
Deuteronomist writers, it indicated the power binding two beings to each other, and thus a communal bond (corresponding to
the Latin *religio* and *pietas*). Ḥesedh was in this way the bond of
unity and affection itself, a bond or "covenant" which as it were
acquired a legal stability. Ḥesedh and *bᵉrîth*, community of love
and covenant, were almost synonymous in practice. They were
used as twin words which evoked mental associations with each
other. (Deut vii. 2–9, 12; 1 Kings viii. 23; Neh i. 5; ix. 32; Ps l. 5;
Ex xx. 6; Deut v. 10; 2 Sam xxii. 51.) Ḥesedh was the principle
making the covenant into a bond of affection, a legally established community. Marriage was the human reality in which
ḥesedh, love, and *bᵉrîth*, covenant, acquired their privileged
meaning, and enabled the Old Testament to speak about God's
covenant of grace. It was precisely because the prophets had
shown that Israel was unfaithful to this covenant, while Yahweh's
ḥesedh lasted for ever (Is lv. 3; Ps lxxxix. *passim*), that the idea
of Yahweh's one-sided, undeserved ḥesedh grew up. Despite the
unfaithfulness of Israel, Yahweh was still intent upon winning a
reciprocated faithfulness from his bride.

There is another marriage concept which must be taken into
account in this connection—the concept of *'ahābhāh*, love or
amor, in the sense of *anhelare*, that is, of being impelled by a
violent and powerful voluntary desire for preference.[42] If we include this concept we find that marriage—expressed in terms of
'ahābhāh (love), ḥesedh, and *bᵉrîth*—originated in a spontaneous
feeling and desire, led on to a definite choice, and was regulated
by a covenant and established in the loving faithfulness of ḥesedh.

According to ancient Near Eastern custom, the man took the

[42] D. W. Thomas, "The root *'āhabh*, love, in Hebrew," *ZAW*, 57 (1939),
pp. 57–64. See also E. Jacob, *Theology of the Old Testament*, London
(1958).

initiative in love.[43] Moreover, *'ahābhāh*, as elective love, was love of the superior being for the inferior, and thus, in the ancient Near East, love of the man for the woman, and not of the woman for the man.[44] (This is why Paul was later to speak of the man's duty in love to the woman, and only of obedience on the part of the woman to the man.) But this choice on the part of the man was an ornament for the woman, making her splendid and worthy in his eyes, whatever she might be in herself— and thus for others (Deut vii. 8, 13; vii. 7; Is xlix. 15). However, this relationship also demanded that the wife should conduct herself in accordance with her election by the man. But man is made in the image of God, and the principle therefore holds good that God's *ḥesedh* for us must have a visible form in man's *ḥesedh* for his fellow-man, since this *ḥesedh* is, as it were, a *ḥesedh 'elōhîm*, a divine love. (2 Sam ix. 3; 1 Sam xx. 14.) We may therefore say that what was in force in the covenant of grace applied particularly to the partner in marriage: "You shall love Yahweh, your God, with all your heart, and with all your soul, and with all your might" (Deut vi. 4).

Included in the general category of covenant relationships, marriage also created what amounted to a blood-relationship between the husband and wife. In ancient nomadic society, this relationship made *šālôm* (peace) between the related parties (Gen xxvi. 28–31; 1 Kings v. 12; Job v. 23; Is liv. 10) who, by their contract, were incorporated into the ancestral tribe. Married life was thus characterized by peace relationships.

Yahweh was always the witness in the making of covenants. He was therefore also witness in the covenant relationship of marriage (Mal ii. 10–16; see also 2 Kings xi. 4). In the words of

---

[43] Yahweh's initiative in the making of the Covenant is clear. See Deut vii. 8, 13; iv. 37; x. 15; 2 Sam xii. 24; Jer iii. 1; Mal i. 2; Hos xi. 1; xiv. 4. All these are texts in which the idea "I (Yahweh) will love (you) freely" (Hos xiv. 4) is prominent.

[44] There is only one reference to the love of a woman for a man, i.e., 1 Sam xviii. 20.

Malachi the Old Testament not only shows this, but also to some extent foreshadows the words of Christ: "From the beginning it was not so" (Mt xix. 8; see also Gen); for in his vigorous opposition to marriage—incidentally a "mixed" marriage—following a divorce Malachi says: "She is your companion and your wife by covenant. Has not the one God made them one flesh and [one] life [= one 'living body,' that is, one living being]?" (Mal ii. 14–16).[45] What is more, the covenant went hand in hand with an oath. The oath of the covenant gave marriage, as a covenant relationship, its legal permanence—both partners swore to be everlastingly faithful to each other,[46] "for better or for worse," as the Anglican marriage vow puts it. Love was thus a commission. The partners in marriage were especially committed to mutual fidelity.

The marriage act itself was an intimate "knowing" of the woman. (Gen iv. 1, 17, 25; xix. 8; Num xxxi. 17–18 etc.). The Hebrew word used to denote the sex act was the same as that used by Hosea to characterize Yahweh's intimate relationship with Israel in the covenant of grace. (Hos iv. 1, 6; vi. 3, 6; xiii. 4.) For Israel, this relationship was a state of being known and loved by Yahweh, who aroused and indeed created love for himself in his people. This "knowledge" of the woman on the one hand points to the man's initiative in love, but on the other hand equally denotes the woman's loving response.[47] In Hebrew, "knowing" means a personal knowledge based on experience, association, and intercourse. Sexual intercourse, then, as denoted by the word "knowing," was an intimate form of "being familiar" with some-

[45] See note 7 of this chapter. [Translator's note.]

[46] See the principal passage concerning the divine covenant expressed in terms of marriage: "You . . . who have despised the oath in breaking the covenant" (Ezek xvi. 59). See also Deut vii. 6–8, although this passage should not be read in terms of the marriage image.

[47] Hosea's account is probably typical here: Yahweh was angry because of Israel's infidelity, but he would bring her back to himself after testing her. The covenant would be established once again, and then Israel would "know" Yahweh (Hos ii. 20).

one, and although the form of personal relationship which has become possible in our own time since the emancipation of woman was not known in the ancient Near East, it was undoubtedly an intensely personal act.

Viewed in this light, then, the statement of Genesis, "They become one flesh" (ii. 24), gains immensely in depth. It can be seen to mean "they become one life" in the Semitic and anthropological sense of the word "life," according to which mankind is a "living body," one life in which two beings are united in marriage by faithful, human love which expresses itself in mutual help, support, and solicitude.[48] Malachi, as we have already seen, anticipated Paul's later affirmation: "Even so husbands should love their wives as their own bodies" (Eph v. 28) in adding "Take heed to your life [that is, your wife] and let none be faithless to the wife of his youth" to the text already quoted above, referring to man and wife as one flesh and one life.[49] The ideal of such a covenant relationship clearly included lifelong fidelity, since it was precisely in order to expose Israel's infidelity to Yahweh that the prophets made an appeal to the image of marriage. "Yahweh is God; there is no other besides him" (Deut iv. 35, 39; vii. 6-8)[50]—it is just this fundamental meaning of the divine covenant which was expressed by the image of marriage. The worship of other gods was adultery. Thus it was indirectly stated that the marriage bond should be indissoluble, even though Israel was to make compromises in her legislation.

Precisely this *eidos*, this essential ideal form of marriage, was used in the Old Testament as a means of revealing the covenant of grace. But the very use of this image provides, in a roundabout way, a deeper insight into the Old Testament vision of marriage. It supplies a necessary addition to what we know about

[48] Gen ii. 18; Jer ii. 2 ff.; 1 Sam i. 5-18; see also, indirectly, the imagery of the Song of Songs.

[49] See note 7 of this chapter. [Translator's note.]

[50] See also note 40 of this chapter. (Deuteronomy cannot be seen in the light of marriage or the marriage image.)

marriage as a divine institution from the Genesis texts. Both creation and the covenant throw light on actual and everyday
marriage, and so there can be little doubt that, if a close interconnection between creation and the covenant itself can be established, an even deeper insight should be gained into the reality of
marriage.

THE PERSPECTIVE OF SALVATION HISTORY:
MARRIAGE AND BELIEF IN THE CREATION

Marriage can be seen from various points of view. It can be experienced directly as a secular reality. This experience can also
be seen explicitly in the light of a vital faith in God's creation.
Finally, marriage can also be experienced from the vantage-point
of faith in God's covenant of grace with man.

Faith in the creation encompasses much more than the universal human awareness of creation as an implication of our
gratuitous being-in-the-world. It is also a remarkable fact that,
although no evidence of this universal awareness of creation appears anywhere in the Bible, the peculiarly Israelite belief in the
creation broke through forcibly at a definite moment in Israel's
existence. That faith in creation which is typical of Israel had no
place in the message of the earlier prophets, even in Hosea, the
chief witness of the revelation of God's covenant of grace in
terms of married love. It was only through her experience of
God's saving activity that Israel's awareness of herself as a creature became that belief in creation which is so characteristic of
the Old Testament—and which broke through almost violently
in Deutero-Isaiah and the books related to it. Although the word
bārā' (creation) was not used for the first time here, it would
appear at this point to have become used as a technical term of
central importance. "Creation," in other words, was used exclusively for Yahweh's activity, either in his creation of the world
or in his saving actions. God's saving activity was itself a creation, and creation gained its deepest dimensions of faith when

seen in the perspective of man's experience of God's powerful saving activity.[51] The God of the covenant was seen as the Creator, and Israel was to confess her faith in the formula: "God of Israel, the Creator." This formula points to the fact that God's activity made everything new.

We should not, however, forget that the idea of creation in the later editing of the first chapters of Genesis goes back to the idea of *bara'* that we find in Ezekiel and Deutero-Isaiah. The first chapters of the book of Genesis give an account of God's initial covenant activity. They tell of God's creation of the world as a place for man to live in. In this world man was to be intimately associated with God. He was, by virtue of his created state, to serve Yahweh and to be faithful to him; and so God's creation was the first fundamental covenant, the preliminary phase in salvation history. As the whole of the Old Testament is a proclamation of God's saving actions, a making present of his past activity, the early history of mankind should be seen as the preliminary stage which was to lead to the covenant that Yahweh made with Israel. This early history resulted in the promise made to Abraham: "Go from your country and your kindred and your father's house to the land that I will show you. And I will make of you a great nation" (Gen xii. 1–2). This promise marked the end of this early history and the beginning of the specific salvation history of Israel.

When viewed in this way, it is clear that the creator of man and woman is the God of Israel, that is, the God of the covenant. This covenant of love is the theme of all God's saving

[51] See, among others, H. A. Brongers, *De Scheppingstradities bij de profeten*, Amsterdam, (1945), although not all of Brongers' conclusions are acceptable; P. Humbert, "Emploi et portée du verbe *bara'* dans l'Ancien Testament," *TZ*, 3 (1947), pp. 401–22; G. von Rad, "Das theologische Problem des alttestamentlichen Schöpfungsglauben," *Werden und Wesen des Alten Testament, BZAW*, 66 (1936); J. van der Ploeg, "Le sens du verbe hébreu *bārā'*," *Mus*, 59 (1946), pp. 143–57. The technical word *bārā'* occurs almost exclusively in Deutero-Isaiah, in the Priestly tradition of Genesis, and a few times in Ezekiel and the Psalms.

activity and the deepest meaning of the creation. The prophets' use of the image of marriage as a means of expressing the covenant of God in human terms is also easy to understand in this perspective. The God of revelation did not choose to reveal himself through a medium open to purely natural apprehension or experience, but through a medium itself deeply and inextricably affected and touched by him, the God of salvation who created mankind as man and woman. The community of marriage, as a gift of creation from the God of the covenant, was a first draft of the finished picture of grace, God's covenant with men. The use of marriage as an image of the covenant was therefore subject to "divine inspiration"—an inspiration which was, we may say, derived from the everyday reality of marriage. The marriage relationship between man and woman was therefore a "mystery" which by creation was implicit even in so-called "natural" marriage, with the result that among all peoples it appeared to have a *religious* significance. The gift of marriage was not simply a good gift of creation, but also a personal gift of salvation from God.

The religious significance of marriage was open to misinterpretation because this personal gift of salvation remained anonymous outside the sphere of the revelation of God's word. Sacred prostitution, including that which took place in conjunction with the ancient rites of fertility, and indeed every form of expression which gave an absolute value to sexuality, of necessity threatened to obscure man's religious view of marriage outside the sphere of the revelation of the word. As we have already seen, this revelation aimed first of all to strip marriage of the pagan religious elements surrounding it, and then—by bringing it in contact with Yahweh—to return it to its true value as something *created by Yahweh*. And so it is clear both that the saving significance of marriage was a reference to the "Wholly Other," the sovereign and free God, and at the same time that this significance—seen from within marriage itself—referred to something transcending marriage.

This reference to something totally *other* was apprehended by the whole of religious mankind, but in the absence of a public or official revelation of the Word its inner meaning was frequently misinterpreted. The true value and the precise meaning of marriage became apparent when this wholly other and transcendent God revealed himself. Creation sets things at their proper value as belonging to this world, but at the same time as being the work of God, that is, as existing within God's secure protection. Thus, precisely by putting a distance between himself and man, the God of salvation, God the Creator, simultaneously gave marriage a deeper dimension, the fullness and still purely secular value of which would be brought more clearly to light only in the later course of divine revelation.

"I WILL MAKE OF YOU A GREAT NATION": MARRIAGE AND THE CHRIST WHO WAS TO COME

The foregoing reflections on the subject of creation and the covenant in the context of marriage gain an even deeper significance when seen in the light of the New Testament, and this deeper meaning will not come from without, but from within. Although the Old Testament should in the first place be read for its own message, we should certainly fail to appreciate the distinctive quality of the covenant were we not to reread the Old Testament from the perspective of Christ. This was, after all, the basic intention and concern of the New Testament writers themselves.[52]

In his epistle to the Galatians Paul wrote: "Now the promises were made to Abraham and to his offspring. It does not say, 'And to offsprings,' referring to many, but referring to one, 'And

[52] See H. Renckens, *The God of Israel*, New York (Sheed and Ward, 1966); for a theological exposition, see also E. Schillebeeckx, *Openbaring en Theologie* (Collected Essays, Volume I), Bilthoven (1964), pp. 13–26 and 112–40. An English translation of this work is in preparation.

to your offspring,' which is Christ" (iii. 16). The blessing of creation on marriage, "Be fruitful and multiply," gained, in Abraham especially, a new dimension in the context of salvation: "I will make of you a great nation" (Gen xii. 1–2; xiii. 16). As we have seen, this marked the end of the early history and the beginning of the specific salvation history of Israel. Marriage as an institution for the founding of a family thereby also gained a very clear saving significance, a striking and subservient function in the history of God's covenant with his people.

The Old Testament covenant seen as God's loving faithfulness implied that marriage and the family in Israel were closely related to God's promise of salvation. Indeed, this promise of salvation would have been proved false were it not for marriage and the family. We have already seen that, in Israel's vision of life, God's covenant was again and again made actual and perpetuated in birth. This idea is woven like a golden thread through the priestly passages of Genesis. The key-word linking the blessing of creation on marriage and the covenant blessing, and showing creation to be purposefully orientated towards the history of salvation, is the Hebrew term *tôledhôth*. This word can be translated as the "genesis"—the "history of becoming" or the "genealogy"—both of God and of "God's image," man. The Priestly account of the creation ends with the words: "These are the *tôledhôth* of the heavens and the earth when they were created" (Gen ii. 4). These words are immediately followed by the "*tôledhôth* of Adam" (v. 1), the patriarchs of the period before the Flood. But the renewed creation which took place after the Flood is linked to the first *tôledhôth* of the creation of heaven and earth in the covenant with Noah: "These are the *tôledhôth* of Noah" (vi. 9).

The Priestly passages in Genesis provide no separate account of the Fall. What they do is to draw certain conclusions from the Yahwist vision of the accumulation of sins committed in the period between Adam and Noah, during which the world reverted to primordial chaos (vii. 11; viii. 2). Yahweh, so to speak, set about doing his work all over again. Noah became the new "first man" and, like Adam, "walked with God" (vi. 9). This creation was an explicit covenant (ix. 9) and God gave a renewed blessing to the marriage of the new "first man and woman" (ix. 7). This is followed by the "*tôledhôth* of the sons of Noah" (x. 1) in which the author aimed to link the father of the Semites (Shem, the son of Noah) with the father of mankind, Adam. This in turn is followed by the "*tôledhôth* of Terah" (xi. 27), the father of Abraham, which leads into the covenant with Abraham and the "creation of Israel." In this way the constitution of the people of God and the history of Israel's salvation was linked with the first day of creation, through the *tôledôth* between Adam and Noah (v. 1–32) and then between the son of Noah, Shem, and Abraham (xi. 10–32). Israel's creation marked the completion of creation itself, and the beginning of the *tôledhôth* of Israel's salvation history: "These are the *tôledhôth* of Isaac, Abraham's son" (xxv. 19), and "these are the *tôledhôth* of Jacob" (xxxvii. 2). Marriage and the family clearly occupy a position of central importance in this succession of *tôledhôth* of creation and covenant history.

The evangelist Matthew, strongly inspired by the Old Testament, was conscious of this golden thread of the *tôledhôth* running through the Priestly passages in Genesis and followed it directly: "These are the *tôledhôth* of Jesus Christ, the son of David, the son of Abraham" (i. 1). Creation, the history of Israel's salvation, and the appearance of the man Jesus, the Christ, form a single, powerful historical unfolding of the mystery which was hidden in God before all ages.

Paul also followed this same thread when he wrote: "The promises were made to Abraham, and to his offspring . . . which is Christ" (Gal iii. 16). The blessing of creation became salvation in the blessing on Abraham and his descendants, and was given a deeper meaning in the blessing on King David: "For thou, O Yahweh, God, hast spoken, and with thy blessing shall the house of thy servant be blessed for ever" (2 Sam vii. 29).

Marriage and the family thus acquired their dimension of "createdness," and at the same time their status as instruments of the covenant, events actively in the service of the kingdom of God and without which the promise made to Abraham could have no future. Marriage and the family were therefore, and in a very special way, orientated towards the "promise to Abraham" and so ultimately towards Christ himself. In my opinion this is so important that, in any study of Mary, Jesus' mother, we ought to consider not only her virginity, but also her real married state, since she was a perfect virgin both as a spouse and as a mother.

In the Old Testament the simple fact of having children was not a fact of salvation. The foundation of a family was not itself decisive. Although it is true that this idea was brought sharply into focus only in the New Testament—the children of Abraham were those who were born "of faith" (Gal iii. 7)—the Old Testament was not entirely unaware of it. Not only did Abraham believe, against all hope because of his wife's barrenness (Gen xv. 2–6), but he also made the fulfilment of the Promise impossible from the human point of view by his act of obedience in faith, his sacrifice of Isaac, the "son of the Promise" whom God had finally given to him (Gen xxii. 1–18). In this the primacy of the religious attitude, "God will provide," is clearly expressed (Gen xxii. 8, 14). In other words, "you shall be a great nation" had to be experienced as an unmerited gift of God. It was a gift to man's obedience in faith (Gen xxii. 15–18). The natural foundation of the family was lifted onto a higher plane by man's faith in Yahweh, and this is why in the Old Testament such special emphasis was placed on barren marriages which were made fruitful by faith in Yahweh, for whom nothing was impossible.

This idea was later to be formulated by the author of the epistle to the Hebrews: "For he [Abraham] looked forward to the city which has foundations, whose builder and maker is God. By faith Sarah herself received power to conceive, even when she was past the age, since she considered him faithful who had promised [i.e., God]. Therefore from one man, and him as good as dead, were born descendants as many as the stars of heaven and as the innumerable grains of sand by the sea-shore" (xi. 10–12). Salvation comes to us from God in human, historical forms. In other words, it is a divine salvation in secular form, and at the same time it is the salvation of a community of human beings scattered in time and space. Because of this, marriage, in its family aspect as well, had a subordinate function with regard to God's covenant activity. Because there have been men in the world who were created with an orientation towards Christ, marriage—the principle within this world for the perpetuation of mankind on earth—is also, in faith, an instrument of salvation in the service of this actual orientation of men towards Christ. Every man, the fruit of marriage, in this way becomes the "son of God's promise," and this is perhaps the Old Testament basis for the Christian sacramentalising of the still secular institution of marriage.

I stress *perhaps*, however, because it is hardly possible to find anything in the Old Testament which explicitly or consciously gives a messianic meaning to procreation or the founding of the family. It is true that the idea of the "great, innumerable nation" was not only an idea of the covenant, but also a Davidic and finally a messianic idea. Nonetheless we can, and indeed must, say that, just as birth, circumcision, and bringing up in the faith in Yahweh were closely associated with each other, in the definitive covenant there is a need for a close synthesis between birth, baptism, and Christian education. The founding of a family, the birth of children, and their upbringing—all human events—were borne up, within the unity of creation and the covenant, by faith that Yahweh would accomplish his salvation in them and carry out his plan. We may therefore conclude with Paul: "For it is written that Abraham had two sons, one by a slave and one by a free woman. But the son of the slave was born according to the flesh, the son of the free woman through promise. Now this is an allegory" (Gal iv. 22–8). Secular marriage thus acquired a religious significance in and through faith. Every marriage, including civil marriages, is Christian— whether in the full sense, the pre-Christian sense (as an orientation towards), the anonymous sense, or, lastly, the negatively Christian sense (when the Christian dimension to marriage is explicitly rejected).

To sum up, we may say that the Old Testament view saw marriage fundamentally as a secular reality and therefore as a good gift of God. But Yahweh was a God of salvation. Both in its aspect of specifically human and personal relationships between man and wife and its family aspect, marriage in Israel entered the history of salvation which was directed towards Christ. Both marriage and the family thus had the function of serving the plan of salvation which led to Christ.

CONCLUSION: SALVATION HISTORY AS A MARRIAGE DRAMA AND MARRIAGE AS A PROPHETIC FIGURE

The use of marriage as an image of the community life of Israel with Yahweh is rich in theological content. It is, however, important to remember that this is only one of many images used in the Old Testament to express the same relationship between God and man. Among these are the father and son relationship, the king and subject relationship (the image of the kingdom of God), and the lord or master and servant or slave relationship.[53] In the master and servant relationship, it is the inequality of the partners which strikes us, an inequality which, although cer-

---

[53] Another image with earlier origins than that of marriage can be found in Deuteronomy. See W. L. Moran, "The Ancient Near Eastern Background of the Love of God in Deuteronomy," *CBQ*, 25 (1963), pp. 77-87. The mutual love between God and his people was not conceived in Deuteronomy as an analogy of married love, as it was in Hosea, but as an analogy of secular, political friendly relations between the king and his people. This relationship was dependent on a covenant love, and was expressed in affectionate obedience and loyal service to the king.

tainly present in Israelitic marriage, is never emphasized in the Old Testament marriage image when this is used to express the communion of God with his people. In the context of the covenant at least, married love and fidelity pointed above all to a communion or dialogue between two partners. The subordinate position of the wife was never particularly stressed, apart from the fact that the husband, Yahweh, always took the initiative, and—in his sovereign freedom—overwhelmed his chosen bride with gifts. In any case, the marriage image was more suitable than the other images used in the Old Testament for the purpose of expressing the religious interpersonal relationship, the direct and intimate dialogue, between God and his people, who were God's "beloved." The various images were thus complementary to each other.

Moreover, one striking feature of the use of the symbolism of marriage for the covenant of grace is that it coincided with the emergence for the first time of a clear theology of the history of salvation in the eighth century B.C.[54] The image of marriage, a secular, human, and changing reality, pointed less to the covenant as such than to the dialectic of the covenant of grace—to the concrete historicity of life in communion with Yahweh, the God of history. The dynamic and indeed dramatic course of man's relationship with God, and of God's sovereign and free saving activity with man, was clearly illuminated in the marriage image. This image was used especially for the purpose of expressing this concrete historical truth. Hosea, Jeremiah, Ezekiel, and Deutero-Isaiah, all of whom used this image, saw the course of Israel's history as a tortuous, but nonetheless continuous, line with a beginning, a middle, and, in the future, an end.

The beginning was situated in the early period of love, the time of the betrothal and the wedding which followed it. Hosea (ii. 17), Jeremiah (ii. 2), and Ezekiel (xxiii, 3, 8, 19, 21) each

[54] See A. Néher, "Le symbolisme conjugal: expression de l'histoire dans L'Ancien Testament," *RHPR*, 34 (1954), pp. 30–49.

placed his own individual emphasis on this phase, but each set it in the period between the deliverance from Egypt and the entry into the promised land, that is, during the sojourn in the desert.

(The tradition of the murmuring of the people of God in the desert was apparently not known to these prophets, although of course Ezekiel toned down the idealistic picture of this time of early love and recognised in it an hereditary taint.)

This, then, was the time of God's and Israel's youthful love for each other, their honeymoon—the time when Israel's "whoredom" with Egypt was no longer possible, and her "whoredom" with the Baal of Canaan not yet possible. According to these prophets, God did in fact make it impossible for Israel to be unfaithful to him, Yahweh, by committing adultery, and this shows that they sensed Israel's inherent weakness as Yahweh's spouse. It was only when Yahweh placed Israel in a historical situation where it was impossible for her to be guilty of "whoredom" that everything went well. (There was in this, too, as we have seen, an element of the corrective punishment which Yahweh was to impose upon faithless Israel.)

Israel's marriage in the desert is thus the point of reference from which the later course of the nation's life should be viewed. The patriarchal period, the sojourn in Egypt, and the Exodus were (we may say) the birth, the youth, and the "marriageable age" of the people of God. Israel's day-to-day married life, with all its ups and downs, began from the time that the nation settled in Canaan. The trust in himself which Yahweh demanded of Israel when he led her through the desert, and which Israel herself, according to this tradition, placed without reserve in him at that time, should have been the norm for Israel's married life with God. The past—the wedding—was the model for the further course of their life together. It was in Yahweh, and in no one else, that Israel was to place her hope and trust. From this point of reference Israel's present life was judged to be adultery and infidelity, committed in spite of Yahweh's constant love for her, a love which penetrated to her very heart. This opened up a perspective into the future, a perspective of either salvation or disaster. If Israel were to seek help and protection from others, let her do so—but in that case she would discover that, if Yahweh was "not a God" for her, she would eventually be ruined, helpless, and reviled. Infidelity in response to Yahweh's love would bring its own punishment. On the other hand, if she returned to Yahweh—and this was only possible because he never regarded her leaving him as a permanent divorce—he would prove to her that all good gifts, including profane ones, were dependent upon him and upon him alone.

What is remarkable, in any consideration of the present and the future of Israel's life, is that the marriage covenant between Yahweh and Israel was placed "in the background"—that it was situated in the past as a milestone, a firm, unshakable reality established once and for all time. For the present and the future the image of children was used more than that of two partners in marriage. Israel of the present was, of course, the fruit of Yahweh's and Israel's marital love for each other in the desert, and the present stage of Yahweh's and Israel's relationship with each other was concerned with the children of that love. Love itself was the *prōton*, the constitutive initial phase, of the relationship, existing at the very beginning as an unassailable, constant, and indissoluble reality. The infidelity and defection took place in the "children of Israel," for Israel was a mother who bore faithless and renegade children (Hos ii. 4, 6, 7). The ultimate vision, then, also points to the return of Israel's children (Is xlix. 20–21; liv. 1). And so there was no question of a permanent divorce, only of a temporary separation, and this was not because in the last resort Israel's dispositions were basically good, but because Yahweh was eternal and unshakable in his love. Hosea and the other prophets saw the course of salvation history as above all a "happy ending," with the exception of Ezekiel, who in chapter xxiii merely allows the final result to be guessed at—the two wives Judah and Israel, the one people of God, were "stoned to death" according to the law for their divorce from Yahweh.

It is precisely when the covenant of grace is understood as a marriage between Yahweh and Israel that this flexible, far-reaching vision is possible, for Israel is essentially a *historical* quantity. On the other hand, it is precisely this marriage image which implies that Yahweh personally participated in Israel's history. The changeable nature of marriage is therefore the best available vehicle for conveying as a message the dialectic of the history of salvation and of disaster.

It is also remarkable that the first time (as far as we know) that the marriage image was used in the Old Testament to express God's love for Israel, the purely allegorical aspect was transcended—a concrete, secular marriage between two Israelites, Hosea and Gomer, became the prophetic symbol of the historical love-dialogue between God and his people. Even where the book of Ezekiel describes the concrete history of Israel's salvation and disaster in her relationship with God allegorically as a marriage, it is more than mere allegory. It is an image pointing to a reality which for men could hardly be expressed differently, but which is every bit as real as the vicissitudes of married life. Moreover, the image is more remarkable still, in that—in Ezekiel—it implies too an ethical message for the concrete married life of the Israelites. If the Old Testament is read first of all on its own, and then afterwards in the light of the New Testament and of the later history of the church, it is impossible not to sense that the Old Testament was already aware of an intimate relationship between concrete human marriage on the one hand and, on the other, true piety or the relationship of man with God—that concrete marriage in the Old Testament has a certain "sacramental" quality.

Moreover, this realisation is a universal fact in religious mankind. But in this connection we must be careful to bear in mind that the full light of the Old Testament revelation could only come to bear on this reality when it had first inculcated the idea of the one God, the absolute transcendence of the God who was above sexuality. The sacramental quality of marriage could not become visible in its purest form until the reality of marriage was first seen as a secular, creaturely reality, stripped of all myths and rites referring to a "non-God"—or (more accurately) to the one, true God whom men had so misrepresented and so fashioned according to their own image that it was difficult for them to conceive and to experience marriage "in God's image." For this reason the Old Testament had first to strip marriage of all its pagan religious connotations. In this way, it is possible to see in the Song of Solomon, as it first appeared and was understood in Israel, the culminating point of the process of demythologization of human erotic love and sexuality. It is then possible to see the same Song—in its later Jewish, and still later Christian, rereading and interpretation—as the culminating point of man's attempt to express the inexpressible dialogue of love between God and his people, the church that he was to adorn as his bride and make permanently his own. But this prophetic allegorical usage was more than an image leaving marriage as something purely secular. Marriage, precisely as marriage, would of itself appear to have a prophetic form.

2

The Old Testament Ethos of Marriage

Creation and the covenant dominate the ethics of Israel. This is explicitly formulated in Deuteronomy, which contributed so much to the moral and religious way of life of the people of God.

And now, Israel, what does Yahweh, your God, require of you, but to fear Yahweh, your God, to walk in all his ways, to love him, to serve Yahweh, your God, with all your heart, and with all your soul, and to keep the commandments and statutes of Yahweh, which I command you this day for your good? Behold, to Yahweh your God belong heaven and the heaven of heavens, the earth and all that is in it. [Creation.] Yet Yahweh set his heart in love upon your fathers, and chose their descendants after them, you above all peoples, as at this day. [Covenant.] [Deut x. 12–15].

Just as the moon and the stars, heaven and earth received their *ḥûqqôth*, their conditions of existence, their appointed limits, on the day of their creation, so too man was tied to the plan of creation and covenant. (Jer xxxi. 35; xxxiii. 25; Ps cxlviii. 5–6; cxix. 89–93; Hos viii. 14; Jer xxvii. 5; Ps c.; Is xxii. 11; xliv. 21; Deut xxxii. 6–15.) In his case, however, the association was one of free obedience in which he, unlike the things of creation, was able to default (Jer viii. 7; xviii. 14). But in addition God freely chose to favour Israel more than all other nations, although she had no claim to preference—indeed, the very contrary was the case (Amos ix. 7; Deut vii. 6–8; Ezek xvi. 4–5). Through this covenant, obedience to God's will was the essence of Israel's spirituality: "You shall be holy to me, for I, Yahweh, am holy, and I have separated you from other peoples, that you should be mine" (Lev xx. 26).[1] God's blessing was on a life that was faithful to creation and the covenant: "And because you hearken to these ordinances, and keep and do them, Yahweh your God will keep with you the covenant, and the steadfast love . . . he will love you, bless you, and multiply you; he will also bless the fruit of your body and the fruit of your ground, . . . in the land which he swore to your fathers to give you" (Deut vii. 12–13).[2]

The marriage ethos of Israel was also experienced in this perspective. But marriage is an actual institution, a reality set within a definite historical and social framework, and it was experienced as such by the Hebrews before the demands of faith in Yahweh came upon them through the Prophets and the Deuteronomic writers. It was also a reality which they encountered among the people with whom, directly or indirectly, they came into contact—the people of Mesopotamia. It was therefore only very gradually that Israel was able to give a concrete form to the ideal of marriage presented in the cult of Yahweh. It was only with difficulty that the ancient Near Eastern pattern of marriage was, under the influence of faith in Yahweh, freed in Israel from elements which were not in keeping with creation and the covenant. What is more, it was inevitable that the pure marriage ideal should be lived in social and historical forms which were Semitic rather than biblical, that is to say, in the framework within which God's Word comes to us, but which is not, as such, a standard for us, as God's Word is. A Semitic anthropological form is by no means the same thing as a biblical anthropological form, which is a vision of man that reveals God's Word to us and binds us.

The welfare of the clan was fundamental to the Old Testament ethos of marriage. Tribal well-being was the ethical norm for all

[1] See also Lev xi. 44; xix. 2.
[2] The word "covenant" has many other shades of meaning, including that of "keeping the commandments."

sexual conduct, and it provides the key to an understanding of all kinds of regulations in Israel concerning sexual matters—those, for example, dealing with the marriage of brothers and sisters-in-law (Deut xxv. 5–10) and the case of Onan (Gen xxxviii. 1–11). But the ethics of the clan acquired a new significance with the revelation of the true God, Yahweh. God himself made the nation his own, and for this reason every sin against the well-being of the clan came to be a sin against Yahweh himself, a breaking of the covenant. This was why Onan did evil in the sight of God —he had no care for Israel's seed, her posterity. This too was why the Israelites were forbidden to "do as they do in the land of Egypt . . . (or) Canaan" (Lev xviii. 1–5). The people of those lands did not know Yahweh.

At this point I propose to go a little more fully into a few of the fundamental themes connected with the Old Testament ethos of marriage and the social structure of marriage in Israel. In this I shall treat them in the light of theological speculation on the reality of marriage.

MARRIED LOVE AND FOUNDING A FAMILY

The book of Genesis stated the inner meaning of marriage to include both married love—"They become one flesh," in the Semitic and anthropological sense of the word—and the founding of the family—"Increase and multiply." There has been great difference of opinion among exegetes concerning this question. Some maintain that in Israel and in Judaism the only purpose of marriage was procreation, and that there was no question of any inner, genuinely human intercourse between husband and wife.[3] Other exegetes claim emphatically that procreation was embodied, in Israel too, in married love.[4] In my opinion, this problem is in itself alien to the ancient Near Eastern way of looking at things. Marriage is a complex entity in which the different factors that

[3] See especially H. Preisker (Bibliography, Part II).
[4] See B. Reicke (Bibliography, Part II).

we are in the habit of distinguishing are in fact undifferentiated.

It is, of course, indisputable that the founding of a family, the perpetuation of the family name through its sons, was strongly emphasized in Israel. Fertility was regarded as the greatest blessing that God could bestow on marriage. (Gen iv. 1; Ruth iv. 13; iv. 11; 1 Sam i. 5–13; 2 Macc vii. 22–3.) In the enclosed life of the clan, in which the members lived solely for the clan and its perpetuation, this may have been influenced initially by the absence of an explicit belief in personal, authentic survival after life on this earth. Later on, it may also have been influenced by God's covenant with Abraham and, in him, with the whole nation —and, in the Jewish period, perhaps also by the messianic expectations of that time. All the same, the root of all this is the link between sexuality and procreation—a link which is immediately and spontaneously apparent—as well as the basic experience that marriage, as an institution belonging strictly to this world, was bound to be lived as something serving to strengthen tribal solidarity when it took place within the society of a clan. It is thus clear that childlessness and widowhood (without remarriage) were inevitably regarded as real calamities, making the childless wife or the unmarried widow "as nothing" in the eyes of the tribe. (Judg xi. 34–40; 1 Sam i. 5–6; 2 Sam vi. 23; Gen xx. 17–18; xxx. 23; Lev xx. 20–21; Deut xxv. 6; Hos ix. 11–14; Is xlvii. 8–9; iv. 1.) To have no children meant that one's own name was "blotted out of Israel" (Deut xxv. 6). Furthermore, for the perpetuation of the family name, God's blessing on a marriage was, as we have already seen, shown above all in sons. (Ex xxxiv. 23; xii. 48; Gen xxxiv. 15–26; xvii. 10–23; 1 Sam i. 11.) Motherhood was the adornment of a woman (Gen xvi. 10; Job xlii. 12–16; Ps cxxvii. 3–5; cxxviii. 3; cxliv. 12), and as her children's mentor the mother had a position of fundamental importance in the family. (Prov i. 8; iv. 3; vi. 20; x. 1; xv. 20; xvii. 25; xix. 26; xxiii. 22–5; xxx. 11, 17.)[5]

[5] See also Gen xxviii. 7; xxxvii. 10; Ex xxi. 15, 17; Lev xviii. 7; Num vi. 7; Deut xxvii. 16; xxi. 18; 1 Kings xix. 20; Ps xxvii. 10; cix. 14.

Although children are given such prominence in any reference to marriage in the Old Testament, and far less is said about love between the husband and wife, this does not mean that married love was regarded as of purely secondary importance. The central position in the divine institution of marriage given by Genesis to the "one flesh" (in the characteristically Semitic usage of the word) in the account of the creation can be traced back to facts of human experience. Two strange human beings come together to found a new clan and in this way they become "blood relations," or "one flesh." Originally the "one flesh" alluded to the new "one tribe" on a basis of the new bond of unity between a man and a woman under the man's leadership and authority. The view of the family as being under the man's leadership is fundamental in the Old Testament—it is precisely this basic human and cultural idea that, thanks to God's revelation, was lived out in terms of faith in Yahweh.

In the ancient Near East nothing like what we in nineteenth- and twentieth-century Western society might call an intimate "communion of souls" existed between man and woman in marriage. But it is important to make a distinction between what may be called the ancient "popular ideology" and human existential experience. Our own legal codes have much more to say about children and the family in connection with marriage than about married love, but this in no way implies that this love is a matter of purely secondary importance in present-day society. Throughout the whole of Israel's popular ideology it is possible to detect the clear note of everyday human experience. It was, after all, faithful married love which in Israel became one of the means of revealing the covenant of grace between God and his people. This image would have been meaningless if marriage itself had not been lived as a covenant of love.

It is moreover remarkable that procreation played no part at all in this image of the covenant of grace. The Bible is generally silent about the reality of the intimate and private side of marriage, but now and then something breaks through. Elkanah, the father of Samuel, for example, protests to his wife Hannah, who has been complaining because she has no children from him: "Am I not more to you than ten sons?" (1 Sam i. 5–8). Instead of paying Laban the normal *mōhar* or dowry for his daughter Rachel, Jacob served his future father-in-law for seven years, and we are told that "they seemed to him but a few days, because of the love he had for her" (Gen xxix. 20). 1 Sam xviii. 20 is the only place in the whole of Scripture where we are told that the woman loves the man.[6] There are also references to "lovesickness" (2 Sam xiii. 2, 25; Song ii. 5; v. 8). We have already seen that this frank assertion of loving and even of "petting" (Gen xxvi. 8–9) can be found in the Yahwist accounts, the Books of Samuel, and the Song of Solomon (which is so closely connected with this tradition).

Married love is also strongly affirmed in the Wisdom literature of the exile, though here it is given a markedly moral and religious slant. Even Israel's law protected the demands of early married love—after the betrothal or wedding, the man was released from various public duties for a year, "to be happy with his wife" (Deut xxiv. 5).[7] In the rather anti-feminist tradition of the rabbis there is nevertheless one rather different story. It tells of a happy marriage which had been childless for ten years and could therefore, according to custom, be dissolved by the husband. He consequently prepared a festive meal to celebrate the separation, and told his wife to take the most precious possession in the home with her when she left him. Waiting until her erstwhile husband was asleep, she had him—the most precious possession in the house—taken away to her new home![8]

It is clear, then, that in Israel too the heavy stress on the family does not mean that married love was put right in the background, even though it was not regarded, at least in theme form, as the

[6] See also 2 Sam i. 26.
[7] See also Deut xx. 7.
[8] Midrash Rabba 1. 4, quoted by J. Leipoldt, *Die Frau in der Antike und im Urchristentum*, p. 72.

primary function in the institution of the family. We do know
from the case of Samuel's father and Hannah that love could
make even a childless marriage meaningful. Israel herself came
eventually to apprehend the meaning of the childless marriage
which she had at first so despised. Not only was it deemed that
"to die childless is better than to have ungodly children" (Sir
xvi. 1–3), but the "barren woman who is undefiled" and the
"eunuch whose hands have done no lawless deed" were thought
blessed (Wis iii. 13–15).[9] Unlike the case of Samuel's father, the
fertility of the childless in these texts is shown in their virtue. As
a result of the social and religious situation in which the writer
and the intended readers of this book were living, Wisdom reacted against the myth of the large family, at least as an end in
itself. The mere fact of having a large number of children—or
only a few—made no difference; what mattered was the moral
and religious attitude involved. The childless state of marriage,
and thus Israel's "popular ideology" too, were given a relative
value in this moral and religious focus—neither the stranger nor
the eunuch were excluded from the eschatological kingdom (Is
lvi.). Here Christ would exceed man's wildest expectations and
subordinate both married love and the foundation of the family
to love for the kingdom of God: Who had said that eunuchs
might enter the kingdom of salvation? I say to you: "There are
eunuchs who have made themselves eunuchs for the sake of the
kingdom of heaven" (Mt xix. 12).

The people of Israel, then, experienced marriage as a commission to found families, but carried out this task in the light of
"one flesh"—of personal relationship within marriage. This phenomenon is one which is normally encountered among nomads
and peasant communities, where married love is a silent but nonetheless real background. But all this was something concerned
primarily with this world rather than with the next.

Yet there is one question in connection with this fundamentally
healthy Old Testament conception of marriage which remains
unanswered, namely that concerning the laws of cleanliness in

[9] See also Wis iv. 1–2.

relation to all sexual matters, such as menstruation, the nocturnal emission of semen, and so on. From these laws it would certainly seem as if sexual life was subject to all kinds of religious taboos[10] which cast a certain shadow on Israel's essentially healthy view of marriage.

MONOGAMY AS THE IDEAL TO WHICH ISRAEL ASPIRED

In the age of the patriarchs the prevalent form of marriage was relative monogamy with a tendency towards bigamy, in which a man kept one chief wife and one concubine. That this was the normal pattern in Mesopotamia is clear from the *Codex Hammurabi*. The custom gradually became widespread in ancient Israel and, in the days of the judges and the kings, almost unrestricted polygamy prevailed, especially at the higher levels of society.[11] The possession of many wives was a sign of power, prestige, and economic prosperity (2 Sam v. 13; 1 Kings xi. 1–8).

With the Deuteronomic writers came a clear protest against the harem system (Deut xvii. 17). This tendency to oppose polygamy is also apparent in the Genesis account of the creation, and it is probably not accidental that, in the vision of the history of saving events given in Genesis, polygamy begins with Lamech, who was descended from Cain (Gen iv. 19). As we have already seen, the Greek translation of the Pentateuch reinforced this monogamous tendency: "They become one flesh" (Gen ii. 24). In Judaism, and certainly among the Alexandrian Jews, the keeping of concubines was increasingly criticized. This tendency became even more pronounced in the ascetic circles of the "community of Damascus," as is apparent from the finds at Qumran, where concubinage was roundly condemned as unchastity. But even in the Wisdom literature the monogamous marriage was clearly regarded as both normal and ideal. (Prov v. 15–19; xii. 4;

---

[10] See, for example, Lev xv.

[11] Deut xxi. 15–17 legally recognises bigamy. See also Judg viii. 30–31; Gen iv. 19–22; 1 Sam i. 2.

xviii. 22; xix. 14; xxxi. 10–13; Ps cxxviii. 3; Eccles ix. 9; Sir
xxvi. 1–4.) No other possibility appears to have been envisaged.[12]
Some scholars are of the opinion that polygamy had virtually
disappeared in Israel by the beginning of the Christian era.[13]
Others, however, regard this as too rosy a view of the situation.[14]

Even in a polygamous marriage one wife was regarded as the
"chief wife" or beloved, where the other was frequently called
the "hated," the "less beloved,"[15] and occupied a position subordinate to that of the first wife, who automatically thought of
her as her rival or "enemy." (1 Sam i. 6; see Gen xxx. 1; xxix.
30–31.)[16] But, besides his relationships with his own concubines,
a husband was allowed to enjoy all kinds of relationships with
girls and slave-girls whose status was not recognized as one of
legal marriage. (Ex xxi. 7, 10; Gen xvi. 2–4; xxx. 3 ff.; Deut xxi.
10–14; Num xxi. 9; Hos iii. 2.)[17] It is doubtful whether it is
possible to form any concrete picture from these legal provisions
of how marriage was in fact experienced by pious Israelites.
What the older laws permitted was not always accepted as good
or fitting by pious Jews of the post-exilic period. Moreover, the
historical, social, and religious character of many of the laws
relating to marriage emerges clearly from the fact that what was
first permitted was forbidden by later laws.[18] After the exile it
became very difficult to reconcile polygamy with the ethics of
marriage seen from the standpoint of faith in Yahweh, and those

[12] Tobit viii. 7 (Greek–RSV); vii. 12; Mal ii. 13–16 (combined in this
case with a reaction against a mixed marriage after divorce).

[13] SB, pt. 3, p. 647.

[14] Herod I, who was in fact not a Jew of pure blood, had ten wives, some
of them simultaneously, but he was held in contempt because of it. He
accounted for his conduct by appealing to the "custom of the patriarchs."
(Josephus, *Antiq.* 14. 12.1; 15. 9.3; 17. 1.2, quoted by J. Leipoldt, p. 77.)

[15] See Deut xxi. 15–17; Gen xxix. 30; Is lx. 15. See also 1 Sam i. 6; Gen
xvi. 4–5.

[16] For the law relating to this, see Deut xxi. 15–17.

[17] There was a legal distinction between polygamy and concubinage: compare Deut xxii. 29 with Ex xxi. 7–8, and Deut xxii. 23 with Lev xix. 20.

[18] Compare Gen xx. 12 and xxxviii. 13–28 with 2 Sam xiii. 13. See also
Ezek xxii. 10–11.

who practised it were probaby despised. Initially it would appear that to bring children, and especially sons, into the world and thus to perpetuate the family name was regarded as a more fundamental commandment than that of monogamy (Deut xxi. 15–17),[19] although it is clear from the Bible that considerations of prestige, political motives, and even lust were not lacking in the case of polygamous marriages (1 Kings xi. 4–8; 2 Sam xv. 16; etc.).

Polygamy and the keeping of concubines were also encouraged by the position of social inferiority occupied by women in the ancient Near East, and especially in the Jewish world. In this male civilisation much more was permitted in the sexual sphere to the man than to the woman, who was strictly bound to monogamy. In cases where a woman would have been punished for adultery, a married man was normally acquitted, so long as his offence was not committed with a woman who was subject to the authority of another man. The idea that the woman was there "to bear children" was, in this type of society, and certainly in the ideology of the people, of overriding importance. In certain respects this inequality between man and wife in married life reflects a lower appreciation of the woman's role than that, for example, of the pagan Greeks and Romans. Another example of this inequality is that divorce was possible for the husband, but not for the wife. The great evil in post-exilic Israel was not really polygamy as such, but so-called "successive polygamy"—a husband was able to annul his marriage, send his wife away, and enter into a new marriage.

THE HUSBAND'S RIGHT TO DIVORCE

In principle, proven adultery between a man and another married or betrothed woman was punished in Israel, both the guilty parties normally being put to death after trial (Deut xxii. 2–5).

19 This is also the basis of the idea of the "law of the levirate" (Deut xxv. 5–10).

The wife was subject to her husband's rule, with the result that a third party had no right to her (Deut xx. 5–7; xxviii. 30). Furthermore, according to sound Yahwist doctrine, marriage was a divine institution in which God himself gave the woman to the man as his life's companion and, as Israel interpreted it, placed her under his authority. No other man was therefore permitted to lay any claim to a married woman.

The conviction that God gave the woman to the man and thus bestowed a measure of indissolubility upon marriage was one which developed very slowly in Israel. Pious Jews lived according to this vision, but in official Israel its deeper implications were never fully realised. Initially divorce was the almost unrestricted right of the man. The woman, on the other hand, was neither able nor permitted to repudiate her husband (Judg xix. 2–10).[20] The law, however, in the spirit of the Mosaic cult of Yahweh, moderated this unrestricted right and regulated it. A man might repudiate his wife only if he found "some indecency" in her (Deut xxiv. 1).[21] In that case, it was sufficient for the husband to give her a "bill of divorce," in which he declared that she was henceforth no longer his wife (Deut xxiv. 1–4; Jer iii. 8; Is l. 1). With this the marriage was annulled and both were free to remarry. The precise meaning of "some indecency," or "something shameful," was not clear, however.[22] Apart from the dispute over the interpretation of the phrase, there were also difficulties in connection with its translation. In an ancient Aramaic translation, the Targum of Onkelos, it was rendered as "for the sake of an offence against a word," that is, if the wife did not obey her husband.[23] The Book of Sirach also appears to follow this interpretation, in demanding the repudiation of a wife if she does not do as her husband directs (Sir xxv. 25–6). In practice,

[20] She could, of course, flee from him (Ex xxi. 11), in which case she was not given a bill of divorce and could not, according to custom, remarry.

[21] See also Sir vii. 28; xxv. 36; xlii. 9.

[22] See, among others, J. Bonsirven, *La divorce dans le Nouveau Testament*, Paris and Tournai (1948), especially p. 24.

[23] See J. Leipoldt, p. 75.

the law was widely interpreted. But when at the approach of the Christian era—no doubt partly due to the influence of the looser customs of the Greeks—repudiation became a frequent occurrence (probably because under Roman occupation the death penalty for adultery could not be carried out by the Jews themselves), the rabbis took up a firm position. Two divergent schools of thought emerged at this time. The school of Rabbi Shammai was of the opinion that the only valid reason for divorce was adultery or unchastity. The school of Rabbi Hillel, on the other hand, interpreted the text in accordance with actual practice and, in the view of this school of thought, all kinds of reasons, some of them quite insignificant, were considered sufficient for the legitimate repudiation of a wife and the annulment of a marriage.[24] According to the law, a man had to leave a wife who had committed adultery, otherwise he would make himself an accessory to the sin. Pious Jews frequently sent such a wife away "quietly" (Mt i. 19).

After the exile, at the time of the reform carried out by Ezra and Nehemiah, sharp protest was heard in certain quarters against divorce. We find in the book of Malachi: "For I hate divorce (repudiation), says Yahweh, the God of Israel."[25] Here, however, it was a question of a qualified divorce, in which no appeal could be made to Yahwist legislation. After the exile, many Jews contracted new marriages with daughters of pagan soldiers and citizens, repudiating their first, Israelite wife ("the wife of your youth") in order to improve their position. That was what constituted an offence against good Yahwist practice. Marriage was indissoluble in the Old Testament after the exile, at least when it implied the legal support and privilege of Israel's faith. What

[24] See SB, pt 1, pp. 312 ff. According to Rabbi Akiba, falling in love with another woman was sufficient reason.

[25] Mal ii. 16. See also the whole passage, ii. 10–16. This is a case of qualified divorce (see later). The translation is that of the RSV, which accords with that of the *BJ*. The Douai mistranslates this text: "When thou shalt hate her, put her away, saith the Lord [Yahweh]." Marital fidelity is also praised in Prov v. 15–19 and Eccles ix. 9.

we have here is, as it were, a "privilege of faith" working in the opposite direction. According to Malachi, and thus according to the reforming spirit of Nehemiah, marriage in the Old Testament might not be annulled in favour of a new marriage with an "unbeliever," that is, with a woman who did not belong to Yahweh's people. (Paul was later, in the light of the same vision, to declare a non-Christian marriage dissoluble in favour of a Christian marriage.) This brings us to the question of the Old Testament judgment on mixed marriages.

MIXED MARRIAGES IN THE OLD TESTAMENT

There were very many mixed marriages in Israel (Gen xxxviii. 2; xlvi. 10; xli. 45; xxvi. 34; Ex ii. 21),[26] in spite of the common experience that a marriage with a "stranger" brought all kinds of trouble. (Gen xxvi. 35; xxviii. 8; xxxi. 14; Judg xiv. 3.) Originally, a "stranger" was somebody from outside one's own tribe or clan, and this was in itself an indication that no marriage should take place, especially if it is borne in mind that even within Israel a man preferred to find a bride from among his own blood-relatives. (Gen xx. 12; xxiv. 15; xxviii. 9; xxix. 12; Num xxvi. 59.) Such a wife would always be subject to the protection of the entire clan. If she were given in marriage to a stranger, she would place herself in an unprotected position (Gen xxix. 19; Num xxxvi. 1-12). Social factors, then, undoubtedy played an important part.,

But an even more important part in the matter of mixed marriages was played by Israel's religion. Israel was above all a "holy people."[27] She was "set apart" from other nations, and consequently also remarkable among them in her way of life. She was "different" from all other peoples, and for this reason mixed

[26] See also the Book of Ruth; Num xii. 1; 1 Kings vii. 14 etc. Many mixed marriages took place in the age of the Judges—see especially Judg iii. 6.

[27] See, among many other texts, Ex xiii. 12; xix. 10, 14; Lev xi. 44; xix. 2; xx. 26; Deut vii. 6; xiv. 2.

marriage was an abomination for Israel. A stranger did not simply come "from a different nation." He or she came also "from a different god." One's own tribe or nation and one's "own god" (henotheism) were intimately connected. (Ruth i. 15; 1 Sam xxvi. 19; 1 Kings xviii. 24; 2 Kings xvii. 26; Judg xi. 23–4.) The non-Israelite peoples were pagans whom Yahweh would wipe out. (Ex xxiii. 23; Deut vii. 1–8; xxv. 17–19 ctc.) Even the Deuteronomic writers began to oppose mixed marriages for religious reasons: "For they [mixed marriages] would turn away your sons from following me [Yahweh], to serve other gods" (Deut vii. 4).[28] The basic reason for opposing mixed marriages was, however, the danger which they constituted for the education in faith in Yahweh of Israel's children,[29] who belonged to Yahweh and had to live according to the commandments of the covenant (Deut vii. 6–11).

After the exile, the religious view was propounded with increasing emphasis as the Israelites began more and more to leave their Jewish wives and marry "strangers." Both Ezra and Nehemiah worked resolutely for the purity of the Yahwist ethos of marriage. (Ezra ii. 59–62; ix. 1–10, 44; Neh vii. 61–4; xiii. 23–9.)[30] The "holy" people was on no account to "mix itself with the peoples of the lands," the strangers (Ezra ix. 2). Should the "holy remnant," now returned from exile, defile itself with strangers? (Ezra ix. 8, 13, 14.) Ezra tore his clothes because of this abomination, which was also the cause of the disappearance of the "holy language of Judah" (Neh xiii. 23–30). Mixed marriages were infidelity to Yahweh and to the covenant of Israel's election. They broke the covenant, and this was why Nehemiah, in his zeal, "cleansed them from everything foreign" (Neh xiii. 30).

All this may well sound rather like what we would call apartheid, but for Israel, and especially for post-exilic, Jewish Israel,

---

[28] See also Ex xxxiv. 12–16. The commandment against mixed marriage acknowledged only one exception (Deut xxi. 10–14).

[29] See also Mal ii. 15.

[30] Mal ii. 10–16, already quoted, dates from the same period.

the "set apart," secular reality of the people could not be separated from the reality of salvation—her election as the one,
chosen people of God. Malachi, who in this precise context made
Yahweh say that he hated the repudiation of Jewish wives, also
provided the real Yahwist objection to mixed marriages, namely
that the fruit of the "one flesh" or "one life" of man and woman
in marriage brought about by Yahweh himself was precisely the
"children of God": "Has not he [Yahweh] made them one flesh
and one life? And what does he desire? Godly offspring [= children of Yahweh]" (Mal ii. 15–16).[31] The basic and essential
dogmatic meaning of this Old Testament vision is undoubtedly
that faithfulness to God takes precedence, even in marriage,
should this ever lead to infidelity in religion; and moreover that
in a mixed marriage it is a grave matter of conscience for the
parents to bring up the children in this religion. How this duty
was to be reconciled with the conscience of the other party in a
mixed marriage is a problem which was not posed in Israel; it is
a problem which has arisen out of modern man's sensitivity towards the validity of his fellow-men's convictions.

[31] But see notes 7 and 8 of Chapter 1 and note 25 of this chapter.

3

The Old Testament Solemnisation
of Marriage

As with all peoples and in all religions, the way in which marriage was solemnised in Israel was a function of her particular social pattern.

We could call Israelite betrothal and marriage "civil" but for the fact that, because of her faith in creation, Israel saw the hand of God in everything. For this reason it would be anachronistic to apply our modern term "civil marriage" to Israel. The secular, civil reality of marriage was for Israel always the "work of God's hands," into which the partners entered praising God. In its Semitic sense, this *berākhāh* (blessing) meant that God was actually present with those who undertook a secular activity in praise of him. It would therefore be more accurate to say that the solemnisation of marriage in Israel was not a religious or ritual matter. Its proper place was not in the synagogue or the temple, and it had nothing to do with the service of the word or of sacrifice. Israel's priests and Levites had no part in it. The celebration of a marriage was a private, family matter, although —once concluded—it was protected by Israel's laws. In this sense, then it is possible to speak of a "civil" marriage ceremony; marriage remained firmly in the midst of everyday, secular life.

In Israel marriage was first and foremost a transaction or arrangement between two families; the fathers, in consultation with

their wives, conducted the negotiations and made the final decision. (Gen xxi. 21; xxiv. 1–4; xxxviii. 1–2; xxix. 18; xxvi. 34–5;
xxvii. 46; xxxiv. 4; Judg xiv. 1–3; i. 12–13; 1 Sam xviii. 7–21; 2
Chron xxiv. 3.) The parents preferred to choose partners for
their children from among those of the family circle who were
related to them by marriage,[1] at least within the limits permitted
by Israel's legislation.[2] It was not, therefore, so much a matter
of the bridal couple mutually agreeing to marry, as of the parents
giving their consent to the marriage after mutual discussion. We
tend to see the essence of marriage in the mutual agreement of
the partners, but we ought not to be surprised by this. Marriage
itself is evolutionary in form, as man gradually acquires a deeper
insight into all genuinely human values. In Israel's family life
especially the will of the father held good for the will of his
son or his daughter. "To do the will of the father" was a family
expression in Israel (an expression which was, of course, applied
in the Gospel of St. John to Christ's relationship with the Father).
The real agreement of the children in the case of marriage was
therefore their obedience to their parents. The children's own
consent to marry was implicit in this obedience, which was automatic in the Israelite pattern of society. We should be even less
surprised by this when we remember that boys and girls married very young in the ancient Near East—according to the
rabbis, a girl had to be at least twelve and a boy at least thirteen
to marry. (A boy "came of age" at the age of thirteen.) Of
course, this does not mean that the parents did not take their
children's own wishes into account in the marriage arrangements
(Gen xxiv. 8, 58; Judg xiv. 2), and certainly not all children were
equally submissive (Gen xxvi. 34–5).

Essentially what was involved was the making of a covenant
between two families. This covenant was made orally by the
parents, and the son was implicated in it by his automatic obedience to his parents. In the ancient Near East a girl had absolutely

---

[1] Gen xxiv. 4; xxix. 19; Judg xiv. 3; Tobit iv. 12 (Greek–RSV); vi. 14
(Vulg.–Douai); vii. 12–13 (Greek–RSV).
[2] See the summary in Lev xviii. 6 ff.

no say in affairs. Through marriage she simply came under the control of another man, her husband. According to the standard formula, she came "under the rule of the master." (Hos ii. 18; Ex xxi. 3; Deut xxiv. 4; xxii. 22; 2 Sam xi. 26 etc.) It would, of course, be wrong to claim that no marriages in the ancient Near East began with love. Life is after all stronger than theory. Nonetheless, it goes without saying that such marriages—covenants made between two families with the daughter as the issue of the negotiations—did not normally begin with love, but that this love was a commission which originated with the solemnisation of the marriage itself.[3]

On betrothal the young man generally paid the girl's father the *mōhar* (the dowry or bride-price). With this the betrothal was concluded (Gen xxxiv. 12; Ex xxii. 16; 1 Sam xviii. 25).[4] Although this did not mean that the marriage had been finally solemnised, intercourse with a third party after the betrothal—and the unlawful repudiation of the betrothed—was regarded as adultery (Deut xxii. 23-7; Judg xv. 6; 2 Sam iii. 14; Hos ii. 19-20), even though conjugal intercourse was not yet permitted between the betrothed man and woman. After the exile, and perhaps even earlier, marriages were legally confirmed in writing.[5]

The climax of the marriage feast was the procession in which the bride was taken to the bridegroom's house.[6] The significant action here consisted of a giving and a taking—the bride's father

[3] See Gen xxiv. 67. This point should not be passed over too lightly. In contrast to the post-Exilic period, especially in later Judaism (2 Macc iii. 19), Israelite girls of an earlier period had a great deal of freedom.

[4] See also Deut xxii. 29; Hos iii. 2. There is a good deal of controversy over the precise meaning of this sum of money. It is not certain—indeed, it is unlikely—that it was a genuine purchase amount, the sign of a marriage by purchase, in which the woman was more or less merchandise. This seems not to have been the real meaning of the marriage ceremony in Israel. The sum of money was rather a seal of a genuine covenant. See De Vaux, pp. 26-9.

[5] Tobit vii. 16; viii. 24 (at least according to one version, which is followed in Vulg.-Douai).

[6] For details, see Judg xiv. 11 ff., Gen xxix. 2 ff.; 1 Macc ix. 39; Ps xlv. 14-16. See also Mt xix. 15; xxv. 1-13; Lk xii. 35-8; Jn iii. 28-9.

gave his daughter away, and the bridegroom's father took her for his son.[7] Wedding hymns were sung during the procession (Ps xlv.; Jer xvi. 19). When she left her parents' house the bride was blessed by her father or by her relatives and friends.[8] The festivities lasted at least a week (Gen xxix. 27–8; Judg xiv. 12 f.).

According to the Jewish and rabbinical literature of the post-Christian Jewish world,[9] which to some extent went back to the very earliest Christian period, marriages were solemnised in the following way. The betrothal (*qiddûšîn*, also *'erûšîn*) took place, as in more ancient times, by the handing over of the *mōhar*, or sum of money, by written document (*kethûbah*), or else—in theory at least—by sexual intercourse. In the minds of the people, the word "betrothal" (*qiddûšîn*) was later associated with "sanctification" (the stem *qdš*, holy)—the custom of dedicating something to the temple, which made it taboo to anyone else. The "formula of dedication" used on betrothal amounted to this: "Be sanctified to me (as my wife) by means of this sum of money."[10] The obligations of the betrothed couple before the solemn taking of the bride from her parents' house to that of her bridegroom were kept less strictly in Judah than in the rest of the country. The blessing of betrothal was expanded into a much longer prayer ("Be praised, Yahweh, our God . . .") of the type that is familiar to us from other Jewish ceremonies. Yahweh's sanctification of Israel was associated with marriage in this blessing. In the north of Palestine sexual intercourse was forbidden during the period between the betrothal and the marriage itself. In Judah, on the other hand, betrothal and marriage practically coincided.[11]

---

[7] See Gen xxix. 12 ff.; xxv. 30; xxx. 4, 9; xxxiv. 11; xxxviii. 2; Ex ii. 21; xxi. 4, 10; xxxiv. 16. There is no word for "marriage" in the Old Testament.

[8] Gen xxiv. 60; Tobit vii. 15 (according to one version); ix. 6 ff. This blessing, with which Raguel gave his daughter Sarah to Tobias, was taken over into the liturgy of the marriage service of the Catholic Church.

[9] See Neubauer, *Beiträge;* SB, pt. 2, pp. 372–99.

[10] Neubauer, pp. 195–8; SB, pt. 2, p. 396.

[11] Neubauer, pp. 57 ff.

The marriage feast (*miśeteh, śimeḥah:* feast, rejoicing, drinking) was simply one long drinking-bout.[12] The cup of wine was blessed again and again by the bridegroom's father during the feast. Here too there were no priests present, although round about the year 140 the Rabbi Simon ben Gamaliel demanded that the marriage document should also be signed by priests or Levites as witnesses. After the festival the couple was taken to the *ḫûppāh*, or bridal tent, where they were able to be alone together for the first time.[13] This undoubtedly came about under the influence of the Greek practice of leading the bride into the bridal apartment. At this time, both the bride and the bridegroom wore garlands.

We may conclude very briefly. The solemnisation of marriage in Israel and in Judaism was a family affair, experienced in faith in Yahweh.

[12] SB, pt. 2, p. 372.
[13] Neubauer, pp. 55 ff. and 224 ff.

Part 2

MARRIAGE IN THE MESSAGE
OF THE NEW TESTAMENT

Introduction

In the Old Testament marriage was above all experienced as a secular reality seen in the perspective of faith in the creative God. In the centuries immediately preceding the Christian era, however, a certain gloom hung like a dark cloud over Israel's optimism in creation. Although the nation's optimistic belief in creation remained fundamentally untouched, it is apparent (from the Book of Ecclesiastes, for example) that a certain dissatisfaction and uneasiness crept into everyday secular life.

In the New Testament man's consciousness of sin and his need for redemption are even more strongly emphasized. The contrast between the unredeemed state and the state of salvation, between death and life, and between sin and grace, is sharply drawn in the light of a completely new experience—that of the mystery of Christ. The New Testament vision is essentially soteriological. In other words, the world is seen from the point of view of man's state either of being redeemed or of being unredeemed.

Even here, though, it is only a question of a change of emphasis. Faith in the creation remained intact in the New Testament vision. Paul's words in 1 Tim iv. 4: "Everything created by God is good, and nothing is to be rejected if it is received with thanksgiving; for then it is consecrated by the word of God and prayer," are a pure echo of the Old Testament optimism in creation that was founded on faith in God's creative word (or on the Gospel, perhaps?) and on man's use of the gifts of creation with God's *berākhāh*, that is, while praising and thanking God for those gifts. This optimism in creation was, in the New Testament, illuminated by the light of the glorified Lord—everything was the Lord's, Paul declared, and Christians might therefore make use of all things in gratitude (1 Cor x. 25–6; cf. Ps xxiv. 1). Like the pious Israelite of the Old Testament, the man who was redeemed in Christ might enjoy everyday secular activities, even eating and drinking, as a thankful entry into God's good creation, to the glory and honour of God (1 Cor x. 31). But the Old Testament idea of creation within the history of salvation was to be experienced Christologically in the New Testament. Not only was the Old Testament title "God of Israel"—Israel's characteristic confession of her faith in creation—also used in the New (Mt xv. 31; Lk. i. 68; Acts xiii. 17; Heb xi. 16; 2 Cor vi. 16); not only did God remain in the New Testament the "God of Abraham, Isaac and Jacob" (Lk xx. 37; Mk xii. 26; Mt xxii. 32; Acts iii. 13; vii. 32), that is, the God who revealed himself in the lives of the pious fathers (Acts iii. 13; v. 30; vii. 45; xiii. 17 ff.; xiv. 14; Heb i. 1; viii. 9; see especially Heb xi. 1–40); but he also became, and this above all, the "God of our Lord Jesus Christ" (Eph i. 17) and the "God and Father of our Lord Jesus Christ" (Rom xv. 6; 2 Cor i. 3; xi. 31; Eph i. 3). The mystery of Christ is seen against the all-important background of the Old Testament belief in creation. What is at issue in the New Testament is the "plan of the mystery hidden for ages in God who created all things" (Eph iii. 9), and the work of the "one God and Father of us all, who is above all, and through all and in all" (Eph iv. 6).

But the reality of creation is lived by Christians in the light of Christ's appearance which creates everything anew. This gave rise to a new sensitivity towards the realities which belong to this world. As a result of this, the Old Testament's essential optimism in creation became for the time being no more than a backdrop to the New Testament writings, so that the essentially *Christian* secularisation of natural, human facts and values was obscured. The *newness* of the appearance of Christ was the focus of all attention.

4

The New Testament Teaching on Marriage

The Gospels provide us with two fundamental statements made by Christ himself on the subject of marriage. The first is an affirmation of the plan of married life within the economy of creation to which Genesis had already given clear assent. Through this affirmation the Old Testament idea of marriage was brought to fulfilment (Mk x. 2–12 and parallels). The second is a specifically eschatological statement, where the quest for the kingdom of God takes precedence over marriage, so that celibacy appears, with marriage, as a characteristic Christian subservience to the kingdom of God (Mt xix. 12). These two fundamental affirmations are thus a direct extension of the two Old Testament confessions of faith: that of creation, and that of the covenant of grace. It is precisely because the covenant, as the redemption of mankind by Christ, occupies a central position in the New Testament consciousness of faith that I propose to analyse marriage first from the point of view of the covenant of grace.

MARRIAGE AND CHRIST'S COVENANT OF GRACE WITH THE CHURCH

The Covenant with the Heavenly Bridegroom at the Second Coming

The prophetic image of marriage used as a means of revealing the covenant of grace recurs in the New Testament, where it is applied to Christ, and therefore to the definitive covenant. In the New Testament marriage is used first of all as a means of revealing the eschatological or heavenly glorification in which Christians, together with Christ, are to celebrate the eternal wedding-feast with God.[1] So important is this idea that, apart from the parables in which the kingdom of heaven is portrayed as a wedding-feast, the Greek term *gamos* (marriage) is, with only two exceptions (Heb xiii. 4; Jn ii. 1–2),[2] not used in the New Testament books with the primary meaning of marriage between human beings, but rather to denote the eschatological wedding of Christ and his redeemed.[3] It is not simply one particular category of Christians (namely, those who are entrusted with Christ's work of salvation by celibacy) which can enjoy this bridal relationship with Christ, but all the baptized without distinction.

The idea of "becoming one"—"the two shall become one flesh" (Gen ii. 24)—also has a background function in the image of the eschatological wedding-feast of the Book of Revelation. The beginning and the end of time, the *prōton* and the *eschaton*, flow together in the Genesis image of the "one flesh" (Rev xxi; xxii. 4.). In this long passage of Revelation, which is introduced by the *leitmotif* "I saw a new heaven and a new earth" (xxi. 1), the image of paradise and that of the holy City of Jerusalem are intermingled. Creation ("one flesh"), the covenant or "holy City of Zion" ("prepared as a bride adorned for her husband," xxi. 2), and the redemption or wedding in heaven between Christ and his church, all come together in this passage to form one single vision of salvation. Paul proclaims the same idea in his own way in Eph v. 22–33, although here it is applied to the church on earth.

Similarly the wedding-feast at Cana, which was graced by the presence of Jesus himself (Jn ii. 1–11), should not be seen first

---

[1] Rev xviii. 23; xix. 7–9; xxi. 2, 9; xxii. 17. In the parables in which the kingdom of heaven is compared to a wedding: Mt xxii. 2–14; xxv. 1–12; Mk ii. 19; Lk xiv. 8, 16–24. Finally: 2 Cor xi. 2–3.

[2] In the John passage—in the account of the wedding-feast at Cana—the use of the word *gamos* is probably not an exception. See also p. 109.

[3] See the textual references given in note 1 above and note 5 below.

and foremost as a sign of the Christianisation of secular marriage, but rather in the prophetic tradition as an "image-in-action" here on earth of the inception of the messianic wedding-feast.[4] On the basis of the saving significance of marriage—already present in Israel—as an image of God's covenant of grace, Jesus' aim, by his presence at the wedding in Cana, was to describe the kingdom of God prophetically as a heavenly wedding-feast. Christ himself is frequently called the "bridegroom" in the New Testament.[5] Just as woman, according to Genesis, was taken from man to form "one life" with him, so the church, Christ's beloved, appeared from the open wound in Christ's side (Jn xix. 34–7). As Augustine was to say later: "Christ died so that the church might be born" (*In Joh. Evang.*, Tr. 9, no. 10 [*PL* 35, 1463]).

In this connection it is important to bear in mind that, as in the Old Testament, marriage was here used only as a means of expressing and of making humanly clear Christ's intimate relationship with the redeemed people of God, his church. These references are not in any sense direct New Testament statements about everyday secular marriage itself; but, as in the Old Testament, the revelation of the New Covenant—expressed in images taken from marriage—was to place the secular reality of marriage in an orbit within which it would catch a strong reflection of light. Paul stated this explicitly. The mystery which he called "great" (i.e., important) was not marriage itself, but the covenant relationship between Christ and his church expressed in terms of human marriage, insofar as precisely this relationship was implicitly suggested in the text of Genesis which discussed "the two who are one flesh."

There are, however, transitional texts in the New Testament in

4 See, for example, J. Charlier, *Le signe de Cana*, Brussels and Paris (1959); K. Schmidt, *Der Johanneische Charakter der Erzählung vom Hochzeitswunder in Kana*, Leipzig (1951); H. Van den Bussche, "Het wijnwonder te Cana," *CG*, 3 (1952), pp. 193–225; A. Feuillet, "L'heure de Jésus et le signe de Cana," *ETL*, 36 (1960), pp. 5–22.

5 See note 2 of this chapter and Mt ix. 15; Mk ii. 19; Lk v. 34–5; xii. 35–6; Jn iii. 29.

which the eschatological wedding-feast is not applied to the eschatological kingdom, but in which this kingdom at the end of time is seen to have begun already in the church, and therefore with it the wedding-feast of salvation. In Christ's wedding-feast with his eschatological community, the Gospel of St. John regards John the Baptist as the "bridal page," the "friend of the bridegroom" (Jn iii. 29) or *šošebîn* who prepared the marriage ceremonies and conducted them, and who above all led the bride in the bridal procession to the husband's house.[6] This "page of honour" also prepared the bridal bath and helped the bride to array herself for the wedding. Similarly, according to 2 Cor xi. 2, Paul is as apostle the bridal page who espouses those who believe in Christ to him and presents them to Christ. In the exegesis of the Jews there was a tradition which compared Yahweh's "presenting" of Eve to Adam (Gen ii. 22) with the function performed by the bridal page at a Jewish marriage ceremony. This image was taken over by John (Jn iii. 39), just as Paul took it over in 2 Cor xi. 2 and above all in the central text of Eph v. 21–33, in which Christ fulfils the functions both of the bridegroom and of the bridal page, Paul insisting here that Christ himself (*autos*) presents the bride, the church, to himself (*heautōi*).

Christ's Bridal Relationship with the Church on Earth

The Pauline text to which we have just made allusion is not entirely alien to the New Testament vision as a whole, but it does have something which is quite distinctive to Paul himself:

Be subject to one another, out of reverence for Christ. Wives, be subject to your husbands, as to the Lord. For the husband is the head of the wife as Christ is the head of the church, his body, and is himself its Saviour. As the church is subject to Christ, so let wives also be subject in everything to their husbands. Husbands, love your wives, as Christ loved the church and gave himself up for her, that he might

[6] See M. Boismard, "L'ami de l'Epoux (Jn iii. 29)," *A l'encontre de Dieu* (*Mémorial A. Gelin*), Le Puy (1961), pp. 289–96. See also SB, pt. 1, pp. 503–4.

sanctify her, having cleansed her by the washing of water with the word, that he might present the church to himself in splendour (as a glorious bride), without spot or wrinkle or any such thing, that she might be holy and without blemish. Even so men should love their wives as their own bodies. He who loves his wife loves himself. For no man ever hates his own flesh, but nourishes and cherishes it, as Christ does the church, because we are members of his body. For this reason a man shall leave his father and mother and be joined to his wife, and the two shall become one. This is a great mystery [= this mystery has a deep significance] and I take it to mean [= but I for my part relate it to] Christ and the church; however [= be this as it may] let each one of you love his wife as himself, and let the wife see that she respects her husband. [Eph v. 21–33.]

Two assertions strike us immediately in this text, and they are both basic. Not only does Paul say something about Christ's bridal relationship with his church in the context of Genesis, but he also says something directly relating to married life itself in the perspective of this covenant relationship, namely "Love your wives, as Christ loved the church." All this serves in Paul to give theological support to the wife's subjection to the husband. I propose to go into this in the section dealing with the properly historical aspects of the New Testament ethos of marriage. Here, however, I shall discuss only the two affirmations noted above.

"This is a great mystery" (Eph v. 32). In Paul, a "mystery,"[7] *mystērion,* in conjunction with the Hebrew *sôdh,* means a hidden

[7] Different writers bring out different shades of meaning in Paul's concept of *mystērion.* See especially: K. Prümm, "Zur Phänomenologie des paulinischen Mysterion und dessen seelischer Aufnahme," *Bbl,* 37 (1956), pp. 135–61; C. Mohrmann, "Sacramentum dans les plus anciens textes chrétiens," *Etudes sur le Latin des chrétiens,* Rome (1958), pp. 233–44; M. Verheijen, "Mysterion, sacramentum et la Synagogue," *RSR,* 45 (1957), pp. 321–37; E. Schillebeeckx, *De sacramentele heilseconomie,* Antwerp (1952), pt. 1, pp. 35–47; E. Vogt, " 'Mysteria' in textibus Qumran," *Bbl,* 37 (1956), pp. 247–57; K. Steur, *Dogmatisch tractaat over het huwelijk,* Bussum (1947); A. Ruiters, "Kleine Dogmatiek van het huwelijk," *SC,* 35 (1960), esp. pp. 82–94. The exegesis of Eph v has a long history, of which a good outline is provided by P. Colli, *La pericopa paolina ad Eph v. 32 nella interpretazione dei SS. Padri e nel Concilio di Trento,* Parma (1951).

divine decree which is revealed in a veiled manner in the course of time. A "mystery" or "secret," which is therefore something revealed by God in the history of salvation, also in Paul implies the veiled manner of revelation and at the same time points to the "deeper significance" of an event (or of anything else). "This is a great mystery" therefore means that Paul is concerned here with something that has a very deep significance, and that says much more than would appear at first sight. On what does he base this? It is clear that he bases it directly on the Genesis text: "Therefore a man leaves his father and his mother, and cleaves to his wife, and they become one flesh" (Gen ii. 24). This Old Testament text has a very deep significance. We have already seen that marriage, which Genesis is here discussing, was used even in the Old Testament as an image for a more profound bond of unity and affection between two partners—the covenant between Yahweh and Israel. But Paul follows this line of argument still further: "But I for my part relate it to Christ and his church" (Eph v. 32). In his view the "great mystery" revealed in a veiled manner in Gen ii. 24 is thus quite concretely the "one flesh," the living bond of unity and affection between Christ and his bride, the church.

Gen ii. 23 provides a type of this living bond between Christ and his church. In this text we are in the direct line of the Old Testament prophets, in which the divine covenant is referred to in terms of married life, although of course our vision is made more profound by reason of our Christological perspective. Whether this was originally intended by the writer of Genesis is, of course, another question. The interpretation that the text provides a type in this way can be disputed, and Paul was well aware of this—this is shown by the phrase "be this as it may" which immediately follows (v. 33). But quite apart from the question as to whether the Genesis text did or did not in fact include an indirect reference to the "one life" of Christ and his church, Paul states that husbands ought in any case to love their wives, as Christ loved the church (v. 33, taken together with v. 25). Whether this was implied in the Old Testament or not, Paul certainly saw human marriage in the context of Christ's bridal relationship with the church. And a great deal can be learned from this relationship about man's relationship with woman in marriage.

"Love, as Christ loved the church" (Eph v. 25). With reference to the example of love between man and woman in marriage, Paul enlarges upon the great love which Christ had for his church. Going back (consciously or unconsciously) to Ezekiel xvi, in which God's love for Israel was described, the bride whom he cleansed and washed and arrayed most beautifully, Paul describes all that Christ's love did for his bride, the church. Inspired by this love for the church, Christ's first concern was to make his chosen bride as glorious as possible. What we have here is a joining together in love of the church with Christ, the Holy One. Christ gave up his life to gain a beautiful bride who was worthy of this bond of love: "He gave himself up for her, that he might sanctify her, cleansing her by the washing of water with the word, that he might present her to himself as a glorious bride, without spot or wrinkle or any such thing, that she might be holy and without blemish" (v. 25–7). Using the image of the wedding preparations, Paul speaks of Christ as the one "who was delivered up for our sins." (Rom iv. 25; Gal i. 4; ii. 20; Acts xx. 28; Tit ii. 11–14; Eph v. 2; 1 Tim ii. 6.) Christ's redemption made mankind into the church. Although there are echoes of the ancient custom of the "bridal bath" and the arraying of the bride in her wedding garments in Paul's words, the apostle's first thought is for baptism (the "washing of water with the word"), by means of which every man and woman is separately incorporated into the church.

Two images are thus closely interwoven in this passage: Christ's death, through which he prepared the church as a glorious bride for himself, and baptism, a "becoming immersed" in Jesus' death, through which one enters the church personally and in this way one also becomes a corporate member of the bride of Christ. It is clear that Paul, knowing only Jesus Christ and him crucified, while thinking and speaking of marriage, was at this point carried away by the mystery of Christ, although he did not forget his real theme, which was that of marriage. He saw the church as the body of Christ, as he had already said previously in the same epistle (Eph i. 23; ii. 16; iv. 12–16; v. 23, 30).[8] And who does not nourish and cherish his own body?

There are echoes of Old Testament ideas here as well. The Genesis text referring to the "one flesh" in connection with marriage was in Paul's mind (see v. 31 ff.) and, what is more, it had already been developed, in what might be called a pre-Pauline perspective, by Malachi: "Has not he [God] made them one flesh and one life? . . . So take heed to your life and let none be faithless to the wife of his youth" (Mal ii. 15–16).[9] Paul says that, just as Christ cleansed, cared for, and cherished the church, his body, with which he formed "one flesh," in the same way "men should love their wives as their own bodies" (v. 28). The biblical idea of the "one flesh," stemming from Genesis, clearly dominates the whole of this passage (v. 22–31). "No man ever hates his own flesh" (v. 29). To love one's wife is to love "one's own flesh," "as Christ does the church," his body (v. 29), of which we are individually fully incorporated members. And then the idea of the "one flesh," which has dominated the whole of the exposition, breaks through explicitly in a direct reference to the Genesis text, which is interpreted by Paul as a mystery-revelation of the reality of the unity of Christ with his church or of the one "mystical body." (In this context it should be noted that Paul here uses "flesh" and "body" interchangeably without any difference of meaning.) He had already called the "Adam" of the story of creation the "type of the one who was to come" in Rom v. 14.

[8] See P. Benoit, "Corps, tête et plérôme dans les épîtres de la captivité," *RB*, 63 (1956), pp. 5–44; A. Feuillet, "L'église, plérôme du Christ d'après Eph i. 23," *NRT*, 78 (1956), pp. 449–72, 593–610.

[9] See note 7 of Chapter 1 and note 25 of Chapter 2.

Therefore, according to Paul's typological exegesis, the "deeper significance" is not only situated in the ancient text itself. It also has a referential content: the "one flesh" of Genesis has a deeper significance which, in Paul's view, refers to the living unity between Christ and his Church.

But in any case Genesis still says that man and wife are "one flesh," and so, "be this [= this typology of Genesis] as it may, let each one of you love his wife as himself [= as his own flesh]" (v. 33). In other words, whatever the typological meaning of this text may be, the literal meaning of Gen ii. 24 is in any case the "becoming one" of man and wife, and hence the idea that husbands must love their wives "as themselves." The personal relationship of marriage is of course seen from the point of view of the husband who, according to ancient custom, occupied the leading position as head of the marriage, but nonetheless remains firmly based on love. Paul's reservation with regard to his typological exegesis in no way cancels out his personal view (expressed in v. 25) that husbands must love their wives in the same way that Christ loved the church.

It is as if Paul had been struck by the thought that the wife is the "body of her husband" (the idea of "becoming one" in Genesis) precisely because he had already called the church the "body of the Lord" as many as four times in the Epistle to the Ephesians before he came to the admonitory part in connection with marriage. Thus his ecclesiological exposition of the church as the "body of the Lord" was the direct inspiration for the passage on marriage in Eph v. 22–33. In Eph v. 2 he had just been discussing Christ, who "loved us and gave himself up for us." Eph v. 22–23 may thus be regarded as a commentary on this in terms of marriage.

The covenant relationship between Christ and his church is a marriage relationship, and it was represented by Paul according to the various phases of marriage—loving surrender (v. 25), cleansing (v. 26), the marriage ceremony (v. 27) and the union

and loving care of married life (v. 29–31).[10] The Jews and the
Gentiles were, in a proleptic or anticipatory sense, the church,
which was actually made into the church by Christ himself. The
"becoming one," a fundamental affirmation of the Old Testament
belief in creation in the context of marriage, which had already
been used by the Old Testament as a means of revealing God's
covenant of grace, was extended by Paul into the mystery of
Christ and his church. In this vision, creation, the covenant, and
redemption are intermingled. Christ is the bridegroom whose
bride is the church. Christ, the one who loves, redeems, and cares
for the church, is presented as a model for the husband in his
married relationship with his wife.

The original idea of the husband's "rib" from which the woman was taken thus acquired an unexpected depth of meaning
in the New Testament. If we can justify theologically man's
creation in grace,[11] we should be able to understand better now
than we were able to understand from the Old Testament[12] that
the concrete gift of creation which is marriage could become the
appointed means of revealing and expressing, in a human and
religious manner, God's covenant of grace with men in Christ,
and that this use of the image could illuminate some of the deepest aspects of marriage itself. Although the Councils of Florence[13]
and of Trent[14] did not base the sacramental character of marriage
on Eph v. 31–2, they certainly associated it with this text. Viewed
in the perspective of the history of dogma, this came about not
because of the word *mystērion*, as used by Paul, and rendered in
the old Latin translations as *sacramentum* or *mysterium*, but because of the Old Testament vision which was carried through
into the New Testament Christological vision of the unity within

10 See P. Benoit, *Les Epîtres de la Captivité (BJ)*.

11 See "De zin van het menszijn van Jesus, de Christus," *TT*, 2 (1962),
especially pp. 154–9.

12 See above, pp. 15 ff.

13 DS 1327 (DB 702).

14 DS 1797 (DB 969).

the salvation history of creation, the covenant, and the redemption. This vision was based on the Genesis idea of creation contained in the "one flesh," on the prophetic idea of the covenant, and on the Pauline idea of redemption. (Eph v. 22–33, and not simply v. 31–2.) The sustained use of the image of marriage in order to express man's bond of unity and affection with God, and indeed—as in the case of Hosea—the use of a *de facto* marriage, disclosed, within this use of revelation, a deeper dimension in marriage itself.

Of course, it is only within the church, under the charismatic guidance of the church's teaching authority, that the Old and New Testaments can be recognised as the *locus theologicus* for the sacramental character of marriage. But on the other hand the church and her teaching authority are regulated and inspired in this recognition by the implicit wealth of the biblical data, which are illuminated in the Christian practice of married life. In a special way, characteristic of the Christian life of married people, the reality of Christ's redemption, the bridal relationship between Christ and the church, is made actual and present in marriage itself. The moral and religious task confronting Christian married couples is therefore to enter intimately into precisely this redemptive love-relationship existing between Christ and his church. (I propose to discuss the second idea that runs through the whole of this passage—the idea of the husband as head of the wife—separately at a later stage.) Moreover, what has been positively stated here is not denied, at least as far as its content is concerned, by Reformed Christianity, although Protestant Christians have formally rejected the sacramental character of marriage. A Catholic may therefore recognise and respect the marriage of two baptized Protestants as a sacrament.

In the meantime, Paul was directly concerned only with exhortations to Christians in connection with their married lives. All that he had said in the passage in his Epistle to the Colossians parallel to that in the Epistle to the Ephesians was: "Wives, be subject to your husbands, as is fitting in the Lord. Husbands, love

your wives and do not be harsh with them. Children . . . Fathers
. . . Slaves . . . Masters . . ." (Col iii. 18–iv. 1; cf. 1 Pet ii. 18–iii.
7). Each member of this larger kinship group was given a suitable
exhortation. The passage in the Epistle to the Ephesians (extending in fact from v. 21 to vi. 9) has the same intention—wives,
husbands, children, fathers, servants, and masters are given exhortations appropriate to their status here as well. The introduction
to this passage embraces all these categories of people (v. 21):
"Be subject to one another, out of reverence for Christ." Although what follows is in the form of an exhortatory exposition,
the exhortation is dogmatically more firmly based than that contained in the epistle to the Colossians. To act "as Christ did
towards the church" gains a deeper meaning from the definitive
and perfected covenant. Marriage has a symbolic value, as a making actual and present of salvation already accomplished, and this
making present is to be imitated in marriage itself.

In contrast to Yahweh's bride Israel, who as such was still able
to be unfaithful to her husband, the church, as the bride of
Christ, is confirmed in salvation. Marriage is therefore an image
of the indissoluble and mutually faithful covenant relationship
between Christ and his church. God gave his definitive assent to
mankind in Christ. In the same Christ he gave mankind's positive
and sanctified response, with the result that Christ's church is
eternally associated with God. Christ's love was so strong that it
was able to arouse reciprocal love in us. What is more, Christ's
love triumphed over all trials, over all disappointments and set-
backs, and was stronger than all the rebuffs of the human partner.
He loved us "while we were yet sinners" (Rom v. 8). "Much
more" does he love us, "since we are now justified by his blood"
(Rom v. 9) and baptized in him.

The consequences of this mutually faithful bridal relationship
between Christ and his church were (intentionally) not developed by Paul in the passage from the epistle to the Ephesians
discussed in this section, but the total New Testament appreciation of marriage will be made clear when viewed in the light of

the definitive redeeming love of Christ, who had already inaugurated the *eskhata* (last things). This we must now reconsider.

THE PRIMACY OF THE BRIDAL RELATIONSHIP WITH CHRIST, EVEN IN MARRIAGE ITSELF

In our discussion of marriage in the Old Testament we have already come to the view that marriage, although a secular reality, pointed beyond itself to something else, to something "Other." It refers to something that transcends marriage, not to a mystical marriage in a supernatural, divine world, but to historical facts—to the historically first fact of the divine constitution of marriage (the Genesis account of the creation), and subsequently to the saving fact of the covenant of grace. Now we know that the "something Other" to which marriage, transcending its purely worldly dimension, refers is the mystery of Christ, the covenant relationship between Christ and his church. This transcendence itself has a twofold meaning: first, a real transcendence of marriage on the part of some Christians in celibacy dedicated to God; and secondly, the transcendence of marriage by "marrying in the Lord."

"Unmarried for the Kingdom of God"

Christ's bridal relationship with his church—the field in which the kingdom of God is prepared—is stressed to such an extent among Christians that, under the impetus of a divine charism, it can completely displace marriage from the personal sphere of interest of some Christians. This recoiling of a secular reality in the face of the coming of the kingdom of God is of such fundamental significance (the secular reality itself undergoes a crisis when it occurs) that only an authoritative pronouncement by Christ himself can explain this inner potentiality and tension of eschatological salvation which is already inaugurated. This authoritative statement on the part of Christ is provided in Matthew's Gospel.

Judaism had distinguished two categories of eunuchs or unmarriageable persons: "eunuchs by birth or from heaven" and
"eunuchs by men."[15] Christ added a third category: "There are
unmarriageable men who have made themselves unmarriageable
for the kingdom of heaven. He who is able to receive this, let
him receive it" (Mt xix. 12). This passage occurs only in Matthew, but even an exceptionally critical exegete such as Herbert
Braun sees it as a statement or *logion* of Christ himself.[16] Matthew
allows this statement to follow another affirmation by Jesus concerning the radical indissolubility of marriage (xix. 3–9).[17] Christ
reacts to the astonishment which this strict view of marriage—an
even harsher teaching than that of the school of Shammai—causes
the apostles by saying that not everyone can understand this indissolubility of marriage. But it is in keeping with Christianity;
indeed, there are even those who do not marry for the sake of
the kingdom of God. The passage dealing with the indissolubility
of marriage is merged with the passage about the Christian possibility of celibacy. (This fusion may perhaps be Matthew's own.)
Because of this, the reasoning would appear to be as follows.
That the Christian experience of marriage may sometimes impose
a practical (i.e., a situational) celibacy because of the indissolubility of marriage should cause no surprise. For there are even
believers who choose voluntarily not to marry at all in order to
give themselves exclusively to the kingdom of God, and this is
even more difficult to understand and to put into practice.[18] In

---

[15] SB, pt. 1, pp. 805–6.

[16] *Spätjüdisch-häretischer und frühchristlicher Radikalismus. Jesus von
Nazareth und die essenische Qumransekte*, pt. 2 "Die Synoptiker," BHT,
24–2 (1957), p. 112, *n.* 3; p. 113, *n.* 1.

[17] *Vv.* 10–11 provide the transition to *v.* 12.

[18] It seems to me incorrect to apply this text solely to the sacrifices that
can be demanded of the Christian by marriage which is indissoluble. (See
J. Dupont, *Mariage et divorce*, pp. 170 ff.). On the other hand, Dupont ad-
mits that Christ's *logion* stood on its own before it was recorded in Matthew's gospel and had in view all those Christians who wished to live as
virgins for the sake of the kingdom of God (p. 220).

other words it is a gift of God, since that is the meaning of the
biblical phrase: "To whom it is given."

The early Christians of the apostolic age took these words of
Christ to heart. In reply to a question put to him by the Christians of Corinth,[19] Paul concluded his long exposition with the
following all-embracing summary: "So that he who marries his
betrothed does well; and he who refrains from marriage will do
better . . . But in my judgment she [the woman] is happier if she
remains as she is [i.e., unmarried]. And I think that I have the
Spirit of God" (1 Cor vii. 38–40).[20] At first it would appear as if
Paul's attitude towards the celibacy of women is subtly different
from that which he takes toward the celibacy of men. It is only
when he speaks of women that he adds "At least in my judgment," just as he had said a little earlier: "Concerning the unmarried, I have no command of the Lord; but I give my opinion
as one who by the Lord's mercy is trustworthy" (vii. 25). But it
emerges clearly from vii. 26 ff. that by "virgins" Paul meant both
men (vii. 27–8a) and women (vii. 28b).

It does, of course, seem remarkable that Paul received "no
command from the Lord" on this score, but it would appear
that he was not familiar with Christ's own pronouncement (Mt
xix. 12), as some exegetes claim.[21] It would certainly have suited
his argument better to appeal to the words of Christ himself. This
is the more remarkable because—in the same context, discussing
the indissolubility of marriage—he does refer (vii. 10) to a statement made by Christ himself (which is, moreover, linked in
Matthew, at least, with Christ's *logion* concerning Christian celibacy to form one connected passage). The argument that Paul
now puts forward for religious celibacy is: "The unmarried man
is anxious about the affairs of the Lord, how to please the Lord;

[19] "Now, concerning the matters about which you wrote. [Paul then
quotes from the Corinthians' letter:] It is well for a man not to touch a
woman" (1 Cor vii. 1).

[20] See also the whole passage, vii. 1–40.

[21] See, for example, E. Stauffer, *Die Botschaft Jesu damals und heute*,
Berne (1959), pp. 79 ff.

but the married man is anxious about worldly affairs, how to please his wife, and his interests are divided" (vii. 32–3). He says the same with regard to women: "The unmarried woman or girl is anxious about the affairs of the Lord, how to be holy in body and spirit; but the married woman is anxious about worldly affairs, how to please her husband" (vii. 34). In conclusion he says: "I say this for your own benefit, not to lay any restraint upon you, but to promote good order and to secure your undivided devotion to the Lord" (vii. 35).

What Paul says here is substantially the same as what is said in Christ's pronouncement: remain unmarried "for the sake of the kingdom of heaven" (Matthew), in order to be "anxious about the affairs of the Lord" and to give one's "undivided attention to the Lord" (Paul). The differences are only in shades of meaning. In Mt xix. 10–12 celibacy is seen as an exception, and rather as a state which is linked with an office in the kingdom of God. Paul, on the other hand, desires celibacy as the state of life for all Christians, although he agrees that it is nonetheless a separate charism. What is more, he has a certain respect for the difference in psychological orientation between married and unmarried people, and—at least in his choice of words—he conceives religious celibacy to be to some extent a form of "self-sanctification" (vii. 34). But celibacy "for the sake of the kingdom of heaven," like the "leaving everything and following Christ" in the synoptic gospels, has a directly apostolic character. This is particularly so in the case of Mark, who clarifies the theme of "following Christ" with the words "for my sake and the gospel's" (Mk viii. 35).[22] It is thus a question of being intimately and personally tied to the Lord in apostolic service to the church, for which everything is left behind: "Leave house or brothers or sisters or mother or father or children or lands, for my sake and for the

---

[22] Mt xvi. 25 and Lk ix. 24 have only "for my sake." See, for the "following of Christ," J. Kahmann's study, "Het volgen van Christus door zelfverloochening en kruisdragen," *TT*, 1 (1961), pp. 205–26. Religious celibacy is a form of carrying one's cross and following Christ.

gospel" (Mk x. 28–9). There is no explicit mention of celibacy in this text of Mark, as there is in Mt xix. 12, but celibacy is essentially implied (or indeed concretely implied for the apostles, who were already married) in the "leaving of everything." Only Luke has, in this parallel text: "If any one comes to me, and does not hate his own father and mother, and *wife* and children, . . . he cannot be my disciple" (xiv. 26).[23] ("Hate" here is a Hebraism for "to love less than." This is explained in the parallel text of Mt x. 37.)

The kingdom of God makes sovereign claims which take precedence over everything else. Now that Christ has appeared among us, to say "I have married a wife" is no longer a valid excuse when the kingdom of God makes an appeal to us (Lk xiv. 20). The synoptic tradition of religious celibacy is therefore so clear that Paul must have been in touch with it. His expression "anxious about the affairs of the Lord" seems to me to be obviously in the same direct line as all of the tradition of Christ that was later to be recorded in the synoptic gospels.

In view of the coming of the eschatological Kingdom, marriage was "put in its proper place" by Christ—in the sphere of life which belongs to this world. We have already seen how the earlier revelation of Yahweh to Israel first demythologized marriage by taking it out of its mythical framework and putting it back into the secular order of creation, so that it could later be used to refer to Yahweh's covenant of grace from the perspective of faith in the same God, Yahweh. Similarly, the eschatological primacy of redemptive grace was affirmed by the revelation of Christ, first of all, and marriage was accordingly interpreted as belonging to this transient world; it was only later that Christians were to become more clearly aware of the repercussions of this revelation on Christian marriage. In the words of Christ: "The sons of this age marry and are given in marriage;

---

[23] In contrast to Mt xix. 29 and Mk x. 29. The presence of the word "wife" in some editions of Mt xix. 29—as, for example, in the Vulgate—seems critically unsound.

but those who are accounted worthy to attain to that age and
to the resurrection from the dead neither marry nor are given in
marriage, for they cannot die any more, because they are . . .
sons of God, being sons of the resurrection." (Lk xx. 34–6; Mt
xxii. 20; Mk xii. 25.) Marriage is here clearly situated in this
world—the "sons of the resurrection" (eschatological celibacy)
are contrasted with the "sons of this age."

Christ himself, "born not of the will [sexual intercourse] of
man" (Jn i. 12–13), showed by his appearance in this world the
birth of the new era which in principle marked the end of the
old. Paul, anticipating the *Eskhaton*, applied Christ's eschatological statements proleptically to Christian life on earth, insofar as this was Christian: "In Christ Jesus you are all sons of
God, through faith . . . There is neither Jew nor Greek, there is
neither slave nor free, there is *neither male nor female*, for you
are all one in Christ Jesus" (Gal iii. 26–8). And so being a Christian means that already in this earthly life he rises above merely
secular relationships. Certain consequences result from this.

We are bound to conclude from this statement of Christ
(which was taken over by Paul) together with his statement
about remaining unmarried "for the sake of the kingdom of
heaven," that the charism of religious celibacy has an eschatological significance—that some Christians have already entered,
proleptically, and in a special way, into the state of being "sons
of the resurrection." They have already renounced concern over
this transient world for another—concern over the coming of
the eschatological kingdom. Apart from exceptional cases, this
was something quite new to the Jews, and especially to the
rabbis. Marriage was regarded as an obligation in Judaism, and
anyone who had not married by the age of twenty was deemed
to have committed an offence against the law of God.[24]

Paul himself had a rather markedly personal view concerning

[24] SB, pt. 2, pp. 372–3; pt. 3, pp. 368 and 373. See also H. J. Schoeps,
"Ehebewertung und Sexualmoral der späteren Judenchristen," *ST*, 3, Lund
(1949), pp. 99–100.

the eschatological character of Christian celibacy, which was also inspired by the strong feeling and expectation in the primitive church that Christ's second coming would not be long delayed. Paul was of the opinion that secular things should be allowed to take their own course, "for the present distress"[25] because "the time is short" (1 Cor vii. 29). In such circumstances it was better not to marry than to marry, and there was no point in throwing oneself headlong into worldly affairs in view of the short time that Christians would have to wait for Christ's return. In a word, "those who deal with this world [should behave] as though they had no dealings with it. For the form of this world is passing away" (1 Cor vii. 31). Paul desired all Christians to live in this state of eschatological tension. It is obvious too that his attitude was also determined by the situation in which the Christian community found itself in the port of Corinth, where the inhabitants tended to live riotously. "To live a Corinthian life" (*korinthiazein*) was a common phrase inspired by the libertine behaviour which prevailed in this port.

On the other hand the Christians of Corinth tended to live extremely ascetic lives. This was, of course, a dangerous tendency, since the Hellenistic world's dualist view of man could give rise to all kinds of "spiritual" views of marriage.[26] This situation had

---

[25] 1 Cor vii. 26. This phrase has been interpreted in various ways: "because of the persecutions threatening the church" (J. von Allmen, *Maris et femmes d'après saint Paul*, p. 15); "because of the difficult situation of Christians in the port of Corinth" (P. Menoud, "Mariage et célibat selon saint Paul," p. 24); "because of the tensions between this aeon or world and the coming aeon" (W. Grundmann, *TWNT*, pt. 1, pp. 349–50; and X. Léon-Dufour, "Mariage et continence selon saint Paul," p. 325); "because of the oppression at the end of time"—this may have already begun or it may still be about to happen (H. Schlier, in *TWNT*, pt. 3, p. 145). It would seem that *enestōs* always means "present," and never "imminent." Paul was in any case concerned with the *thlipseis* or the "oppressions of this aeon," the time of the ending of the old aeon and the beginning of the new. This time of the church was an eschatological time characterized by eschatological sorrows and distress.

[26] See the various commentaries on 1 Corinthians. See also L. Cerfaux, *L'Eglise des Corinthiens*, Paris (1946); W. Grossouw, "Een bijbelse theol-

caused the Christians of Corinth to ask Paul several different questions (1 Cor vii. 1, 25; viii. 1; xii. 1; xvi. 1), which will be dealt with in the section on the New Testament ethos of marriage. One, however, is relevant to our present discussion: What do you think of the proposition "It is well for a man not to touch a woman"? (vii. 1). Paul knew which way the wind was blowing, and at first reacted sceptically to such a clear inclination towards fanaticism (rather as Pascal did, when he said "Yes, I agree, but *qui fait l'ange fait la bête*"). His reply was a qualified "yes," "but because of the temptation to immorality, each man should have his *own* wife and each woman her *own* husband" (vii. 2). Husband and wife should therefore give to each other that to which each was entitled as a married person (vii. 3). Initially Paul solved the problem as the rabbis had solved it, although in a different context—in order to devote himself to prayer, the husband should live for a time in abstinence, and afterwards come together with his wife again (vii. 5).[27] Paul regarded this as a concession on his part (5b–6). In view of the trend of these first few verses, some exegetes think it possible that it was not permission to return to normal marital relationships which Paul regarded as a concession on his part, but (bearing in mind the excessive tendency towards asceticism among the Christians at Corinth) the very opposite, namely temporary abstinence.[28] Further on he was, of course, to develop the au-

ogie van het huwelijk," *TL*, 45 (1961), pp. 261–8; "Enkele bijbeltheologische opmerkingen over het huwelijk," *Werkgenootschap Kath. Theologen in Nederland, Jaarboek 1961*, Hilversum (1963), pp. 63–78; see also under "Korinte," *BW*, cols. 960–1.

[27] According to the rabbis, regular times were necessary in married life during which intercourse was an obligation. (See SB, pt. 3, pp. 368 ff.). There were also necessary periods of continence for prayer and the study of the Law. (See pt. 3, p. 372.) The rabbis regulated these times in detail. Paul, on the other hand, left this to the individual conscience of the Christians in Corinth.

[28] M. Thurian, *Marriage and Celibacy*, Naperville, Ill. (Allenson, 1959), interprets verses 5b–6 as a concession on Paul's part to the ascetic tendencies among the Christians of Corinth which, if properly understood, could be

thentically Christian eschatological idea of celibacy (vii. 6 ff.) which we have just discussed.

However, most exegetes see in Paul's "indulgence" a concession to married persons to return to normal married relationships after a period of abstinence. Psychologically he was forced into a difficult position by the question put to him by the Christians of Corinth. He both had to, and wanted to, safeguard Christ's commandment concerning the indissolubility of marriage, and all the various possible consequences of it (vii. 10–11); on the other hand, he wanted to encourage Christians to be self-sacrificing enough to embark on the charism of total continence (vii. 7–8). For even though it was good "not to touch a woman," this did not imply that divorce was permitted. In this passage Paul was addressing people who were already married—people therefore for whom abstinence was not simply a matter of course (vii. 2). In such circumstances it was better to keep to normal marital relationships (vii. 5 and vii. 9, 36), and to interrupt them only temporarily and then only for the sake of prayer, since married couples are bound to please each other and they have a right to each other (vii. 3–5, 33). Paul was clear enough in his affirmation of the goodness of marital relationships. His use of the term "concession" in this connection can be understood if viewed in the light of a totally different, transcendent vision of marriage—a vision in which marriage is no longer a necessity in the Christian order of salvation, as it was in Israel and in Judaism.

Marriage is not the last word for the Christian. Yet this transcendence of the kingdom of God is given its form not only in celibacy, but in the life of married people as well. This is Paul's own, distinctive vision. He received, it is true, no commandment about it from Christ, but nonetheless he deemed it to be right (vii. 26), and believed it to be true to the inspiration of the Holy Spirit (vii. 40). Married Christians could not be considered

---

interpreted in the light of his eschatological motivation, but which were in fact misunderstood.

to have sinned if they did not follow this counsel (vii. 28, 37, 39); but Paul was conscious that he was speaking for their own Christian well-being (vii. 35).

Paul's own life of abstinence was not the celibacy of an unmarried man, or of a widower. In all probability it was the celibacy of a man who had either left his wife or had been left by her on his conversion.[29] This fact makes it possible to understand not only why Paul laid such particular stress upon the so-called "Pauline privilege," but also why he at the same time advocated—with some degree of insistence—total abstinence as a universal ideal for all categories of Christians. He wished the *agamoi*, those who were not married, the widows and widowers, to remain unmarried (vii. 8; vii. 39-40). Those who were betrothed, but who were hesitant about the final legal step of marriage itself, that of taking their future partner into their home, should, if they were spiritually strong enough to manage it, refrain from taking this step: "He who marries his betrothed does well; and he who refrains from marriage does better" (vii. 38). As for the *parthenoi*, the young men and girls of marriageable age who were still neither betrothed nor married, and thus still "available" and able to go in either direction (vii. 25 ff.)—he wanted them to follow his counsel and stay as they were (unmarried) "for the present distress" (vii. 25-8).

Finally, married Christians—and this included those who were living together as man and wife (vii. 3-5, 10), those who were living apart (vii. 10), and those who were living together but were separated by their faith (vii. 12-16)—ought to "live as though they had none (= no wife)" (vii. 29). This was Paul's most earnest desire, and he offered himself as an example (vii. 7, read in its context). It is clear that, unlike the Synoptists, Paul generalised from the ideal of total abstinence, and even saw it as a positive possibility for married Christians. He was, however,

---

[29] A great deal has been written about this subject. See P. Menoud, "Mariage et célibat," *RTP*, 39 (1951), p. 23, and X. Léon-Dufour, "Mariage et continence," p. 321, for brief summaries of the various hypotheses.

completely realistic about this, and although he regarded abstinence in marriage as an ideal attitude, he realized that it was a
charism (vii. 2 taken with vii. 7). For him sexual relationships
remained the norm in marriage: "The husband should give to
his wife her conjugal rights, and likewise the wife to the husband" (vii. 3), "Do not refuse [intercourse to] one another, except perhaps by agreement for a season, that you may devote
yourselves to prayer; and then come together again" (vii. 5).
These texts, in which conjugal intercourse is recommended, are
not contradicted by the statement: "Those who have wives live
as though they had none" (vii. 29). Paul's aim was only to
demythologize sexual intercourse from the point of view of
eschatological salvation. This is quite clear from the context:

Those who have wives live as though they had none, and those who
mourn as though they were not mourning, and those who rejoice as
though they were not rejoicing, and those who buy as though they
had no goods, and those who deal with this world [should behave]
as though they had no dealings with it. For the form of this world is
passing away. [vii. 29–31.]

Christians weep and rejoice, they occupy positions in the
world of commerce, they have normal marital relationships with
their wives, but all this played down, muted, by the Christians'
expectation of the eschatological Kingdom; for it is not, after all,
the last word to be said on the subject of human life. This is
why Paul was able to say, quite simply, in a passage which contains his very first statement concerning marriage: "For this is the
will of God, your sanctification: that you abstain from immorality; that each one of you know how to take a wife for himself
in holiness and honour, not in the passion of lust, like the heathen
who do not know God" (1 Thess iv. 1–8). Despite the widespread feeling that the end of time was fast approaching, Paul
could say quite calmly: There must be no panic; work must
continue as usual, and so must normal married life. Later on he

was to proclaim total abstinence as the ideal for those who wished to commit themselves exclusively to the work of the gospel.

There is, in 1 Cor vii, no trace of the strained, tense spiritual view of marriage which many scholars have thought they could detect in it. Paul's attitude towards married Christians is sound and realistic. But his vision is characterized by an inner Christian need to give marriage an explicitly relative value—in Paul marriage always evokes the prospect of total abstinence. Seeing the intimate relationship between the two states of life, he is unable to discuss marriage without making at least a passing reference to the other, eschatological way of life. The fundamental tendency in 1 Cor vii is Paul's stripping marriage of the absolute value which it had in the Old Testament.[30] Here he is not so much discussing celibacy as the newness of total abstinence which Christianity proposes as a possibility for every Christian, whatever his status in life may be. Anyone who denies that Paul, deeply concerned as he was for the kingdom of God, did not regard a life of complete abstinence as the ideal state is bound to do violence to these texts.

It is, of course, indisputable that he came later (in Eph v) to a deeper insight into the Christological significance of marriage itself and its meaning within the life of the church, but this does not mean that his basic intuition of 1 Cor vii was swept aside. Whereas Genesis said that it was not good for man to be alone, Paul—astonishingly enough for a Jew—reached the point where he could state that it was indeed good for man to "be alone"! (See vii. 25–6.) This complete change of mind can be understood from a consideration of Eph v, from which it is clear that every Christian is embodied in Christ's marriage covenant with his church and lives in communion with this covenant. Total abstinence is here a symbolic action, but—unlike the exceptional action of Jeremiah's continence, which symbolized the sterility of God's faithless people (Jer xvi)—it is an action which

---

[30] See Léon-Dufour.

expresses the perfect attachment in exclusive faithfulness to God and Christ, and thus the fruitfulness of the marriage covenant between Christ and his church. Here Paul's significant contribution to dogma is to show that it was no longer possible, within the Christian order of salvation, to define marriage perfectly without at the same time calling upon total abstinence for the sake of the kingdom of God as a correlative possibility. This intrinsic relationship between marriage and Christian celibacy and abstinence is so close that, as we shall see later, the sacramental aspect of marriage was to be acknowledged explicitly in the light of virginity in the course of the history of the church. The two states of life were to have an intimate effect upon each other in Christianity.

For this reason it is inconceivable that some "new existential experience," the discovery of new aspects of marriage which escaped those who experienced it at an earlier period, should make the New Testament vision of Christian celibacy appear relative or incomplete in any respect. When we come to consider this question later on we shall see that the charism of celibacy presupposes various different mental, physical, and social components, but that Christianity will never be able to close its ears to the authentic biblical call to total abstinence as a possibility which forms an intrinsic and essential part of Christianity itself. The superiority of this exclusive love of Christ in total abstinence is not simply a matter of subjective experience, even though in concrete terms it does amount to this for each individual, since the value of the individual's celibacy can only be measured by his moral and religious experience of it. Above all it is an objective form in which the eschatological kingdom appears in this world. The dogmatic and historical link between Genesis (the divine institution as a good natural gift, implicitly confirmed in 1 Thess iv. 1–8) and Eph v (marriage as an image of the covenant between Christ and his church) is 1 Cor vii (total abstinence as making marriage a relative value in the light of the *Eskhaton*).

In all this I have no intention of denying that in Paul's choice of certain words because of the context some historically conditioned factors are also at work in 1 Cor vii. But I do certainly mean that they are *also* at work, because the importance of these texts is not thereby restricted solely to the earliest period of the church's history. Christ's first coming, and his Second Coming— even though this might still be in the distant future, for "with the Lord one day is as a thousand years, and a thousand years as one day. The Lord is not slow about his promise" (2 Pet iii. 8–9) —made human existence and its involvement in a worldly history qualitatively different. Paul gave a relative value to secular human existence, and even to secular Christianity; by so doing he put marriage "in its place" (in both senses of the phrase) within the framework of Christianity, stressing that there is no question of marriage in the eschatological kingdom, and that in consequence marriage can never be the last word—the be-all and end-all—for the Christian.

This, then, is the dogmatic and scriptural essence of Paul's vision. What will emerge from this—but here we are leaving the sphere of biblical theology proper and entering that of so-called speculative theology—is that Christian celibacy, as a proleptic affirmation of the "sons of the resurrection" and thus "for the sake of the kingdom of heaven" or "for the gospel," was to be a sign for the whole church. This sign was to have an important message for married as well as for celibate Christians, even (and indeed especially) at a time when Christianity as a whole—in contrast to Paul, whose vision was not quite fully developed, or at least was determined by the situation prevailing in the Corinth of his own time—came authentically to affirm the profound human and Christian value of interpersonal relationship in marriage, and to gain a deeper insight into specifically Christian secular life. What is more, this Christian secular life was, in a highly characteristic way, so emphatically Christian within marriage itself that it could at a later stage be termed "sacramental" in the real and in the Catholic and technical sense of the word.

"Marriage in the Lord": the Christian Secular Life of Marriage

If the covenant of the redemption and the church's wedding-feast with Christ, especially as seen eschatologically, put secular marriage "in its proper place," this very covenant also put marriage in its place within the plan of salvation. Although 1 Cor vii chronologically precedes the text of Eph v, I have chosen to discuss the content of Eph v before discussing that of 1 Cor vii because I thought it better to reverse the normal sequence for the purpose of this study.

First of all, it is important to note that on the one hand Paul calls marriage (which is "good," 1 Cor vii. 38) "better" (vii. 9) than remaining unmarried, while on the other hand he calls celibacy (which is equally "good," vii. 37) "better" than marriage (vii. 8). The qualification "better" is in this context obviously determined by the prevailing situation—for one person marriage is the better concrete choice, for another abstinence. But over and above this personal situation and vocation of the individual, Paul, as we have seen, regards Christian celibacy as in itself more desirable than marriage from the point of view of eschatological love, and places it above marriage because it is a state permitting complete and exclusive dedication to the kingdom of God and an affirmation of the transcendence of this kingdom over the world. This interpretation contains the implication that Paul takes the distinctive task of married Christians within this world seriously.

What does Paul mean, then, when he says that marriage is "good," or even (for some people) "better"? This mystery, which was more profoundly analysed according to its saving dimension in the epistle to the Ephesians, is grappled with in the epistle to the Christians of Corinth. In 1 Cor vii. 39 Paul says that believers who are baptized "in the Lord" are similarly married or marry "in the Lord." Being baptized "in the Lord" has a different meaning in Paul from marrying "in the Lord." His general attitude

towards the affairs of this world and men's status in the world
is that men should remain as they were when they became Christians by baptism and allow the things of this world to take their
course. His general policy, then, is: "Let everyone lead the life
which the Lord has assigned to him, and in which God has called
him" (1 Cor vii. 17; see the examples in vii. 18), and "every one
should remain in the state in which he was called" (vii. 20). If
he was a slave when he was baptized, then he should remain a
slave (vii. 21–2).

These texts express a manifest "indifference" towards the
structure of human society in this world. All that Paul asks of
Christians is that they should experience this state of bondage "in
the Lord," that is, as Christians. He did not attack the social
phenomenon of slavery as such, as did, for example, Spartacus.
He maintained that it was possible to be a Christian in every
worldly situation, even as a slave. This remains true, even though
Paul was not aware of all the later social consequences of Christian influence on the affairs of this world. He was in no sense a
social reformer.[31] He left the hierarchical structure of human
social relationships which prevailed in the world of his day as it
was, but exhorted Christians to experience these relationships "in
the Lord," that is, as believing Christians. Hence slaves were bound
to serve their masters as though they were serving the Lord.[32]
In the same way, he left the pattern of marriage in the world as

[31] On the other hand, however, Christianity did bring about a change in
man's inner attitude towards life (by means of brotherly love, for example),
so that in the long run slavery itself could in fact be abolished, on condition
that there was at the same time a change in the economic situation. Paul
was himself well aware of this possibility. See his epistle to Philemon about
Philemon's slave Onesimos, who had run away from him. Accepting the
pattern of life as it was, Paul sent the slave back to his master, but added
that "if you have understood the meaning of Christianity, you will give
Onesimos his freedom, so that he can help me in my apostolate."

[32] The slave who was a Christian was a "freedman of the Lord" and the
freedman who was a Christian was a "slave of Christ" (1 Cor vii. 22). For
this reason, slaves were to serve their masters "in the Lord" (Col iii. 24;
Eph. vi. 6–8).

it was, even though its form had been conditioned by the social and historical framework in which it was set, but said that a Christian should experience marriage—within that pattern and form—"in the Lord," that is, as a Christian. A Christian wife should be subject to her husband "as to the Lord" (Eph v. 22) or "in the Lord" (Col iii. 18). Similarly Christian children should obey their parents "in the Lord," as if they were obeying Christ (Col iii. 20).

"Marriage in the Lord," then, must mean this: a normal, secular marriage, but taken up into the sphere of salvation. In the context of 1 Cor vii. 39, however, it also carries the practical implication that the Christian should marry a Christian. The expression "marriage in the Lord" thus implies that Paul regarded marriage both as a secular matter and as something to be experienced as a Christian. It seems to me, therefore, that it would be scripturally inaccurate to read anything more into this text; it is, in fact, less rich in content than Eph v. 22–33. If 1 Cor vii. 39 ("marriage in the Lord") were to be taken as the biblical foundation for the sacrament of marriage, it would be equally necessary to regard the state of "slavery in the Lord" as a sacrament. Taken in context, however, it is clear that Paul's immediate and explicit intention is that "being in the Lord" should here have quite a different meaning from the sacramental state of being "in the Lord" at baptism or on receiving the eucharist. In the writings of the Church Fathers, it is true, the term "marriage in the Lord" was for a long time to mean marriage with another Christian; but this was a reaction against mixed marriages. We ought not to read too much into this text.

On the other hand we should be careful not to underestimate the importance of the text. Certainly "marriage in the Lord" does include, in Paul, a kind of respectful indifference towards the social patterns of this world as such; and in any case he had no wish to take marriage out of its secular sphere and to cover it in mystical obscurity. But at the same time Paul did not mean that the Christian, in experiencing marriage in its existing social structure—"in the Lord," that is, as a Christian—should sanctify himself in spite of his married status. He was to sanctify himself precisely as a married person. Just as the Christian slave's obedience to his master is really obedience to Christ, so the Christian wife's obedience to her husband is also, according to Paul, obedience to Christ—but it is an obedience "in the Lord" in a deeper sense than that of the slave to his master. Paul says of the husband-wife relationship, as distinct from the relationship of the master and the slave:

> For the husband is the head of the wife as Christ is the head of the church, his body, and is himself its saviour. As the church is subject to Christ, so let wives be subject in everything to their husbands. [Eph v. 22–4.]

The phrase "in everything" contains a clear echo of the pattern of behaviour prevalent in Paul's own time, and further on I shall examine the question as to whether this historical pattern of behaviour is essential to the Pauline affirmation itself. In the immediate context of our present question, however, we must content ourselves with the statement that Paul in any case regarded the husband as the representative of Christ in respect of the wife, who was the representative of the church—with the result that, although they were both of the same order, the married relationship between man and wife "in the Lord" had a deeper meaning than (for example) the relationship between master and slave "in the Lord." In marriage, the husband, as the representative of Christ, has a soteriological significance, a saving function with regard to the wife—"as Christ is the head of the church, his body, and is himself its saviour."

And so Christ's redemptive love is made actual and present in the personal relationship of marriage, and this takes place in the manner of marriage itself. In other words, Christ's love is made present by married Christians as married persons—in their state of being married, and in their conjugal relationships as these are experienced within the pattern of social behaviour prevailing at the time. Experience of marriage "in the Lord" does not imply any extrinsic addition to secular marriage. Paul saw the Christianisation of marriage—that is, the making Christian, not of the secular structure of marriage, but of its natural and human interrelationships, although these are always experienced within ordinary secular patterns of life—as an entirely intrinsic process. It is therefore possible to say that in this respect marriage comes within the scope of the "new creation" (2 Cor v. 17; Gal vi. 15). The so-called "household codes" or rules of domestic life, expressing the ethos of the family which was widespread among both Jews and Gentiles at the time, were embodied into Christianity by Paul. In this way they entered the kingdom of God, suitably amended and inwardly transformed by being "in Christ." This universally valid ethos acquired a totally new spirit from its acceptance into Christianity—a spirit which was to be expressed in concrete actions. "Do not be conformed [in your conduct] to this world, but be transformed by the renewal of your mind, that you may prove what is the will of God, what is good and acceptable and perfect" (Rom xii. 2).

In marriage it was a question of secular *Christian* love. And so we find Paul speaks of the *agapē*, the Christian love deriving from grace, that permeates the relationship of ordinary, secular marriage (Col iii. 19; Eph v. 25; 1 Cor vii. 4–5). It is by means of this *agapē* that the human interrelationships of secular marriage itself are inwardly transformed. It is true that Paul does say that the natural *taxis*—the natural domestic order, to a great extent determined by existing social and historical conditions—should be preserved in the family, and that because of this the husband is the head of the wife in the family. On the other hand, however, if this relationship is experienced "in the Lord," it will be inwardly transformed by that Christian *agapē* which will enable the husband to treat his own wife as a "sister," that is, as a sister in the Lord (1 Cor ix. 5).[33] In this way the position of total au-

[33] See the Greek text.

thority over the wife which the husband enjoyed in marriage in the world of that time underwent an inward change. Permeated by Christian charity, the ordinary secular relationships of the family were not cancelled out, but subjected to a complete metamorphosis. Love achieved a position of authority.

A parallel process took place in the "natural" relationship of the master to the slave existing in the society of those days. This relationship too was inwardly transformed by Christian love—it became so permeated by the new spirit that in the long run, with the coming of new economic situations, slavery itself could be abolished. The social and historical conditions prevalent in the ancient world resulted in a slave being "naturally" regarded as a *res* or "thing," and his running away from his master as theft or a violation of the laws of property. Paul himself fully accepted this "natural" order, and sent the slave Onesimos who had run away back to his master. In spite of this, though, he considered this slave in the Lord to be a "beloved brother" (Philemon 16; Col iv. 9) and insisted that his master's human relationship with Onesimos should be Christian. Christian love made not only the inner intention, but also purely profane human interrelationships, totally different. This is true too of Paul's view of ordinary secular relationships in marriage and the family. Accepting the "secular" nature of these relationships—a condition which was in fact the result of human evolution—he nonetheless believed that these ordinary secular human interrelationships became totally different "in the Lord." We must now turn to a consideration of this vision in connection with Paul's ethos of marriage.

Did Paul regard "marriage in the Lord" as a charism, as he regarded Christian celibacy? The text of 1 Cor vii. 7 is ambiguous: "I wish that all were as I myself am [i.e., living in total abstinence]. But each one has his own special gift from God [charism], one of one kind and one of another." It is beyond dispute that in this text Paul is maintaining that Christian celibacy is a charism. Having regard to the context, is he also claiming the same for marriage? Opinion is very divided among exegetes on this point. There are, however, many, both Protestant and Catholic, who maintain—albeit hesitantly—that marriage as Christian marriage is, according to Paul, a charism (that is, a gift received from the God of salvation).[34] In my opinion, Paul did not have this directly in mind. The fact of the matter is this, however: Are we, or are we not, bound to accept this as an implied consequence after careful consideration of Paul's total vision? He himself never calls the love, the *agapē* which must transform marriage, a charism. Marriage is a particular expression of Christian love; in marriage this love acquires a distinctive pattern of its own and an irreplaceable form—this seems to me really to be quite explicit in Paul's thought. But whether or not marriage itself is a special charism can scarcely be established directly from the Pauline texts. On the other hand, it is certainly possible to feel implicit in these texts something of what was later to be known in the church as "the sacramental nature of marriage." According to Paul the various charismata are included among the *pneumatika* (1 Cor xii). They originate in the Holy Spirit and as such are a *diakonia* or duty to the Church community (1 Cor xii. 7; xiv. 26).

Thus, just as there is a non-charismatic celibacy, resulting from natural and noble motives, or even from ignoble and selfish motives, as well as a purely charismatic celibacy, so also should it be possible to speak—in the Pauline tradition—of charismatic and non-charismatic marriage. We may in any case conclude that the expression "marriage in the Lord" presupposes and emphasizes the ordinary, secular reality of marriage, and at the same time explicitly states that this secular reality is inwardly taken up into the sphere of salvation. At a later stage (in Eph v) Paul was to reveal the deeper significance of this phrase "marriage in the

[34] See especially W. Michaelis, "Ehe und Charisma bei Paulus," *ZST*, 5 (1928), pp. 426 ff.; B. Allo, *Première Epître aux Corinthiens*, Paris (1956); J. von Allmen, "Maris et femmes," p. 18; K. Barth also inclines to this view: *Church Dogmatics*, pt. 111–4; for the opposite view, see, among others, H. Lietzmann, *An die Korinther*, Tübingen (1949).

Lord." This scriptural conclusion seems to me to be of the greatest importance from the ecumenical point of view, since the
Reformation threatened to diminish the Christian saving dimension of marriage expressed by the Catholic Church in the words
"sacrament of marriage."[35] For their part, though, some Catholics threaten to diminish the primary secular reality of marriage, at least in all its consequences.[36] What also emerges from
this consideration of the New Testament teaching on marriage is
that religious celibacy is in no way conditioned by some historical underrating of marriage, and that consequently Christian
celibacy does not decline in value and ultimately disappear as
marriage becomes more and more appreciated at its true worth.
The very opposite is in fact true: the greater the decline in
Christian celibacy, the less Christian marriage is valued. As a
brother of the community of Taizé, Max Thurian, rightly said
some years ago: "When the vocation of celibacy is underrated,
that of marriage is underrated too."[37]

[35] Some Protestant theologians even go so far as to call marriage a kind
of "necessary evil," an inferior form of Christian life. See E. Stauffer,
TWNT, I, p. 650; H. Preisker, *Christentum und Ehe in den ersten drei
Jahrhunderten*, Berlin (1927), p. 127; R. Bultmann, *Theologie des Neuen
Testaments*, Tübingen (1958), p. 199.

[36] I propose to deal with Catholic diminutions of marriage as a secular
reality in greater detail in a later volume of this work.

[37] *Marriage and Celibacy*, Naperville, Ill. (Allenson, 1959).

5

The New Testament Moral Teaching
On Marriage

THE ABSOLUTE INDISSOLUBILITY
OF MARRIAGE

The difference between the patristic view of the indissolubility of marriage and the view which came into prominence in the church in the twelfth and thirteenth centuries may be briefly summarised as follows. According to the church Fathers, marriage as a *sacramentum* in the older sense of a "life commitment" or an "oath of fidelity" was something that *might not* be dissolved, since it involved a personal commission to live married life in such a way that the bond of marriage was not broken. The indissolubility of marriage was a task which had to be realized personally. According to the later, scholastic concept of the *sacramentum*, on the other hand—a concept developed in the twelfth and thirteenth centuries especially from the idea of ontological participation in the covenant between Christ and his church—marriage was seen as something that *could not* be dissolved. There was in marriage an objective bond which—once made—was exempt from any action or interference on the part of man. These two visions—the patristic view of marriage as a moral obligation and the scholastic view of marriage as an ontological bond—are not mutually exclusive, but rather mutually implicit. Both the patristic and the scholastic doctrines are firmly based on Scripture. Since the Catholic Church at present both defends and practises these two complementary views of marriage, it is important to ascertain precisely what this biblical point of view is. It is even more important when we remember that Catholic recognition of the sacramental aspect of marriage is intimately related to Catholic affirmation of the indissolubility of marriage.

Jesus' Statement

Christ's statement on the indissolubility of monogamous marriage was absolute in an unprecedented way:

And Pharisees came up to him and tested him by asking, "Is it lawful to divorce one's wife for any cause?" He answered, "Have you not read that he [the Creator] who made them from the beginning made them male and female, and [the Creator] said, 'For this reason a man shall leave his father and mother and be joined to his wife, and the two shall become one'? So they are no longer two but one. What therefore God has joined together, let no man put asunder." They said to him, "Why then did Moses command one to give a certificate of divorce and to put her away?" He said to them, "For your hardness of heart Moses allowed you to divorce your wives, but from the beginning it was not so." [Mt xix. 1–8.][1]

Therefore: "Whoever divorces his wife and marries another, commits adultery against her" (Mk x. 11–12)[2]; and "he who marries a woman divorced from her husband commits adultery" (Lk xvi. 18). In none of these texts is there any mention of an exception. Christ—and, following his teaching, the early apostolic

---

[1] See also Mk x. 1–12; Lk xvi. 18. Paul, referring to Christ's *logion*, affirms this in 1 Cor vii. 10–11.

[2] Unlike the other synoptists, who had only the Jewish legal practice of the male right to repudiation in mind, Mark interpolates a parallel text referring to the wife's repudiation of her husband. This practice was accepted in the Greco-Roman world, and the influence of Greco-Roman civilisation in this particular case was moreover already being felt in Palestine. See also 1 Cor vii. 10–11.

church—allowed no scope whatever for divorce. This was in complete contrast to the teaching of the Old Testament and in express opposition to the Law of Moses. (Deut xxiv. 1–4; see Mt. v. 31; xix. 7.) It also ran directly against the practice of the whole ancient world. We have already seen that in Jesus' time there was both a strict and a more lenient interpretation of the deuteronomic law, and both allowed a man to put his wife away if he had discovered "some indecency" in her. The school of Rabbi Shammai regarded adultery and moral misconduct as the only acceptable grounds for divorce; but the school of Rabbi Hillel held that all kinds of reasons, even quite trivial ones, were sufficient grounds for legal divorce, and it was this second interpretation of the law which was in fact practised. The Pharisees wanted to force Christ to choose between these two schools so that on the basis of his answer they could accuse him either of laxity or of shortsighted and narrow rigorism, and thus inflame the people against him, the leading question being: "Is it lawful to divorce one's wife *for any cause?*" (Mt xix. 3). But Christ overrode the views of both schools by referring to the great marriage charter of Genesis. Marriage was indissoluble and there was no legal ground for divorce whatever; in view of the fact that marriage had been brought about by God himself, it could not be dissolved by any secular authority. "In the beginning it was not so," that is, in the beginning divorce was not permitted—Jesus was referring here to the initial phase of man's history or at least to the time before the Mosaic law. In any case, the essential meaning of this phrase is that God did not have this as his original intention when he established the institution of marriage by his creation of mankind as man and woman.

Certainly Christ's aim was not to make some kind of social statement concerning the question as to whether divorce was known or unknown in the history of man before the Mosaic period. In any case, what he asserted was that the essential indissolubility of marriage was far from being something totally new, arising only from the eschatological redemption, but on the contrary had its roots in the human essence of marriage itself as called into existence by the Creator who from the very beginning had been the God of salvation. Jesus asserted the will of the Creator as against the law of Moses.

One conclusion and one only can be drawn from these four quoted passages in Scripture: the bond of marriage cannot be dissolved by divorce. There are, however, two texts, both to be found only in Matthew's gospel, which would appear, at least at first sight, to constitute an exception to this. The first is: "And I say to you: whoever divorces his wife, *except for unchastity*, and marries another, commits adultery" (xix. 9); and the second is: "But I say to you that every one who divorces his wife, *except on the ground of unchastity*, makes her an adulteress; and whoever marries a divorced woman commits adultery" (v. 32). It would be almost impossible to estimate how much has been written about these verses in Matthew from the time of the Fathers until the present day. Does Matthew in fact claim that full divorce is permissible for Christians after one of the partners in marriage has committed adultery?

One of the points of difference between the Catholic and the Reformed Churches is the divergent interpretation of this text. Although it is not possible to speak of a clear consensus among the Reformed Churches, in general Protestant exegetes do tend to regard these two texts as saving clauses. In the non-Uniate Eastern Churches, too, remarriage after adultery committed by the other party is permitted. This does not mean, however, that adultery is regarded by any Christians as sufficient grounds for divorce. In any case of upset or disharmony in Christian marriage the Reformed Churches also maintain that "the only solution which is legitimate within the kingdom of God is a mutual return to God's order."[3] Divorce is therefore never recommended. But there are, for the Reformed Churches, some situations in which divorce with permission to remarry is the only practical solu-

[3] J. Rinzema, *Huwelijk en echtscheiding*, p. 140.

tion: "There are no grounds for divorce for Christians, only situations in which divorce is inevitable."[4]

As we shall see, the Council of Trent firmly opposed any such interpretation, although its condemnation was—for historical reasons—expressed indirectly. The Catholic Church refuses to accept any grounds whatsoever for divorce in the case of sacramental and consummated marriage. All that the Council of Trent did was to confirm a long tradition in the church—that Matthew was speaking only of judicial separation "from bed and board," without any possibility of remarriage.[5]

In the middle of the second century Hermas referred to a practice in the church characteristic of the whole period before the first Council of Nicea: the husband had to repudiate his wife if she committed adultery and persisted in it, but he was not permitted to remarry; moreover, he was guilty of sinful conduct if he refused to take his wife back again on her repentance.[6] Hermas also added to this that the same was applicable both to

[4] This is the statement of a representative of the Reformed Churches, J. Rinzema, *Huwelijk en echtscheiding*, p. 146. In fact the Reformed Churches in general accept two possible grounds for divorce—adultery and wilful desertion—although there is much more doubt concerning the second. See, among other works, the pastoral letter of the General Synod of the Dutch Reformed Church concerning marriage (*Herderlijk schrijven van de Generale Synode der Nederlandse Hervormde Kerk over het huwelijk*), The Hague (1952).

[5] The interpretation of "separation from the body" goes back to Jerome, *In Matt.* 19. 9 (*PL*, 26. 135).

[6] Hermas, *Pastor* (*Mand.* 4. 1. 5–8). The practice that the unfaithful party had to be repudiated was fairly general in the first three centuries. From the fourth century onwards, however, this obligation began to lapse. Repudiation of the guilty party was still permitted, but remarriage was still not allowed, as in the ante-Nicene period. Nonetheless, the rules of excommunication which previously applied to remarriage were abolished. See J. Arendzen, "Ante-Nicene Interpretations of the Sayings on Divorce," *JTS*, 20 (1919), pp. 230–41. For the question of excommunication on remarriage after separation because of adultery, see, among other works, the *Canones Apostolorum* which are included in the *Constitutiones Apostolicae*, VIII, 47, can. 48. See also Funk, *Didaskalia et Constitutiones Apostolicae*, Paderborn (1905), pt. I, p. 579.

the wife and to the husband, although if adultery was committed by the husband the wife was not obliged to send him away.[7] Apart from the obligation to send the guilty party away, it would appear that, according to the practice of the subapostolic and the ancient church, a straightforward breach between the partners in marriage did not give the innocent party the right to remarriage, even if the other party was guilty of grave misconduct. This practice was in accordance with what Paul himself, appealing to Christ's *logion*, advocated as a duty for the Christians of Corinth: "To the married I give charge, not I but the Lord, that the wife should not separate from her husband (*but if she does,* let her remain single or else be reconciled to her husband)—and that the husband should not divorce his wife" (1 Cor vii. 10–11). Remarriage was not permitted in the apostolic church, no matter what reasons were given for the separation. The *Decretum pro Armeniis* of the Ecumenical Council of Florence was later to call this a separation "from bed and board" (from the *torus*).[8] No other line has in fact ever been followed in ecclesiastical legal practice. There have been very few dissentient opinions.[9]

This apostolic and subapostolic practice gives us clear evidence that the two texts in Matthew were not understood as constituting an exception to the indissolubility of marriage. It is therefore clear that, despite the difficulty presented by these texts, the apostolic church concluded from Christ's *logion* that marriage was absolutely indissoluble, and this made it difficult to interpret the Matthaean texts as a saving clause. This extrinsic reasoning is moreover reinforced by an analysis of the texts themselves.

---

[7] See, for example, Tertullian, *De monogamia*, 10 (PL, 2. 942–3); Justin, *Apol.* 2. 2 (PG, 6. 443–7).

[8] "Quamvis autem ex causa fornicationis liceat tori separationem facere, non tamen aliud matrimonium contrahere fas est, cum matrimonii vinculum legitime contracti perpetuum est" (DS 1327 [DB 702]).

[9] Ambrosiaster, *Comm. in 1 Cor.* 7. 10 (PL, 17. 218). Lactantius, who was not a theologian, says more or less the same in his *Epitome* 66 (PL, 6. 1080).

In the first place, there is some evidence to indicate that the two texts, which are peculiar to Matthew, are secondary. This does not mean that they are later interpolations, as some exegetes have claimed,[10] but rather that Matthew brought Christ's original *logion*—as reproduced in Mark and Luke—up to date in view of a definite problem existing in the Jewish Christian communities. The clause in Mt v. 32 is completely absent from the text of Lk xvi. 18, which gives Christ's *logion* in a more original form, and the interpolation in Mt xix. 9 is also lacking in the earlier text of Mk x. 11.[11] We are, then, fully justified in assuming that the clause does not go back to Christ himself; but this does not mean that Matthew introduced into the church an exception to something concerning which Christ himself had made an unqualified pronouncement.

Some modern exegetes have looked for a solution in the real meaning of the word *porneia* (unchastity). *Porneia*, as a translation of the Hebrew word *zenûth*, may mean not only adultery on the part of the wife,[12] or unnatural sexual intercourse, or even the marriage of an Israelite and a pagan, but also marriage which conflicted with the conditions laid down by Leviticus (Lev xviii. 1–20), or even with the rabbinical definitions of the law. All these were called "unchastity." On a basis of the various possible meanings of *porneia*, J. Bonsirven[13] reached the following solution. If

10 See J. Dupont, *Mariage et divorce*, pp. 83–4; especially *n.* 2, in which the author refutes the hypothesis of a post-apostolic interpolation.

11 See, for example, H. Braun, *Spätjüdisch-häretischer und frühchristlicher Radikalismus*, BHT, pt. 2 (1957), p. 89, *n.* 3; p. 109, *n.* 1; p. 110, *n.* 4. This author, however, concludes that Matthew impairs the authentic tradition of Jesus. The priority of Mark is moreover denied by J. Bonsirven, *Le divorce dans le Nouveau Testament*, p. 27.

12 See, for example, Num v. 11–33.

13 *Le divorce dans le Nouveau Testament;* see also " 'Nisi fornicationis causa.' Comment résoudre cette 'crux interpretum' ?", *RSR*, 35 (1948), pp. 422–64. Many exegetes follow Bonsirven's interpretation, including H. Cazelles, "Mariage," *DBS*, 5 (1957), p. 934; M. Berrouard, "L'indissolubilité du mariage dans le Nouveau Testament," *LV*, 4 (1952), p. 26. See also J. Kahmann, "Evangelie en echtscheiding," *NKS*, 49 (1949), pp. 11–18.

the Matthaean texts are considered in connection with Acts xv. 20, 29 and xxi. 25, in which Christians are required by the apostolic synod to refrain from all "unchastity," then the *porneia* in Matthew ought to mean marriage in conflict with the Jewish definitions of the law—for example, a marriage within one of the degrees of consanguinity recognised by the Jews. Matthew wrote his gospel principally for Christians who had been converted from Judaism in Palestine and Syria, and not for converts from the Gentile world. The Jews who became Christians continued to follow the Jewish laws of marriage, while the Gentiles who were converted to Christianity kept the Greco-Roman laws of marriage. This inevitably led to a conflict, which the first council of the apostolic church solved by means of a compromise—Christians from the Gentile world were not bound by the Jewish laws, but they were subject, for the sake of peace, to the Jewish laws relating to *porneia*.

Porneia, then, was a marriage that was null and void according to the Jewish law, and thus also according to the canon law of the primitive church following the apostolic decision of Acts xv. 20–29. Consequently Matthew did not envisage any exception to the absolute ban on divorce, but only said (in parenthesis, as it were) that a marriage which was validly contracted in accordance with the Greco-Roman laws, but which was in conflict with the prevailing Jewish impediments to marriage, was henceforth to be regarded as concubinage as far as Christians as well as Jews were concerned. In such a case a Christian was bound to repudiate his wife, since she was not really his wife at all. There was absolutely no question of divorce on grounds of adultery. This, he holds, is confirmed by 1 Cor v. 1, which clearly refers to a transgression of the marriage law as stated in Lev xviii. 8, the very law which was enforced by "canon law" in the apostolic decree (Acts xv. 28).[14] *Porneia*, then, included all the various associations listed in Lev xviii.

[14] There is considerable disagreement among exegetes concerning the structure of this "apostolic decree." What it comes down to ultimately is that there were probably two apostolic councils, but for theological reasons

This interpretation of the word *porneia* would appear to be generally accepted by exegetes. It does not, however, necessarily follow that the word was used in this wide sense in Mt xix. 9 and v. 32, since, if this were the case, the passages would be virtually meaningless. In any case J. Dupont has clearly demonstrated that the interpolation "except on the ground of unchastity" did not in the context relate to *de facto* invalid or illegal marriage, but was clearly connected with the saving clause in Deut xxiv. 1. This connection is apparent from the strikingly Semitic phrase in Mt. v. 32, *parektos logou porneias*, which was obviously intended to be a literal translation of the technical term used in Deut xxiv. 1, namely, *ᶜerewēth dābhār*. It is also clear that the entire context of Mt xix. 9 was dominated by the heated controversy that was raging in Jesus' time between the school of Rabbi Hillel and that of Rabbi Shammai.[15] And so the conclusion which emerges is that *porneia* referred to those cases of fornication or unchastity for which divorce was permitted according to the school of Shammai (i.e., adultery or moral misconduct on the part of the wife).

Several other interpretations have been suggested in recent years. Dupont has continued in the direction of Jerome, but has

these were reported by Luke as one as far as their content was concerned. If this is so, then the first council must have been attended by all the apostles, including Paul, and the debate conducted under the leadership of Peter. The principal topic for discussion at this first council must have been the significance of the Mosaic law for Christians, and especially the importance of circumcision (Acts xv. 1–12). A second council must have taken place within the community of Jerusalem, headed—in the absence of Peter—by James. The main topics for debate must have been the relevance to Christians of the dietary laws and *porneia* (Acts xv. 13–39). See, among other works, S. Giet, "L'assemblée apostolique et le décret de Jérusalem," *RSR*, 39 (1951), pp. 203–20; P. Benoit, "La primauté de saint Pierre selon le Nouveau Testament," *Ist*, 2 (1955), pp. 305–34; J. Dupont, "Pierre et Paul à Antioche et à Jérusalem," *RSR*, 45 (1957), pp. 42–60, 225–59. The consequence of this is that—in all probability—the apostolic decree came chronologically after Paul's first epistle to the Corinthians and also after that to the Galatians.

15 J. Dupont, *Mariage et divorce*, pp. 29 and 87.

presented this view in a new way. According to Dupont, *porneia*, on grounds of which the husband was permitted to repudiate his wife, does not mean the "unchastity" that the husband might commit by contracting an illegal marriage (as Bonsirven claims), but the unchastity of which his wife had made herself guilty. In such a case the wife was repudiated according to Jewish custom, but the separated husband continued to live in continence for the sake of the kingdom of God.[16]

Another interpretation has been advanced by Hulsbosch.[17] Like Dupont, he accepts the traditional view that *porneia* refers here to adultery. Jesus, however, did not intend in this case to make a pronouncement as to whether divorce was permitted or not. He wanted rather to show who was in fact the guilty party in this case of putting asunder what God had joined together. His aim was to point out that a *de facto* separation did not change in any way the divine plan of marriage. What violated the unity of marriage was not divorce, but intercourse with a third party—in other words, adultery. According to Hulsbosch, therefore, the meaning of the two texts is this: "Whoever repudiates his wife, except in the case of misconduct, and marries another with whom he has intercourse, disrupts the unity with his first wife that was decreed by God. The addition: 'except in the case of misconduct,' is important, because in such a case of misconduct this unity has already been destroyed and the statement is not applicable to this particular case."[18]

This is certainly in accordance with Mt v. 32, which says that

---

[16] As has already been indicated, this is no doubt the significance of the merging together by Matthew of what were originally two separate *logia* on Christ's part (Mt. xix. 1–8 and xix. 9–12). See J. Dupont, *Mariage et divorce*, pp. 161–220. For a criticism of this, see M. Zerwick in *VD*, 38 (1960), pp. 193–212; M. Boismard in *RB*, 67 (1960), pp. 463–4.

[17] A. Kuiters, "Kleine Dogmatiek van het huwelijk," *SC*, 35 (1960), especially pp. 111–50. The exegetical section of this appears under the name of A. Hulsbosch.

[18] A. Kuiters, p. 125.

"whoever repudiates his wife, except in the case of misconduct, is the *cause* of her committing adultery." In the case of repudiation because of adultery, it is clear that the wife is herself the cause of the breach in the marriage. From the context it was clearly Jesus' aim to find out who was really the guilty party in an unsuccessful marriage—if the wife had not committed adultery, and her husband nonetheless repudiated her, then he was really guilty of his wife's subsequent sin with a third party. Jesus' intention, then, was to teach men the essential meaning of adultery, and in the case of misconduct this statement no longer has any meaning, since it is clear that the marriage is already violated. This view provides an adequate interpretation of Mt v. 32, since this text makes no mention of the husband's remarrying or not remarrying after repudiating his wife. It does, however, run into difficulties with Mt xix. 9, as this text refers clearly not only to the moral and religious breach of marriage, but also to the legal consequences—whether such a person was or was not permitted to marry again. This was a question that was immediately raised by the Jewish notion of "repudiation," and it is clear from the whole context that it was included in the problem.

Other modern exegetes have shown that the Greek words translated—in the RSV and in the AV/Douai respectively—as "except on the ground of" or "saving [excepting] for the cause of" (Mt v. 32) and "except for" or "except it be for" (xix. 9) do not, in this context, have any limiting meaning. In other words, the passage in Mt xix. 9 means: "Whoever repudiates his wife— this is not permissible even because of adultery or unchastity— and marries another . . ." In Mt v. 32 the word *parektos*, though normally used in an exclusive sense, has an inclusive sense, so that the text means: "Even in the case of a husband repudiating his wife because of adultery, she is driven even further into sin."[19]

---

[19] Well-known exegetes such as Vogt, Sickenberger, Allgeier, and others support this view. For a summary of their exegesis, see V. Holzmeister. "Die Streitfrage über die Ehescheidungstexte bei Mt.," *Bbl*, 26 (1945), pp. 133–46, and J. Dupont, *Mariage et divorce*, pp. 98 ff.

According to this view, Matthew must have wished to impress even more upon his Jewish readers that adultery was no reason for divorce. This interpretation is in no sense normal, though it is to some extent plausible from the philological point of view. It may not be possible to accept it on its own, but it is in any case clear enough from the preceding passage in Mt xix. 1–8 that in this respect Christ completely did away with the law of Moses.

Let us bring together all the elements which the various interpretations have established beyond dispute. First, exegetically the clause is of secondary importance. The interpolation has its original setting in a particular society, and—in view of the fact that it occurs only, and twice, in Matthew—this setting is to be found within the Matthew tradition, i.e., in Jewish Christian circles. The Greek words of the clause as it appears in Mt v. 32, *parektos logou porneias*, would seem to be a literal allusion to Deut xxiv. 1, which refers to divorce on grounds of "some indecency." In view of all this, and especially of the fact that Matthew was writing for Jewish Christians, it seems clear that he was not thinking of the Greco-Roman custom (according to which the wife could also take the initiative) but of the Jewish custom (according to which only husbands could send their wives away because of unchastity). The interpolation, then, is concerned only with unchastity on the part of the wife (contrary to Bonsirven, because contracts of marriage which were null and void also involved the husband). Consequently it should be clear that, if this secondary interpolation is interpreted as a saving clause, this not only impairs the absolute value which Mark, Luke, and Paul all placed on Christ's *logion*, but also does a certain violence to the whole context of Mt xix. 9. The deuteronomic saving clause of Mt xix. 9 would, in this case, be in flagrant contradiction to what was said in the preceding verse, xix. 8, about the abolition of this Mosaic law relating to the "putting away" of one's wife. Jesus simply refused to accept this sending away— even in the case of *porneia*, when it was permitted under the old law—and, in contrast to the Old Testament saving clause, asserted the will of the Creator.

The whole passage would have become quite meaningless if the evangelist had included this exception in the verse that followed. What is more, if Mt xix. 9 is taken to mean that Jesus was siding with the followers of the school of Shammai, who permitted divorce on grounds of adultery, then the astonishment expressed in the apostles' answer would be incomprehensible— "then it is not expedient to marry" (xix. 10). Their astonishment is only explicable if Christ in fact rejected all possibility of the dissolution of marriage. His rejection is reinforced by the statement: "Not all men can receive this precept, but only those to whom it is given" (xix. 11). It is clear too that Matthew regarded total abstinence as a possibility within marriage as well, since he linked the passage referring to those who were "unmarriageable for the sake of the kingdom of God" (xix. 12) directly to that relating to the indissolubility of marriage. The interpolated clause, which is peculiar to Matthew, is clearly connected with this merging together of the two originally distinct passages—something else that occurs only in Matthew. From a consideration of the context in Matthew itself (and so not only because of Mark, Luke, and Paul), we are bound to conclude (and whatever the interpolation may mean in the positive sense, we can and must, for purely exegetical reasons, only conclude negatively) that the inserted clause cannot be interpreted as forming an exception to the absolute indissolubility of marriage.

It is, however, more difficult in this case to establish the positive meaning of the interpolation because of its secondary character—as a later addition to an existing *logion*. In the primitive church it did happen that wives were sent away or abandoned, but remarriage was impossible. Paul based this ban on remarriage on Christ's *logion* (1 Cor vii. 10–11). It is therefore clear that the Jewish concept of "repudiation," which essentially incorporated the "possibility of remarriage," was in Christian circles divided by Christ's radical ban, so that repudiation on the ground of *porneia* was still permissible, but without the possibility of remarriage. This was further confirmed by Paul (in 1 Cor vii. 10–11) and by Hermas. The whole of the subapostolic practice of the church—repudiation without remarriage—and the closely related case of 1 Cor vii. 10–11 in the apostolic church argue strongly in favour of Dupont's view, despite the fact that this author has probably over-systematized the matter. The interpolation in Matthew is a saving clause which refers only to the "sending away" of wives, and not to "remarriage." As far as its content is concerned, the implication in Mt xix. 9 is the same as that of the less problematical interpolation in Mt v. 32. The meaning of Mt xix. 9 is, however, far less obvious, in view of the fact that the content of Mt v. 32 is closely bound up in xix. 9 with an affirmation of remarriage. Nonetheless, the idea is clearly expressed that repudiation on grounds of adultery can be understood, even if remarriage is out of the question.

Christ not only expressly condemned divorce (showing, in other words, that the indissolubility of marriage is a moral imperative); he also said that any divorce which might possibly take place had no effect whatever on the bond of marriage itself (pointing out, in other words, that the indissolubility of marriage is an objective bond). The church Fathers were to emphasize the first aspect of indissolubility, the scholastics the second. Both aspects are biblical and will have to be accorded their rightful place in our synthetic examination of the subject later on. Paul summarised Jesus' view of the indissoluble bond of marriage in these words: "A woman is bound to her husband as long as he lives. If the husband dies, she is free to be married" (1 Cor vii. 39; see also Rom vii. 2–4).

Christ went even further than this and made conjugal fidelity a matter of inward moral significance:

You have heard that it was said, "You shall not commit adultery." But I say to you that every one who looks at a woman lustfully has already committed adultery with her in his heart. [Mt v. 27.]

Jesus' view of marriage bears undeniable witness to a radical attitude towards the principle of the holiness of marriage. On the other hand, we cannot fail to be struck by the gentleness and mercy which Jesus showed in his attitude towards sexual weakness, in contrast to the severity which he showed towards the piety of the Pharisees. (Mt xxi. 31–2; Lk vii. 36–50; Jn viii. 3–9 and viii. 11.) This redeeming mercy was also applied to married life and human sexuality.

The Becoming One of Man and Wife and the Community of Faith

On the other hand, Paul provides us with what is evidently an exception to the indissolubility of marriage. Moreover, it is clear from this exception that the absolute indissolubility of marriage is applicable only to Christian marriage.

> To the rest I say, not the Lord, that if any *brother* has a wife who is an unbeliever, and she consents to live with him, he should not divorce her. If any woman has a husband who is an unbeliever, and he consents to live with her, she should not divorce him. For the unbelieving husband is consecrated through his wife, and the unbelieving wife is consecrated through her husband. Otherwise your children would be unclean, but as it is they are holy. But if the unbelieving partner desires to separate, let it be so; in such a case the brother or sister is not bound. For God has called us to peace. Wife, how do you know whether you will save your husband? Husband, how do you know whether you will save your wife? [1 Cor vii. 12–16.]

"Let it be so!" The question is: Should this "separation" be understood in the Jewish sense of the dissolution of marriage, or in the new Christian sense of separation without remarriage? In the first place, we should be concerned with the so-called "Pauline privilege" which conferred preferential legal treatment upon the believing party; in the second, it is probable that Paul was generalising from his own case. What is in any event clear is that Paul certainly did say that, in the case of marriage between two Christians (1 Cor vii. 10–11), those who were in fact separated were not permitted to remarry. This assertion was based on Christ's own dictum. In the case of a mixed marriage, to which he was referring in the passage under consideration (vii. 12–16), he was speaking on his own—but nonetheless apostolic—authority, and permitted separation. The contrast between the two texts shows that in the second case "separation" implies the dissolution of the marriage: "the brother or sister is not bound in such a case" (vii. 15). Although Paul does not say explicitly that the baptized party is permitted to remarry after separation, this is certainly implied in the text.

However, it must be admitted in this connection that Paul's manner of expression is to some extent forced: "he [or she] is no longer enslaved," implying that cohabitation with such a person is slavery for the believing partner. Since Christ has called the believer to peace, he may therefore withdraw from slavery in such a case. There is no clear statement to the effect that the believing party is free in the sense of being permitted to remarry.[20] This is, however, the unanimous interpretation of the exegetes—the believing party was perfectly free to remarry after separation. Paul saw this as an exception not only in respect of vii. 12–13, but also in respect of vii. 10–11. If a Christian took the initiative in the separation, either with regard to a fellow

[20] The text is nonetheless interpreted by almost all exegetes as a release from the bond of marriage. But not so long ago, besides several Protestant scholars, a Catholic exegete raised the question as to whether there is really any reference in 1 Cor vii. 12–16 to the "Pauline privilege": see P. Dulau, "The Pauline Privilege; is it promulgated in the first Epistle to the Corinthians?", *CBQ*, 13 (1951), pp. 146–52. In its defence of the Pauline privilege, the Catholic Church has never explicitly and directly based its teaching on 1 Cor vii. 15. See DS 768 and 778 (DB 405 and 408), and (*Casti Conubii*) DS 3712 (DB 2236). Only a declaration of the Holy Office, dated 11 July 1886, explicitly connects the "Pauline privilege" with this text of Paul. It will be necessary to examine how far this privilege is connected with the apostolic "power of the keys" in the synthesis that follows.

Christian (vii. 10–11) or with regard to a non-Christian (vii. 12–13), then this separation could have no legal consequences—that is to say, the marriage remained indissoluble and remarriage was not permitted. The exception here is only that if the initiative in separation was taken by a non-believer—and Paul was thinking here especially of non-Christian Gentiles—then the marriage really was dissolved. In basis the moral obligation applied to the Christian, with the result that the bond of marriage remained un-impaired even when there was a breach in his marriage with a non-Christian partner.

Paul continued to use the Jewish technical term "sending away" if the husband took the initiative; and, according to Jewish law, the husband was the only party who was permitted to take the initiative. If it concerned a wife, who could not herself write a bill of divorce, he continued to make use of the technical term "abandonment of," or "departure from," the other party. In other words, even when the separation was accompanied, according to Jewish custom, by a "bill of divorce," this legal action had no effect whatever on the bond of marriage if the initiative had been taken by the believing party—whether by the Christian husband's giving a bill of divorce, or by the Christian wife's leaving her husband and thus forcing him to issue a bill of divorce. All this indicates incidentally that separation without any possibility of remarriage was recognised as a reality in the apostolic church. The "Mosaic practice" of the bill of divorce seems to have con-tinued among the Jewish converts to Christianity, but it took on a new meaning.

At first sight, however, this interpretation does present one difficulty. Although he was acting within his apostolic authority, Paul does appear to regard the absolute statement, proclaimed by Jesus as the will of the Creator, as applicable only to the marriages of baptized persons. It does look as if this is a rather Christian concept of the Creator. But in fact Paul, who always regarded a genuinely historical dictum made by Christ as an inviolate norm that was never contradicted by the heavenly Christ,[21] did not even here restrict the meaning of Christ's *logion*. Indeed, it is possible to say that Paul made Christ's *logion* more radical in meaning. The synoptic *logion* embraces the idea of "one flesh," the single living communion which was the God of creation's intention in marriage.

For a Christian believer this communion *in faith* is an essential element in marriage. Paul had in mind those people who were already married before they became converted to Christianity. Even then an existing marriage remained in force—unless the non-Christian partner did not wish it to continue or else made the marriage too difficult for the believing partner; but in an exceptional situation of this kind the marriage was dissolved on the very grounds of this principle of marriage itself, the biblical "one flesh," the living communion which was peace. Faith is of such essential importance in marriage, and forms such an indispensable element in its constitution, that there must have been a kind of *error substantialis* (fundamental mistake) in the conclusion of the contract if a non-Christian no longer desired to live with a believer in marriage. Paul did not say that this marriage was dissolved by subsequent remarriage, as the canonists maintain in connection with the "Pauline privilege," but that this marriage dissolved itself because of the factual situation—it was terminated as a marriage by the fact that the non-Christian partner no longer wished to live with the believing partner. We are confronted here with the self-dissolution of marriage in the interests of the baptized partner's life of faith.

It is a biblical datum that the marriage of a baptized person—a "brother" or a "sister" is a member of a community of faith, and thus a person baptized in faith—has a deeper and more radical meaning than the marriage of an unbaptized person, although the latter is certainly a real marriage. For, whereas marriage is formally indissoluble as far as a baptized person is concerned, it is

---

[21] E. Hirsch, "Eine Randglosse zu 1 Kor. 7," *ZST*, 3 (1925-6), pp. 50-60. This point is dealt with very clearly.

dissoluble as far as an unbaptized person is concerned. (Even the marriage of a baptized person is thus indirectly dissoluble, via the unbaptized party.) The basis of absolute indissolubility is therefore to be found in Christian baptism. And so "the will of the Creator" to which Christ referred means that marriage, as a human reality, is a reality that includes a religious relationship with God—the saving relationship that was concretely provided in Christ—and thus formally falls to the share of man by faith and baptism.

Marriage is a covenant reality.[22] Eph v. 25–32 was therefore able to say that the communion to which Genesis and Jesus' *logion* about the indissolubility of marriage referred had a more profound meaning, and pointed to the indissoluble unity between Christ and his church. Jesus' *logion* about the "one flesh," on which the indissolubility of marriage is based, is essentially connected with the communion of Christ and his church. This does not mean that Paul established this connection explicitly when he confirmed separation in marriage with an unbaptized person; but this vision is certainly implied in the sheer dynamism of these texts. That is why I believe that the strongest biblical basis for the sacramental aspect of marriage is to be found in 1 Cor vii. 15 —the self-dissolution of a marriage with an unbaptized person when this person refuses to live with the believing partner.

The marriage of the unbaptized person is in no way reduced in status by this view—on the contrary, Paul forbade separation if the unbaptized partner wished to continue with the marriage with the Christian partner. This view simply indicates that marriage has a special character for a baptized person. It is quite different from the situation in which a marriage "dissolves itself" on moral and religious grounds because of persistence in adultery;

---

[22] Paul here disregards the question whether or not there is salvation for those who are not of the community of faith. Salvation comes from Christ, and salvation falls to the share of him who believes in Christ and is baptized in him. These formal statements do not therefore aim to deny the religious character of "Gentile" or "Jewish" marriage. Their further and more precise formulation is not the function of biblical exegesis, but of theology.

for in that case not only is violence done to the moral obligation, but the objective bond of marriage remains, in this biblical vision, unimpaired. This can only mean that baptism is the real and concrete bond in Christian marriage—baptism continuing to have an effect in the establishment of the marriage, and, resulting from this, the moral obligation to be "one flesh." The real bond, exempt from human intervention, is present in marriage by virtue of Christian baptism. This real bond is still present in the marriage of an unbaptized person, or in marriage with an unbaptized person, insofar as the mystery of Christ is not denied. Such a marriage can therefore be called an implicitly Christian marriage —an implicit reality which automatically disappears if there is an explicit denial of the mystery of Christ. And so if the unbaptized partner wishes to continue to live with the Christian husband or wife, this marriage remains—according to Paul—undissolved.

If, on the other hand, the unbaptized partner is explicitly confronted with the historical reality of Christianity—in this case the wife (or husband) who has been converted to Christianity—and yet refuses to continue in this living communion with her, it is evident that he is denying the implicit relationship to Christ of the marriage, and consequently also denying the real and indissoluble bond which this relationship confers upon the marriage.

It will be better to analyse the dogmatic implications of Paul's view before I proceed, in my synthesis, to discuss the power of jurisdiction which hierarchical authority has over marriage. This is to ensure that the relative indissolubility of marriage is not interpreted in a "positivist" or a purely juridical sense, by means of a simple appeal to the church's "power of the keys." The power of the keys is in any case not an authority existing independently from the authority of Christ. The two are intimately linked.

Paul did not base his reasoning on his apostolic authority, but on the objective saving reality of marriage which he, as Christ's apostle, clarified and interpreted. As a result of this, the marriage contract of unbaptized persons undoubtedly has an inner tendency towards absolute indissolubility because of this implicit relationship with Christ; but, on the other hand, it can give way to a marriage that acquires an explicit relationship with the mystery of Christ and his church on a basis of baptism. The distinct character of the marriage of a baptized Christian also emerges even more clearly from 1 Cor vii. 14, 16, in which Paul says that the unbaptized partner in marriage is "consecrated" by the holy state of the baptized partner, and that the children of such a marriage are also "holy."

What does this signify? In the first place it is an established fact that the Jewish idea of the "uncleanness" or impurity of the Gentiles[23] was taken over by the Christians of the apostolic church and associated with the idea of the purifying effects of washing by the water of baptism. In other words, non-Christians were "unclean."[24] However, there was no need for the baptized partner to be concerned lest he should be "defiled" by an "unclean" partner's impurity, Paul reasoned. In Paul's view the very opposite was the case, for the baptized partner purified the unbaptized partner. His proof of this was that the children who were born of such marriages were "holy"; Paul clearly did not expect the Corinthians to contradict this, but rather assumed that it would be accepted in the community. There was, then, an assumption on Paul's part that the children of such mixed marriages would be "holy." Reasoning, by means of an analogy, from the fact that the children of a mixed marriage were sanctified, he went on to show that there *could* also be a consequent sanctifying effect (see vii. 16) upon the unbaptized partner.

The core of Paul's train of thought is therefore quite clear: a Christian member sanctifies the entire family. At the same time it is also apparent that in this passage the children—and not merely either the husband or the wife—are assumed not to have been baptized, otherwise the whole power of Paul's argument to prove

---

[23] See A. Büchler, "The Levitical Impurity of the Gentile in Palestine before the Year 70," *JQR*, 17 (1926-7), pp. 1-81.

[24] This is presupposed in Mt viii. 7; Jn xviii. 28; 1 Cor vii. 14 and Acts x. 28.

his point is lacking.[25] This means that the "holiness" of the children is fundamentally attributable to their being members of a family with a Christian father or mother; so there is a "holiness" which is not due to personal baptism, although this holiness does in the end go back to someone who is baptized.

I do not propose at this point to provide a historical survey of the patristic and scholastic attempts to overcome this difficulty. What is, however, immediately apparent is that the terminology of 1 Cor vii. 14 is derived from the ritual terminology of the later Jews. This means that the text as such did not envisage a personal, moral-religious holiness—this, according to the New Testament view, was the result of faith and baptism, and was in actual fact associated only with adult Christians—but rather an "objective holiness" independent of personal faith.[26] Later Jewish thought also made—in connection with the baptism of proselytes —a distinction between those children who were "sanctified" and those who were "not sanctified." The children who were "not sanctified" were those born to the parents before they were converted to the Jewish faith. Such children required the baptism of proselytes. The children who were "sanctified" were those born after their parents had gone over to the Jewish faith. These children were not baptized, since they were regarded as forming an integral part of the whole Jewish family, and thus as belonging to the people of God.

This historical evidence makes it clear that, despite the fundamentally different dogmatic content of Christian baptism, the early Jewish converts to Christianity continued—as far as terminology and ritual practice were concerned, at least—to be closely associated with the practices of the Jewish baptism of proselytes. We may assume with a high degree of probability

[25] See J. Jeremias, *Infant Baptism in the First Four Centuries*, Philadelphia (Westminster, 1961); O. Cullmann, *Baptism in the New Testament*, Naperville, Ill. (Allenson, 1958).

[26] See H. Braun, "Exegetische Randglossen zum 1. Korintherbrief," *TV*, 1 (1948-9), especially pp. 39 ff.

that the phrase "he was baptized with all his family" implied that the children were also baptized. Jeremias has established this on a basis of sound reasoning, but it is not relevant to the passage under consideration at present. What is of importance, however, is the fact that the primitive church continued for some time not to baptize the children born to parents who were already baptized. This practice was based on the analogy of the Jewish baptism of proselytes. The fact that there were some children who were baptized (if they were born before their parents' baptism) makes no difference to our certainty that in this passage Paul assumed that the children were not baptized. Otherwise, all his reasoning is pointless.

And yet he called these children "sanctified" and assumed that everyone would accept this. (The phrase "but as it is they are holy" in vii. 14 may be understood in the sense of "you know, they really are holy!") According to the passage as a whole, this is so even if only one of the parents was baptized. This view is closely connected with the Jewish and the Jewish-Christian idea of family solidarity and with the idea of "corporate personality" which was so fundamental to Jewish thought, and which meant that for God too the family was a single entity. For this reason, when the father of a family was converted to Christianity it generally happened that "he was baptized with all his house."[27] On the other hand, if the family was already Christian the birth of a child was regarded as an "incorporation into the Christian family." For a short period during apostolic times baptism was not administered in a case such as that, either at birth or when the child had reached adulthood. This is a fact, and it requires a theological explanation.

At this stage in the historical development of the teaching on baptism, birth into a Christian family—to two Christian parents—was experienced as the sacramental equivalent of baptism. The

[27] See Acts xvi. 30–34. The phrase "you and all your house" appears (with slight variations) in Acts xvi. 31; xvi. 34; xviii. 8; xi. 14; 1 Cor i. 16. In Acts xvi. 14–15, there is reference to a woman and "all her household."

theological explanation for this is that the essential core of the "external sign" of baptism is incorporation into the visible community of the church, made concrete by immersion in water; but that initially even this concrete sign appeared to be "plastic." Birth into a Christian family—that is to say, being accepted into a Christian sphere of life—fulfilled as such the fundamental idea of baptism as an incorporation into the visible community of the church. This situation did not dispense with the necessity of baptism, but was experienced as "baptism." The children were, so to speak, baptized in the baptism of their parents, who formed the Christian environment into which the children were accepted and incorporated.

That is why the "sanctification of the children" in 1 Cor vii. 14 does not have a purely ritual significance, despite the presence (in the background at least) of later Jewish ideas. On the other hand, the text undoubtedly lays emphasis on a state of having been sanctified (*hēgiastai*, in the perfect tense). It seems to me that there is no justification for interpreting this in the sense of "external purity"—an interpretation which is, in fact, based on a fear of coming into conflict with the dogma of the necessity of baptism for salvation. The objective condition of holiness is peculiar to the saving effect of baptism, and in particular to incorporation into the new people of God—the saving community which constitutes the sphere in which Christ's redemptive grace is effective in a highly concentrated form, as a powerful influence felt, so to speak, "in one's own home." This condition, then, gave members of the Christian community both the power and the duty to enter intimately into the faith and the love of this community, to confess their membership of it. It was a condition of having been saved that was factually present in the Christian community of the family for those children who were not born before their parents' baptism, but who were born and brought up after their parents had been baptized.

This, in any event, appears to have been the experience of Christians at the time of Paul's first epistle to the Corinthians (i.e., in the year A.D. 54). There is no *a priori* reason for attributing to the church in apostolic times as well-developed a dogmatic awareness as we now possess with the texts of the church's councils in our hands.[28] In any case the background of the Jewish idea of sanctification, which continued to have a powerful effect among the Jewish converts to Christianity, makes the Christian view of that period quite clear. As Paul says, in a different context, but drawing on the same background thought: "If the dough offered as first-fruits is holy, so is the whole lump; and if the root is holy, so are the branches" (Rom xi. 16). Instead of forcing these texts to fit the required interpretation, the study of dogma has in fact far more to gain from trying to understand more fully the significance of the necessity of baptism as an incorporation into the community of the church during this very tentative initial period of the church. In this way it should be possible to learn how to assess theologically those "frontier" situations which are often capable of revealing in a distinctive and "flexible" way the real significance of a requirement posed by dogma.

Paul assumed that it was known that the children born to baptized parents, or to a baptized father or mother, were really sanctified, even if they did not receive baptism with immersion. From this, he went on to discuss the different situation of the unbaptized partner in marriage. In that instance, the fact that the unbaptized partner was an adult formed an essential element in the constitution of his personal response to faith, and the mere fact of his being incorporated into a Christian family did not of itself mean that he personally became converted to Christianity. This was expressed by Paul in the question: "Wife, how do you know whether you will save your husband? [= whether you will bring him to the Christian faith]. Husband, how do you know

[28] It is not always easy for us to trace the motives for certain actions in apostolic times. An example of this is the practice alluded to in 1 Cor xv. 29—that of "being baptized on behalf of the dead." The idea of "family solidarity" appears to play a part here too.

whether you will save [= convert] your wife?" (vii. 16). In such a case, a personal conversion, or repentance (*metanoia*), was necessary. This would be completed in baptism, through which salvation was accepted in faith. In the practice of the ancient church a difference was in fact experienced between the "sanctification of the children," which was objectively accomplished by the baptism of water or by the baptism of incorporation into a Christian family, the "local" community of faith, and the "sanctification of the unbelieving partner in marriage." This was so even though there was, in the latter case, an objective condition of holiness—the state of being sanctified, indicated by the use in 1 Cor vii. 14 of *hēgiastai* in the perfect tense—based on the possibility of the eventual personal sanctification of the unbelieving partner. Life in a Christian community of faith was, in other words, an objective offer of grace for the non-Christian partner in marriage.

For an adult, entry into a Christian circle could only be the result of a call to "conversion," which culminated in faith and in baptism by water. It was precisely to this end that the baptized partner had to direct his "zeal" as a believer.[29] Peter also speaks of marriage between a Christian wife and an unbaptized husband. Here, the wife's "zeal" for the faith is regarded as forming part of the total Christian experience of the domestic relationship between the husband and the believing wife: "You wives be submissive to your husbands so that some, though they do not obey the Word, may be won without a word, by the behaviour of their wives, when they see your reverent and chaste behaviour" (1 Pet iii. 1–2).

[29] For the idea of "zeal" in the faith, which is of such importance for Paul in the case of mixed marriages, see J. Jeremias, "Die missionarische Aufgabe in der Mischehe (1 Cor 7. 16)," *Neutestamentliche Studien für R. Bultmann*, Berlin (1957), pp. 255–60. The author does not accept the usual translation "Wife, how do you know whether you will save your husband?", but prefers, for philological reasons, the translation: "Perhaps (who knows!) you can, O wife, save your husband." Even though the eventual meaning may be the same, this translation fits far less well than the usual translation after the preceding verse.

We may therefore conclude that 1 Cor vii. 12–16 not only closely follows the thought of Jesus' synoptic *logion* concerning the indissolubility of marriage, but makes it far more radical by revealing its full depths. It does this by throwing light on the idea of "peace" within the "one flesh" of marriage, and showing how Christian baptism causes the contract of marriage to become an indissoluble, objective bond. Moreover, it is clear from the text that marriage is essentially a commission—a task of apostolic sanctification proceeding from the partners in marriage to each other, and to the children and the family as a whole. Marriage does not simply enter salvation; by so doing it also becomes an instrument of salvation effective within the personal relationship of marriage. When we come to consider the increasing value placed upon the interpersonal relationship aspect of marriage—as is the case in modern marriage especially—it will no longer be possible to look to this Pauline text for the full effects of the vision of marriage it presupposes, even though it will still be necessary to be guided by Paul throughout the attempted synthesis. In my opinion 1 Cor vii. 12–16 offers the most compact "theology of marriage" in the whole of the New Testament.

Jesus' statement concerning the indissolubility of marriage, made on a basis of the Old Testament view of creation that marriage was "one flesh"—a single, living communion—is shown by 1 Cor vii. 12–16 in its full saving significance. There is an intimate connection between this indissolubility and baptism; as a result of this close interconnection the marriage of unbaptized persons has —in a sense—a lesser value (though it is in no way inferior), and lacks the special and distinct significance which characterizes the marriage of baptized partners. In its orientation towards salvation, what is usually known as "natural" marriage undoubtedly has a similar significance, but in this case an implicit one. However, if this orientation towards salvation is denied by the unbaptized partner, the marriage may be dissolved in favour of the "peace" into which salvation has incorporated the baptized partner. From this it is once again apparent that salvation in Christ, the communion with Christ, transcends married life. The moral conse-

quences of this are very great indeed, as I shall try to show at a
later stage. On the other hand, it also means that this priority is
made interior in married life itself—that married life is transformed from within by the communion with Christ, who is the
saving omnipotence of the living God in history. The dogmatic
consequences of this will also be made clear in my consideration
of marriage in the history of the church.

What is striking is that, according to Paul's view, the possibility of dissolution is *naturally* present in the case of a marriage
between a baptized and an unbaptized person, but that the baptized partner may not take the initiative in the matter of dissolution. This is, of course, in tune with the apostle's view of the
objective bond which baptism brings about—via the marriage
contract—in marriage. It was only in the course of history that
it later emerged that, if only one partner was baptized, this "one-
sidedness" in marriage was bound to have repercussions on the
effects of baptism within the marriage bond. At a later stage,
too, another problem came to be considered: Does such a case
constitute an authentic sacrament of marriage? The solution of
this problem will inevitably depend on whether the so-called
"Pauline privilege" is only one manifestation of a definite reality
which, according to circumstances, embraces other possibilities
and variations that were not envisaged as such by Paul.

This brings us face to face with the fact that the Roman Catholic Church dissolves marriages between baptized and unbaptized
persons, even if the unbaptized party wishes to continue the
marriage. As we shall see later on, the ecclesiastical administration
of the law in fact considers every marriage in which an unbaptized party is involved to be ultimately dissoluble in the interest of the baptized party's faith, even if such a marriage was
concluded with the Church's permission and after a dispensation
from the impediment to marriage—the *disparitas cultus*—which
made this marriage invalid according to canon law. We shall also
be confronted later on with the even more difficult situation in

which the Church follows the legal practice of dissolving, in certain cases, a marriage concluded between two baptized parties—in other words, a sacramental marriage—if this is not sexually consummated. Undoubtedly what is in evidence here is that ecclesiastical legal practice is in this case based on the view that the biblical idea of "one flesh" ("what God has joined together" according to Christ's synoptic *logion*) gains its full significance in the explicit connection between Christ and his church, and insofar as this marital "becoming one" also gains its full form (full, that is, in the anthropological and physical sense of the word).

Paul's view of marriage has already shown that these problems cannot be solved simply by having recourse to a purely "positivist" appeal to the church's jurisdiction or "power of the keys," as the jurists and canonists are in the habit of doing, however right this may be for them. Ecclesiastical law itself must be based on dogmatic insight, and the idea of "one flesh" promulgated in the Old Testament, deepened by Jesus, and clarified by Paul, must always be the guiding canonical principle, the full scope and meaning of which can certainly be interpreted by the church, but never changed. The church's power of the keys is in no sense a high-handed authority, but a power bound to the word of the historical and risen Christ. In this way the Bible remains a critical authority from which the jurisdiction of the church is unable to emancipate itself.

In the course of history, however, the real scope and full implications of this "one flesh" as the basis of the indissolubility of marriage have been revealed through new problems in changing situations. There is also little doubt that in the future fresh problems will arise which will bring out new aspects of this idea, and which the church, guided by the vision of the Bible in the light of the tradition of faith, will be able to interpret authoritatively. Moreover, in cases such as these, particularly if they are concerned with the *dogmatic* dissolubility of a marriage which the unbaptized partner does not deny, it will be necessary to take justice into account—the humane and moral obligations that may well be present in fact—despite the fact that the marriage may be open to dissolution. In these cases, a purely dogmatic insight that there is a possibility of dissolution cannot provide the final answer to the concrete problem. But this discussion has already drawn us far from the sphere of biblical theology and into the territory to be explored in a later volume of this work.

Paul's Opposition to Mixed Marriage

In the preceding sections we have considered Paul's views on the marriages of Gentiles who were already married before one of the two partners became converted to Christianity. "Mixed marriages" of this kind were, of course, inevitable in the earliest Christian period, and Paul had only good to say of them. His reaction to "mixed marriages" contracted by those who were already baptized with non-Christians was quite different.

> Do not be mismated with unbelievers. For what partnership have righteousness and iniquity? Or what fellowship has light with darkness? What accord has Christ with Belial? . . . What agreement has the temple of God with idols? For we are the temple of the living God. [2 Cor vi. 14–16.]

Today we may well be astonished by this black-and-white picture, and by the note of triumph at the end: We are on the side of right. It is of course true that Christians of the first century had little feeling for the good in other people and their religions, whereas the spirit of the present age impels us today to acknowledge the good in others, and even to see only our own shortcomings. Paul, however, saw things in a totally different light. For him the central fact of existence was that the mystery of Christ had appeared—that redemption had come in Jesus. The "saints" were those who had turned to Christ in faith and baptism. Everything else faded into insignificance beside the explicit acknowledgement of this central fact of salvation. Christianity really appeared to the Gentile world of that time as a sun in the darkness—a phenomenon that "set the world on its head," as the Gentiles themselves put it: *hoi tēn oikoumenēn anastatōsantes* (Acts xvii. 6), surely a remarkable definition of Christians as the people who "set the world in an uproar." Both Gentiles and Christians themselves felt that Christianity was something quite unique. And indeed, it is unique, even today. What Paul said then is still applicable today. The Catholic Church still regards a marriage with an unbaptized person as invalid in principle. It is not a marriage unless the impediment to marriage has been removed by an ecclesiastical dispensation, and even then it is still dissoluble.

The New Testament of course says nothing directly about "mixed marriages" in the modern sense of the phrase (that is, marriages between Catholic and non-Catholic Christians). This particular problem will be dealt with in a later volume.

PATTERNS OF BEHAVIOUR

"The husband is the head of the wife": Biblical Assertion, or Simply Social Pattern?

We have already touched on the basic principle of the ethos of marriage in the New Testament in connection with the problem of "marriage in the Lord" in the context of 1 Cor vii. 39. The apostolic and the ancient church accepted man's ethical awareness as it was in Jewish and Greco-Roman society during the first century. But this ethical consciousness was incorporated into the Christian spirituality of "being in and with Christ," and thus of faith and love, and was inwardly transformed and corrected. Christians were, in everything, "in the Lord" (Col iii. 18).

This is particularly clear from the "household codes" of the New Testament.[30] These rules were modelled on the secular

---

[30] See Col iii. 18–iv. 1, 5; Eph v. 22–vi. 9; 1 Tim ii. 8–15; v. 3–8; vi. 1–2; Tit ii. 1–10; 1 Pet ii. 13–iii. 7. These lists or "moral rules" have been called "household codes" (in German, *Haustafeln*, in Dutch, *huisspiegels*).

household codes of the Hellenistic, and especially of the Judaeo-Hellenistic, world. A form-critical analysis of these lists, which provide ethical standards for all kinds of social relationships—relationships between husbands and wives, parents and children, masters and slaves, rulers and subjects—shows that they go back to the household codes common in the popular ethics of the Hellenistic world.[31] These codes summarized the civil duties of man as a "political being," that is, as a citizen, or member of a human society. They included man's relationship towards God (since the worship of God was regarded as a political duty or civic virtue) and his relationship towards his native country (that is, towards the authority of the state) as well as relationships between husband and wife, parent and child, brother and mother, and relationships with relatives, friends, strangers, and slaves. If these civic virtues originally had a religious basis, in conjunction with the religion of the family, they were eventually "secularised"—that is, they became ethically based on "human nature" and on the human conscience.

Even before Christianity these secular household rules had made their influence felt in the Jewish world (e.g., Tobit iv. 2–23; Sir vii. 20–39), where they became intermingled with Jewish elements.[32] The New Testament took over these household codes in broad outline, but always left out the first civic duty, that of the worship of God, in view of the fact that man's relationship with God transcended his other duties and was based on revelation and faith. In this way, "religion" and "ethics"

See E. G. Selwyn, *The First Epistle of St. Peter*, London (1946), pp. 419–39; K. H. Schelkle, *Die Petrusbriefe. Der Judasbrief*, Freiburg i. Br. (1961), especially pp. 96–8; H. Schlier, *Der Brief an die Epheser*, Düsseldorf (1959), pp. 250–52; 287–8.

[31] Epictetus, *Dissert.* 2. 14. 8, Seneca, *Epist.* 94. 1, and Stobaios, *Anthologia*, 1. 3. 53, are especially typical, the last-named expressing the Stoic doctrine of civil duties.

[32] That the immediate substratum in the New Testament "codes" (see note 30 above) is Judaeo-Hellenistic is clear from the Jewish element, the "fear of God." See, for example, Eph v. 21, 33.

were formally distinguished, however much each was implied in the other. For the rest, "natural," secular ethics were taken over, based on God, and gradually Christianised.

This secular character is most in evidence in Paul's first use of household codes (Col iii. 18–iv. 1). All that is said here is that these ethics must be experienced "in the Lord." In Eph v. 22–33 the relationship between man and wife, following closely on the principles of these domestic rules, is interpreted in the religious sense (that is, "as Christ and his church"). 1 Pet ii. 13– iii. 7 contains many traces of Christian influence,[33] without of course Paul's theological superstructure. The planning of domestic life is the planning of a house that is the temple of God (1 Pet ii. 1–10). These household codes give the clearest possible indication of the transformation of ethical elements already present in secular society and taken over by Christianity. For they show that these ethical rules of conduct—which the New Testament raised to the level of "commandments"—were not simply experienced "in the Lord," as in Col iii. 18–iv. 1, chronologically the earliest of the New Testament household codes; the motivation of these rules became more and more explicitly Christian. Christians were exhorted to love each other "as Christ loved his Church," and to be subject to each other "as the Church is subject to Christ." The slave's submission to his master—the ethic and practice of the period—was raised to the level of a following of Christ (1 Pet ii. 19 and 21–5). And so the motivation of the current code of behaviour became formally Christian.

In other words, the "natural" code of the period was not simply viewed according to its divine basis, nor was it merely experienced as such "in the Lord." According to the New Testament, it was more than this—it acquired from Christ a formally Christian motivation. The New Testament household codes are therefore theologically the best proof that we have of the fact that a Christian moral theology was already in process of growth

[33] 1 Pet ii. 13; ii. 17; ii. 20b; iii. 1–2; especially iii. 7; iii. 5–6; iii. 10, 12.

in the New Testament—on a basis of an ethical appreciation already existing in society, and in connection with the planning and regulation of social life, both in the smaller community of the then prevalent extended family and in the greater community of the state.

This immediately poses a delicate problem. Are we confronted here with a Christian confirmation of existing ethical forms which are thus presented in the New Testament as an unchangeable norm? Or is this just a call to experience "in the Lord" and from Christian motives the ethical values and social structures already present in society? And, if this latter is the case, is it not also the case that the New Testament, by not rejecting the contemporary situation but simply giving it a Christian motivation, has in effect put it forward as a principle that the actual, existing social structures of this world should be preserved? This question becomes particularly significant when it is considered in the context of the New Testament assertion that the husband is the "head of the wife," and of the wife's subordinate position and factually inferior social status in the ancient world which resulted from this assertion.

Before I attempt to throw light on this problem in the New Testament, a preliminary theological observation will not be out of place—especially since this observation will also prove to be in itself a conclusion from an examination of the New Testament, thus providing further substantiation of the claim that theology is regulated by the Bible.

Both in the tradition of the Old and New Testaments and in the subsequent tradition of the church, it is evident that a "human" tradition also existed alongside the divine tradition. This human tradition not only went back a long way; it is also true to say that the faithful community was, initially at least, not necessarily always explicitly aware *per se* of the distinction between the "human" and the "divine" traditions in its assertions. In the assumptions on which the community of the faithful lived, and on which it based much of its thought and action, there was not only a whole area of convictions that went back to the revelation of God's word, but also a not inconsiderable group of convictions derived from the universally received ideas of a definite period of time. These convictions formed the communal property of human awareness at a given period and were only replaced when new situations and fresh discoveries showed them to be outdated.

It is only when a social or economic change takes place in human values that the believing community feels impelled to examine whether—first—the convictions that it has inherited really go back to an inner demand made by revelation or by a basic human and ethical awareness; whether their source is in fact purely human; or whether—finally—they originated in an essentially religious truth expressed thematically, either in conceptual terms borrowed from an out-of-date view of man and the world, or in outdated social structures which have in the meantime been replaced by newer ones.

Something of this kind faces us today in the matter of the married woman, in view of the changed outlook on woman in the modern world and the completely new social position which she occupies both in public life and in the circle of her own family. And so the question has arisen: Are the affirmations which the Bible makes about woman and marriage really "biblical" (that is, are they really divine declarations with the force of commandments), or are they merely structures set in an ancient historical and social framework, which Christians of that period experienced "in the Lord"?

A comparison of the structure of domestic life in the New Testament with domestic life in the secular world of the period shows that the New Testament structure contains data which are social and historical. This, however, provides no solution to the problem—at least, not to the problem of whether it is a "biblical" assertion that the husband is the "head of the wife," certainly the most important in this connection. In any case, it cannot be denied that the wife's position in the New Testament was broadly speaking very similar to the low social position of the married woman in the whole of the ancient world.[34] This is clear from minor details. A man, for example, "married," whereas a woman was "given in marriage" (e.g., Lk xvii. 27; xx. 35). A husband was to love his wife, but neither Paul nor Peter says in his epistles that a wife is bound to love her husband. She was to be "subject" to him (Col iii. 18; Eph v. 21–2; 1 Pet iii. 1, 5; Tit ii. 5).[35] This, however, still proves very little. It may well mean that the assertion "the husband is the head of the wife" was experienced by Christians in terms of contemporary social patterns, but this still does not prove that the assertion itself is anything more than an experience "in the Lord" of already present, changeable social relationships.

In a nutshell, the problem is this: Is the statement, "the husband is the head of the wife," an authentically biblical assertion, based on revelation, which was of course bound to be experienced in accordance with and within existing social structures? Or is it not a biblical assertion at all, but merely something taken over from the ancient idea of the *pater familias* and expressed in Christian terms? It is by no means easy to answer this question. First it will be necessary to examine the New Testament facts themselves, and then we shall have to go into Paul, the first epistle of Peter, and the Pastoral Epistles, since this theme is not present in the Synoptic tradition or in John (a fact which is in itself important).

In the *Corpus Paulinum* there is a double series of texts referring to this question: "the husband is the head of the wife" (1 Cor xi. 3; Eph v. 23) and "wives, be subject to your husbands"

---

[34] There were, of course, many gradations within this relatively lowly position. Despite the authority of the *paterfamilias*, the Roman wife enjoyed a fairly privileged position, higher than that of the Jewish wife, or even than that of the Greek wife. See J. Leipoldt, *Die Frau in der Antike und im Urchristentum*, Gütersloh (1953).

[35] On the other hand, however, Paul could say quite simply in his epistle to Titus: "They are to train the young women to love their husbands and their children" (Tit ii. 4), although the word used here is not *agapāin*, as for men, but the general and secular word *philandros*.

(Col iii. 18; 1 Cor xiv. 34; Eph v. 21–2; see also 1 Pet iii. 1; Tit ii. 5). This latter, this *hupotaxis* (subjection or submission) of the wife to the husband, is also to be found in the secular Greco-Roman and in the Judaeo-Hellenistic household codes. It expressed the idea, universally current in those days, of the wife's status in the *oikos*, that is to say, in marriage and in the family. It was, therefore, not an expression of the general subordination of woman in society. In 1 Pet iii. 1, Eph v. 22 and Tit ii. 5—all "household code" texts—there is explicit reference to the wife's subjection to her own husband, and consequently no direct mention of woman's subordinate position in contemporary society. What was at issue here was the wife's real place in the *taxis* (plan) of domestic life.

This was also the context in Eph v. 22–32. Eph v. 21 ("Be subject to one another out of reverence for Christ") forms an introduction to the exposition of the household codes which follows, and does not invalidate the idea of the wife's submission to the husband, as may at first sight appear. It would be completely alien to Paul's thought to suggest that he meant that the husband should also be subject to the wife. He required a mutual subjection on the part of the following groups of categories of person—husbands and wives, parents and children, masters and slaves. Even when the husband is called the "head of the wife" in Eph v. 22–3, it is quite clear that this was meant in the *domestic* sense. According to the whole context of Eph v. 22–33, the husband is the "head of his *own wife*."

In 1 Cor xi Paul appears to take quite a different point of view, both with regard to the subjection of the wife to the husband and with regard to the husband as the head of the wife. In xi. 3 the man is quite simply called the head of the woman, and the entire context refers to the subordinate position of woman in society and in the church. "But I would have you know that the head of every man is Christ; the head of the woman is the man;[36]

[36] Douai version. Some translations (e.g., the RSV translation) have "her husband," which limits Paul's general assertion to the relationship of marriage and the family. See my critical examination of the text.

and the head of Christ is God" (xi. 3). The same thought is re-sumed in xi. 7, though now from the perspective of the concept of the "image and glory of God": "The man is the image and glory of God; but the woman is the glory of the man." It is true that Paul expresses this idea in general terms, but he certainly sees this general assertion in the light of conjugal relationships. Even in xi. 3 he states that Christ is the head of *every* man, but not that the man is the head of *every* woman. The absence of the word "every" in the second phrase can scarcely be without sig-nificance. What is more, "the man," with the Greek article, can-not mean men in general, but a concrete and particular case— "the man of the woman" is therefore "the husband of the wife," and so "the head of the wife is her husband." All the same, this text is completely divorced from any context of marriage. It cannot be denied that the text does to some extent generalise, even though it does so via marital relationships. It will therefore be necessary to examine this text before going on to discuss Eph v. 22 ff., in which the man is called the head of the family.

We have to assume that—allowing for certain gradations— woman was illiterate and had no part to play in social life, both in the Jewish and in the Greco-Roman world. She was supposed to remain silent, and her place was in the home, by the cradle and at the loom. The household codes accepted—as an ethical rule of conduct in all families which were properly regulated according to the spirit of good citizenship—that wives were obliged to be subject to their husbands. The Judaeo-Hellenistic codes even added "in everything." We may set Josephus' text, "The wife, says the Law, is subject to the husband in all things,"[37] beside that of Paul, "As the Church is subject to Christ, so let wives also be subject in everything to their husbands" (Eph v. 24). What Paul aimed to do in 1 Cor xi, in connection with the proper regulation of the practice of religion, in which women had to be silent and to veil their heads, was to provide a

[37] Josephus, *Contra Apionem*, 2. 24.

theological basis for woman's social status and for the accepted code of behaviour which this status demanded. The pains to which he went to establish this theological basis are a clear indication of the fact that he had to go against certain strong tendencies.

It is undisputed that human values and social relationships were beginning to change in the secular world, both before and during the first century A.D., despite the existence and widespread use of the household codes in the secular sphere. A new orientation was taking place in the way that (in particular) the Greeks felt towards their fellow-men and the things that surrounded them. They were becoming aware, no doubt partly because of the contacts which Alexander's conquests had established between Greece and the known world, of the differences between themselves and other men. They were also beginning to look at the everyday things that had long been familiar to them with new eyes. Politics were becoming less and less the activity of the ordinary man and citizen and more and more the concern of "world rulers," and for this reason ordinary Greek citizens began to focus their attention on the people and the things that immediately surrounded them in their own environment.

Everyday sufferings and joys were observed with increasing interest. Epictetus, for example, comments on the growing popularity in his time of the custom of addressing girls as "madam" or "my lady" from the age of fourteen onwards.[38] A certain courtly respect for women, which up to this time had been less conspicuous, was making itself felt throughout the entire Greek world. Lovers called each other "lord" and "lady" precisely in order to testify to their mutual subjection and to their loyalty to each other. The husband remained the *paterfamilias*, but a change was taking place in the sphere of human

[38] *Kyria*, "lady" or "madam," as the counterpart of *kyrios*, "lord" or "sir." See J. Leipoldt, *Die Frau*, p. 47. For the influence of the successive schools of Greek philosophy, see Fustel de Coulanges, *La cité antique*, Paris (n.d.), especially the chapter "Nouvelles croyances religieuses," pp. 136 ff.

feelings, and husband and wife were gradually coming to treat each other more as equals. The ancient social structures were not swept aside as yet, but they were filled with a new spirit—a spirit of increasing equality. It is possible to detect expressions of what we should now call "female emancipation" in the world of Greek women of this time. In literature, for example, we see the beginnings of the theme of marriages of love.

The citizens of the international port of Corinth were, in Paul's time, in many ways ahead of people elsewhere. The progressive women's "movement" developed in Corinth into an unrestrained non-conformity. The women who were converted to Christianity assumed airs even in the Christian community which scandalised their fellow-Christians. Their greater freedom expressed itself, for example, in their appearing unveiled at public religious meetings, and in their rising to speak at these meetings together with the men.[39] To the Jewish converts to Christianity especially this was something quite new and unknown, and it aroused their suspicions. Paul's epistle to the Corinthians is therefore a reaction against the kind of behaviour that was threatening the normal domestic order and harmony. Was he defending an outdated social order and family pattern against the threat of a new and freer way of life? Or was he trying to show that there was much more in the older pattern of life and behaviour than simply outdated forms? This is the problem with which we must deal.

As I have already said, Paul was looking for convincing and conclusive arguments. For this reason, he points to the structure of creation. "For man was not made from woman, but woman from man. Neither was man created for woman, but woman for man" (1 Cor xi. 8–9). In 1 Tim ii. 13, too, he refers to Genesis: "For Adam was formed first, then Eve." He bases his argument not only on the creation, but also on the fall of man: "Adam was not deceived, but the woman was deceived and became a transgressor" (1 Tim ii. 14). He also uses the Old Testament, and in particular the Law of Moses, in his argument against the loose

---

[39] See L. Cerfaux, *L'Eglise des Corinthiens*, Paris (1946).

morals of the Corinthians: "As in all the churches of the saints, the women should keep silence in the churches [= in your meetings]. For they are not permitted to speak, but should be subordinate, as even the Law says. If there is anything they desire to know, let them ask their husbands at home" (1 Cor xiv. 33–5). This argument based on the Bible is clearly used to confirm Paul's main line of argument, that of ecclesiastical custom, since he stresses "as in all the churches of the saints" (see also 1 Cor xi. 16). Here he is no doubt referring to the Christian communities of Palestinian Jews in which the older social structures were more firmly rooted.

In a similar context, he also refers to the "traditions even as I have delivered them to you" (1 Cor xi. 2). It is clear from the context that the Corinthians kept these traditions, with the exception of that of the subordination of women in the community, since he makes an immediate appeal to Christology, in the text which follows: "The head of every man is Christ; the head of the woman is the man; and the head of Christ is God" (1 Cor xi. 3), which should be compared with "Wives, be subject to your husbands, as to the Lord" (Eph v. 22) and "Wives, be subject to your husbands, as is fitting in the Lord" (Col iii. 18). In Eph v. 22 ff. Paul insists that women should be subject to their husbands "for the husband is the head of the wife as Christ is the head of the church. . . . Therefore, as the church is subject to Christ, so let wives also be subject in everything to their husbands."

The whole of this argument has an unaccustomed ring, giving the impression that Paul is defending a thesis that he feels he cannot fully substantiate and must consequently reinforce with numerous supporting pieces of evidence. It is obvious that he wholeheartedly accepts the custom of women veiling their heads, but he defends this practice as a sign of the subordinate position of woman in society by a mass of arguments which seem laborious and forced. The original significance of this veiling of the head is not easy to trace.[40] The custom was in fact

---

[40] See R. de Vaux, "Sur le voile des femmes dans l'Orient ancien," *RB*, 44 (1935), pp. 397–412.

regarded in contemporary society as an expression of the fact that the woman was the possession and property of the man who had veiled her. Originally, however, it would seem as if the veil was used as a kind of protection to ward off the evil spirits from which the "weaker sex" especially needed to be guarded. It would also seem as if Paul had heard of this, since he comments that women must wear a veil on their heads "because of the angels" (1 Cor xi. 10).[41] But it cannot be denied that the necessity for women to be veiled is Paul's conclusion from the premise that "man was not created for woman, but woman for man" (xi. 9). This is why women must wear a veil. The argument may well be called a "biblical" argument, since the *exousia* or "power" (xi. 10) which the wife has on her head—the veil as a sign of marital power—would appear to be a translation of the Hebrew *meme-šālāh*, and thus an allusion to Gen iii. 16 in which the woman is placed, after the fall, "under the husband's power."

A new element, this time a philosophic argument derived from the Stoics, adds weight to this reasoning: "If a woman will not veil herself, then she should cut off her hair; but if it is disgraceful for a woman to be shorn or shaven, let her wear a veil" (xi. 6). The conclusive force of this argument eludes us, but for Paul it was clearly something like an appeal to the "natural law." According to the Stoics a woman "naturally" had long hair; consequently she ought not to go against nature and allow her hair to be cut off. The Greeks who read Paul's epistle understood this. Paul regarded the veil as being as much a "natural law" as long hair, and held that a woman who refused to wear a veil might just as well allow her hair to be cut off. The Corinthian women were conscious of the shame of having their heads shaven, but they did not regard it as ridiculous not to wear a veil. For Paul, however, both were "unnatural." The impression is inescapable

[41] This reference by Paul is clearly to something that had already for a long time been stripped of its ancient mythical elements. Since he is speaking here about religious meetings, it is obvious that he is thinking concretely of the angels who were present during prayer, an idea that recurs frequently in the first century A.D. and in the writings of the Fathers.

—Paul attached as much importance to this custom as to something very sacred indeed: "Does not nature itself teach you that for a man to wear long hair is degrading to him, but if a woman has long hair, it is her pride?" (xi. 14–15).

This was the argument of the Stoics. But Paul went further: "For a man ought not to cover his head [when he prays], since he is the image and glory of God; but woman is the glory of man . . . woman [was created] for man. That is why a woman ought to have a veil on her head, because of the angels" (xi. 7–10). The biblical argument of the woman's subjection to the man was based on a divine punishment after the fall. In this text, however, Paul goes back beyond the original sin of man to the situation in paradise when the man was created as "God's image" and the woman was created indirectly, being "taken out of the man."

This final rabbinical and biblical argument marks the end of Paul's reasoning. Strangely enough, however, he does not look back over the series of weighty arguments that he has put forward convinced that he has proved his point beyond all doubt. On the contrary, he feels impelled—with a feeling of slight irritation—to conclude his case with a sentence which is highly charged with meaning and which in fact sums up the whole of his plea: "But, if any one is disposed to be contentious, *we* recognise no other practice, nor do the churches of God" (xi. 16). This is really the only argument which is fully to the point. The practice of wearing a veil was, in other words, a venerable custom both among the Jews and among the Jewish converts to Christianity. Paul attached great importance to it because, in his own time especially, it had a profound religious and symbolic value. It stressed the modesty of women before God, and was above all a social symbol of woman's subordination to man (this latter was, of course, a basic conviction of Paul's). His zeal for the veiling of women was the result of his zeal for the idea that the man is the head of the woman.

In itself, the veil is simply a fact of secular or of religious society; it possesses no constant value. Even in our own time, men remove their hats on entering church. This is a purely social and religious symbol, important to us today as an expression of respect. In one particular society and at a given period of time, the custom of wearing a veil may be extremely significant; at a later age, and in a later society, this significance may have been lost. But there is always the difficulty of transition between the two cultures. In a transitional period of this kind, a custom may be renounced for good reasons, but it may also be repudiated for less good reasons—a desire to pursue the latest fashion, a refusal to conform to established ideas, a lack of sensitivity for the condition of man, or an attitude which sets greater store by external change than by basic and intrinsic values.

Paul was in fact fighting for something which was—from the point of view of culture and society—a lost cause, but it would be wrong to accuse him of being a reactionary on that account. He had abundant reasons for suspecting that what lay behind this attitude toward the veiling of women in Corinth was a basic lack of seriousness towards religious and moral values. This accounts for his heated partisanship and his rabbinical search for arguments which probably made little impression on the Greek mind.

The pastoral epistles show clearly how this lack of modesty was to be revealed in quite a different way in an already "settled" religious community. What we have here is a case of secular fashions in head-dress among women "in church":

[I desire that women, when they pray, should] adorn themselves modestly in seemly apparel, not with braided hair or gold or pearls or costly attire but by good deeds, as befits women who profess religion. (1 Tim ii. 9–10; see also 1 Pet iii. 3–4.)

In order to stress the relative value of the social and historical elements in this epistle, we might go so far as to say—though this is merely a debating point—that its author reaped the results of Paul's zeal for women's head-dress! On the other hand, it must be admitted that Paul was under Christ's sway and the rest was only of relative interest to him. He does not provide a "theology" of cultural and social change, or even any basic principles that underlie the changes which take place in human life and ordinary secular structures. What he does offer is that basic eschatological vision which every "theology" of society must take into account if it aims to be a Christian theology. What concerned Paul above all was man's "being in Christ," what animated and inspired the Christian. As far as the rest was concerned, the *taxis* or social order, he desired only that "all things be done for edification" (1 Cor xiv. 26). His view is confirmed by the comment with which he concludes his plea that women should be silent in the Christian community: "all things should be done decently and in order" (1 Cor xiv. 40). This "order" (*taxis*) does not directly imply orderliness or discipline; it is only the consequence of Paul's more profound view of "order" as "hierarchical structure." Structures of this kind were very dear to Paul:

For just as the body is one and has many members, and all the members of the body, though many, are one body, so it is with Christ. For by one Spirit we were all baptized into one body—Jews or Greeks, slaves or free—and all were made to drink of one Spirit [= we have all been saturated by the one Spirit]. For the body does not consist of one member, but of many. If the foot should say . . . And if the ear should say . . . But as it is, God arranged the organs in the body, each one of them, as he chose . . . [1 Cor xii. 12–18.]

This passage, which continues by discussing the functions of the members of Christ's body (xii. 12–31), is a good example of one of Paul's favourite themes. It is a fruitful source, but it can easily be misused if it is taken to explain actual historical structures in terms of theology.

What we have learnt so far is that Paul's view of woman certainly contains elements which were without question determined by existing social conditions, and that to some extent the apostle was undoubtedly aware of these himself. The conclusion to his argument about the need for women to veil their heads—"be this as it may, I want women to be veiled because of their subordinate position with regard to men"—is echoed in Eph. v. 25–33, in which Paul is not directly concerned to interpret marriage as an image of the covenant between Christ and his church, but concerned rather to demonstrate that the wife is subject to the husband in marriage. What he gives us here is the exact counterpart to his argument in favour of the veil. The difference, however, is that the biblical argument—that the woman is taken from the man and thus forms one flesh with him in subjection to him—is here developed according to its relation with Christ and with the church: just as Christ and his church form one flesh, but Christ is nonetheless the head of the church (an idea which Paul had been developing throughout his epistle to the Ephesians), so also is the husband the head of the wife.

These are really the same ideas as those in 1 Cor xi. 3–16, but they have been thought over again in the light of the new idea of Christ as the head of the church. It is noticeable that Paul ends his theological argument here in Eph v. 25–33 too with a certain doubt—"that at least is my view," which is the implication of the sentence "But I take it to mean [= but I for my part relate it to] Christ and the church" (v. 32), and "However [= be that as it may] let each one of you love his wife as himself; and let the wife see that she respects her husband" (v. 33). Moreover, it is clear that, just as in 1 Cor xi. 3–16, the argument of Eph v. 25–32 (which, incidentally, occurs within the framework of a moral exhortation similar to that of the "household codes") was intended as a defence, based on formal theological lines, of the domestic relationship between man and wife that was generally accepted within the various Christian communities—a relationship which was, it should be remembered, threatened by the prevailing spirit of the age, especially in the case of the Greek Christians.

These formal theological themes are advanced with great sincerity by Paul, but he does somehow give the impression of feeling that they are not entirely convincing as a theological basis for these social relationships. (This is why, in my discussion of this passage in the section dealing with the New Testament teaching on marriage, I passed over the ultimate purpose of this text, since it to some extent distorts the legitimate image of marriage in order to defend the position of the husband as the "head of the wife.") We may therefore conclude that the New Testament ethos of marriage does contain changeable social elements, but that the relative value of these elements is recognised, even though this recognition sometimes takes a veiled form.

If scriptural statements of this and of a similar kind are to be properly understood, it is important not to forget that as a rule women received no education during the first century. I am referring to statements such as "I permit no woman to teach" (1 Tim ii. 12) because she is susceptible to heresies (1 Tim iv. 7; 2 Tim iii. 6). These are in no sense *a priori* statements, but they occur in the pastoral epistles, and these could assume that the already well-organized communities to which the epistles were addressed had gained a great deal of experience. The same kind of statement is also to be found in the secular writings of the Greeks of this period—the man's place was in the gymnasium, instructing and being instructed in physical and intellectual pursuits, whereas the woman's place was in the home, at the cradle and the distaff. The pastoral epistle, 1 Timothy, says very much the same thing:

[During instruction] let a woman learn in silence, with all submissiveness. I permit no woman to teach, or to have authority over men; she is to keep silent. For Adam was formed first, then Eve. And Adam was not deceived, but the woman . . . Yet woman will be saved through bearing children, if she continues in faith and love and holiness, with modesty. [1 Tim i. 11–15.]

This, then, is the same conduct which is expected of women by the secular Greek writers but, in the case of Christian women, experienced "in the Lord." To construct a theology of marriage on a basis of such texts—to refer to the "primary significance" of the married woman and to conclude from this that Christianity cannot, for example, accept the idea of married women working away from home—would be to violate the first principles of sound biblical exegesis.

Nonetheless, though it should by now be clear that the wearing of the veil, the insistence that women should keep silent in the community, and the similar rules of conduct which were put forward by Paul on a theological basis were really determined by existing social and historical conditions, the basic assertion of Paul—that the man is the head of the wife who is subject to her husband—is in no sense disproved by this. This, then, is the essential problem facing us: Is this doctrine, advanced not only by Paul but also by Peter (1 Pet iii. 1–7), a biblical *datum?* Or is it only a biblical *mode of thought and expression,* and as such merely a variable social and historical quantity? Contemporary thought makes this problem extremely important. Article 16 of the *Declaration of Human Rights* states that husband and wife have equal rights, before, during, and after marriage. Since the Second World War, the clause "the husband is the head of the matrimonial union" has been struck out of the legislation of most European countries. This has happened in Belgium, for example; but Holland, in contrast to the general tendency, has upheld the principle.[42] Does this modern tendency do violence to a biblical datum, and should Christians, taking their stand on the Bible, oppose it?

[42] A very clear exposition of this can be found in E. A. Luyten's inaugural address, *Hoofd der echtvereniging. Enkele rechtsvergelijkende beschouwingen naar aanleiding van de pivaatrechtelijke emancipatie der gehuwde vrouw in de wetgeving van Nederland en enige andere Europese landen,* Nijmegen (1960) ("The head of the matrimonial union. Some considerations arising from the emancipation of the married woman in the legislation of private law in the Netherlands, compared with that in some other European countries").

In the first place, it is of importance to note that Paul does not employ the term "head of the family" or *pater familias*. He refers to the husband as the "head of the woman," although it is evident that the husband exercises authority over the children.[43] This does, however, indicate that it is not simply a formal question of man as head of the family, but a more fundamental question of man as head of the woman, even though what is in the end implied is that the man is the "head of his wife." The generalisation, the "head of the woman," is derived from the Genesis account, and the fact that Paul refers his proposition to the account of the creation—this emerges from his argument in connection with the veiling of women—provides us with one element for the solution of this problem. His general proposition and his particular proposition (the place of the woman in marriage and the family) are fundamentally one, despite a certain distinction.

This is clearly so, because he advances the same biblical arguments for both: the woman must be veiled during religious meetings because "the head of a woman is her husband" (1 Cor xi. 3), and the woman must be subject to the man in marriage because "the husband is the head of the wife" (Eph v. 22–3). This position, the "head of the woman," has a biblical basis: "the woman was taken out of man." This is one element—the first—in the solution of the problem, since it is clear that Paul regards the actual social status of woman as something ordained by creation. His evidence for this is the account provided in Genesis; but it is characteristic that he blends data from the older Yahwist account of the creation with the more recent Priestly tradition.

The Yahwist account in Genesis offers an "androcentric" view of creation. First man was created, then woman. This account was, in its very formulation, dependent upon the actual social status of woman which was prevalent at the time when the tradition gained its form. First the 'ādhām was created; later, a second being was taken out of this 'ādhām, and these two beings were,

---

[43] Paul speaks of the obligations of the children towards the parents, and conversely of the obligations of the father—in the exercise of his authority —towards the children (Col iii. 20–21).

in their relationship to each other, *'iš* (man) and *'iššah* (woman). The *'ādhām* was later identified with the *'iš*, the man, and the woman was at this period regarded as a kind of "second edition" of the man.[44] The view revealed by this account of the creation without doubt relies on the actual, historically conditioned status of woman at the time. It is a biblical view, but the assertion itself is not biblical, in the sense that it is revelatory, but rather a framework within which divine revelation could come to men.

The Priestly account in Genesis is quite different. In this account, the *'ādhām* existed from the very beginning as two persons in a complementary sexual relationship with each other,[45] and there is no mention of the man being the first being and the woman being the second, "taken out of the man." The Priestly account also says that this "mankind" (that is, man-and-woman) is the "image of God."

It is remarkable that Paul should follow the androcentric conception of the Yahwist account and the idea of the "image of God" of the Priestly account, but interpret this "image of God" in the light of the Yahwist tradition: "The man is the image and glory of God, but woman is the glory of man. For man was not made from [= was not taken out of] woman, but woman from man. Neither was man created for woman, but woman for man" (1 Cor xi. 7–9). That the man is the image of God and the

---

[44] The Aristotelian idea that woman was "as a failed man" (*De generatione animalium*, II, 3) was taken over, along with many other of Aristotle's ideas, by the medieval Christians. Another fact that was well known was that *'ādhām*, originally a generic name meaning "mankind" (Gen i. 27–8), was later used as a proper name, without the article, and identified with the man (Gen iv. 25). The transition from the generic to the proper name is particularly striking in Gen v. 1, 3–5, where *'ādhām* is used as a proper name ("Adam"), and in Gen v. 2, where it is used in the generic sense.

[45] The *'ādhām*, or human being, who was created consisted of two complementary and related beings, the *zākhār* (male), and the *neqêbhāh* (female), that is, man and woman. The derivation of these words is obscure, but it would seem that the first means the "sharp" one, that is, the being with the penis, and the second the "split" one, the being with the vagina. The *zākhār* is only called "man" (*'iš*) in contrast with the *neqêbhāh*, as *'iššah* or woman.

woman the image (or glory) of the man is therefore a rabbinical
and Pauline confusion of two distinct and unequal categories of
data: a social and historical datum which conditioned the Old
Testament view, resulting in the androcentric idea that woman
was "taken out of the man," was interpreted in the light of a
theological datum, namely that of mankind as the image of God,
with the result that the social and historical datum itself became
theology.

It is now clear what Paul means when he says that the man is
"the head of the woman." *Kephalē* (head) can be the translation
both of *rô's* (head) and of *resîth* (beginning or principle). It is
true that *kephalē* was not used by the secular Greek writers to
mean *arkhē* (beginning or cause). On the other hand, however,
the Hebrew *rô's* (head) was translated only once by *arkhē*
(beginning or principle) in the Greek Septuagint, and normally
by *kephalē*, whereas *arkhē* was used to translate *resîth* (beginning
of first principle).[46] This confusion did not escape Paul. *Kephalē*
(head) is used by Paul, in the context of the relationship between
man and woman, to mean none other than what he was aiming
to demonstrate in 1 Cor ix, namely, "first the man, then the
woman," since the woman was taken out of the man. This becomes even clearer in 1 Tim ii. 13: "Adam was formed first
(*prōtos*), then (*eita*) Eve." Thus *kephalē* here has not so much
the meaning of "head" as of *arkhē*—the first, both chronologically and hierarchically.

I do not wish in any way to deny that *kephalē* has the meaning of "head" in Paul, but simply to point to the fact that the
meaning of "first" and "priority" is very prominent here, just as it
is in the Latin *caput* and the French *chef* as well as the English
"head" itself. "Head" therefore does not simply point to an
organic unity between the "head," the man, and the "body,"
the woman, in Eph v. 22–32. It indicates above all a hierarchy in

[46] See S. Bedale, "The Meaning of *kephalē* in the Pauline Epistles," *JTS*,
5 (1954), pp. 211–15.

this organism—the first and leading function of the man, and the second and subordinate function of the woman.

To this contemporary social pattern, in which the man had priority over the woman, Paul gave a theological substructure by means of an appeal to the Yahwist account of the creation, in which the woman's position and function are a reflection of her position and function in the social system of that time—something which was to be completely overcome in the later account of the creation. In other words, although Paul had recourse to Genesis, the actual source of his assertion was still an actual social situation in which woman occupied a subordinate position. This is apparent from his argument in 1 Cor xi. 8–9, which is based on the second and older Genesis account, in which the woman was fashioned from the man's rib.[47]

Summarising the results of our investigation so far, we can say that Paul gave a theological superstructure to a factual situation which was reflected in the household codes and was accepted as a human ethos—the situation of the wife's subjection to her husband—and to the generally inferior and secondary position of woman in society, and that he did this by referring to the second and older Genesis account of the creation, in which the assertion of the woman's subordinate position was itself a reflection of an actual social situation.

This, however, still does not settle the matter finally, since Paul says in Eph v. 23: "the husband is the head of the wife as Christ is the head of the church." Many scholars have concluded from this that the ultimate establishment of the husband as the head of the family is a New Testament datum, by virtue of this analogous relationship between Christ and the church. This is, I feel, rather

---

[47] Both the general statement, "the head of the woman is the man" (1 Cor xi. 3) and the particular statement, "the husband is the head of the wife" (Eph v. 23), are based on the same Yahwist account of the creation, in which the general and the particular intersect. In Rom vii. 2, *hupandros gunē* means a "woman placed below the man," in other words, a married woman. This is certainly the main assertion, but the subordination of woman in general was at the same time undoubtedly in Paul's mind.

too hasty a conclusion. In 1 Cor xi. 3 Paul had already called the man the "head of the woman." I have already discussed in detail what Paul means by this, in my analysis of his defence of the actually subordinate, "veiled" position of woman in society. It is obvious that the epistle to the Ephesians, which continually stresses the point that Christ is the head of the church, makes use of this analogy when the "household codes" are introduced at the end of the epistle, and thus the woman's subjection to the man, as the "first," and her "head."

Paul does, of course, emphasize that this situation should be experienced "in the Lord," as he does in the parallel text of Col iii. 18, in the phrase "as is fitting in the Lord." How better could he express this fact in the epistle to the Ephesians, with its repeated references to Christ as the head of the church, than by the analogy "as Christ is the head of the church"? The chief function of the man is not somehow *inferred* from the mystery of Christ as a kind of conclusion here; what Paul does is to associate the *already existing and generally accepted* position of the man as head with Christ—and there is all the difference in the world between the two. Moreover, it is already clear in 1 Cor xi that this function of the man was not a theological fact, but a situation that was already present in society to which Paul gave a theological superstructure.

We are obviously bound to conclude, therefore, that Paul is saying no more than that Christians should experience the existing social structure of marriage and the family "in the Lord"— that, in other words, the married man should "follow Christ" in marriage and family life, and the married woman should "follow the church." The biblical and dogmatic fact of the unity existing between Christ and his church and the dogmatic influence of this unity on the unity—the "one flesh"—of man and woman in marriage on the one hand, and, on the other, Paul's attempt to provide a purely social datum—the man as "head" and the woman as "subject," occupying a subordinate position—with a theologi-

cal basis, cut across each other in this passage in the epistle to the
Ephesians.

It is of course true that it is only now, when we are confronted
with the problem of marriage in its present form, that we are in
a position to make this scriptural distinction clear and to deal
with it thematically. It is also true that Paul was not conscious of
it, or at least not fully conscious—at a later stage I shall attempt
to show that he was to some extent aware of this distinction. But
the constant rereading of Scripture at different periods of man's
development, and in the light of the particular situation in which
a reader is placed, does not of itself result in "enegesis" rather
than exegesis. The modern situation is only a stimulus which
confronts us with this particular problem.

In the first place, we must always bear in mind that marriage is
a secular reality which has entered salvation. As a *human* reality,
this datum is based on the essence of man as an essence that only
is itself, only becomes itself, within history. As a community of
parents and children, marriage has essentially a social aspect—it is
a community which of its very nature calls for a unifying or
leading principle. In an androcentric society, a "man's world,"
this principle is automatically ascribed to the man. I do not mean
to claim that today the woman is the unifying principle, but
philosophical and other studies more and more emphasize both
the husband and the wife, in their marital unity of one flesh, as
the main principle of marriage and the family.[48]

It will be necessary to go into this question in the synthesis
which follows, since it certainly does not come within the scope
of the purely biblical examination of the subject. Whether the
man or the woman should occupy the position of authority in
marriage and in the family is a matter of human and historical
significance. It is in any case not an arbitrary question, but arises
from the essence of marriage itself. In this sense a "natural law" is

[48] This view has clearly not yet penetrated to the sphere of legislation,
which still aims to safeguard the separate personal rights of the husband
and the wife.

involved, the inviolable norm which exists in the human values of married life; but the content of this particular norm is a question of a growing historical insight. There are societies in which the woman is the head of the family, though these are exceptional. But is this fact less "natural" than the fact of the man as the head?

This brings us to the problem of the meaning of "natural" and its evolution, which is a question that can only be answered in the synthesis. For the present I can do no more than say that the revelation of salvation does not change the essentially human and historical significance of these values. Revelation can only confirm man's consciousness of the "natural law" in this—in his search for what is objectively and essentially human in varying circumstances. But of course the whole question turns on the precise meaning of the "natural law" in this particular case, namely that of marital relationships. Moreover, it will be obvious that, before Paul, or the teaching authority of the church, can be said to *confirm* a "natural law," this natural law must first show itself as such.

How can a natural law be actually confirmed by salvation or revelation so long as the precise demands of this natural law are not apparent to the community? Revelation, it is true, does in actual fact confirm the "natural law," but for us (*quoad nos*) it cannot confirm anything that does not appear to be natural law at the time. Reflecting as a theologian on the assertions made by the exegetes, one can but say that Paul only confirms the assertion that the husband is the "head of the wife" as a natural law in the light of salvation, if it is clear that we are actually—in this instance—dealing with a natural law. So long as this is not apparent or evident—indeed, so long as it is not fully substantiated—we can only conclude that there is nothing to prove that Paul can demonstrate any more in Eph v. 22–4 and 1 Cor xi than that the Christian is bound to experience actual contemporary family relationships "in the Lord."

In Paul's own time the man, as husband and father, was the head of the wife and of the whole family. For this reason Paul was able, in his revelation of the relationship between Christ and his church, in which Christ was in fact the head, not only to disclose the very profound meaning of Christian marriage as "one flesh," but to use this reality as a suitable image for the ethos generally accepted at the time of the wife's complete subjection to her husband. In other words, it is a delicate operation which must be carried out here in connection with the dogmatic datum: the relationship between Christ and his church was made present in a special way in Christian marriage, but the idea of "head" and "subjection," which is real in the case of the relationship between Christ and the church, was in marriage only a fact determined by social and historical conditions. Paul was able to combine the two aspects of the one image, but from the exegetical and the theological point of view it is by no means evident that the man was established as head of the family *by revealed truth*, or that revealed truth confirmed a natural law to the effect that the "husband is head of the wife."

At this stage of our examination of the subject it is hardly possible to reach any definite conclusions at all. The foregoing does not in itself refute the idea of the man as head of the family. All it does is to say that Paul can be regarded as having sanctioned a natural law in the light of salvation only if it is clear that there is a question of such a natural law being involved in the human and historical significance of the family. Whether this is so or not will have to be made clear in our phenomenological and philosophical analysis of the relationship between husband and wife in marriage and the family. Even in the case of church pronouncements in which the man is called head of the family we are no nearer to a solution of the dogmatic part of the problem, unless such statements are borne out by an appeal to Paul. The defence of this principle can have the same significance as Paul's defence of the veil—that is, it may be meaningful but at the same time determined by social and historical factors, at least so long as it is not clearly evident that we are faced with an ethical norm of "natural law," or so long as it does not provide an intrinsically comprehensible justification which compels us to follow the particular value judgments concerned.

We may therefore conclude that what is involved in Paul's assertion, "the husband is the head of the wife," is an experience "in the Lord" of an existing pattern of society and of family life, in which an absolute—though historically conditioned—datum of "natural law" may be implied. Moreover, Paul's tendency to provide these hierarchical structures which were already present in society with a "theological" basis, and thus to give them an independent value, is clearly expressed in this assertion, with the result that we get the impression that we are dealing here with a constant and unchangeable structure bestowed on marriage by God himself. In the New Testament there is as yet no explicit recognition that revelation does not exclude the growth of human awareness, or the development of the historical significance of the values in this and similar spheres of life which have, in the first instance, a secular and existential significance.

That Paul does tend to provide existing situations with a theological superstructure is confirmed by the fact that it is apparent from the texts themselves that he is himself conscious of the relative value of his own assertions. Paul, who obviously insisted on his assertion, "the husband is the head of the wife," being accepted without question and put into practical effect by his Christians, nonetheless realised that it was necessary for him to bring out the various shades of meaning present in it. Although, as we have already seen, he was generally content to allow ordinary secular structures to take their own course, and merely to impress upon Christians the need to experience them as Christians, he clearly felt impelled, in the light of his own experience of the mystery of Christ, to place his universal vision in perspective. His general statement in the epistle to the Galatians is evidence of this: "Now [that is, in Christ] there is neither Jew nor Greek; there is neither slave nor free; there is neither male nor female [= neither man nor woman]." (Gal iii. 26–8; see also 2 Cor v. 17 and Mt xii. 25.) In the particular case of the conjugal duties of the husband and the wife, he also stated the principle of the equality of the two persons (1 Cor vii. 3–4 ,12), thus breaking completely with the double morality that conceded more to the husband than to the wife. In addition to this he also modified his thesis that the husband was the head of the wife—"for man was not made from [= taken out of] woman, but woman from man" and "man was not created for woman, but woman for man" (1 Cor xi. 8–9)—in its immediate context by saying: "*Nevertheless*, in the Lord, woman is not independent of man nor man of woman; for as the woman was made from man, *so man is now born of woman*. And all things are from God" (1 Cor xi. 11–12). The inferior position of the woman, assumed in the Old Testament, though certainly not substantiated by the biblical theology of the Genesis account, is interpreted in the light of Christian experience—"in the Lord"—as a complementary interrelationship —"man is *born of* woman." From Christianity Paul came to a more anthropological view of human relationships. We have already seen how, in the light of Christianity and of Christian love, which makes use of the human interrelationships of ordinary secular structures, Paul inwardly transformed this human fellowship, and saw the woman, though subject to the man, as his "sister" in Christ. Paul was not aiming to reduce all social relationships to the same level, but rather to permeate them with the leaven of a Christian and transcendent vision. This was evident in what he had to say concerning the relationship between masters and their slaves. He was no Spartacus—not even a Christian Spartacus—but an eschatological Christian. Christian experience "in the Lord" of the actually present, existing, human and social relationships of subordination changes the real and basic meaning of this subordination for Paul. (He also attributes to Christ subordination to the Father; "subordination" is for him a matter of "hierarchical order" and has in itself no unfavourable connotation.) "Love your wives as Christ loved the Church" (Eph v. 25)—this task which husbands had with regard to their wives inwardly transformed the male position of authority and gave it a primacy of love.[49] At the same time it is important not to lose sight of the fact that Paul is here referring to *agapē*—to Christian love as a gift of God in the Spirit. The New Testament ethic is not distinguished by new norms for marriage and sexuality, but by a Christian view of man as having been received into Christ's redeeming grace. The Petrine text, "Likewise you husbands, live considerately [in marriage] with your wives, bestowing honour on the woman as the weaker sex, since you are joint heirs of the grace of life" (1 Pet iii. 7), is a typical expression of this vision. The epistle of Peter, from which this text is taken, combines a secular and a Christian datum. "Give honour to the woman as the weaker sex" is a characteristic example of the new sensitivity which was emerging in the Hellenistic world even before the coming of Christianity, but the epistle bases this courteous treatment of women on the conferment of grace equally on both men and women in Christ. There is no equality of nature between man and woman in society, but an all-embracing equality in dignity of the sexes "in the Lord."

One of the results of this Christian leavening of the "natural" social relationships is that women obtained a place in the very early apostolic church which must have caused something of a sensation in contemporary society. In the first place, Christ himself, acting in complete contradiction to contemporary custom, had talked with women in the street. The apostles were astonished by this behaviour on Christ's part, but they dared not draw his attention to it. (Jn iv. 7–11, 27; see also Mt viii. 14 ff.; Lk xiii. 10–17; viii. 1–3.) Initially, women were also permitted to speak in the community of believers. (Acts ii. 17–18; even 1 Cor xi. 5, in contrast with 1 Cor xi. 34.) They too were charismatically inspired (Acts xxi. 9). Women also took part in the election of Matthias to the ranks of the apostles (Acts i. 14, 26). There were many women in the service of the gospel (Col. iv. 15; 1 Cor i. 11; Rom xvi. 1, 6, 12, 15; Phil iv. 2), and widows occupied a promi-

---

[49] See also V. Heylen, "Het hoofd van het gezin," *TT*, 1 (1961), pp. 309–28.

nent place in the community (1 Tim v. 9).[50] Indeed, they even
gave instruction in the faith (Acts xviii. 26). This was, of course,
entirely alien to the Jewish spirit, and, although it was to some
extent intelligible to the Hellenistic world, it nonetheless represented a distinct break with the established views of the time on
the position of woman in society. It was only as a result of certain less happy experiences that the pastoral epistles show evidence of a reaction against it.

It is quite clear, then, that the Pauline (and, for that matter,
the Petrine) assertions concerning the subjection of the woman
to the man are not dogmatic reactions on Paul's part, but a question of ecclesiastical and hierarchical pastoral guidance within a
definite historical setting—a policy in pastoral matters which required arguments to substantiate it and to make it meaningful.
The theological lesson to be drawn from this is that having established that this is basically a question of a variable social and
historical factor does not in fact clear the matter up once and for
all—there still remain the question of the church's conduct in
pastoral affairs, and the question of personal decision on grounds
of individual conscience. Whether or not the attitude which Paul
adopted in this matter is—from the Christian point of view—the
only possible one, is quite a different question. In the history of
the church there are many cases of the hierarchy taking a
"Pauline" attitude, and in such cases the doctrinal background is
mingled with an appreciation of the factual situation as a function
of the church's pastoral guidance. The policy actually followed
by the church in these cases is not the only one that she could
have followed, but it deserves respect as a corporate decision on
grounds of conscience on the part of the authoritative body. And
so, both in the case of Paul and in the case of papal documents
dealing with problems relating to this world, it is important always to distinguish between the "ethical norm" and the concrete

[50] Although this was at the same time also conditioned by social factors
in the Hellenistic world. Widows who did not remarry enjoyed a high
status in Hellenistic society.

"moral obligations" which are at once conditioned by the prevailing situation at the time and also present themselves as the ethical "rules of behaviour" in a given period.[51]

The Condemnation of Porneia

Christianity of the New Testament period accepted the "household codes" as rules of conduct in domestic life, but, as we have seen, they were deepened in the light of man's community with Christ and, where necessary, brought into line with Christian thought. The New Testament also shows a sharp reaction against both the sexual excesses of the Hellenistic world and the Manichean heretical views of marriage according to which women especially were regarded as corrupt. This is particularly noticeable in the pastoral epistles. In the first epistle to Timothy, for example, we read that these people—i.e., those who held heretical views of this kind—rejected marriage and the use of certain foods, although "God created [these] to be received with thanksgiving by those who believe and know the truth. For everything created by God is good, and nothing is to be rejected if it is received with thanksgiving; for then it is consecrated by the word of God and prayer" (1 Tim iv. 3–5; see also 1 Thess iv. 3–6). The epistle to the Hebrews has this to say about marriage: "Let marriage be held in honour among all, and let the marriage bed [= married life] be undefiled; for God will judge the im-

---

[51] In my anthropological analysis of the morality of married life I shall attempt to show how this distinction has not always been kept sufficiently in mind in connection with sexuality and marriage. An absolute ethical norm is above all an idea which is "open," pointing to the inalienable rights and duties connected with the dignity of the human person. An ethical "rule of behaviour" is, or may be, a concrete "moral obligation" which at the same time presupposes an appreciation of the actually existing situation, and which is also able to change if the situation itself changes. The ethical norm, the appreciation of human values, on the other hand, does not change, though it does develop. But this ethical norm only—and always—achieves authentic form *within* a concrete obligation and is therefore, even as norm, dynamic.

moral and adulterous" (Heb xiii. 4). In the first epistle to the
Thessalonians, Paul says: "Each one of you [should] know how
to take a wife for himself in holiness and honour, not in the
passion of lust, like heathen who do not know God" (1 Thess iv.
4–5). Chaste living within marriage as well—which here certainly
does not mean abstinence, but chastity in marital relationships—
is therefore a question of man's practical experience of God:
"Whoever disregards this [that is, these admonitions concerning
the Christian experience of married life], disregards not man but
God, who gives his Holy Spirit to you" (1 Thess iv. 8).

Nowhere in the New Testament is there any explicit commandment that marriage should be monogamous or any explicit
commandment forbidding polygamy. This presented no concrete
problem: monogamous marriage was accepted as a point of departure. Sexual intercourse outside marriage (Jn viii. 41; 1 Cor vi.
12 ff.), sodomy, and homosexual relationships were condemned as
sinful (Jude 7; Rom i. 24–7). So were prostitution (1 Cor vi.
12 ff.), which at that time was still practised in the temple, and
pederasty (1 Cor vi. 9). The sexual aberrations—*porneia* in all
its forms—so common in the cities of the Greco-Roman world
were briefly but decisively repudiated by the New Testament.

In connection with the rejection of prostitution in the New
Testament, there is a passage in Paul which shows clearly how
the author had an anthropological view of marital relationships—
the "becoming one" of marriage—and at the same time provided
a Christological background for this:

The body is not meant for immorality, but for the Lord, and the
Lord for the body. And God raised the Lord and will also raise us up
by his power. Do you not know that your bodies are members of
Christ? Shall I therefore take the members of Christ and make them
the members of a prostitute? Never! Do you not know that he who
joins himself to a prostitute becomes one body with her? For it is
written, "the two shall become one." But he who is united to the
Lord becomes one spirit with him . . . Do you not know that your

body is a temple of the Holy Spirit within you, which you have from God? You are not your own; you were bought with a price. So glorify God in your body. [1 Cor vi. 12–20.]

This passage ought to be an inspiration to us in our dogmatic consideration of the whole question of marriage in Paul. The apostle recognised that the Christian is closely bound to the glorified Christ even in his physical being. To emphasize this, Paul refers to the resurrection in which our bodies will reflect the glory of Christ's "spiritual" body, and this destiny is already in a sense present for our bodies by virtue of baptism. Belonging to the "body of the Lord," the Christian's own body is, so to speak, the body of Christ, so that he no longer has control of it, to use it against the will of Christ. Intercourse in marriage is a "becoming one flesh." Association with a harlot is an offence against the "one spirit" which the Christian has become with Christ. The "one flesh" which the Christian forms with Christ in belonging to his body, the church, is here seen to be "one spirit," not in the later, "ghostly" sense of "spiritual," but in the original New Testament sense—the baptized Christian forms a *living community* with Christ. Paul is not seeking to establish a connection here between the "one flesh" which baptized partners in marriage form and the "one spirit" of the marriage covenant of the believer with Christ. All that he does is to contrast fornication with the living community with Christ. These are mutually exclusive, and Paul expresses this fact by contrasting "one flesh" and "one spirit." There is, as Eph v. 22–32 so clearly shows, no contrast between the "one flesh" of married Christians and the "one spirit" which the believer forms with Christ. This idea is a very rewarding one from the dogmatic point of view; and, from the anthropological point of view, the text implies that the sex act is not a superficial one, in which the person remains outside—on the contrary, the person is deeply involved. That is why intercourse with a prostitute is not—as the Corinthians, with their false conception of freedom, thought it to be—a "liberation" (1 Cor vi. 12–16), but rather an enslavement, of the person. True liberation consists in subjection to Christ. Paul was thinking here of the temple of Aphrodite at Corinth, in which those who gave themselves to a prostitute believed that they were dedicating themselves to the deity. This "personal" character of religious prostitution in the temple was prominent in Paul's mind throughout this argument. The idea of the body as the "temple of God" was, moreover, already well-known in Hellenistic philosophy, and had become a current term among the fashionable thinkers of those times. But this "theistic" view was given a deeper meaning by Paul: Christ had bought our bodies by his redemption, so that they belonged legally to him. In other words, they were no longer *sui iuris*, having the rights of a freeman, but *iuris Christi*—they belonged legally to Christ. (The terminology is reminiscent of that used in connection with the ransoming of slaves, vi. 20, who were regarded as bodies—*sōmata*—or things.) This vision was to have a deep influence on marriage teaching.

It should also be noted that the problem of the relationship between married love and the foundation of the family or "pro-creation" is not dealt with in the New Testament. It was assumed that there would be love between both the partners and the children in Christian family life. The problem of not wanting children is not discussed at all in the New Testament. Paul in fact only deals with love (especially in Eph v. 22–33) and with the need to experience sexuality in a Christian way (especially in 1 Cor vii) in his basic expositions on the subject of marriage. The problem of "children" in marriage appears not to have existed in the apostolic church, in contrast with the patristic period, when attempts were made to find a solution to such problems by abandoning unwanted children as foundlings or even by abortive means which may or may not have been effective.

The pastoral epistles show how the New Testament idea of Christian celibacy for the sake of the kingdom of God began to acquire its first concrete institutional form, and it is worth re-marking that it occurred precisely in connection with those who

held office in the church—*episkopoi, presbuteroi,* and *diakonoi.*
True celibacy was not imposed as a condition of acceptance to
office in the church, but office-bearers were forbidden to contract a second marriage on the later death of their wives, or on
separation on grounds of conversion to Christianity.[52] What is
more, widows who were assigned to a function within the church
were not permitted to remarry (1 Tim v. 9), whereas young
widows who had no function within the church were advised to
remarry (1 Tim v. 14). It is clear, therefore, that the celibate
ideal, which had been advanced by Paul especially, tended to be
associated above all with those who held office in the church,
for not remarrying was seen, in 1 Cor vii, as we have already
noted, to be in accordance with the universal eschatological call
to complete abstinence.

[52] 1 Tim iii. 2 (the *episkopoi*); Tit i. 6 (the *presbuteroi*); 1 Tim iii. 12
(the *diakonoi*).

Conclusion to Part 2

It would be quite impossible for me to summarize in a few words the whole New Testament conception of marriage with its dogmatically comprehensive and ethically oriented content. All that I can usefully do here is to draw attention briefly to a few points which spring to mind, since these may help to point the way in the exploration of the experience of marriage in the course of the church's history which follows.

Marriage is a secular reality with a distinctively human significance which must be experienced "in the Lord." It is not simply a fact of creation, but something which has entered salvation. Baptism has conferred a special and separate meaning on marriage. On the other hand, it is not possible to define Christian marriage without at the same time referring to the eschatological call to abstinence. A remarkable tension is disclosed in the New Testament: on the one hand there is a decisive assertion of the goodness of a morally directed sexual life within marriage, an assertion which even stresses the mutual loving sexual obligations of marriage which may not be neglected for ascetic reasons; but, on the other hand, there is a reference to the *Eskhaton* which is present in marriage itself, and because of which Christian marriage is deprived of the absolute value that it possessed in the Old Testament.

What is also especially striking in connection with the New Testament view of marriage is the definitive aspect of marriage as a commitment. It is a venture for life, a bond which is not only a call personally to forge marriage into an existential union of marital interrelationship and personally to grow together in loving fidelity into an indissoluble unity, but also—on a basis of the structure of creation made even firmer by baptism—an objective union transcending free self-dissolution and existential disruption. This fact is a unique aspect of the Christian revelation of salvation—a unique fact which, in its absolute and unconditional quality, has no natural foundation apart from the saving fact of baptism, and which can only be approached and understood as a datum or revelation. This biblical view seems the clearest basis for the sacramentalism of marriage—the phenomenon which occurs only in the sacraments of the church, whereby a secular reality, with its distinctive historical significance, is inwardly transformed into a religious reality. This definitive surrender to another person, without any foreknowledge of what may happen in the future, is the human manifestation of man's definitive surrender to the other being, God. According to Jesus' Synoptic *logion*, marriage means a consecration for life to a fellow human being—in this case, to one's chosen partner in life. Paul in his turn interpreted this as a consecration in the same sense as Christ devoted his life to the church. In utter devotion man consecrates himself, by virtue of the baptism which he has received, to God in Christ. The indissolubility of Christian marriage is connected in the most intimate way with the definitive Christian character of the community of grace with God. For this reason the New Testament ideal of marriage may be seen to reflect the unconditional and absolute quality which by definition is peculiar to the reception of grace as man's making a gift of himself to the living God. But an equally clear conclusion is that this demand can be accepted in marriage only from within the community of grace with God; outside the explicit confession of Christ it must, inevitably, have a relative value. This is apparent from the so-called "Pauline privilege," which really does no more than to say that it is only Christian marriage which possesses this distinctive, separate, and absolute value—a value which is present only as a tendency in the marriages of unbaptized persons.

The church has given form to this biblical vision of marriage throughout the course of history. It has done this in historically developing forms, some of which have been more fortunate and more successful than others. In Volume II I shall try to trace this historical growth, at least in its clearest and most crucial aspects, in the life of the church, before going on to provide a systematic exposition of marriage.

Bibliography

N.B.—Footnotes in the text frequently refer to books listed in this bibliography. If only one work of a particular author is listed here, all that is given in the footnote is the author's name and the page reference of the book listed in this bibliography. If, on the other hand, two or more works by the same author are referred to, the short title is given in the footnote, so that it is clear which of the author's articles or books is meant. Only in cases where a point of detail is commented upon does the footnote give the full reference. In cases where a book or an article is quoted or referred to outside the chapter or section in which it is listed in this bibliography, it is given as a full reference in the footnote, in order to avoid confusion.

GENERAL INTRODUCTION: THE MODERN PATTERN OF MARRIAGE AS AN OPPORTUNITY FOR GRACE

AGIER, E., *Désintégration familiale chez les ouvriers,* Neuchâtel (1950).
ANSHEN, R., *The Family. Its Function and Destiny,* New York (1949).
ARCHAMBAULT. P., *La famille, oeuvre de l'amour,* Paris (1950).
BURGESS, E. and LOCKE, H., *The Family: From Institution to Companionship,* New York (1953).
CLEMENS, A., *Marriage and the Family. An Integrated Approach for Catholics,* Englewood Cliffs (1957).
DOUCY, L., "Gedanken zur Soziologie der Familie." *Vom Wesen und Geheimnis der Familie,* Salzburg (1953), pp. 90 ff.
FREYER, H., *Theorie des gegenwärtigen Zeitalters,* Stuttgart (1956).
HÄRING, B., *Ehe in dieser Zeit,* Salzburg (1960).

HILL, R., "A Critique of Contemporary Marriage and Family Research," *SF*, 33 (1955), pp. 268–77; "Sociology of Marriage and Family Behaviour 1945–1958," *CS*, 7 (1958).

HOFMANN, A., and KERSTEN, D., *Frauen zwischen Familie und Fabrik*, Munich (1958).

HOURDIN, G., "La famille et la civilisation moderne," *Famille d'Aujourd'hui* (1958), pp. 35–53.

KINSEY, A. C., *The Sexual Behavior of the Human Male*, Philadelphia (1948); *The Sexual Behavior of the Human Female*, Philadelphia (1953).

KÖNIG, R., *Materialien zur Soziologie der Familie*, Berne (1946); "Soziologie der Familie," ed. A. Gehlen and H. Schelsky, *Ein Lehr- und Handbuch zur modernen Gesellschaftskunde*, Düsseldorf and Cologne (1955²).

KWANT, R. C., *Het arbeidsbestel. Een studie over de geest van onze samenleving*, Utrecht (1959).

DE LESTAPIS, S., *Amour et Institution familiale*, Paris (1948).

MÖRSDORF, G., *Gestaltwandel des Frauenbildes und Frauenberufs in der Neuzeit*, Mainz (1958).

PICARD, M., *Die unerschütterliche Ehe*, Zürich (1952).

PRINGENT, R., *Renouveau des idées sur la famille*, Paris (1939).

DE ROUGEMONT, D., *Passion and Society*, London (1940).

SCHELSKY, H., *Wandlungen der deutschen Familie in der Gegenwart*, Stuttgart (1954²).

THOMAS, J., *The American Catholic Family*, Washington (1956).

VIERKANDT, A., *Gesellschaftslehre*, Stuttgart (1928²), esp. pp. 447 ff.

ZIMMERMANN, C., and FRAMPTON, N., *Family and Society*, New York (1935).

*PART I: MARRIAGE IN THE DIVINE REVELATION
OF THE OLD TESTAMENT*

BEER, G., *Die soziale und religiöse Stellung der Frau im israelitischen Altertum*, Tübingen (1919).

BENZINGER, J., *Hebräische Archäologie*, Leipzig (1927), pp. 115–21.

BURROWS, M., *The Basis of Israelite Marriage*, New Haven (1938).

COLE, W., *Sex and Love in the Bible*, New York (1959).

DRONCKERTS, K., *Het huwelijk in het Oude Testament*, Leiden (1958).

EPSTEIN, L., *Marriage Laws in the Bible and the Talmud,* Cambridge, Mass. (1942).

FRAZER, J., *Folklore in the Old Testament,* 3 pts., New York (1954).

GELIN, A., "Passage de la polygamie à la monogamie," *Mélanges Podechard,* Lyons (1945), pp. 135–46.

GRELOT, P., *Le couple humain dans l'Ecriture,* Paris (1961) (*LD* 31).

HORST, F., "Ehe," *RGG³,* pt. 2, cols. 316–18.

JENNY, H., "Le mariage dans la Bible," *MD,* 50 (1957), pp. 5–29.

KORNFELD, W., "Mariage," *DBS,* pt. 5 (1957), cols. 905–26.

DE KRUIJF, Th. C., *De Bijbel over de sexualiteit,* Roermond and Maaseik (1963).

LEIPOLDT, J., *Die Frau in der Antike und im Urchristentum,* Gütersloh (1953), pp. 49–78 ("due Jüdin").

NASH, A. S., "Die hebräische Familie," *Mensch, Geschlecht, Gesellschaft,* Paris and Frankfurt (1954).

MACE, D. C., *Hebrew Marriage,* London (1953).

NEHER, A., "Le symbolisme conjugal, expression de l'histoire dans l'Ancien Testament," *RHPR,* 34 (1954), 30–49.

NEUBAUER, J., *Beiträge zur Geschichte des biblischtalmudischen Eheschliessungsrechtes,* Leipzig (1919–20).

RENCKENS, H., *Israëls visie op het verleden,* Tielt and The Hague (1956).

STRACK, H., and BILLERBECK, P. (see list of abbreviations).

DE VAUX, OP, Roland, *Ancient Israel. Its Life and Institutions,* London (1961), pt. 1, pp. 26–9.

VOLLEBREGT, G., *The Bible on Marriage,* London (1965).

PART II: MARRIAGE IN THE MESSAGE OF THE NEW TESTAMENT

ALFRINK, B., "Paulus en de zin van het huwelijk," *NKS,* 40 (1940), 39–49.

BAUER, J., "Die Ehe bei Musonius und Paulus," *BL,* 23 (1955–6), pp. 8–13.

BARTH, K., *Church Dogmatics,* Edinburgh (1936–   ), esp. III, 4.

BONSIRVEN, J., *Le divorce dans le Nouveau Testament,* Paris and Douai (1948).

CAZELLES, H., "Marriage," *DBS,* pt. 5 (1957), cols. 926–35.

CHANSON, P., *Le mariage selon saint Paul,* Paris (1953).

DELLING, G., *Paulus' Stellung zu Frau und Ehe*, Stuttgart (1931).

DULAU, P., "The Pauline Privilege; Is it promulgated in the First Epistle to the Corinthians?" *CBQ*, 13 (1951), pp. 146–52.

DUPONT, J., *Mariage et divorce dans l'Evangile*, Bruges (1959).

GEYSER, A., "Paul, the Apostolic Decree and the Liberals in Corinth," *Studia Paulina* (in mem. J. de Zwaan), Haarlem (1953), pp. 124–38.

GOICHON, A., "La destinée de la femme selon l'Islam et Saint Paul," *NV*, 30 (1955), pp. 268–82.

GREEVEN, H., "Zu den Aussagen des N.T. über die Ehe," *ZEE*, 1 (1957), pp. 109–25.

GROSSOUW, W., "Een bijbelse theologie van het huwelijk," *TL*, 45 (1961), pp. 261–8; "Enkele bijbeltheologische opmerkingen over het huwelijk," *Jaarboek* 1961, *Werkgen. Kath. Theol. Ned.*, Hilversum (1963), pp. 63–78.

LEENHARDT, F., *La place de la femme dans l'Eglise d'après le Nouveau Testament*, Montpellier (1948); *Le mariage chrétien*, Neuchâtel and Paris (1946).

LÉON-DUFOUR, X., "Mariage et continence selon saint Paul," *A la rencontre de Dieu* (Mémorial A. Gelin), Le Puy (1961), pp. 319–30.

MENOUD, Ph. H., "Mariage et célibat selon saint Paul," *RTP*, 39 (1951), pp. 21–34.

MICHAELIS, W., "Ehe und Charisma bei Paulus," *ZST*, 5 (1928), pp. 426–52.

NEGWER, J., *Die Ehe und Familie in der Heiligen Schrift des Alten und Neuen Testamentes*, Leipzig (1956).

PREISKER, H., *Christentum und Ehe in den ersten drei Jahrhunderten*, Berlin (1927); "Ehe und Charisma bei Paulus," *ZST*, 6 (1929), pp. 91–5.

REICKE, B., "Neuzeitliche und neutestamentliche Auffassung von Liebe und Ehe," *NvT*, 1 (1956), pp. 21–34.

RINZEMA, J., *Huwelijk en echtscheiding in Bijbel en moderne samenleving*, Aalten (1961).

ROBILLIARD, J., "Le symbolisme du mariage selon saint Paul," *RSPT*, 21 (1932), pp. 242–7.

SCHNACKENBURG, P., *Die sittliche Botschaft des Neuen Testaments*, Munich (1954).

SCHROEDER, D., *Die Haustafeln des Neuen Testaments. Ihre Herkunft und ihr theologischer Sinn*, Hamburg (1959).

THURIAN, MAX, *Marriage and Celibacy*, Naperville, Ill. (1959).

Index of Biblical References

Old Testament

Genesis			Genesis (*cont.*)	
i.14ff.	24n.		viii.2	72
i.26	22n.		ix.7	73
i.27–28	12, 190n.		ix.9	73
i.28	22n.		x.1	73
ii.4	72		xi.10–32	73
ii.18–24	12		xi.10–12	75
ii.18	17, 25, 61, 167n.		xi.27	73
ii.20	24		xii.1–2	69, 72
ii.21	21		xiii.16	72
ii.22	17, 110		xv.2–6	74
ii.23	18, 112		xvi.2–4	90
ii.24	21, 22, 67, 89, 108,		xvi.4–5	90
	112, 115		xvi.10	85
iii.6	25n.		xvii.10–23	85
iii.12	25n.		xvii.10–11	24
iii.16	19, 25, 30, 182, 183		xix.8	66
iv.1	23, 66, 85		xix.30–38	25n.
iv.17	66		xx.12	90, 94
iv.19–22	89n.		xx.17–18	85
iv.25	66, 190n.		xxi.21	98
v.1	72, 190n.		xxii.1–18	74
v.1–32	73		xxii.8	74
v.1–3	23		xxii.14	74
v.1–2	12, 19		xxii.15–18	74
v.2	24, 190n.		xxiv.1–4	98
v.3–5	190n.		xxiv.4	97
v.3	22		xxiv.8	98
vi.9	73		xxiv.15	94
vii.11	72		xxiv.16	29n.

Genesis (*cont.*)

xxiv.58	98
xxiv.60	18, 23, 99*n.*
xxiv.67	29*n.*, 98*n.*, 100*n.*
xxv.19	73
xxv.30	100*n.*
xxvi.8–9	29*n.*, 87
xxvi.28–31	64
xxvi.34–5	98
xxvi.34	94
xxvi.35	98
xxvii.27–9	22
xxvii.46	98
xxviii.7	85*n.*
xxviii.8	94
xxviii.9	94
xxix.2*ff.*	99*n.*
xxix.12*ff.*	100*n.*
xxix.12	94
xxix.14	18*n.*
xxix.18	98
xxix.19	94, 98*n.*
xxix.20	29*n.*, 87
xxix.27–8	100
xxix.30–1	90
xxix.30	90
xxx.1	90
xxx.3*ff.*	90
xxx.4	100*n.*
xxx.9	100*n.*
xxx.23	85
xxxi.14	94
xxxiv.4	98
xxxiv.11	100*n.*
xxxiv.12	99
xxxiv.15–26	85
xxxvii.2	73
xxxvii.10	85
xxxvii.27	18*n.*
xxxviii.1–2	98
xxxviii.1–11	84
xxxviii.2	94, 100*n.*
xxxviii.13–28	90*n.*
xxxix.1–23	25*n.*
xli.45	94

Genesis (*cont.*)

xlvi.10	94
xlix.3–4	22
xlix.8	22

Exodus

ii.21	94, 100*n.*
xii.48	85
xiii.12	94
xix.10	94
xix.14	94
xx.2	14
xx.6	64
xxi.3	99
xxi.4	100*n.*
xxi.7–8	90*n.*
xxi.7	90
xxi.10	39, 99*n.*, 100*n.*
xxi.11	92*n.*
xxi.15	85*n.*
xxi.17	85*n.*
xxii.16	99
xxiii.23	90*n.*, 95
xxiv.7	64
xxiv.15–16	13
xxxiv.12–16	90*n.*, 95*n.*
xxxiv.16	100*n.*
xxxiv.23	85

Leviticus

xi.44	15*n.*, 83*n.*, 94*n.*
xv	89*n.*
xviii.1–5	84
xviii.6*ff.*	98*n.*
xviii.7	85*n.*
xviii.8	148
xix.2	15*n.*, 83*n.*, 94*n.*
xix.20	90*n.*
xx.20–21	85
xx.26	15*n.*, 83, 94*n.*
xxi.7	36

Numbers

v.11	33*n.*
vi.7	85*n.*
xii.1	94*n.*

Numbers (*cont.*)

xxi.9	90
xxv.3–8	13
xxvi.59	94
xxxi.17–18	66
xxxvi.1–12	94

Deuteronomy

iv.35	67
iv.37	65*n.*
iv.39	67
v.10	64
vi.4	65
vii.1–8	95
vii.2–9	64
vii.4	95
vii.6–11	95
vii.6–8	66*n.*, 67, 82
vii.6	15*n.*, 94*n.*
vii.7	65
vii.8	65*n.*, 66
vii.9	63
vii.12–13	83
vii.12	64
vii.13	64*n.*, 65
x.12–16	24
x.12–15	82
x.15	65*n.*
xiv.2	15*n.*, 95
xvii.17	21*n.*, 89
xx.5–7	92
xx.7	87*n.*
xxi.10–14	90, 95*n.*
xxi.15–17	89*n.*, 90*n.*, 91
xxi.18	85*n.*
xxii.2–5	91
xxii.22	99
xxii.23–7	99
xxii.23	90*n.*
xxii.29	90*n.*, 99*n.*
xxiv.1–4	92, 143
xxiv.1*ff.*	36
xxiv.1	92, 149, 152
xxiv.4	99

Deuteronomy (*cont.*)

xxiv.5	87
xxv.5–10	84, 87*n.*, 91*n.*
xxv.6	85
xxv.17–19	95
xxvii.16	85*n.*
xxviii.30	92
xxxii.6–15	82

Judges

i.12–13	97
iii.6	94*n.*
viii.30–31	89*n.*
ix.2	18*n.*
xi.23–24	95
xi.34–40	85
xiv.1–3	97
xiv.2	98
xiv.3	94, 98*n.*
xiv.11*ff.*	99*n.*
xiv.12*ff.*	100
xv.6	99
xvi.4–22	25*n.*
xix.2–10	92

Ruth

i–iv	94*n.*
i.15	95
iv.11	23, 85
iv.13	85

1 Samuel

i.2	89*n.*
i.5–13	85
i.5–18	67*n.*
i.5–6	85
i.5–8	87
i.6	90, 90*n.*
i.11	85
xviii.7–21	97
xviii.20	29*n.*, 65*n.*, 87
xviii.25	99
xx.14	65
xxvi.19	95

2 Samuel
i.26	87
iii.14	99
v.1	18n.
v.13	89
vi.23	85
vii.29	73
ix.3	65
xi.26	99
xii.24	65n.
xiii.2–15	29n.
xiii.2	87
xiii.13	90n.
xiii.25	87
xv.16	91
xix.12–13	18n.
xxii.51	64

1 Kings
v.12	65
vii.14	94n.
viii.23	64
xi.1–8	89
xi.4–8	91
xiv.24	13
xvii.24	95
xix.20	85n.

2 Kings
xi.4	65
xvii.26	95

2 Chronicles
xxiv.3	98

Ezra
ii.59–62	95
ix.1–10	95
ix.2	95
ix.8	95
ix.13	95
ix.14	95
ix.44	95

Nehemiah
i.5	64
vii.61–4	95
ix.32	64
xiii.23–30	95
xiii.23–9	95
xiii.30	95

Job
v.23	65
xxxi.15	24
xlii.12–16	85

Psalms
v.7	63, 64
xxiv.1	106
xxvii.10	85
xxxiii.20	19
xxxvi.5	63
xlv.	100
xlv.14–16	99n.
xlvi.5	19
xlvii.4	52n.
xlviii.9	63
l.5	69
lxxxvi.5	64
lxxxix	64
c	82
cvi.7–45	64
cix.14	85n.
cxiii.9	23
cxix.89–93	82
cxxvii.3–5	85
cxxvii.3	23
cxxviii.3	85, 90
cxxxix.14	15
cxliv.12	85
cxlv.8	64
cxlviii.5–6	82

Proverbs
i.8	85
ii.16–17	56
ii.17	63
iv.3	85

Proverbs (*cont.*)

v.	56
v.2–14	56
v.3	60
v.15–18	60n.
v.15–19	89, 93n.
v.15	56
v.18	56
v.19	60n.
v.20	56
vi.20	85
vi.31	60n.
vii.4–27	56
vii.17	60n.
vii.19	55
x.1	85
xii.4	89
xv.20	85
xvii.25	85
xviii.22	55, 89
xix.14	55, 89
xix.26	85
xxiii.22–5	85
xxx.11	85
xxx.17	85
xxx.18–19	21, 55
xxxi.10–31	55, 56, 58, 90
xxxi.10	55

Ecclesiastes

ix.9	90, 93n.

Song of Songs

ii.5	87
ii.9	60n.
iv.5	60n.
iv.11	60n.
iv.12	30, 60n.
iv.14	60n.
iv.15	60n.
v.8	87
vii.11	30
viii.6–7	21, 30
viii.7	60n.
viii.8–10	30

Song of Songs (*cont.*)

viii.14	60n.

Isaiah

i.21–6	52n.
iv.1	85
v.1	52n.
xxii.11	82
xl–lv	49
xliii.7	24
xliv.21	82
xlvii.8–9	85
xlix.7	63
xlix.15	65
xlix.20–1	79
l.1	49, 50, 52, 52n., 92
liv	51
liv.1	79
liv.1–3	50
liv.3	51
liv.4	50
liv.5	50
liv.6–8	49–50
liv.6–7	52n.
liv.10	65
lv.3	64
lvi	88
lviii.7	18n.
lx.15	90n.
lxii.5	52n.
lxiii.7	63, 64

Jeremiah

i.5	24
ii.2ff.	67n.
ii.2	77
ii.18	43
ii.20	13, 43
ii.34	43
iii	43
iii.1–2	13
iii.1	44, 49, 65n.
iii.7–8	44, 49
iii.8	92
iii.12	63

Jeremiah (*cont.*)

iii.12–13	44
iii.20	44
v.24	24*n.*
viii.7	82
xiii.27	13
xvi	130
xvi.19	100
xvi.20–1	23
xviii.14	82
xxvii.2	35*n.*
xxvii.5	82
xxviii.10	35*n.*
xxxi.2	44
xxxi.3*f.*	44
xxxi.22	44
xxxi.35–6	24*n.*
xxxi.35	82
xxxii.18	64
xxxiii.25	24*n.*, 82
xliii.5	63
xliv.19	26

Ezekiel

xiv.20–21	23
xv	45
xvi	45, 113
xvi.4–5	45, 82
xvi.4	46
xvi.6–7	45
xvi.7	45
xvi.8–14	45
xvi.8	45, 46, 63
xvi.15–34	46
xvi.20	48
xvi.20–21	23, 23*n.*, 47
xvi.35–43	63*n.*
xvi.38–42	63
xvi.40	46
xvi.59	66
xvi.60	46
xxii.10–11	90*n.*
xxiii	45, 46, 48, 79
xxiii.3	77
xxiii.8	77

Ezekiel (*cont.*)

xxiii.19	77
xxiii.21	77
xxiii.24–5	63*n.*
xxiii.25	63
xxiii.48–9	48

Hosea

i–iii	34
i–iv	43
i.1–9	36
i.2	37
i.10	37
ii.2–13	38
ii.2	38
ii.3	39
ii.4	38, 74
ii.4–17	36
ii.5	38
ii.6	38, 79
ii.7–15	39
ii.7	38, 79
ii.8	38
ii.12	39
ii.13	39
ii.14–5	39
ii.16	37, 39
ii.16–7	38
ii.16–23	39
ii.17	77
ii.18	99
ii.18–25	36
ii.18*ff.*	63*n.*
ii.19–20	39, 99
ii.20	66
ii.23	39, 40
iii.1–5	37, 40
iii.1	41
iii.2–4	41
iii.2	90, 99*n.*
iv.1	66
iv.6	66
iv.13*f.*	43
v.8–11	35
vi.3	66

Hosea (*cont.*)
vi.6	66
viii.4	37
viii.14	82
ix.1	43
ix.11–14	85
xi.1	65*n.*
xi.1–11	41
xi.12	63
xii.9	37
xiii.4	37, 66
xiii.9	37
xiv.1	37
xiv.4	41, 65*n.*

Joel
ii.13	63

Amos
ix.7	82

Micah
vii.18	63

Malachi
i.2	65*n.*
ii.10–16	65, 93*n.*, 95*n.*
ii.13–16	90*n.*
ii.14–16	20*n.*, 23, 66
ii.14	63
ii.15–16	96, 114
ii.15	95*n.*
ii.16	93*n.*

Apocrypha

Tobit (RSV)
iv.12	98*n.*
vii.12–13	98*n.*
vii.12	90*n.*
vii.15	100*n.*
vii.16	99*n.*
viii.6	60
viii.7	60, 90
ix.6*ff.*	100*n.*

Tobit (Douai)
vi.14	98*n.*
vi.16–22	61
vii.15–16	62
viii.4	61
viii.5	60, 61
viii.19	60
viii.24	99*n.*

Wisdom of Solomon
iii.10–iv.6	59
iii.13–15	88
iii.13*f.*	59
iv.1–2	88*n*
iv.1	59

Wisdom of Solomon (*cont.*)
iv.3	59
viii.1	59
viii.9	59
viii.16	59

Sirach
vii	16
vii.19	56
vii.28	92*n.*
ix.3–9	56
ix.8	29, 56
xvi.1–3	88
xxiii.18–27	56
xxv.1	55
xxv.2	xxx
xxv.8	55–6
xxv.13	58
xxv.16	58
xxv.19	58
xxv.24	58
xxv.25–6	92
xxv.28	56
xxv.36	92*n.*
xxvi.1–4	56, 90

Sirach (*cont.*)

xxvi.1	55
xxvi.3	55
xxvi.6	58
xxvi.13	55
xxvi.14	55
xxvi.15	55
xxvi.16	55
xxxvi.22	55
xxxvi.24	55
xxxvi.24–6	19
xxxvi.25	55

Sirach (*cont.*)

xlii.9	92*n*.
xlii.9f.	59
xlii.13	58
xlii.14	58

1 Maccabees

ix.39	99*n*.

2 Maccabees

iii.19	99*n*.
vii.22–3	85

New Testament

Matthew

i.1	73
i.19	93
v.27	154
v.31	143
v.32	144, 147, 149, 150, 151, 152, 154
viii.14*ff*.	199
ix.15	109*n*.
x.37	123
xi.31–2	155
xii.25	197
xv.31	106
xvi.25	122
xix.3	143
xix.3–9	120
xix.7	143
xix.1–8	142, 150
xix.9	143, 144, 147, 149, 150, 151, 154
xix.8	66
xix.10–12	122, 153
xix.12	88, 107, 120, 121, 122
xix.15	99*n*.
xix.29	123*n*.
xxii.2–14	108*n*.
xxii.20	123, 124
xxii.32	106

Matthew (*cont.*)

xxv.1–13	99*n*.
xxv.1–12	108*n*.

Mark

ii.19	108*n*.
ii.19	109*n*.
viii.35	122
x.1–12	142
x.2–12	107
x.11–12	142, 147
x.28–9	122
x.29	123*n*.
xii.25	124
xii.26	106

Luke

i.68	106
v.34–5	109*n*.
vii.36–50	155
viii.1–3	199
ix.24	122*n*.
xii.35–8	99*n*.
xii.35–6	109*n*.
xiii.10–17	199
xiv.8	108*n*.
xiv.16–24	108*n*.
xiv.20	123
xiv.26	123
xvi.18	142, 147

Luke (*cont.*)

  xx.34–6   124
  xx.37   106

John

  i.12–13   124
  ii.1–11   108
  ii.1–2   108
  iii.28–9   99*n.*
  iii.29   109*n.*, 110
  iii.39   110
  iv.7–11   199
  iv.27   199
  viii.3–9   155
  viii.11   155
  viii.41   202
  xix.34–7   109

Acts

  i.14   199
  i.26   199
  ii.17–18   199
  iii.13   106
  v.30   106
  vii.32   106
  vii.45   106
  xiii.17*ff.*   106
  xiv.14   106
  xv.1–12   149*n.*
  xv.13–39   149*n.*
  xv.20–29   148
  xv.28   148
  xviii.26   200
  xx.28   113
  xxi.9   199
  xxi.25   148

Romans

  i.24–7   202
  iv.25   113
  v.8   118
  v.9   118
  v.14   114
  vii.2   192*n.*
  vii.2–4   154

Romans (*cont.*)

  xii.2   136
  xv.6   106
  xvi.1   199
  xvi.6   199
  xvi.12   199
  xvi.15   199

1 Corinthians

  i.11   199
  v.1   148
  vi.9   202
  vi.12*ff.*   202
  vi.12–16   203
  vi.12–20   202, 203
  vii   130, 131, 132, 133, 204
  vii.1   121*n.*, 126
  vii.1–40   121*n.*
  vii.2   126, 127, 129
  vii.3   xxiv*n.*, 126, 129
  vii.3–4   198
  vii.3–5   127, 128
  vii.4–5   137
  vii.5   126, 127, 129
  vii.5b–6   126
  vii.6*ff.*   127
  vii.7   139, 142
  vii.7–8   127, 128, 129, 138
  vii.8   128, 133
  vii.9   127, 133
  vii.10   121, 128
  vii.10–11   126, 142, 146, 153, 154, 155, 157
  vii.12   198
  vii.12–16   128, 155, 156, 161, 166, 167
  vii.15   159
  vii.17   134
  vii.18   134
  vii.20   134
  vii.21–2   134
  vii.22   134*n.*
  vii.25*ff.*   121, 126, 128
  vii.25–6   130

1 Corinthians (*cont.*)

vii.25–8	128
vii.26	125*n.*, 127
vii.26*ff.*	121
vii.27–8a	121
vii.28	128
vii.28b	121
vii.29	124, 128, 129
vii.29–31	129
vii.31	124
vii.32–3	122
vii.33	127
vii.34	122
vii.35	122, 128
vii.36	127
vii.37	128, 133
vii.38	128, 133
vii.38–40	121
vii.39	128, 133, 135, 154
vii.39–40	128
vii.40	127
viii.1	126
ix.5	138
x.25–6	106
x.31	106
xi	127, 178, 189, 190, 195
xi.2	181
xi.3	176, 178, 181, 189, 193, 199*n.*
xi.3–16	186
xi.5	199
xi.6	182
xi.7	178, 192
xi.7–9	190
xi.7–10	182
xi.8–9	180, 198
xi.9	182
xi.10	182
xi.11–12	198
xi.14–15	183
xi.16	178, 183
xi.34	199
xii	139
xii.1	126

1 Corinthians (*cont.*)

xii.12–18	185
xii.12–31	195
xiv.26	185
xiv.33–5	181
xiv.34	176, 199
xiv.40	185
xvi.1	126

2 Corinthians

i.3	106
v.17	137, 197
vi.16	106, 171
xi.2–3	108*n.*
xi.2	110
xi.31	106

Galatians

i.4	113
ii.20	113
iii.7	74
iii.16	72, 73
iii.26–28	124, 197
iv.22–8	75
iv.27	51
vi.15	137

Ephesians

i.3	106
i.17	106
i.23	114
ii.16	114
iii.9	106
iv.6	106
iv.12–16	114
v	130, 131, 133
v.2	113, 115
v.21	118, 178
v.21–2	177
v.21–33	111, 118
v.22	135, 177
v.22*ff.*	177, 181
v.22–3	177, 189, 117, 135
v.22–4	195
v.22–31	114

Ephesians (*cont.*)

v.22–32	177, 191, 203
v.22–33	108, 110, 115, 173, 204
v.23	20, 114, 176, 192, 192*n.*
v.24	178
v.25	113, 115, 137, 198
v.25–7	113
v.25–32	186
v.25–33	159, 186
v.26	115
v.27	46, 115
v.28	20, 67, 116
v.29	114
v.29–31	115
v.30	114
v.31*ff.*	114
v.31–2	116, 117
v.32	111, 112, 186
v.33	112, 113, 115, 186
vi.1–9	118
vi.6–8	133*n.*

Philippians

iv.2	199

Colossians

iii.18	135, 171, 181, 193
iii.18–iv.1	118, 173
iii.19	137
iii.20–21	189*n.*
iii.20	135
iii.24	134*n.*
iv.9	138
iv.15	199

1 Thessalonians

iv.1–8	129, 131
iv.3–6	201
iv.4–5	202
iv.8	202

1 Timothy

ii.6	113

1 Timothy (*cont.*)

ii.9–10	184, 185
ii.11–15	187
ii.12	187
ii.13	180, 191
ii.14	180
iii.2	205*n.*
iii.12	205*n.*
iv.3–5	201
iv.4	105
iv.7	187
v.9	200, 205
v.14	205

2 Timothy

iii.6	187

Titus

i.6	205*n.*
ii.5	177
ii.11–14	113

Hebrews

i.1	106
viii.9	106
xi.1–40	106
xi.16	106
xiii.4	108, 202

1 Peter

ii.18–iii.7	118, 173
iii.1–7	188
iii.1	100, 177
iii.3–4	184
iii.7	199

2 Peter

iii.8–9	132

Jude

7	202

Philemon

16	138

Revelation

xviii.23	108n.
xix.7–9	108n.
xxi.1–22	108
xxi.1	108

Revelation (*cont.*)

xxi.2	108n.
xxi.9	108n.
xxii.17	108n.
xxi	108
xxii.4	108

VOLUME II

Marriage in the History
of the Church

Abbreviations

AAS	*Acta Apostolicae Sedis*
AER	*The American Ecclesiastical Review*
AQOK	*Die ältesten Quellen des orientalischen Kirchenrechts,* ed. H. Achelis and J. Flemming, Leipzig (1891, 1904)
ASS	*Acta Sanctae Sedis,* Rome (1865–)
Bijd	*Bijdragen*
CCOF	*Codificazione Canonica Orientale: Fonti,* Vatican City (1930–)
CIC	*Corpus Iuris Canonici*
COH	*Het christelijk Oosten en Hereniging*
Comp	Gregory IX, *Compilatio Decretalium*
CSEL	*Corpus Scriptorum Ecclesiasticorum Latinorum,* Vienna (1866–)
CT	*Concilium Tridentinum: Diariorum, Actorum, Epistularum, Tractatuum nova Collection,* ed. Soc. Goerresiana, Freiburg (1901–)
DB	H. Denzinger, *Enchiridion Symbolorum, Definitionum, et Declarationum de Rebus Fidei et Morum,* Freiburg; ed. C. Bannwart, S.J. (1908–$13^{10\text{-}12}$) and others (1921–$57^{13\text{-}31}$)
DCA	*Didascalia et Constitutiones Apostolorum,* F. X. Funk, Paderborn, 2 parts (1906)
DPI	*Decretales ps.–Isidorianae et Capitula Angilramni,* P. Hinschius, Leipzig (1863)
DS	H. Denzinger, *Enchiridion Symbolorum.* Freiburg; ed. A. Schönmetzer, S.J., (1962^{32})

DTC	*Dictionnaire de Théologie Catholique*, Paris (1903–)
EL	*Ephemerides Liturgicae*
ETL	*Ephemerides Theologicae Lovanienses*
FRBE	K. Ritzer, *Formen, Riten und religiöses Brauchtum der Eheschiessung in den christlichen Kirchen des Ersten Jahrtausends* (Liturgiegeschichtliche Quellen und Forschungen, 38), Münster (1962)
FS	*Franziskanische Studien*
GCS	*Die griechischen christlichen Schriftsteller der ersten drei Jahrhunderte*, Leipzig–Berlin (1897–)
HCDO	C. J. Hefele and H. Leclercq, *Histoire des conciles d'après les documents originaux*, Paris (1907–)
IEG	J. B. Pitra, *Iuris Ecclesiastici Graecorum Historia et Monumenta*, 2 pts., Rome (1864–8)
IGR	J. Zepos and P. Zepos, *Ius graeco-romanum*, 3 pts., Athens (1931–)
Irn	*Irénikon*
JTS	*Journal of Theological Studies*
MBG	*Münsterische Beiträge zur Geschichtsforschung*
MD	*La Maison-Dieu*
MGH	*Monumenta Germaniae Historica*, Hanover–Berlin (1826–)
–AA	*Auctores Antiquissimi*
–C	*Capitularia*
–E	*Epistulae*
–LC	*Leges III, Concilia*
–SRM	*Scriptores Rerum Merovingicarum*
MS	*Medieval Studies*
M–SC	J. D. Mansi, *Sacrorum Conciliorum Nova et Amplissima Collectio*, 60 pts., Florence-Venice-Paris (1759–)
MSR	*Mélanges de science religieuse* (Lille)
MTZ	*Münchener theologische Zeitschrift*
NAADG	*Neues Archiv fur der Gesellschaft ältere deutsche Geschichtskunde*
OS	*L'Orient Syrien*
PG	J. P. Migne, *Patrologia Graeca*, Paris (1857–66)
PL	J. P. Migne, *Patrologia Latina*, Paris (1844–64)

PLSL	A. Altaner, *Patrologie: Leben, Schriften und Lehre der Kirchenväter*, Freiburg (1950²)
PW–RKA	*Paulys Realenzyklopädie der klassischen Altertumswissenschaften*, ed. V. G. Wissowa and W. Kroll, Stuttgart (1893–)
QLP	*Questions liturgiques et paroissiales*
RHE	*Revue d'Histoire Ecclésiastique*
REDC	*Revista Española de Derecho Canonica*
RSR	*Recherches de science religieuse*
RTAM	*Recherches de théologie ancienne et médiévale*
SCG	St. Thomas Aquinas, *Summa Contra Gentiles*
Sck	*Scholastik*
SG	L. C. Mohlberg, *Sacramentarium Gelasianum* (Rerum Ecclesiasticarum Documenta), Rome (1960)
DSDM	H. Singer, *Die Summa Decretorum des Magister Rufinus*, Paderborn (1902)
ST	St. Thomas Aquinas, *Summa Theologiae*
StG	*Studia Gratiana*
TLL	*Thesaurus linguae latinae*
VS–S	*La Vie Spirituelle* (Supplément)
WW	*Wissenschaft und Weischeit*
ZKT	*Zeitschrift für katholische Theologie*
ZSSR	*Zeitschrift der Savigny-Stiftung für Rechtgeschichte*

Introduction

It is important here, at the beginning of the second volume of this work, to bear in mind that our study will be principally concerned with the way in which marriage, as a secular reality and as a contract concluded and celebrated civilly and by the family, came within the sphere of the church; with the eventual division that occurred between marriage in the church and civil marriage; and with the inevitable consequences of this division. At the same time an attempt will be made to trace the path of the growing Christian awareness that this secular reality was a sacrament. With the needs of theology and the claims of ecumenism in mind, I shall also give my attention to the problem of the meaning of "church marriage"—in the purely dogmatic sense, and in the concrete canonical sense—in the belief that a different, but nonetheless dogmatically justified, canonical way out of the present dilemma may emerge from this analysis. At the same time it will also become clear that the civil dimension, as an intrinsic element of secular marriage, simultaneously enters the sacramentalism of marriage.

There remains the question of a second analysis of marriage in the course of the history of the church—an analysis, in other words, of the human appreciation of sexuality and marriage and of the church's appraisal of these in the patristic, scholastic, and post-Tridentine periods, and in modern society, together with the historical background to the problem of birth control. This I propose to undertake in a later part of this work. Its publication in separate volumes is, of course, partly responsible for this division; but, on the other hand, I also believe that this second historical analysis is organically closer to the anthropological analysis of the human and Christian ethos of marriage attempted later on, and thus better suited to precede it.

1

The Formation of Church Marriage

In the first Christian centuries, pagan converts to Christianity were for the most part already married when they became Christians. Initially, then, marriage posed no special problems for the church. The marriages of these pagan converts were brought within the Christian sphere of life by baptism. In the case of already baptized Christians who wished to marry, the idea of celebrating these marriages with a separate church ceremony, distinct from the normal civil marriage celebrated in the family or the immediate social circle, did not at first come to mind. Christians did much the same as their non-Christian fellows, the Greeks and the Romans, and later the Germanic, Frankish, Celtic, and other peoples. The ceremonies and popular customs associated with marriage in contemporary society also formed the marriage ceremonies for baptized Christians, and of course many of these customs were eventually brought within the church's orbit. It will be necessary to make at least a general survey of the social customs of each period in the environment of Christianity before we can trace this development.

THE ENVIRONMENT OF THE FIRST FOUR CENTURIES

1. It is important to distinguish clearly between three periods when considering the Roman view of marriage.[1]

[1] See Bibliography, general.

(*a*) According to the views of ancient, primitive peoples, the solemnisation of marriage was a "sacral" event. In the case of both the Greeks and the Romans, marriage was not originally based on interpersonal relationships. Nor was it based directly on the procreative act, leading to the foundation of a family, or on marital and paternal authority, but on the "religion of the hearth," the *focus patruus*. The hearth was the symbol of the deceased ancestors, the household gods—the *manes, lares,* and *penates*. Thus each family had its own household liturgy with its own rites, prayers, hymns, and sacrifices. The domestic hearth was never allowed to go out; it was the providence of this particular family, and no other. Its priest was the *paterfamilias* of the domestic hearth. The care of the household gods was passed on from father to son. The continued existence of the household religion was thus assured by procreation. A barren marriage meant that there was a danger of the domestic religion becoming extinct; as a result, barrenness dissolved marriage. The ancient family was thus, by definition, a religious community—an *epistion* (var. *ephestion*), standing round the hearth, as the Greeks said, assembled round the sacred household fire, the inextinguishable symbol of the household gods.

For a woman, then, marriage meant a transference from one religion to another—from the religion of her father's household to that of her bridegroom's, with its different rites, prayers, and sacrifices. This transference, or conversion, could only be accomplished by means of a religious consecration and initiation. The bride had to be, so to speak, "excardinated" from her own paternal household religion, and incardinated into the new religion of her bridegroom's household. The Roman—and also the Greek —wedding consequently consisted of three essential acts. The first took place in the house of the bride's father. This was the *enguēsis* (or *ekdosis*) or *traditio puellae*, the handing over of the bride. The final ceremony, the *telos*, took place in the bridegroom's house. Between these two ceremonies occurred the *pompē* or *domum-ductio,* the solemn taking of the bride to the house of her bridegroom.

The bride's father made an offering in his own house to the household gods. Then he solemnly agreed to "hand over" his daughter to the *manus* of the bridegroom—to his authority as *paterfamilias.* This *ekdosis,* the giving away or handing over of the bride, was a religious ceremony of excardination and an essential element in the marriage, since the girl had not been received into her parents' house simply because her father had begotten her, but by virtue of the religious ceremony in which she had been accepted by her father after her birth and initiated into the household religion. The first element in the marriage, the *sponsio,* the giving away or handing over of the bride by her father, was thus both a religious and a legal act. This was followed by the taking of the bride to the bridegroom's house. In the procession, the bride, wearing a veil and a garland and arrayed in a white ceremonial garment, was seated in a carriage, while wedding hymns were sung. On arriving at the bridegroom's house, she was not allowed to approach the religion of the new household of her own accord, since this was always kept secret. After a simulated abduction by force, she was carried by the bridegroom over the threshold of his house, which she herself was not permitted to touch. It was at this point that the religious ceremony of marriage took place, the incardination into the new household religion.

The bride was led to the household altar, the sacred hearth, where she was sprinkled with lustral water and permitted to touch the sacred fire. She was received "into the community of water and fire." Prayers were said or offerings were made. Finally, the ceremony which gave its name to the entire sacral marriage service took place, the *confarreatio.* The bride and the bridegroom partook of the wedding-cake, the *far* or *panis farreus,* a loaf made of flour which was the "very holy pledge of the marriage." By this act the bride and groom entered into religious communion with each other through communion with the house-

hold gods. The marriage contract thus consisted of a religious—
and thus legally valid—ceremony: the *traditio puellae*, the *domumductio*, and the *confarreatio*. These ceremonies were more or
less parallel both in the case of the ancient Greeks and in the
case of the Romans.

Marriage was therefore originally a religious act, an initiation
of the woman into a different religion. To solemnise a marriage
was to "offer" it (*thuein gamon*). It was therefore a liturgical
service, an offering, not originally to the great gods of Olympus
or the Capitol, but to the household gods of the family (*lares* and
penates) or family ancestors (*manes*). (At a later stage, the ceremony was divided into a domestic liturgy and a public rite in
the temple to the great gods.) Marriage was therefore a living
community *in humanis* and *in divinis*: "Uxor socia humanae rei
atque divinae," "nuptiae sunt divini iuris et humani communicatio." (*Digesta*, xxiii, 2; *Codex Justiniani*, ix, 32, 4.) This structure of marriage would appear, despite certain differences in detail, to have been the original basic pattern of the marriage
contract in Indo-European society.

It was the principle of the household religion which provided
the basis for the monogamous and essentially indissoluble character of marriage. As the Greeks and Romans gradually lost sight
of this principle, the idea of the indissolubility of marriage became less potent. The "aim" or deeper meaning of marriage was
originally not seen in sexual gratification or in interpersonal relationship, but, as the later sacramental formula of the marriage
charter expressed it, "in order to bring forth little children," as
already in Demosthenes (*Kata Neairas*, 122). But this must be
understood above all in the religious sense, that is, in the light of
the need to perpetuate the family's religion by means of human
descendants, for it was the husband and father who was the real
"priest" of the household—a son was "the saviour of the paternal
hearth" (Aeschylus, *Khoëphoroi*, 264). A birth was in itself only
a material fact; the real formal birth in the family was the religious and legal act by which the father acknowledged the son,

or refused to acknowledge him and repudiated him. This acceptance took place on the ninth or tenth day following the birth, when the infant was ritually initiated into the household religion. "Relationship," then, meant sharing in the community of the same household gods (Plato, *Nomoi*, 5).

The authority exercised by the father, or *paterfamilias*, over the wife, children, slaves, and all the family's possessions was originally unlimited in Greek and Roman society. But the father's authority was always dependent on the ultimate authority of the household gods—the *lar* was the real *paterfamilias* (Plautus, *Mercator*, 5.1.5). Religious conviction was the factor which governed everything in the home. On the basis of her initiation, the wife was under her husband's control. Originally it was only the religious rite of the *confarreatio* which gave the husband this right over his wife, so that he had her "in his hand." Even when other forms of marriage came into use (see below) this form of marriage still remained valid, but the wife was no longer regarded as being under her husband's "hand." This "sacral" marriage made the man "father," *paterfamilias*, even if he had no children. In our modern sense of the word, "father" means the founder of a family, the *genitor*. The *paterfamilias*, however, was anyone who was not dependent upon any other person and who had authority over a family and a domain—he was therefore also the *pater*, the father, of his slaves. Although they were not equal as far as authority was concerned, husband and wife enjoyed an equal dignity. Woman was far more "emancipated" in Greco-Roman society than, for example, in Semitic society. The wife stood beside her husband as co-priestess. The husband's priesthood in fact ceased when his wife died. In obedience to her husband, the wife was the mistress of the house. All ethics were therefore fundamentally the enclosed and private ethics of the family. But the family was the nursery bed, the fertile soil, in which the ethics of society as a whole were raised. New confederations came into being—*curiae*, or *phratriai*, *gentes*, tribes, and finally cities and *civitates*. In this way, the ethics of the family spread and gradually gained a wider influence.

When men eventually came to realise that there was one God who held heaven and earth and all *gentes, civitates,* and *familiae* in his hand, and transcended all the household, tribal, and state gods, the "ethics of the family" became world-wide. Love, which had initially been restricted to the family circle, within the sphere of influence of the household gods of the individual family —had been, in fact, a sort of "group egoism"—became a love which embraced the whole of mankind. The family, the origin of the whole of society, was originally also the source of a morality which sought to find its own distinctive and authentic meaning.

Initially, a marriage contracted by mutual agreement (*consensus*) and without any other formalities was unheard of in a religious society of this kind. Any child born of a marriage brought about purely by mutual consent was simply called a bastard—such a child was "not born by the hearth" (Demosthenes, *Pros Makartaton,* 51). In this society, adultery was the greatest of sins, because it endangered the household religion and could result in the gradual withering away of this religion. It might cause members of the family to neglect the worship of their ancestors, almost unconsciously, and thus leave them "out in the cold."

(*b*) From the seventh to the fifth centuries B.C. a revolution slowly but surely took place in Greek and Roman society. This was accompanied by a "secularisation," a process during which social institutions were gradually dissociated from their original religious foundations. The *turannis* came into being—a form of authority not based on religious convictions, but on the authority of a mere man over his fellow-men. This of course meant that the priesthood was also divested of its authority. Authority was henceforth based on the will of the people and their general welfare was safeguarded by legislation, and no longer by "sacral" traditions. This secularisation of social institutions was almost automatically accompanied by a spread of "atheism"; although the earlier household religion continued to exist as a formal institution, it was no longer a potent religious force. The codex of the "twelve tables" is an early, tentative example of the will of the people. The inviolable authority of the father of the family was preserved, but already certain restrictions were being introduced.

What is more, the "sacral" form of marriage, contracted by the ceremony of *confarreatio*, was no longer practised among the people; the new form of marriage was based on the inclination of the intending partners and concluded by means of their mutual consent. Initially, patricians regarded this kind of marriage as worthless and denied that the husband had his wife "in his hand" on a basis of such a marriage. In their opinion, only a religious rite was able to confer full authority in marriage upon the husband. In the long run, however, the marriage of mutual consent gained the same legal status as the older religious marriage, in that the husband's matrimonial authority was brought about by means of *coemptio* (a fictitious purchase) or by means of *usus* (that is, by the wife's living with her husband for at least a year after their mutual agreement to marry). This gave the marriage of mutual consent in effect the same standing—with regard to the husband's authority—as the ancient rite of *confarreatio*, though it is important to note that marriage by *emptio* or *usus* was not a new manner of marrying, but the manner in which the husband acquired his legal authority over his wife in a marriage by consent, but without the ceremony of *confarreatio*.

By praetorian legislation this social revolution eventually gained a distinctive and new form, which meant complete secularisation of marriage and the family. Philosophers began to ponder the real ontological significance of religiosity. Gradually the vague notion of one single supreme Being developed, and the household gods and the gods of the city and the state fell into ill-repute, although this form of religiosity survived as a "custom" without any inner inspiration. Religious traditions no longer supplied the ethical standard for society—this was provided by the philosophers who speculated about "human nature." "Common human nature," subjected to the scrutiny of philosophy and the human conscience, took the place of the priestly traditions of the family.

The inevitable result of this was that the household and national gods declined in prestige. Morality was divorced from religion. The "natural law" became the chief subject for human investigation. The idea gained ground that all men were brothers— that they were citizens of the world, and not restricted to individual clans and families or limited to separate cities and states. Man's humanity was discovered (Zeno) and his personal existence. This growth towards the secularisation of marriage was, moreover, completed in the Greco-Roman period under the influence of Christianity, which declared itself to be a religion that was "not of this world."

But, before going more deeply into this, we must first consider briefly the subject of marriage at the very beginning of the Christian era in imperial Rome.

(*c*) Among the Romans at the time of the Empire the betrothal was arranged by the fathers of each family (the *stipulatio*). This was sometimes done while the children were still very young. This betrothal was a contract without any form of law. Contacts with the East, however, had led to the adoption in the West of the custom of the *arrha* in betrothals. This entailed the giving of a pledge, or *arrha*, which often took the form of an engagement ring. Tertullian was the first to give evidence of this custom in the West (*Apol.* 6, 4–6 [*PL*, 1, 302–4]).[2]

The marriage itself was accompanied by various ceremonies. The form of marriage to which I have referred in the foregoing section, involving the ceremony of the *confarreatio*, and the later custom of *coemptio* or *usus* as a condition of matrimonial authority in the case of marriages by mutual consent and without religious rites, both disappeared in imperial Rome. Marriages were

---

[2] In Africa, this was probably a survival from the ancient Phoenician civilisation.

concluded at this time without any form of law, and merely by mutual consent, though in traditional circles this was supplemented by the ancient religious customs. The two concrete elements necessary to make the marriage valid were the *consensus*, or mutual consent of both partners, and the *domum-ductio*, or leading of the wife to her husband's house. The *domum-ductio* and the community of the partners, the *individua vitae consuetudo*, together formed, at least for those who were not slaves, a *matrimonium iustum*, a valid and lawful marriage. They gave, in other words, concrete form to the mutual consent to marry. In the Christian era, stated Justinian finally, the mutual consent of both partners was sufficient for a valid marriage without any further formalities: *nuptias non concubitus, sed consensus facit;* in other words, marriage was not brought about by *usus*, or actual sexual intercourse, but by the partner's mutual consent (*Digesta* xxxv, 1, 15).

This classic Roman constitutional law of marriage should not, however, be understood in the full sense which it was to acquire in canon law. According to ecclesiastical law, the partners' mutual consent to marry binds them for life. According to this Roman law, however, their mutual consent simply created a condition which lasted only as long as the partners persevered in this mutual agreement. The *Codex Theodosianus* (Lib. iii, tit. 7, lex 3 [Krüger, Berlin, 1923, fasc. 1, p. 106])[3] laid down that every marriage concluded by mutual consent of the partners in the presence of several friends as witnesses was valid; all further secular and religious practices surrounding it were expressly placed outside the framework of the legal validity of marriage. What clearly emerges from this legislation is that, however firmly established the marriage of mutual consent may have been by this time, the religious ceremonies were still commonly practised, even though their essential meaning may have been forgotten. At the same time it is also clear that both priestly au-

[3] The date of this particular marriage law is 428.

thority and temporal power were excluded from the essential act of marriage, which was a strictly personal and family affair.[4]

Various customs, now frequently of a superstitious nature, continued to surround the wedding feast itself. On the eve of the feast the bride was dressed in white, as a Vestal virgin, with a fiery red veil (the *flammeum*) and a garland of flowers. On the morning of the feast the auguries were consulted and, if they were favourable, the partners' consent to marry each other was heard: "Did she (he) wish to become a mother (father)?"[5] This was followed by the *iunctio dexterarum*, the joining of the bride's and the bridegroom's right hands. Next, either at home or in the temple, an animal was sacrificed, while the bride and bridegroom sat on two seats which were bound together and covered by a sheepskin. Then the priest pronounced a prayer over the couple who passed round the altar.

After a symbolic abduction of the bride, the solemn entry into the bridegroom's house took place. On her arrival at the new dwelling, the bride smeared the doorposts with oil and fat and decorated the doors. She was lifted over the threshold and received by her husband "into the community of fire and water." On the following day the young wife made an offering to the *lares* and *penates* and received the "morning gift" from her husband. During the period of the Roman emperors the marriage document, the *tabulae nuptiales*, came into use for the first time. It was this document which stated that marriage was undertaken "in order to bring forth children." This usage came from the East, quite possibly via the Phoenician civilisation in Africa.[6]

(*d*) Although there was a certain distaste for marriage in Greece from the sixth century onwards,[7] it was nonetheless regarded as a civil and religious duty, especially for the perpetua-

---

[4] See Esmein and Génestal, *Le mariage en droit canonique*, pt. 1, p. 4.

[5] "An vellet sibi mater (aut: pater) familias esse?" (Cicero, *Topica*, 14).

[6] This is first mentioned by Suetonius, *De viris illustribus*, 5. 29; see also Tertullian, *Ad uxorem*, 2, 3 (PL, 1, 1292–3); *De virginibus velandis*, 12, 1 (PL, 2, 106); Augustine, *Sermo* 9, 11, 18 (PL, 38, 88); *Sermo* 51, 13, 22 (PL, 38, 345).

[7] See Bibliography, 1.

tion of descendants. In the classical period, the courtship of the bride was followed by betrothal. Among the citizens of Athens, marriage itself took the form of an agreement or contract (*enguēsis*) between the bride's "lord" or "master" and the bridegroom. This lord or master gave the dowry in the presence of witnesses. The contract included both the *ekdosis,* the handing over of the bride, and the *gamos,* the wedding feast, or feast of the inception of married life. Although, according to Attic law, this contract was purely a legal matter, the marriage feast was celebrated as a religious event. Before the feast the bride and bridegroom went in procession to a place to which water from sacred wells or springs had been taken for the "marriage bath" of the bride and bridegroom. The bride dedicated her playthings or a lock of hair to the goddess. All kinds of offerings were made to the "wedding goddess" at the wedding feast itself, but it was only in the Hellenistic period that priests were associated with the feast.

During the festive meal everyone present was adorned with a garland of myrtle leaves. The unveiling of the bride probably took place towards the end of the eating and drinking, and it was then that the bridegroom gave his bride his wedding presents. The feast concluded with a drink offering and various blessings. The *pompē,* or solemn taking of the bride into the bridegroom's house, took place during the night. Her reception there was accompanied by all kinds of popular ceremonies, culminating in that of her being ushered into the bridal chamber. Either a sacrifice or an entry in a kind of register of marriages served as evidence of a valid marriage.

In the Hellenistic period these ceremonies came under the influence of Eastern customs. The marriage itself included a hallowing by priests, who also took part in the marriage offering and gave instruction to the bride and bridegroom.

2. In the Near East, in Babylonia and Assyria, marriage was formally a legal contract,[8] the evidence of which was the mar-

[8] See Bibliography, 1.

riage document. The other ceremonies were merely complementary to this valid contract of marriage. The betrothal, which
was concluded by the giving of an *arrha* or dowry (a symbol of
taking possession of something), had a greater binding force in
the East than in the West. Both the form of betrothal confirmed
by the giving of an *arrha* and the form of marriage confirmed
by a written contract were later taken over by the West—the
first after the time of Constantine, the second in imperial Rome.

The written declaration also played an important part in every
contract in Egypt. Although Egypt had initially taken the practice of the *ekdosis* from the Greeks, this was replaced in imperial
times by the *sunkhorēsis*, a written contract of marriage between
the bride and bridegroom. Men and women had equal rights in
this in Egypt. In the ancient world, Egypt was the first to regard
marriage as an agreement between the couple proposing marriage. As a result, in Egypt the way was opened in the Hellenistic
period for the real formation of "marriages of love." At the time
of Alexander the Great, and possibly from early times, the priest
had a function to fulfill in Eastern marriages in connection with
the marriage document. He was not present in a purely religious
capacity, to hallow the union, but rather in a jurisdictional, official capacity.

CHRISTIAN MARRIAGE IN THE EARLY CENTURIES[9]

According to the evidence of a contemporary letter, the *Epistula
ad Diognetem*,[10] Christian marriage was much the same as that of
pagans. As a general rule, Christians were bound to conform in
this and in similar matters to the pattern of life of their own environment.[11] The synod of Elvira, held round about the year

9 See Bibliography, 2, 3.
10 See P. Jounel, 1 (Bibliography, 3).
11 Athenagoras, *Legatio pro christianis*, c. 33 (PG, 6, 965); Arnobius, *Adv.
Gentes*, 1, 2 (PL, 5, 719–23); Tertullian, *Apologeticum*, 42 (PL, 1, 490–5);
John Chrysostom, *Homilia* xvi, *ad populum Antiochenum* (PG, 49, 164).

306 (can. 54 [*M–SC*, pt. 2. 14]), also accepted as its point of departure that the marriages of baptized Christians were celebrated like those of unbaptized pagans. The church simply accepted the subjection of her members to the Roman legislature, and matrimonial cases were also brought before the civil lawcourts.

From the very outset, however, the church surrounded the civil and family marriages of her faithful with pastoral care. She wished to protect them from pagan influences of a harmful kind, and in particular from sacrifices to false gods. Not long after the close of the canon of Scripture, Ignatius of Antioch pointed out that it was fitting for the faithful to conclude a marriage only "after the bishop's approval" (*Ad Polycarpum* 5. 2 [*DCA*, pt. 1. 292]). The aim was neither to create a separate marriage procedure for Christians, nor to give the baptized an exceptional civil position in this respect with regard to their non-Christian fellows. It was much more a question of the pastoral care of Christian marriage and of a Christian spirituality of marriage, "so that marriage may be according to the Lord and not according to desire," as Ignatius added to his statement above. Clerical intervention was regarded only as desirable and did not include a jurisdictional act of any kind. What is more, Ignatius' affirmation stands in almost complete isolation in the ancient church and was in fact never put to any great extent into practice. We may safely assume that his statement was in accordance with his "episcopalism."

Marriage was regarded by Christians too as a family affair in the early-church period. Originally it was the parents who decided on the marriage, though in the Roman-Hellenistic period the partners themselves came more and more to make the decision to marry. In the case of marriages between two Christians, clerical intervention was regarded as superfluous. All this goes to show that marriage was above all seen to be a secular reality which had to be experienced "in the Lord." The father of the house was responsible for the Christian way of life of everyone in the household, and thus also for their choice of a Christian partner in marriage. In Syria in the third century, this responsibility was officially assigned to the father. There is no mention of intervention on the part of the clergy (*Syrian Didascalia*, c. 22 [*AQOK*, II, pp. 115, 15–19]).

After Ignatius, Tertullian was the first who is known to have testified to the fact that a marriage concluded without the knowledge of the bishop and the church community was regarded by the faithful in a somewhat unfavourable light.[12] This was no doubt due to Montanist views about the role of the church in marriage. There are no facts to show that these views were also held outside Montanist circles in the first three centuries. In Catholic communities, marriages concluded according to the prevailing social customs were considered to be valid; only clandestine marriages were forbidden. The fact of being married had to be officially controllable (Synod of Laodicea, can. 1 [M–SC, pt. 2, p. 363]). Certain papal decretals, believed to have been made in the second and third centuries, and pointing out the necessity for marriages to be publicly celebrated in church and solemnised by a priest, are not authentic, and in fact date from the ninth century.[13]

Difficulties occurred in the case of slaves, who, according to civil law, were not able to contract a valid marriage with free persons, and whose marriages among each other also had no claim to the title of *conubium* and *matrimonium*, but were regarded as *contubernium* (concubinage).[14] The popes, however, permitted marriages of this kind. Pope Callixtus (217–222) was

---

[12] Tertullian, *De Pudicitia*, 4 (*PL*, 2, 986–7). In Montanist circles, such marriages were even regarded as whoredom. See *De Monogamia*, 11, 1 (*PL*, 2, 943). In his *Ad Uxorem*, 2, 8–9 (*PL*, 1, 1302), Tertullian assumes that it was customary for marriages to be solemnised in a Christian manner.

[13] *Epist. Papae Evaristi*, c. 2 (M–SC, pt. 1, p. 624) = Pseudo-Isidoriana, ninth century (*DPI*, pp. 87–8), *Decretale Callixti II* = Pseudo-Isidoriana, c. 16 (*DPI*, p. 140); Pope Eutychianus, *Exhortatio ad presbyteros* = in fact a sermon of the Frankish synod, dating from the ninth century (see Z*SSR*, Kan. Abt. 58 [1938], pp. 639–65).

[14] See PW-*RKA*, pt. 4, pp. 1164–5.

criticized by Hippolytus because in so doing he went against the civil laws (*Philosophoumena*, 9. 12.24 [*GCS*, pt. 3, pp. 225. 13–17]). It was in this way that the so-called "marriages of conscience" came into being. These were concluded with the permission of the bishops, but they were kept secret from the civil authorities. These constitute the first pieces of evidence that we have, apart from Ignatius, concerning the marriage of Catholics with episcopal permission. The intervention of the bishop was also necessary in the West in other, particular cases—marriage among the clergy[15] and of catechumens.[16] It is clear, then, that these were exceptional cases.

As far as pagan ceremonies were concerned, the clergy was only intent to point out that Christians should refrain from sacrifices, and, although they might rejoice in their celebrations, they were bound to avoid all pagan excesses.[17] Initially Christians both in the West and in the East were opposed to the wearing of the marriage garland. The original significance of this custom—perhaps in the sense of a hallowing—was, however, no longer clear at this time, and its meaning eventually became completely blurred[18]—so much so that the Christian objection to it began to disappear towards the end of the third century. Later the wearing of the garland even began to acquire a Christian significance.[19] In the fourth century, Christians were also employing the custom of the *iunctio dexterarum* in marriage. Tertullian refers to the practice of the marriage document among Christians (*Ad uxorem*, 2, 3 [*PL*, 1, 1292–3]; *De virg. vel.* 12, I [*PL*, 2, 106]), as does Augustine, who also alludes to the custom of the

---

15 F. Vacandart, "Célibat," *DTC*, pt. 2, pp. 2068–88.

16 *Constitutio Apostolica* (*DCA*, pt. 1, p. 354).

17 Tertullian, *De Idol.*, 16 (*PL*, 1, 685); Synod of Laodicea (held at the end of the fourth century), can. 53 (*M-SC*, pt. 2, pp. 571–3), can. 52 (*M-SC*, pt. 2, p. 574); Eusebius, *Hist. Eccl.*, 6, 40, 6 (*GCS*, pt. 2, pp. 2, 598).

18 See K. Baus, *Der Kranz in Antike und Christentum*, Bonn (1940), pp. 98 ff.

19 See, for example, John Chrysostom, *Hom. 9 in I Tim.* (*PG*, 62, 546).

bishop's signing of the document whenever he was present at the family feast (*Sermo* 332, 4 [*PL*, 38, 1463]; see also *Sermo* 9, 11, 18 [*PL*, 38, 88] and *Sermo* 51, 13, 22 [*PL*, 38, 345]). The bishops and priests saw to it that the marriage was experienced in a Christian manner, especially if the parents defaulted in their obligations. At first, however, the church even had to combat the rigorist view that baptized persons were not permitted to marry. This was especially the case in Syria.[20] Round about the year 179, Dionysius, the bishop of Corinth, admonished one of his colleagues not to be too strict in his attitude towards young people—rather than insisting on continence, he should permit them to marry (see Eusebius, *Hist. Eccl.*, 4, 23, 7 [*GCS*, pt. 9, pp. 1. 376]). There is clear evidence of this rigorist attitude until the second half of the fourth century. In reaction against it, the bishops emerge as "marriage brokers."[21] Augustine, on the other hand, refrained from such practices, knowing that the blame for an unhappy marriage could be imputed to the bishop if he had acted as "broker" (Possidius, *Vita S. Augustini*, 27, 4–5 [*CSEL*, 138, 140. 8–20]). The practice of bishops acting as "marriage brokers," at least during the period before the peace of Constantine, must, however, be seen in the light of their pastoral care to prevent mixed marriages.

It is clear from the foregoing that the contract of marriage was, in the first Christian centuries, felt to be a straightforward secular act, but that this contract was nonetheless inevitably accompanied by all kinds of moral, Christian, and ecclesiastical problems. Marriage "in the presence of the church" (*in facie ecclesiae*) was not known at this time, except in non-Catholic

---

[20] See A. Vööbus, *Celibacy, a Requirement for Admission to Baptism in the Early Syriac Church*, Stockholm (1951); J. van der Ploeg, "Spiritualiteit der Syrische monniken," *COH*, 13 (1960–61), pp. 229–45; K. Müller, *Die Forderung der Ehelosigkeit für alle Getauften in der alten Kirche*, Tübingen (1927).

[21] Gregory Nazianzen was also to react against the custom on the part of unmarried persons of delaying their baptism, calling himself a *nymphostolos*, or maker of marriages. See *Orat.* 40, 18 *in S. Baptisma* (*PG*, 36, 382).

Montanist circles, if we leave aside the isolated desire of Ignatius of Antioch, which in any case was ineffective. We have already mentioned the fact that the intervention of the clergy was required only in certain exceptional cases (in the marriages of the clergy and of catechumens). This intervention, however, became more widespread with the course of time.

In the early church, and especially in the East, the bishop was responsible for Christian works of charity,[22] and this social Christian function also implied a particular care for the marriages of orphans who had been neglected by the community of believers.[23] Care for the marriages of these lonely and neglected people was therefore only one of the many branches of the bishop's comprehensive paternal and charitable "care of the poor," even though this duty was in the first place the responsibility of the community. It sometimes happened that the bishop himself conducted the whole marriage of mutual consent, but this again was only in special cases. His intervention was, for example, necessary in the case of a woman who had taken a vow of virginity, but had been unfaithful to this vow and had thereby incurred the punishment of excommunication from the church (*FRBE*, p. 50).

The bishop's guardianship of the poor and the orphans was forbidden by law in the West (see Cyprian, *Epist.* 1, 1, 2 [*CSEL*, III, 2, 466]), but the Eastern practice appears to have entered the West too at about the time that Ambrose and Augustine were bishops. There are many known cases at this time of the bishop's assuming the decisive role of the father as guardian in the marriages of orphans (Augustine, *Epist.* 252 [*PL*, 33, 1069]; *Epist.* 255 [*PL*, 33, 1070]; *Epist.* 254 [*PL*, 33, 1069–70]), and thus concluding the marriage of his protégé. But this only confirms the

---

[22] See G. Krüger, "Die Fürsorgetätigkeit der vorkonstaninischen Kirchen," *ZSSR, Kan.* Abt. 24 (1935), pp. 113–40; see also *FRBE*, pp. 48 ff.

[23] Among other works, the *Didascalia Apost.*, c. 17, refers to this episcopal duty in the East (*AQOK*, "Die Syrische Didaskalie" [*Texte und Untersuchungen*, 10, 1, 87] and *FRBE*, pp. 48–9).

view that marriage was a civil and family matter in which the
father or the guardian was the real subject of the legal proceedings.

It is only in the fourth century that evidence of priestly
prayer and blessing is found in connection with marriage. The
Ambrosiaster defended the goodness of marriage established under God's blessing on the creation of man, which blessing was
in use in marriage in the synagogue and "is likewise practised in
the Church" (*Liber quaestionum novi et veteris Testamenti*
[*CSEL*, 50, 400, 11–14]). These ceremonies—prayers and blessing by the bishop or the priest—were traditionally known, from
the fourth century onwards, as a "marriage service" (a marriage *sub benedictione sacerdotis*). This priestly blessing probably developed from the practice—highly regarded by families—
of a priest, or especially a bishop, going to congratulate the
family in which a marriage feast was celebrated. It goes without
saying that the bride and bridegroom would ask the bishop for
his blessing on their new state in life. This custom developed in
the fourth century into an ecclesiastical ceremony. The practice
of the priest's, or bishop's, blessing and prayer, together with the
influence of the implicit awareness, present at least in the experience, of the particular religious significance of marriage—an
experience which led, at a later stage, to the thetical assertion of
the sacrament of marriage—ought perhaps to be linked with a
text of Paul. Some Christians, living in the expectation of Christ's
second coming, refused to marry or to work. Paul reacted
sharply to this, saying that everything that God had created was
good, having been "sanctified by the word of God and prayer"
(1 Tim. iv. 3–5; see also Heb. 1. 24–5).

With evident reference to this text, Clement of Alexandria
said: "Marriage that is concluded according to the *Logos* (the
word of God) is sanctified if the community of marriage is
subject to God and is contracted with a sincere heart in the fullness of faith ["faith" here is probably used in the sense of marital fidelity] by those who have purified themselves of guilt and

have washed their bodies with pure water and agree in the same hope" (*Stromata* 4, 20 [*PG*, 8, 1338]). Clement's policy was to Christianise pagan practices, and so he saw Christian baptism as the counterpart of the pagan marriage bath. There was, however, no suggestion at this time of a priestly ceremony. The holiness of Christian marriage was seen to be based on baptism. When the church had become more firmly established, and the pagan religions had lost a great deal of their prestige, the church became more receptive towards pagan religious practices in connection with marriage. With the passage of time, Christian marriage was given an outward form of a Christian kind. But the liturgy of marriage only formed a framework surrounding the real marriage which was still contracted civilly within the family circle. The purpose of this liturgical framework was to demonstrate the holiness of the contract; it was prompted by motives of pastoral care and moral solicitude, and included prayers that God should "harmonize" the marriage already concluded (Gregory Nazianzen, *Epist.* 231 [*PG*, 37, 373]).

These Christian practices surrounding the wedding gradually replaced the pagan religious ceremonies originally associated with the family marriage contract. An ecclesiastical form of law for the conclusion of marriage—and thus a "church marriage" in that sense—did not, however, exist at this period. Although, as we have already seen, Christians greatly appreciated the presence of a bishop or a priest as a guest at their marriage feasts, the church regarded it as less fitting that a member of the clergy should be present at a second marriage. (Ambrosiaster, *In 1 Cor.*, 7, 40 [*PL*, 17, 225]; see the Synod of Laodicea, can. 54 [M–SC, pt. 2, p. 574]; Synod of Neo/caesarea, can. 7 [*HCDO*, pt. 1, p. 330].) In such cases, a blessing was never given, thus bearing out the view that the marriage as such was contracted without any ecclesiastical form of law.[24] Marriage "in the Lord" in the first

[24] Many, even, called a second marriage on the part of Christians simply "respectable whoredom"; see, for example, Athenagoras, *Legatio*, 33 (*PG*, 6, 965).

centuries of Christianity meant, as it did for Paul, marrying a fellow-Christian. It also implied, of course, that the marriage itself was, in the prevailing circumstances, to be experienced according to Christian principles. (Ambrosiaster, *In 1 Cor.* 7, 40 [*PL*, 17, 225]; Tertullian, *Ad uxorem*, 2, 2 [*PL*, 1, 1291-2]; *De corona* 13 [*PL*, 2, 96], etc.)

A well-known text of Tertullian has often been quoted in this context, and as often misinterpreted. His words are: "Matrimonium, quod Ecclesia conciliat et confirmat oblatio et obsignat benedictio, angeli renuntiant, Pater rato habet. Nam nec in terris filii sine consensu patrum rite et iure nubunt" (*Ad uxorem*, 2, 9 [*PL*, 1, 1302]).[25] (The translation of this text follows the exposition.) Dating from Tertullian's Catholic period, it would appear that this text points to the existence of an ecclesiastical liturgy of marriage. But it would be wrong to conclude more from the text than it in fact says. There is no suggestion here of a marriage contract before the forum of the church. "*Ecclesia conciliat*" means that the church "founds" Christian marriage. It does not mean that marriage may be entered into only with ecclesiastical permission, or that the bishop or priest, as guardian, should take over the role of the father. (In the West, before Constantine, this guardianship of bishops in special cases was unknown.)

What, then, does this "founding by the Church" mean? The whole of *Ad uxorem* is directed against the contracting of marriages with pagans. The marriage of a Christian woman with a pagan provided the point of departure for this book. With reference to 1 Cor vii. 39 Tertullian says that marriage must be contracted "in the Lord"—that is, as he himself says, "with a Christian."[26] A Christian's marriage with a pagan is "evilly

---

25 *Benedictio* is absent in some mss., which read: "quod . . . obsignatum angeli renuntiant." *FRBE*, pp. 58 ff., gives a good analysis of this text—the exegesis is followed here.

26 "*tantum in Domino*, i.e. *in nomine Domini quod est indubitate Christiano*" (2, 2).

founded" (*conciliare*) and condemned by the church (2, 8). Christians who marry pagans pray to the devil for their partners and withhold their marriages from the church (2, 2). A "church marriage" according to this context is therefore a marriage between two baptized Christians; it is only such marriages which receive the blessing and the consent of the heavenly Father.[27] Contrary to the interpretation which has frequently been suggested, the phrase "*Ecclesia conciliat*" in fact confirms the civil and family basis of the Christian marriage contract, since, according to *Digesta*, the father's consent was necessary for a valid marriage, and this is precisely what Tertullian assumes in his comparison. For baptized Christians, the father of both parties who had to give his consent to the marriage was God. No intervention on the part of the clergy was therefore necessary. The church communities were still small enough at this time to render any separate system of ecclesiastical control superfluous.

The marriage of two baptized Christians was "confirmed by a celebration of the eucharist" (*confirmat oblatio*) and "sealed with a blessing" (*obsignat benedictio*). Does this mean that there was at this period already a nuptial mass with a marriage blessing? It should not be forgotten that the book deals in the first place with the remarriage of a widow with a Christian, and therefore with a second marriage. At this time, and indeed for a long time after Tertullian, permission was never given for a blessing in the case of a second marriage. Tertullian's phrase, "sealed with a blessing," must therefore have a different meaning here. It is clear from the context that it means no more than the prayer, the "communal prayer" of the two partners themselves.[28] The domestic liturgy—family prayer—assured the continued Christian life of the marriage. On the other hand, the phrase "confirmat oblatio" clearly means that the continued Christian

[27] See, for example, "Conciliare nuptias," *TLL*, pt. 4, p. 44.
[28] In a mixed marriage there was no *divina benedictio*, that is, the praise of God in communal prayer by the "singing of psalms and hymns" (2, 8; see also 2, 6).

life of the marriage was also firmly established by the partners'
joint participation in the liturgical worship of the Christian community, and especially in the celebration of the eucharist. Tertullian was therefore not referring to a nuptial mass, which was of a
later date, but to the regular, joint participation of both partners
in the communal Christian celebration of the eucharist. In a
mixed marriage, it was not possible for them to join together in
the celebration of the sacrifice of the mass (2, 8).

The interpolation concerning the angels (*angeli renuntiant*)
does not allude so much to the contract of marriage as such,
but rather to the fact that the angels were the witnesses of Christian marriage, and safeguarded its continued happiness.[29] Pagan
marriages, or marriages between a Christian and a pagan partner,
were, on the other hand, surrounded by "demons and spirits of
misfortune" (2, 4, and 2, 8).

The conclusion, then, is obvious. Tertullian says nothing at all
about an ecclesiastical liturgy of marriage, with a nuptial mass
and a priestly solemnisation of marriage, but is referring to the
Christian experience of marriage which is brought about by both
partners' sharing the same faith, by their joint participation in
the eucharist, by their practice of Christian charity, and by their
praying together at home (see also *FRBE*, p. 66). It is possible,
then, to translate Tertullian's text by paraphrasing it as follows:
"The marriage of baptized Christians is, by virtue of their baptism, a church marriage (*Ecclesia conciliat*), and one that is
moreover firmly established in its adherence to the Christian way
of life (to the church) by the joint participation of the two
partners in the liturgical celebration of the Christian community
and by their being able to pray together at home. The angels are
the witnesses of such a Christian married life, safeguarding its
continued existence. The heavenly Father gives his consent and
his blessing to such a marriage." I do not accept the usual conclusion drawn from this text of Tertullian, but prefer to see it as

---

[29] The ancient church believed that the angels were present, not only at
the sacraments, but also at the communal prayer of Christians.

a confirmation of the civil and family contract of marriage and of the secular character of marriage, which, however, has a special meaning for Christians by virtue of baptism and is sustained and nourished by Christian prayer and by the sacraments (especially the eucharist). Interpreted in this way, Tertullian's text seems to me to be of great dogmatic importance. It represents the intermediate stage between the still undifferentiated biblical assertions about marriage and the later assertion of the sacramental nature of marriage between baptized persons. At this stage, a "church marriage" was still a valid contract of marriage made civilly and in the family between two baptized persons and relating to the secular sphere. There is no direct reference here to a separate ecclesiastical or liturgical solemnisation of marriage. The most that we can say is that the bishop gave his blessing to the married couple if it so happened that he visited them during the wedding feast, and that the addition of his signature to the marriage charter was greatly appreciated.

The first evidence that we have of a nuptial mass with a priestly solemnisation of marriage contracted civilly and in the family dates from the fourth and fifth centuries, in the Roman church. The papal decrees of the fourth century laid down that the lower orders of the clergy were bound to have their marriages solemnised by a priest.[30] For the laity, however, the priest's solemnisation of marriage was more in the nature of a proof of the church's approval of their blameless conduct. Not every layman received this ecclesiastical blessing on his marriage. During the first ten centuries there was no obligation to receive it. The so-called Decretal of Pope Hormisdas (514–523), according to which every Christian was obliged to receive the blessing of a priest on marriage, is not authentic.[31] As late as the ninth cen-

---

[30] The first evidence is that of Pope Siricius (384–99), *Epist. ad Himerium*, c. 8 (*PL*, 13, 1141–3); also Pope Innocent I (404), *Epist. ad Victricium*, c. 4–6 (*PL*, 20, 473–7). Up to and including Pope Pelagius I, this obligation was restricted to the lower clergy.

[31] *Decretum*, to be found in Burchard of Worms (1000–1025), 9, 3 (*PL*, 140, 816).

tury Pope Nicholas I referred, in his well-known *Responsum ad Bulgaros* (866), to the validity of marriages by mutual consent, even if all other ceremonies—family and civil and ecclesiastical— were lacking.[32] As we shall see, it was only in the eleventh century that any change came about.

CHRISTIAN MARRIAGE FROM THE FOURTH TO THE ELEVENTH CENTURIES

Secular Marriage, Contracted Civilly and in the Family

1. When Christianity spread to the *Germanic* tribes, it was some time before the church succeeded in getting her marriage theory of the *consensus*, based on Roman law, accepted. In ancient Germanic law,[33] marriage was seen as a contract between two tribes or extended family groups, rather than as a contract between the bride and the bridegroom themselves. Under this contract, the bridegroom acquired from the girl's father or guardian the *mundium*,[34] or the power giving him the right and the duty to protect and to represent his bride. In the pre-Frankish period, this took the form of a single legal proceeding. Later it was divided into two distinct acts—the betrothal and the marriage itself, the *Trauung* or "handing over of the bride" (in other words, a form of *traditio puellae*). Later still, a second tradition in Germanic law began to emphasize the mutual consent of both partners in marriage. This was the so-called *Friedelehe*, which required no handing over of a *mundium* and no public act.

The Germanic betrothal was a sort of deed of purchase or conveyance between the bridegroom and either the tribe or the sponsor, the *Vormund*, of the bride. It thus bore points of resemblance to the Eastern betrothal by means of *arrha*. By giving

---

[32] c. 3 (PL, 119, 980). A better edition of the text can be found in *MGH-E*, 6, 2, 568–600.

[33] See Bibliography, 2.

[34] *Mundium*, from the Saxon *mund*, peace, protection, has the approximate meaning of our "guardianship."

a *wadia*[35] and other wedding presents or sureties, the bride-groom placed himself under an obligation to take the girl as his wife and to give her a certain part of his possessions by way of a *wittum*.[36] The sponsor, or *Vormund*, betrothed the woman, whose guardian he was, to the bridegroom by giving a certain symbol (*wadia*). The bridegroom gave this *wadia* back, and in this way entrusted his future wife to the holder of the *mundium* until the wedding day. The Germanic people adopted the Roman custom of the ring; but, whereas in the case of the Romans the ring was a pledge of a firm resolve to marry, and thus an en-gagement ring, among the Germanic tribes it was—at least from the eighth and ninth centuries onwards—really the sign of the contract of marriage itself. The wedding ring is therefore of Germanic origin and not of Roman.

The marriage itself began with the drawing up of the marriage document, in which the *wittum* (*dos*) and the dowry for the handing over of the authority over the girl was laid down. Then the "sponsor" gave the girl to the bridegroom with his right hand, and the bridegroom paid him the dowry. This concluded the "handing over of the bride" and all her property to the bridegroom. The bridegroom also gave the *launegild*, a present given in return by way of compensation to the "sponsor."

What is not clear, however, is whether the mutual consent to the marriage was sufficient in itself, if it was not given a con-crete form in the giving of the ring and the wedding presents. The handing over of the bride by her father or guardian (*Vor-mund*) was the most important condition in Germanic law of the validity of the marriage, and, at a later period, Luther was to de-nounce the Council of Trent because it attached less importance to this practice concerning the Christian validity of marriage.

[35] A *wadium*, or *wette*, was a sum of money given in surety—the sign that something, or somebody, had been passed from one person's hand to another's. A *wadius* was the "sponsor" who paid out this surety.

[36] A *wittum*, or *wera* (*weregild*), was a sum paid on purchase or in com-pensation, and indicated that something or somebody was in the protection of whoever paid this sum.

In what is now modern Germany, the ancient Germanic law remained in force, but marriage was accomplished in two stages —the betrothal and the marriage itself. Each different tribe had its own marriage customs, and these were strictly observed with the aim of preventing any later doubts and disputes over the validity of the marriage. A Frank who had married a Saxon wife might, for example, claim that he was not married according to Frankish law and was therefore free to repudiate his Saxon wife and marry again. The *mundium* form of marriage, however, gradually fell into disrepute, and women began to gain a certain degree of emancipation. There is evidence in the *Ruodlieb*, the *Nibelungenlied*, and *Gudrun*, for example, that marriage was concluded by means of the mutual consent of the bride and the bridegroom. The change would appear to have taken place, particularly in Upper Bavaria, by the eleventh century.

By this time, the legal proceedings were enacted, so to speak, in three stages. The first stage was the proposal and the betrothal. This was followed by the mutual consent to marry—the "marriage in the circle"—and finally by the wedding feast, which included the bringing home of the bride, the festive meal, and the solemn entry into the bridal chamber. The father or guardian played a prominent part in the proposal and the betrothal. At the next stage—the marriage by mutual consent within the circle of blood-relations and friends—a third person, an outsider, asked questions which were answered by the bride and the bridegroom, who thus signified that they agreed to marry each other. In this ceremony the man and the woman enjoyed an equal status, but the ceremony of the marriage sword which followed showed clearly that the husband was the master of the house. The third phase, however—the *domum-ductio* of the bride and the consummation of the marriage—gradually came to be regarded as conclusive evidence of the legal validity of the marriage contract. Giving the *wittum* remained important.

2. As with the other Germanic tribes, there were two stages —the betrothal and the marriage itself—in the marriage of the

Franks.[37] The father and the tribe decided in principle upon the betrothal of a girl. (This was the principle of *Geschlechtsvormundschaft*, the guardianship of the generation of the tribe.) At the time of the Merovingian kings this paternal and tribal right was frequently restricted by interventions on the part of the king himself—the king was able to betroth a girl to a man of his choosing by exercising his right of royal command. The betrothal took place by means of the payment of a fixed sum of money. On the conclusion of the marriage itself, the bridegroom handed over the *wittum* in the presence of witnesses, as a sign of his responsibility to protect his wife. The taking of the bride to the bridegroom's house, the *Brautlauf*, was enacted according to a statutory regulation. The public character of marriage was stressed in the Roman Merovingian law of the Franks, especially from the Carlovingian period onwards, and this arrangement was particularly acceptable to the church, even though she was later to come into conflict with the tribes over their exaggerated adherence to the tribal forms of law.

3. All kinds of influences—from the East, from ancient Greece and Rome and the Germanic tribes, but above all from the Western Goths—were present in fifth-century *Spain*. The Western Goths were originally Arians, and were not converted to Catholicism until the end of the sixth century. It was especially via Spain that the form of betrothal by means of the *arrha* (the engagement ring) penetrated to Rome and the whole of the West. After the conversion to Catholicism, affairs of state and ecclesiastical matters in Spain became intermingled, and as a result the law of the church became the law of the state. The decisions of ecclesiastical synods were ratified by the king, while the clergy were preoccupied with interior matters.

For the Western Goths[38] betrothal and marriage were above all tribal affairs, as they were for the Germanic tribes, and thus ne-

[37] See Bibliography, 2.
[38] See Bibliography, 2.

cessitated the handing over of a *mundium*. The most important
proof of a validly contracted marriage was the giving of the
dowry (the *dos*). These customs were also observed by Christians.

4. The *Celts* and the *Anglo-Saxons* originally regarded the
woman simply as merchandise, and marriage consequently above
all as a sort of deed of purchase or conveyance. The price was
paid to the "guardian" (or to the tribe) of the bride. It was not
until the eleventh century that women gained a measure of freedom in the matter of their own consent to the marriage. However, there are indications that, from the seventh century onwards, the sum paid for the purchase of the bride was tending to
become a payment made in compensation for the upbringing that
the girl had received from her parents or her guardian. The
betrothal and the marriage were distinct legal proceedings among
these tribes too.

The Formation of a Non-Obligatory Ecclesiastical Liturgy of Marriage[39]

The priestly marriage blessing or veiling. We have already seen
that there was during the first three centuries a growing realisation in the church that marriage between two baptized persons,
although a secular affair, had a special Christian and ecclesiastical
significance. From the fourth to the eleventh centuries increasing
emphasis was placed on the church aspect of the marriage contract, without prejudice to its legal validity, by surrounding it
with liturgical ceremonies.

1. The first evidence in the churches of *Rome* and *Italy* of a
truly liturgical celebration of marriage dates from the time of
Pope Damasus (366–84) and is provided by Pseudo-Ambrose
(Ambrosiaster) (*Liber quaestionum novi et veteris Testamenti*

[39] See Bibliography, 3.

[*CSEL*, 50, 400, 11–14]). This blessing applied only to the first marriage. The marriage was celebrated by God himself in heaven.[40] The marriage blessing was accompanied by liturgical actions, which in Rome and Italy took the form of the veiling of the bride by the priest,[41] with the result that the "veiling by the priest" and the "marriage blessing" became almost synonymous. This ceremony was extended to form an entire liturgy, as was described by Paulinus of Nola at the beginning of the fifth century. It took place in the church. The father led the wedding guests to the altar, where the bishop celebrated the marriage with an improvised prayer, covering the bride and bridegroom with a veil (*Carmen* xxv [*CSEL*, 30, 238–45]). There is no reference to a nuptial mass. The first apparent evidence of this occurs in the writings of an unknown author during the pontificate of Sixtus III (432–40) in Rome (Anon., *Praedestinatus*, III, 31 [*PL*, 53, 670]). According to Pope Nicholas I (858–67), gifts were offered by the bride and bridegroom during the nuptial mass (*Responsum ad Bulgaros*, c. 3 [*PL*, 119, 980]).[42] Both the bride and the bridegroom received the eucharist. The practice of placing wreaths on the bride and bridegroom was possibly also adopted in Rome and Italy from the East. The ceremony took place on the day on which the bride was solemnly brought from the bridegroom's house. Originally—and elsewhere—it probably took place previously (Cyprian of Toulon, *Vita sancti Caesarii*, 1, 59 [*MGH–SRM*, pt. 3, 481, 15–16]),[43] or in connection with the betrothal.

---

[40] "Primae nuptiae sub benedictione Dei celebrantur sublimiter" (Ambrosiaster, *Comm. in Epist. l ad Cor.*, 7. 40 [*PL*, 17, 238]). This is an allusion to the Genesis blessing over marriage, but would also appear to assume an ecclesiastical practice. See also *Comm. in Epist. l ad Tim.*, 3, 12–13 (*PL*, 17, 497).

[41] Pope Siricius (*PL*, 16, 1171); Ambrose, *Ep.* 19 *ad Vigilium* (*PL*, 16, 1026), "Ipsum coniugium sanctificare oportet velamine sacerdotali et benedictione." The priest now lays the stole over the hands of the bride and the bridegroom.

[42] See also note 57 below.

[43] This may also have been the practice of the Gallican church.

This division between the veiling (or marriage ceremony) and
the marriage feast recognised as legally valid by the state, frequently led to casuistical problems concerning the actual date of
the marriage. Even the fact that the church decided that the
woman had to be given back to the man with whom she had
been veiled[44] is not definite proof that the veiling constituted a
marriage, since the betrothal was at that period often regarded
as strict moral obligation to marry.[45] Later on, the marriage
blessing and the marriage feast proper were more closely connected. After the year 1000 the nuptial mass followed the marriage, which took place in the church porch. This was the case
at least in most countries (*FRBE*, p. 163).

As we have already seen, this liturgical solemnisation of marriage was in no sense a commandment of the church. It was in
fact forbidden to those who did not lead an exemplary life (Innocent I, *Epist. ad Victricium*, c. 4–6 [*PL*, 20, 473–5]; Synod of
Pavia [*MGH–C*, pt. 2, 119, 21–38]). In principle, it was only
applicable to those marrying for the first time, and only for the
clergy was it obligatory. The ecclesiastical solemnisation of marriage only had a bearing upon the moral and religious realisation
of the marriage that had been validly contracted according to
the various statutory or unwritten laws. There was, then, no
obligatory liturgy of marriage in the church before the eleventh
century, except that for the lower orders of the clergy. The
father's consent, or the mutual consent of the bride and bridegroom, according to the prevailing custom of the country, continued to be the essential element in the constitution of a marriage, and in the express words of Pope Nicholas I, the only
essential element. But this papal intervention is a clear indication
that the Germanic and Frankish tribes were already beginning

---

[44] See, for example, the Synod of Pavia (850), can. 10 (*MGH–C*, pt. 2,
119, 39–43).

[45] The marriage blessing was refused to those who had broken the
betrothal in the ancient church of Rome. See the Synod of Elvira, can. 54
(*FRBE*, p. 166).

to feel differently about this question—that the mutual agreement of the partners was a legally valid, tangible consent to marry only so long as it was given a concrete form in the customs and practices of the country, such as the handing over of the bride, the dowry, and so on. For the popes, too, the attendant ceremonies, both secular and ecclesiastical, were clearly elements indicating the presence of actual consent; they were consequently brought forward as evidence in matrimonial lawsuits.[46]

2. Whereas the solemnisation of marriages in the churches of Rome and Italy took the form of a veiling of the bride and bridegroom, the priestly marriage blessing in the churches of *Gaul* took the form of a blessing given in the bridal chamber (*benedictio in thalamo*). This was because the climax of the marriage in these lands was the entry into the bridal chamber. The earliest evidence of this is provided by Stephanus Afer and Avitus of Vienne (Stephanus, *Vita S. Amatoris de Auxerre;* Avitus, c. 494–518, *Epist.* 55 [*FRBE*, p. 204]); they compared the blessing of the bride in the bridal chamber to the blessing received by a virgin on her dedication at the altar. This form of solemnisation was not at first ruled out in the case of second marriages.

Caesarius of Arles laid down that the liturgy of marriage in the church should take place *secundum morem Romanum* (according to the practice of the church in Rome). It is not certain whether he also laid down that a nuptial mass should be celebrated in connection with the marriage ceremony, in accordance with the practice of the Roman liturgy. The ancient Gallican liturgy was replaced in practice by the Roman rite in the Car-

[46] See, for example, Leo I, *Epist. ad Rusticum* (PL, 67, 288). There was no question here of a marriage blessing. The giving of the dowry served as proof of the validity of the marriage. Nicholas I enquired, in connection with the question of the validity of the marriage of King Lotharius II with Waldrada, whether the bride had received a marriage blessing and also whether the dowry had been handed over according to law and justice. (See *MGH–E*, pt. 6, 277). If the dowry had not been handed over, the solemnisation of the marriage in church could scarcely have been held as proof of the validity of the marriage.

lovingian period; in Gaul too, marriages were solemnised by a nuptial mass and by the veiling of the bride and groom, though this was not obligatory. Gaul also adopted the strict Roman attitude towards second marriages.

There was no question at this time of an ecclesiastical handing over of the bride, unless the bishop himself was the guardian of an orphan and consequently had paternal functions to fulfil in the marriage of his ward.

The church, then, had a moral and religious task at this time, and the marriage itself was not conducted according to any ecclesiastical form of law, but rather according to the statutory or unwritten legal practices of the people in each land. The church did, however, issue regulations in connection with the impediments to marriage—incest appears to have been common among the converted Germanic tribes—and the abduction of women. The church also opposed the right of a king to give a girl to a man as he thought fit, at least in cases where the girl was already betrothed to a third party. Marriage with a non-Christian was also forbidden. The synods of the church did not, however, concern themselves at this time with the legal form of the marriage contract.

What did happen for the first time in the eighth century, however, was that a synod laid down that marriages between nobles and lay commoners were to be contracted publicly.[47] In connection with the legal validity of marriage, Pope Leo I clearly complied with the popular practices which were later given a statutory status.[48] In 541 the synod of Orleans forbade marriages to be contracted without the permission of the parents or the guardian (can. 24 [*MGH–LC*, pt. 1, 92, 16–23]). This leads us to conclude that the legal form of marriage was at this time still secular. The priest's function in connection with marriage was therefore in practice limited to the rite of the marriage blessing

---

[47] The Synod of Verneuil: "ut omnes homines laici publicas nuptias faciant tam nobiles quam ignobiles" (*MGH–C*, pt. 1, 36, 16).

[48] See, for example, *Epist. ad Rusticum* (PL, 67, 288–9).

which was eventually performed according to Roman liturgical practice. This continued until the eleventh century.

3. The marriage liturgy of *Spain* was closely related to that of Gaul. The marriage of Christians was accompanied by a priestly blessing in Spain by the fourth century (Pope Siricius, *Epist. ad Himerium* [PL, 16, 1171]).[49] Isidore of Seville was the first to review the Spainsh liturgy of marriage (*De Eccles. Officiis*, 2, 20 [PL, 83, 810–12]).

The ecclesiastical solemnisation of marriage in Spain took the form of a *benedictio thalami*, a blessing of the bridal chamber. The betrothal also had its own liturgy, with the engagement ring as *arrha*. Initially it was the bride and bridegroom who were blessed rather than the ring, though later on the ring itself was also blessed. When the engagement ring was liturgically handed over the man kissed the woman. The betrothal acquired an almost binding character by virtue of this ceremony, which was eventually absorbed into the marriage rite itself. There was no real liturgical ceremony of veiling in Spain, although Isidore does refer to a marriage rite in the church—the bride and bridegroom were joined together by the deacon with a cloth while the priest blessed them. But, initially at least, there was no nuptial mass.

4. In the British Isles during the Celtic and Anglo-Saxon periods, there is no mention in the oldest documents known to us of any marriage liturgy (*FRBE*, p. 237 ff.). It is not until the tenth and eleventh centuries that any marriage rite can be found in the liturgical books. Some of these books refer to a nuptial mass only, others to a special priestly blessing given during the mass, but this does not appear to be the solemnisation of the marriage. There are, in addition, a number of liturgical books which

[49] This evidence should not be accepted without some reservation, since the popes tended, in their letters, to take the liturgical practices of Rome and Italy as their point of departure.

mention a ceremony accompanying the entry into the bridal chamber without the nuptial mass, and this points to the original Gallican and Celtic solemnisation of marriage. The blessing of the ring itself seems, however, to have been peculiar to the marriage rite of the British Isles. The Roman formulae of marriage together with the nuptial mass and the solemnisation of the marriage in the bridal chamber are to be found in a third group of liturgical books.

It is therefore possible to say that, up to the eleventh century, there were two forms of marriage rite in England. The older form was the Gallican and Celtic blessing of the house, the *benedictio thalami*, which was given after the *domum-ductio*, when the bride and bridegroom entered the house of marriage. The bride and bridegroom themselves and the wedding ring were also blessed at the same time. The later form came with the introduction into England of the Roman rite, which was accompanied by the Roman nuptial mass. In some places, the nuptial mass was celebrated in the morning and the ceremony of the blessing of the house took place in the evening. In other places, the blessing of the house was divided, so that the blessing of the ring took place, not in the house, but in the church, incorporated in the ceremonies of the marriage itself. This, however, occurred (during the eleventh century) in Gaul, where the influence of the Celtic and Anglo-Saxon liturgical books was felt in the second half of the eleventh century.

Tendencies within the church to make marriage an ecclesiastical affair: the Pseudo-Isidorian Decretals. An exceptional case occurred in the Frankish empire in the ninth century, in which the liturgy of marriage was associated with the rite of the coronation of a king (*Opera Hincmari* [PL, 125, 811–14]). It was the bishop himself, Hincmar, who performed the ceremony of the handing over of the bride in this case. But this should not lead us to suppose that it marked the beginning of a tendency to make the bishop or the priest conclude the marriage. In fact, a certain change did become apparent at the time of Hincmar. It is, however, necessary to outline the historical events leading up to this evolution.

The eighth century, the time of Pepin the Short, was characterised not only by a Romanisation of the Gallican liturgy, but also by an increased strictness in the discipline of the church. Boniface and Pepin were themselves the advocates of this. Those who broke the rules of the church concerning forbidden marriages were punished both by the church and by the secular arm. Many different measures of public control were brought in to discourage marriages in forbidden categories. The above-mentioned decision of the national synod of Verneuil that marriages should be contracted in public should also be seen in this light. By "public" marriage was meant the keeping of the formalities of marriage as these had been prescribed by the laws of the people or by the statutes of the Empire. In the eighth century, Boniface made an "examination" obligatory before marriage was permitted (Synod of the Bavarian Church, can. 12 [*MGH–LC*, pt. 2, 53]). The priest and the nearest relatives had to be previously informed of the intention to marry, so that they might be able to find out whether or not the marriage came under any of the forbidden categories.

This had already begun to take place a little earlier in England (*Canones sancti Theodori* [of Canterbury] [*FRBE*, p. 250]). It was made obligatory for the whole of the Empire in a *Capitulare* of Charlemagne, which appeared in 802 (*MGH–LC*, pt. II–I, 191). Many were in fact unable to receive the marriage blessing because they had been living in concubinage before their marriage, in which case the priestly blessing was not permitted. In any case, it is possible to establish with certainty that the church of this period, as distinct from the church of the Roman-Gallican and Merovingian periods, placed increasing emphasis upon the public legal form of marriage. The obligatory enquiry on the part of the ecclesiastical authorities prior to marriage was the first symptom of the church's attempt to take over the legal form of marriage. It failed because the ecclesiastical solemnisation of marriage was not in fact obligatory. Moreover the frequent occurrence of the practice of abduction made the church stress the secular legal form of the marriage contract.

The strictly ecclesiastical legal form of the marriage contract came about mainly as a result of the misleading Pseudo-Isidorian writings.[50] These decretals, which originated round about 845, were meant to serve the ends of church politics, but at the same time were directed towards the moral and religious restoration of the entire Frankish church. They aimed to assert the indissolubility of marriage, and to discourage the contracting of marriages within the forbidden categories and above all the frequent occurrence of abduction. For this reason they were obliged to stress the secular forms of law of the marriage contract. The authors of these decretals tried to achieve their aims by falsely attributing their writings to popes in the distant past or to imperial councils, thus giving them the force of a papal document or an imperial statute.

Benedict Levita[51] (in Book III, 179) resumes the efforts of the Pseudo-Isidorian writings to forbid marriage in certain categories and marriage by abduction, and to regulate "according to the laws [that is, the customs of various peoples] and the gospel" (*FRBE*, p. 268)—in other words, in accordance with secular and ecclesiastical practice—the legitimate conduct of the contracting of marriage. The giving of the dowry and the public contract of marriage were regarded as strictly obligatory. The marriage had to be concluded in church in the presence of the people. The enquiry preceding the marriage had also to take place in the church. The betrothal and the giving of the dowry, which had until then been secular matters, coming under civil jurisdiction,

---

[50] See Bibliography, 3.

[51] For the significance of the Pseudo-Isidorian reforms, see P. Fournier and G. Le Bras, *Histoire des Collections canoniques*, pt. I, pp. 127–232; R. von Scherer, *Über das Eherecht bei Benedictus Levita und Pseudoisidor*, Graz (1878).

became ecclesiastical and canonical legal acts. This marked a beginning at least of the adoption and incorporation of secular forms of law into the church—to gear them to the liturgy and make them into canonical norms. It is therefore possible to say that, just as the well-known text of Tertullian, discussed in some detail above, forms an initial step towards the clear recognition of church marriage, at least in the sense of a secular marriage between two baptized persons, the Pseudo-Isidorian writings constitute a new step towards the recognition of church marriage in the sense of an ecclesiastical contract of marriage. These ninth-century writings marked the beginning of this development, not its end.

Benedict Levita finally insists (in Book III, 463) on the obligation to have the marriage solemnised by a priest after the giving of the dowry (*FRBE*, p. 273), and also refers to the *domumductio* and to the question of the mutual consent to marry. It is therefore possible to conclude briefly by saying that, according to Benedict Levita, a marriage was legally concluded if it had taken place in the presence of the father or the guardian (since it was these who gave their consent to the marriage); if it was at the bride's petition; if the dowry had been given; if the priest had blessed the marriage; and, finally, if the handing over of the bride had taken place according to the laws and customs of the people. Even though there was some concern for the woman's freedom, the legality of the marriage was above all dependent upon the consent of the woman's parents, and this consent emerged in the normal course of the marriage contract according to the local laws and customs. It was above all the dowry which set the seal upon this parental consent to the marriage, and formed the visible and tangible legal evidence of this consent. Marriage purely by mutual consent was alien to the whole Pseudo-Isidorian spirit, as indeed it was to all the early medieval Germanic laws and customs of the people.

This tendency was continued by the false decretals of Pseudo-Isidore. A decretal attributed to Pope Evaristus, the first successor to St. Peter, laid even greater emphasis on the necessity of concluding the marriage publicly (chap. 2, *DPI*, pp. 87–8). According to the false decretal of Pope Callixtus, a marriage was considered to be valid so long as the dowry had been given and the priestly solemnisation had taken place (2, 16, *DPI*, p. 140).

These forged documents, which were accepted as authentic until the fifteenth century, eventually found their way into the *Decretum Gratiani*, the medieval "canon law," with the result that the solemnisation of marriage was made canonically obligatory, and also that the secular forms of law of the marriage contract were absorbed into canon law. None of this, however, affected the validity of the marriage contract.

After the Pseudo-Isidorian Decretals, it was perhaps Hincmar, the Archbishop of Rheims, who played the most important part in this development in the ninth century, especially because of his involvement, as a bishop, in a number of prominent matrimonial problems. These were the marriages of Lotharius II with Teutberga (Hincmar, *De Divorcio Lotharii et Teutbergae* [*PL*, 125, 623–772]), of Stephen of Aquitania, a vassal of Charles the Bald, with the daughter of Count Regimund (*De nuptiis Stephani et filae Regimundi comitis* [*PL*, 126, 132–53]), of Baldwin and Judith (*Epist. ad Nicolaum* [*PL*, 126, 27]), and of Argembert and Northildis (*De Divorcio Lotharii*, Resp. 5 [*PL*, 125, 655]). In this reaction to the problems raised by these marriages Hincmar clarified certain fundamental points. Even before the later school of Bologna, he made a clear and essential distinction between the "marriage contract" (*matrimonium initiatum*) and the "consummation" of marriage (*matrimonium consummatum*) in sexual intercourse. On the grounds that marriage was finally consummated in marital intercourse, he held that, if this consummation could not take place, the marriage could be dissolved (Hincmar [*PL*, 126, 149]). If consummation was in fact possible, but did not take place, he held that the marriage was indissoluble from the moment that it had been contracted according to the prevailing forms of law.

From this it is clear that the whole of the marriage feast formed the valid contract of marriage, although certain elements in the feast were more important than others. Here Hincmar was following the views expressed in the false decretals. A valid contract of marriage included the betrothal, the giving of the dowry, and the handing over of the bride (*PL*, 126, 148). Hincmar fully recognised the special authority of the civil laws for the validity and the public nature of marriage.[52] The principal elements in any contract of marriage, according to the laws of use and wont which gradually became statutes, were that it was *a parentibus petita, legaliter desponsata et dotata, publicis nuptiis honorata*, and a *copulae sociatio* (*De nuptiis Stephani*, Ep. 22 [*PL*, 126, 137]).

As we have already seen, Hincmar added the priest's blessing of the marriage in other places. This, however, was no more than God's blessing of creation over every marriage, including those of non-Christians, but pronounced by the priest in the case of Christian marriages, for the sanctification of the marriage (*De divorcio Lotharii* [*PL*, 125, 653]; *De raptu* [*PL*, 125, 1020]). The marriage blessing was not permitted in the case of second marriages; therefore these could be properly contracted "according to the secular laws" (*Epist. 2 ad Nicolaum* [*PL*, 126, 27]). What particularly concerned the church at this period was not so much that marriages should take place according to the rites of the church, but rather that they should take place publicly. They had to take place according to the formalities of the secular law and also according to the tradition of the church which, for Hincmar, was set out in the false decretal which he believed to have been the work of Pope Evaristus, the first successor to Peter. It was partly due to Hincmar's activity that the views on

[52] *De divorcio Lotharii*, Resp. 11 (*PL*, 125, 686–9; *PL*, 125, 653 ff.); *De nuptiis Stephani*, Ep. 22 (*PL*, 126, 135); *Ep. 2 ad Nicolaum* (*PL*, 126, 26): "Post quae voluimus . . . ut iuxta ecclesiasticam traditionem prius Ecclesiae quam laeserant satisfacerent, et sic demum quod praecipiunt iura legum mundalium exequi procurarent."

marriage expressed in the false decretals became so firmly established in the ninth and tenth centuries.

The Movement towards an Exclusively Ecclesiastical Contract of Marriage

If, in connection with the foregoing, we ask the question: What was the relationship between the church and the state in the matter of marriage throughout the first ten centuries?, we are bound to come to the following conclusion. The Fathers of the church implicitly recognised the jurisdictional power of the state in matrimonial affairs. They did, of course, protest against matrimonial laws which they regarded as unacceptable to Christians, but they never claimed that the state authorities should not be allowed to pass any laws at all in connection with marriage which would be binding on baptized Christians. It is true that the Christian emperors usually first established contact with the bishops before legislating in connection with marriage, but there is no evidence to show that the ecclesiastical authorities demanded that the state should be essentially subordinate to the church in this matter. On the contrary, the Fathers of the church again and again drew the attention of the faithful to their duty to obey the laws of the state.[53]

The church fully accepted the situation that marriage was concluded within the family according to tribal customs and was protected by the statutes of the realm. For Christians, too, this constituted real and valid marriage. In 406, the Council of Carthage requested that an imperial law should be passed, forbidding married persons who were separated to contract a new marriage.[54] This is a clear indication of the church's recognition of the state's power to make statutory enactments in matrimonial

[53] Esmein, pt. 1, pp. 6–7; P. Jounel, p. 35.
[54] *Codex can. Ecclesiae Afric.*, c. 3; Bruns, *Canones Apost. et conc.*, p. 186; see Esmein, pt. 1, p. 107.

affairs.[55] Sometimes the emperors asked the bishops themselves to pronounce judgment, but in such cases the bishops were bound to pass sentence in accordance with the tenor of the statutes of the realm.[56] It is therefore possible to assert that the church in practice accepted the legislative and judicial power of the state in matrimonial affairs, including those affecting Christians.

This situation lasted until late in the Middle Ages. It is true that a considerable body of moral and pastoral teaching on the subject of marriage was developed within the church, but the church was not concerned with legislation in matrimonial matters. Even Pope Hormisdas' instruction against clandestine marriages was a pastoral measure, aiming to protect the sanctity and unity of marriage; "No Christian . . . should marry in secret, but must, after having received the priest's blessing, marry publicly in the Lord" (*Decretum* 2 [*PL*, 63, 525]). Clandestine marriages, concluded without witnesses, were nontheless valid. A few centuries later, Pope Nicholas I laid down that it was no sin if the liturgical ceremonies which had grown up around the form of marriage contracted civilly within the family (in fact the sacrament for Christians) did not take place, on condition that there had been a genuine mutual consent to marry.[57] This shows the essence of marriage as independent of the authority both of the state and of the church, and the validity of Christian marriage as dependent only on the mutual consent of the two baptized partners (marriage "in the Lord"). This formed the background to the entire patristic and medieval view of marriage.

[55] The power of the state here was also recognised by Pope Leo I, *Epist.* 167, *ad Rusticum* (*PL*, 54, 1207).

[56] G. Joyce, *Christian Marriage* (Bibliography, 3).

[57] The *Epist. ad consulta Bulgarorum*, c. 3 (*PL*, 119, 980; *MGH–E*, VI, 2, 569 gives a slightly different version) was addressed to the Bulgars who had been converted by the Christian Greeks. As will be seen in the section on marriage in the Eastern Church, the Greeks held that the essence of marriage as a sacrament was to be found in the so-called *stephanōma*, the liturgy of the garland, and had little interest in the theory of mutual consent, at least in the period following that of Justinian, and especially from the eighth century onwards.

Nonetheless, marriage had, by the turn of the millennium, come under the jurisdictional power of the church. The movement towards this transference of jurisdictional power from the state into the hands of the church had begun in the ninth century. This was not due to the church having taken up a basically new position, but to the coming about of a factually different situation. It is impossible to claim on the basis of historical evidence that the church had deprived the state of its power in matrimonial affairs. The Merovingians and Carlovingians certainly did not consciously transfer the jurisdictional administration of marriage to the church.[58]

In the tenth century, the kings lost a great deal of their power, and this may well have been the most important reason for the transference of their jurisdictional power into the hands of the bishops and the church, although other causes also played a part. The feudal system, under which the bishops had the status of overlords, also favoured this transference. It is not clear, however, whether the bishops were feudal lords in their ecclesiastical capacity or purely as secular rulers. In any case, the fact remains that the legislative function of the church in matrimonial affairs acquired a new meaning in the Frankish empire at this time. It became not only moral and pastoral, but also jurisdictional, although no one studied the meaning of this change. The marriage contract, which had previously been outside the church's jurisdiction—that is to say, in itself independent of the hierarchy of the church—now became in a very real sense subject to the hierarchy's jurisdiction.

It is important, however, to remember here that this jurisdictional power did not in any way affect the marriage contract proper. This was quite independent of the church's authority, and was brought about by the mutual decision of the two prospective partners to take each other as man and wife, even if no witnesses were present, or—in accordance with a different practice, which will be discussed at a later stage—by the first act of

[58] Esmein, pt. i, pp. 16 f.; see also p. 23.

sexual intercourse as the expression of this mutual desire to marry. The church was mainly concerned, in the exercise of her jurisdictional power, with the determination of the impediments to marriage and with judging the validity of marriage contracts. All the same, she was at this time more and more pressing in her demands that the mutual consent to marry should be public, and with the passage of time this mutual consent in fact took place less frequently in the family circle and far more often in the presence *in facie Ecclesiae*, that is, in front of the church porch.

The attitude of Hincmar, the bishop of Rheims whose role in various matrimonial disputes has already been discussed, was, I think, characteristic of this final period preceding the eleventh century. In 860 he declared the marriage of Stephen of Aquitania with the daughter of Count Regimund to be canonically invalid, but recognised the right of the secular arm to administer justice.[59] Elsewhere, he referred to a matrimonial case under Louis the Pious. A lady, Northildis, had initiated legal proceedings against her husband, Argembert, at the court. The king referred the matter to an episcopal synod which happened at that moment to be in session. The bishops, however, referred the case back to the secular judges, who were deemed to be the competent authority in this case.[60] In another matrimonial lawsuit, that of Baldwin and Judith, both the church and the civil authorities exercised their jurisdictional powers and both imposed punishments. The guilty parties appealed to Pope Nicholas, who spoke on their behalf to the emperor, although he recognised the authority of the secular power in judgments concerning the validity of marriages.[61]

[59] *De nuptiis Stephani et filiae Regimundi Comitis* (PL, 126, 134): "Et hanc causam rex cum nobilibus viris inter viros nobiles pacificare procuret: vos autem episcopali auctoritate et canonica diffinitione eam dirimere, et ad debitum atque salubrem terminum studeatis producere."

[60] *De divorcio Lotharii et Teutbergae* (PL, 125, 633 ff.). Here the judicial verdict was civil, whereas the duties of the bishop were principally moral and pastoral. See L. Godefroy, *DTC*, under "Mariage," pt. IX-2, cols. 2118–19.

[61] Esmein, pt. I, pp. 22–3.

According to historians, it is by no means easy to interpret these cases correctly: the limits of the state's and of the church's jurisdiction in matrimonial matters at this period have in fact been variously interpreted. A synodal canon, dating from the ninth century, sought to solve the following question concerning the form of law of marriage. Each people had its own practices in marriage. In the case of marriages between partners of different peoples, it was customary to apply both the legal form of the bridegroom's people and that of the bride's. When this was not done, the validity of the marriage remained in doubt. The synod therefore decided that in such cases the legal form that was lacking had to be supplied, since the only criterion which could be applied in judging the validity of the marriage was the keeping of the customary laws and the civil legislation.[62] It is not possible to find anywhere at this period[63] any evidence for the exclusive competence of the ecclesiastical courts. In short, a marriage was valid only if it had been contracted "according to the laws and customs of the Catholics."[64]

In the eleventh and twelfth centuries, we see that the church obtained complete jurisdiction in matrimonial affairs, and even became responsible for the regulation of the purely civil consequences of marriage.[65] As has already been pointed out, this was

[62] Esmein, pt. I, p. 24.

[63] I. Fahrner maintained (*Geschichte der Ehescheidung*, p. 103) that Regino of Prümm was a fervent advocate of the exclusive competence of the church. See *De ecclesiastica disciplina* (anno 906). This view has, however, been the subject of historical controversy.

[64] Bishop Atto of Vercelli, *Epist. ad Azonem* (PL, 134, 109). Ivo of Chartres also said the same. See G. H. Joyce, *Christian Marriage*, p. 54, *n.* 22. The penitential books of the Middle Ages illustrate the way in which the church approached marriage. See, among others, J. G. Ziegler, *Die Ehelehre der Pänitentialsummen von 1200–1350*, Regensburg (1956).

[65] The following books, most of which are listed in the bibliography, are especially valuable for these centuries: Esmein and Génestal, *Le mariage en droit canonique;* Fahrner, *Geschichte der Ehescheidung;* E. Friedberg, *Das Recht der Eheschliessung;* J. Freisen, *Geschichte des Kanonischen Eherechts;* G. Joyce, *Christian Marriage;* A. Smith, *Church and State in the*

not justified in principle, but was rather the result of the development of various historical factors. In some districts, too, the
secular authorities retained full jurisdictional control, even up to
the thirteenth century.

There was considerable diversity in the functions assumed by
the priest at this time in the marriage contracts in Germanic
lands. One fact, however, is quite certain. From the time of the
disappearance of the ancient ceremonies, the part played by the
priest gained immensely in significance. It was usually the priest
who gave the bride to the bridegroom, though in some places he
gave the partners to each other, or conducted the ceremony. The
significance of this is not easy to understand, and it has been
variously interpreted by historians. Some claim that the priest
took over the function of the father or guardian in the handing
over of the bride, whereas others maintain that his part was that
of the third, and neutral, party, whose function was to ask the
two partners for their mutual consent.

On the other hand, Otto Opet put forward the extremely
questionable thesis that the priest's handing over of the bride
went back to a practice of the early church.[66] But Ritzer came to
the following, rather more cautious, conclusions. The first evidence of a liturgical handing over of the bride by the priest is
provided in the nuptial mass of the Spanish West Gothic rite.
From this rite, it passed into the Frankish liturgical books, in
which we find that the father or the guardian of the bride gave
her, before the altar, to the priest conducting the liturgy. The
priest, in his turn, gave the bride to the bridegroom and, while
he was performing this action, read a text from the book of
Tobit (one of the blessings still in our marriage liturgy). Ritzer
considered this to be parallel with a similar practice in the
medieval liturgy of the coronation of a king. In both a particular

---

Middle Ages, Oxford (1913); G. le Bras, "Mariage," *DTC*, pt. IX-2, cols.
2123–317.

[66] O. Opet, *Brauttradition und Consensgespräch im mittelalterlichen
Trauungsritualien*, Berlin (1910), pp. 77–96.

legal action was repeated "by the better hand," in this case, by the priest. In the marriage contract, the legal proceedings enacted by a layman—that is, the father or the guardian (the *Vormund*) —were re-enacted by the priest (*FRBE*, p. 333).

At a later stage, the liturgical formula, "Et ego [i.e., the priest] coniungo vos in nomine Patris, et Filii, et Spiritus Sancti," grew from this practice. The first evidence of this formula dates from the fourteenth century, and was present until recently in the marriage liturgy of (for example) Holland, Belgium, and Germany, but it has since been replaced by the priest's official confirmation of the matrimonial bond made by the partners themselves. The Germanic "guardianship of the generation of the tribe"—that is, the handing over of the bride as a legal action on the part of the bride's father or guardian—gradually disappeared between the twelfth and the fourteenth centuries.

It is obvious that, when the ceremonies of marriage were adopted and assimilated by the church, it was the priest who "married" the bride and the bridegroom. In the marriage "formula" quoted above there was no longer any question of the bride being handed over in the older sense, since it was the priest who handed the bride and the bridegroom over to each other, even though the rubric still referred to a handing over of the bride. There are also liturgical texts of this period in which the idea of a handing over of the bride has become very weak indeed— the priest simply gives the bride and bridegroom to each other.

In broad outline, then, church marriage was conducted at this period in the following way. The priest asked the bride and bridegroom for their consent to the marriage at the entrance to the church. The parents of the bride then handed their daughter over to the bridegroom, and the dowry was given. This was followed by the blessing and giving of the ring, and the priest's marriage blessing. After this everyone went in procession into the church where the nuptial mass was celebrated and a separate blessing (the veiling ceremony or the blessing of the nuptial mass) was given. After the ceremony the priest gave the husband the kiss of peace, which was passed by the husband on to the wife. The blessing of the bridal chamber frequently followed.[67] Practices proper to secular society had thus become fully integrated into the liturgy of the church. Worldly things, symbols, and legal proceedings—the *arrha*, the ring, the dowry, the *iunctio dexterarum*, the veiling, and so on, objects and practices deriving from the popular tradition of the Germanic, Frankish, Celtic, Longobardic, and Gothic tribes—had, partly under Greco-Roman and Eastern influence (especially via the Western Goths in Spain), found their way into the liturgy of the church.

In Rome, however, marriage had already been associated with the celebration of the eucharist from the fifth century onwards. The church, conscious of the central significance of marriage for the faithful, had placed it under the aegis of her central mystery, the eucharist. Indeed, in the rite deriving from Rome, the priest's blessing of the bride formed an integral part of the liturgical celebration of the eucharist—the blessing or the veiling of the bride took place during mass (probably at the conclusion of the canon, after the *Per quem haec omnia*).

A combination of various circumstances led, from the eleventh century onwards, to the growth of the idea of the sacramental nature of marriage. But it was not this idea that caused the church gradually to acquire exclusive jurisdictional power over marriage. The church's acquisition of this jurisdictional power preceded the development of the sacramental idea of marriage— an idea which, moreover, was not originally based on elements in the formal constitution of marriage, but on the priestly liturgy surrounding it, namely the veiling or the priest's blessing of the marriage or the bride.

---

[67] An example of this is to be found in the missal of Rennes (twelfth century), in Brittany, where the new liturgy of marriage had acquired a distinctive form by the end of the eleventh century. See Martène, *Ordo* 1 (*FRBE*, p. 314). For the oldest form of an even more primitive liturgy in the West, see especially Ambrose of Milan, *Epist.* xix, 7 (*PL*, 16, 984).

THE SACRAMENTAL NATURE OF MARRIAGE:
THE ELEVENTH TO THE THIRTEENTH
CENTURIES

The course of the growing realisation that an everyday secular reality—the marriage contract itself—had to be regarded as a sacrament, not because of the liturgy which in fact surrounded it, but because of the nature of the event of marriage itself, occupied several hundred years of thought and discussion from the eleventh to the thirteenth centuries.

Insofar as the early schoolmen were acquainted with the patristic texts by way of anthologies, they were unable to find much inspiration in the writings of the church Fathers, which in fact displayed a distinct antipathy towards everything concerning sexuality.[68] This was especially so because complete ignorance prevailed concerning the remarkable liturgical celebration of marriage in the East. In general the church Fathers related marriage to the miracle of the wedding at Cana, by means of which Christ had, in their opinion, blessed marriage and included it in the plan of redemption.[69] It is true that Tertullian had said that the heavenly Father protected marriage with his gift of salvation (*Ad uxorem*, 2, 7 [*PL*, 1, 1299]), and that Christ was always present in any marriage made "in the Lord" as the factor binding the two baptized parties together: "Where two [are together], there also is he [Christ]; where he is, there evil cannot be" (Tertullian, *Ad uxorem*, 2, 9 [*PL*, 1, 1302]). But Tertullian said this not so much of marriage as such as of the fact that, in a marriage between two Christians, domestic life was able to develop into a true family liturgy. In his *Ad uxorem*, life in the Christian family is depicted very much as monastic life in microcosm. Nonetheless, he did say that God himself ratified the marriage of

[68] The patristic and the scholastic view of sexuality is dealt with in a later volume.

[69] See, among others, Cyril of Alexandria, *Comm. in Joh.*, 2, 2 (*PG*, 73, 223); Epiphanius, *Adv. Haer.*, 51, 30 (*PG*, 41, 941); John Damascene, *De fide orthodoxa*, 4, 24 (*PG*, 94, 2374).

two baptized Christians (*Pater rato habet*). He only saw the consequences of this for the Christ-like life of the married couple, and not for the marital life of Christians. Origen had claimed that marriage was a divine gift of salvation precisely because it was God himself who made the marriage (*Comm. in Matth.*, 14, 16 [*PG*, 13, 1228–9]; see also *GCS*, 10, 323–4), and that marriage was consequently subject to a divine charisma which ensured that the partners in marriage would live together in harmony.[70] But when Pope Siricius saw marriage as having been "founded on God's grace," he was alluding to the goodness of marriage on a basis of God's blessing of creation.[71] It was also said of anyone who lost fidelity in marriage that he lost God's grace (Ambrose, *De Abraham*, 1, 7 [*PL*, 14, 442]).

This is not very much to go on. What is more, Paul's text from his epistle to the Ephesians was not associated with marriage in the first centuries—this text was only used at that time with reference to the church as the bride of Christ (which was, of course, Paul's primary intention). It acted as an incentive to the Fathers of the church, following Paul, to draw attention to the moral and religious demands of Christian married life; for this was the chief pastoral concern of the Fathers in connection with marriage, which they felt to be simply an ordinary fact of life to be accepted by Christians. (Willing and sympathetic acceptance of this fact was exceptional, actually, in the case of the church Fathers.)

Augustine, however, was more radically concerned with the symbolism of marriage in Eph v. 21–32 and, taking this as his point of departure, called marriage a *sacramentum*. *Sacramentum* in this context had a double meaning. Augustine used it in the first place in the sense of an indissoluble bond of "sacral" obligations and in the second in the sense of a sacred sign. As a "sacramental sign" marriage referred to the mystery of the unity exist-

---

[70] Origen, *In 1 Cor.*, Fragment; see *JTS*, 9 (1908), p. 503.
[71] "Illud esse coniugium, quod erat primitus divina gratia fundatum," *Epist.* 36 (*PL*, 20, 602).

ing between Christ and his church. The distinctive quality of
Augustine's view should, however, not be misunderstood by
interpreting it anachronistically on a basis of the thirteenth-
century idea of a sacrament. Both the pagans and the Fathers of
the church saw marriage primarily as a means of founding a
family (*ad procreationem*). Their view of marriage was dominated by the idea of the *bonum prolis*, the legitimate child.

In pagan circles infidelity, adultery, and misconduct in marriage were judged above all in the light of the child. Marital
infidelity and misconduct led to a *confusio prolis*—in other
words, brought strange children into the domestic circle. The
right of repudiation of an adulterous wife was based on this view.
The same idea also played a part in the patristic judgment of
adultery and misconduct in marriage. On the other hand, the
Fathers, taking their stand on the gospel, stated that remarriage
was out of the question if the wife had been repudiated on these
grounds. According to Augustine this view was based on the
presence in marriage of what he called *quiddam coniugale* (*De
nuptiis et conc.*, I, 11, 12 [*PL*, 44, 420–1])—a certain marriage
bond. He did not, however, see this *vinculum* in precisely the
same way as it was seen later, in the Middle Ages. For him it was
not a kind of ontological bond, but rather a bond which made
the *iura matrimonii* permanent. In other words, the obligations
undertaken for life in the marriage contract did not cease to exist
because of infidelity in marriage.

Augustine based the permanence of this moral obligation on
the *sacramentum* of marriage, and the permanence of this *sacramentum* was in turn based on a "sacral" symbolism. It was not
permissible to dissolve marriage, because it was a sign of "more
profound realities"—namely, the mystery of Christ in his church.
From the moment that a marriage was contracted between Christians, it contained this "sacral" element and might therefore not
be dissolved, or the sacral symbolism would be destroyed. In
this, Augustine was completely in accordance with the rest of
patristic teaching—namely, that the indissolubility of marriage

was a moral obligation, a commission to be fulfilled. The contract brought into being a status implying rights and duties which were valid for life. This obligation was reinforced by the sacral symbolism of marriage. Neither adultery nor non-cohabitation deprived marriage of this obligation or invalidated its sacral reference to the mystery of Christ, which was actually destroyed only by remarriage.

Augustine's view of marriage, then, was that the partners in marriage had a lifelong obligation to remain faithful to each other because of the obligations undertaken in the marriage contract, but these obligations were all the more binding because the contract was a *sacramentum*, or sign of the mystery of Christ in the church, and so because in the case of infidelity something sacral was violated. Both the Greek and the Latin patristic texts of the first five centuries generally assert that remarriage after the repudiation of a legal partner was not permissible, even if the repudiated partner was not baptized. (The "Pauline privilege" was apparently unknown.)[72] A separation of this kind completely disrupted the marriage, but did not nullify the fundamental obligations that the partners had taken upon themselves in the marriage contract. This accounts for the distinction between the *bonum fidei* and the *bonum sacramenti* of marriage. The *bonum fidei* commanded the partners to be faithful to each other and condemned every form of misconduct, whereas the *bonum sacramenti* of marriage forbade adultery in the sense of remarriage after separation.

The church Fathers, then, maintained that marriage was in-

---

[72] Certain of the Greek Fathers have frequently been misinterpreted here. John Chrysostom, for example, asserted, in *Epist. I ad Cor.*, 19, 3 (*PG*, 61, 154–6), that the *gamos* might result in a separation, but he did not assert that remarriage was permissible. Cohabitation (*gamos*) with the unbaptized partner could be discontinued in intolerable circumstances. The only Greek Father to approve both remarriage after separation and remarriage after the repudiation of the unbaptized partner was, as we have seen, the Ambrosiaster. There is no mention of the possibility of remarriage in Lactantius, Theodoret, Basil, or Asterius, even though they refer to a dissolution of the *gamos*.

dissoluble because, mainly on a basis of the *sacramentum*, it involved permanent obligations—obligations, on the one hand, not to disrupt the unity existing between the partners and, on the other, not to destroy the sacramental sign of marriage. In the scholastic view of marriage which was elaborated in the twelfth and thirteenth centuries, the *sacramentum* was not seen purely as a symbol, but as an effective symbol which brought something about—an objective bond that could not be broken. According to the church Fathers the dissolution of marriage was not *permissible;* but according to the schoolmen its dissolution was not *possible.* Both views came together in the joint assertion that a marriage entered upon after the disruption of a valid Christian marriage was invalid.

The difference between the two views is this. According to the Fathers, marriage was itself a *sacramentum*, latent and unclear in the case of "natural" marriage, explicit and clear in the case of marriage between Christians. According to the schoolmen, however, the "sacrament"—that is to say, the ecclesiastical contracting of a marriage—in fact brought about this mystical reference in marriage (even though it may have done so on the basis of a religious symbolism of marriage as such). The patristic view that marriage was a moral obligation and indissoluble on a basis of the *Sacramentum*, and the scholastic view of marriage as an objective and indissoluble bond on the basis of a certain efficacity of the sacrament, are therefore complementary. Both saw the sacramental bond of marriage as a saving commission on the partners in a marriage to be existentially faithful.

In classical Latin, indissoluble obligations were referred to by the word *sacramentum*. The fact that Augustine chose to use the word *sacramentum* for "sacred signs" does not alter the fact that *sacramentum* at the same time had an authentically Roman meaning in the context of marriage. The basic meaning of this word in secular Latin usage was "religious commitment" or "*engagement*," and it was from this that all the other meanings were derived—*sacramentum* as an initiation (which, of course, necessarily involves personal commitment), as an oath or *iuramentum* (the oath pointing to the legal aspect of this personal commitment), and finally as the legal and sacral bond resulting from the obligations undertaken under oath.[73]

Tertullian, though not the first to use the secular term *sacramentum* in a Christian sense, provides important evidence of its religious use, especially in the context of Eph v, and there he always employed it in the sense of a sign (*sacramentum-signum*). Before Augustine, the classical *sacramentum-vinculum* (sacrament-as-sacral-bond) is found in this connection only in the writings of the lay Christian, Lactantius (*Epitome* 61[PL, 6, 1080]). The word occurs again with this meaning—that is, the second sense of the word "sacrament"—in the writings of Augustine when he is talking about the *sacramentum* of marriage, and it occurs for the most part in the context of the "three properties of marriage" to which he refers in these works: *De nuptiis et conc.*, I, II [PL, 44, 420]; *De bono coniugali*, 32 [PL, 40, 394]; *De pecc. originali*, 34, 39 [PL, 44, 404]; 37, 42 [PL, 44, 406]; *Contra Jul.*, 3, 57 [PL, 44, 732]; 5, 12 [PL, 44, 810]. In this context the word has the unmistakable meaning of "indissolubility." Just as an excommunicated apostate does not lose his *sacramentum fidei*—the indissoluble obligations of his baptism—(*De nuptiis et conc.*, I, II, *n.* 13 [PL, 44, 421]; *De coniugiis adulterinis*, 2, 5 [PL, 40, 473]), or a priest is not acquitted from his official service to the kingdom of God on relinquishing his office (*De bono coniugali*, 24, 32 [PL, 40, 394]), so a separated man or woman is not released from the *sacramentum*—from the indissoluble obligations which he or she undertook when the marriage contract was concluded. This indissolubility comprised the *sanctitas sacramenti* (the inviolability of marriage).

According to Augustine, marriage was a *sacramentum* because it was indissoluble and inviolable, and therefore holy. Augustine

---

[73] See C. Mohrmann, "Sacramentum dans les plus anciens textes chrétiens," *Etudes sur le Latin des Chrétiens*, Rome (1958), pp. 233–44; see also A. Kolping, *Sacramentum Tertullianeum*, Regensburg (1948).

also held that remarriage after separation was impermissible even according to the human view, the *sensus humanus* (*De coniug. adult.*, 2, 5 [*PL*, 40, 473]).[74] Marriage was therefore, in Augustine's opinion, a natural *sacramentum-vinculum*—a sacral bond of indissoluble obligations. The indissolubility of Christian marriage was, however, more firmly based, because it was not merely a prefiguration, but—according to Eph v—an explicit sign (*sacramentum-signum*) of the mystery of Christ in his church. For Augustine, then, the very essence of marriage, insofar as it was a *sacramentum* or a "sign of the unity of Christ and his church," was the basis of the indissoluble unity—the *sacramentum*—of marriage.

The second meaning of *sacramentum*—as a sacral contract—is echoed clearly in only one text where Augustine alludes explicitly to this symbolic representation (*De bono coniugali*, 21 [*PL*, 40, 387-8]). According to Augustine, marriage to some extent resembled a sacral contract; this made him think both of the inviolability of the obligations in respect to the kingdom of God which are undertaken at baptism, and of the inviolability of the obligations undertaken when office in the Church is freely accepted. He expressed his Christian consciousness of the holiness or inviolability of marriage by means of the word *sacramentum*, which, although it had secular origins, was highly suitable for the purpose. However, it was not this secular reality, but Christ's *logion* concerning its indissolubility, which caused Augustine to affirm the "sacramental" nature of marriage. Moreover, the fact that Paul had—according to the ancient Latin translations—spoken about the *mystērion-sacramentum*, a sacred mystery pointing to a higher reality, was an even greater inducement for him to make this assertion.

The early schoolmen were to analyse the implications of this Augustinian vision on the basis of the liturgy of marriage. I pro-

---

[74] Augustine usually does not concede the *sanctitas matrimonii*, or full indissolubility, to marriage between unbaptized persons. See *de bono coniugali*, 32 (PL, 40, 394).

pose therefore to trace the course, from the eleventh to the thirteenth century, of this development in early scholasticism towards a theological interpretation of marriage, since this formed the basis of what was to become the traditional "treatise on marriage." Two problems cut across each other in the explication of the sacramentalism of marriage. The first is the relationship between the partners' mutual consent to marry and their sexual intercourse with each other—in other words, the problem as to what precisely constituted marriage; the second, and consequent, problem is at what moment was the "sacrament" itself to be found. These two problems will be dealt with separately.

Spiritual Communion and Sexual Intercourse: The Indissolubility of Consummated Marriage

Since the church had in fact taken over complete jurisdiction in matters of marriage, from the tenth to the eleventh century, she was faced in matrimonial lawsuits with the question as to what really constituted marriage as a valid contract between husband and wife. Although Christ had said that marriage was indissoluble, he had not said in what the anthropological reality of marriage precisely consisted. In other words, precisely *what* was indissoluble?

When the church found herself in almost total jurisdictional control of matrimonial affairs, she discovered that it was a highly complex issue. The pattern of marriage at that time was the result of many different ideas and social factors. First, there was the Roman conception of the marriage of mutual consent—marriage by *consensus*. Then there was the Germanic, Frankish, Gothic, and Celtic *mundium* form of marriage, in which the marriage contract was formally regarded as a handing over of the bride by her father to the marital control of the bridegroom. Finally, the very ancient idea that the marriage was not consummated until cohabitation and sexual intercourse had actually taken place played an important part in the minds of all peoples. The *domum-ductio*, or the solemn taking of the bride in procession to the bridegroom's house, was thus regarded both by the Greeks and the Romans and by the Western tribes as the consummation of the marriage contract. In the Middle Ages, these did not exist side by side as three distinct systems of law; they interacted upon each other. Even when the church had succeeded, after considerable difficulty, in getting her Roman point of view (marriage by *consensus*) accepted by the Germanic and Frankish tribes, this *consensus* was—as we have seen —still concretely regarded by these tribes—that is, in the way it was transacted within their own tribal customs, especially in the "handing over of power" and in the official initiation of the "cohabitation."

During the eleventh century the widespread circulation in the West of the texts of the ancient legislation of Justinian brought about a renaissance in Roman law. From this time onwards the theory of the *consensus* was not simply imposed upon the Western tribes by Rome—the Longobardic, Germanic, and Frankish theologians began of their own accord to think about marriage as a *consensus*. This early scholastic speculation about the doctrine of the *consensus* in fact accompanied the first reflections about the sacramental nature of marriage. This speculation took as its point of departure one particular aspect of the Augustinian vision—namely, that marriage derived its profound significance from the *sacramentum*, from the fact that it was a sacred symbolic representation of the unity between Christ and his church. On the other hand, the indissolubility of marriage was closely connected in the Germanic and Frankish lands with the consummation of marriage in sexual intercourse. This confronted the early schoolmen with the problem as to whether the *consensus* or the *copula* constituted the marriage.

Unlike the church Fathers, the scholastics connected sexuality with the constitution of marriage, and were therefore faced with a difficult problem. This came about because they followed—via the writings of the Fathers, and especially of Augustine—the Jewish and ancient view that the primary purpose of marriage

was the foundation of a family (the procreation and the bringing up of children),[75] with the result that they felt obliged to
value sexual intercourse particularly, while on the other hand
they refused to relinquish the Roman idea of the *consensus*.
They had, however, read in Augustine that a true marriage was
possible even without sexual intercourse. (*Contra Jul.*, 5, 16 [*PL*,
44, 816–18]; *De consensu evang.*, II, 1, 1 [*PL*, 34, 1071]).[76] A
better knowledge of patristics would have made them realise that
Augustine was virtually alone in holding this view; but they had
to take this Augustinian fact into account. The ninth and the
preceding centuries gave them no help, since there were two distinct trends of thought there as well. Isidore of Seville had said
that marriage came about by mutual consent (*Etymol.*, 9, 7 [*PL*,
82, 365]), and the popes supported this view;[77] Hincmar of
Rheims, on the other hand, had clearly taken his stand (in the
matrimonial lawsuits in the Frankish lands) on the view that sexual intercourse was necessary for a marriage to be consummated, and even that the mutual consent to marry was not a
sacramentum of Christ and his church if it were not consummated by cohabitation.[78] This gave rise to the idea current in
certain circles that the "marriage" was situated in the *consensus*,
but the *sacramentum* of the marriage in the physical union, of the
partners.

The problem was further complicated by the Germanic and
Frankish view of the betrothal, which brought about a far
stronger bond in the Germanic and Frankish lands than in the
case of the Romans. One occasionally has the impression that a

[75] These problems will also be discussed from the historical point of view
in a later volume.

[76] See also, in connection with the marriage of Joseph and Mary, *De
nuptiis et conc.*, I, 11, 13 (*PL*, 44, 424).

[77] See the letter of Pope Nicholas I to the Bulgars, already mentioned in
note 57 above.

[78] In the letter already discussed, *Epist.* 22, *de nuptiis Stephani* (*PL*, 126,
137) and *De divorcio Lotharii*, Interr. XIII (*PL*, 125, 707–14). See also
Bliemetzrieder, in *RTAM*, I (1929), p. 476.

betrothal, followed by sexual intercourse, was more or less regarded as a marriage, even though this was forbidden. The protagonists of the theory of the *copula* were provided with a specious argument by the fact that the betrothal also contained a form of mutual consent and still could not be regarded as a marriage. The early French scholastics of Chartres threw some light on this question. Ivo of Chartres maintained that according to Genesis sexual intercourse constituted marriage, which was indissoluble on this basis. The school of Chartres, however, also made a clearer distinction between the "betrothal" (the *fides pactionis*, or intention to marry) and the marriage itself (the *fides consensus*, or contract of marriage) (*Epist.*, 99 [*PL*, 162, 118–19]; *Epist.* 167 [*PL*, 162, 170]). The first was dissoluble, though its dissolution was not permissible and was punishable; the second was indissoluble. This view was taken over by the school of Laon.[79] After many changes in the terminology used, Peter Lombard's technical distinction between *sponsalia de futuro* (the betrothal) and *sponsalia de praesenti* (the contract of marriage) finally became accepted as standard.[80] This cleared up the initial confusion as to whether an intention to marry together with cohabitation was not really a valid marriage, even though cohabitation at this stage was not permitted.

It also marked the first step towards an understanding of what in fact constituted marriage, by excluding the betrothal. It was at

---

[79] Here the distinction is between *fides pactionis* and *fides coniugii;* see William of Champeaux, *Sententiae de coniugiis*, ed. Lefèbre, *Travaux et mémoires de l'Université de Lille*, Lille (1898), pt. 6, p. 74. Until Peter Lombard there was no unified terminology; see *Epitome* (*PL*, 178, 1745)— *foederatio de coniugio contrahendo* and *foederatio coniugii;* and Hugh of St. Victor, *De sacramentis* (*PL*, 176, 487)—*pactio et promissio futuri consensus* and *consensus coniugii*. A certain stability came about in the middle of the twelfth century; see Orlando Bandinelli, later Pope Alexander III, *Sententiae*, ed. A. Gietl, p. 274—*ligatio* (or *desponsatio*) *de futuro* and *ligatio* (or *desponsatio*) *de praesenti*.

[80] *IV Sent.*, d. 27, c. 9. See J. Freisen, *Geschichte*, pp. 212–15, 901 ff.; I. Fahrner, *Geschichte der Ehescheidung*, pt. 1, pp. 131–4; G. Le Bras, "Mariage," *DTC*, pt. ix-2, cols. 2140–56.

this time, too, that Ulpianus' classic sentence became known in the West: "*Nuptias non concubitus sed consensus* [or *affectus*] *facit*" (*Codex Justiniani*, Dig., 17, 30)—not sexual intercourse, but mutual consent, constitutes marriage. This rediscovery of the Roman law dealt the protagonists of the theory of the *copula* a hard blow. Hugh of St. Victor, who was the first to write a scholastic treatise on marriage, built up the whole of his vision —which was inspired by Augustine—on this *consensus* theory. (See pp. 320 ff. below.)

Although the theologians, with individual shades of emphasis and meaning, supported the theory of the *consensus*, the canonists, with their feeling for the practical reality of human life, continued to defend the *copula* theory. It is possible to distinguish three schools of thought about the essence of marriage in the confused situation resulting from this. According to one group, the essence of marriage was to be found in sexual intercourse, as defined by Astenasus.[81] The desire for sexual intercourse belonged, according to this group, to the mutual consent to marry. According to the school of thought of which Hugh of St. Victor was the exponent, marriage consisted of a spiritual communion, and of living, being, and acting together. Sexual intercourse was not an essential element in marriage, which continued to be a full marriage even when sexual intercourse played no part. The marriage of Mary and Joseph was the "perfect marriage." Hugh maintained that God had nonetheless given a task of procreation to married persons, but this task was connected with the *officium* of the marriage, not with its constitution.[82]

The third theological definition of marriage had a more social emphasis, and went back to the etymological definition of marriage provided by Isidore of Seville—namely that marriage made

[81] "Coniunctio illa quae est in actu carnali"; see J. Ziegler, *Die Ehelehre der Pänitentialsummen*, pp. 35 ff.

[82] This view was derived from Modestinus' definition in the ancient *corpus iuris civilis*, and given a Christian meaning: "Matrimonium est maris et feminae coniunctio, consortium vitae communis, divini et humani iuris communicatio" (*Dig.* 32, 2, 1).

the woman into a mother,[83] and that marriage was an institution for the bringing up of children. Isidore thus based the constitution of marriage on the partners' mutual consent to marry. It is clear from these three definitions that the early scholastics were not exclusively concerned with the purely juridical question as to when a marriage was in fact legally, and thus indissolubly, contracted.

Marriage was also considered from a more existential point of view; the early schoolmen were very much concerned with the meaning of marriage as a human reality. And in this connection, too, there were the three distinct schools of thought outlined above: the view that regarded marriage as a primarily sexual community; the second view that situated the essence of marriage in the interpersonal relationship of the partners of the marital community, which could be extended to sexual intercourse, but which nonetheless remained a full marriage—and indeed marriage in a very special and even sublime sense—even when sexuality played no part in it; and finally the third view, according to which marriage is regarded socially as the foundation of a human environment in which children could grow up. These three trends of thought certainly impinged upon each other at several points, but no synthesis was reached in the early period of scholasticism.

But the problem as to what in fact constituted marriage as such ultimately became less a controversy between the protagonists of the so-called *copula* theory and those of the *consensus* theory (since both sides were agreed that the essential element was the partners' mutual consent), than a controversy about the relationship between this mutual consent and the community of marriage itself. The two trends of thought reached a synthesis in the middle of the twelfth century—Gratian's Decree synthesized

---

[83] "Matrimonium quasi matris munium, i.e., officium quod dat mulieribus esse matrem"; (*Etymol.*, ix, 8, 19 [PL, 82, 366]). "Mother" here was not so much "the one who bears children" as "the one who brings up the children."

the views of the canonists (the *copula* theory), and Peter Lombard those of the theologians. Gratian expounded the views of the school of Bologna, with the result that his decree was taken to represent the view of the "Roman Church."[84] Peter Lombard's theory, based on the views of the Paris school of theologians, came to be known in the Middle Ages as the view of the "church in Gaul."

According to Gratian's decree, it was indeed the partner's mutual consent which brought about the marriage (c. 27, q. 2; Dictum c. 29, q. 1), but a distinction was made between the *coniugium initiatum* (the contracted marriage) and the *coniugium consummatum* or *ratum* (the ratification of the marriage by sexual intercourse). The first was dissoluble, the second indissoluble.[85] Furthermore, Gratian had no clear distinction between betrothal and the marriage *consensus* in mind. Peter Lombard, however, placed full emphasis on the *consensus* which, in his view, was the *sacramentum* of the unity of Christ and his church (*IV Sent.*, d. 26, c. 6; d. 27, c. 2, 3; d. 28, c. 2), a symbolism extending to sexual intercourse (*IV Sent.*, d. 27, c. 7). The marriage bond was thus already established by the partners' mutual consent (*IV Sent.*, d. 28, c. 3; d. 31, c. 1, 2); but this was clearly distinguished from the betrothal (*IV Sent.*, d. 26, 27; see especially d. 27, c. 4). This mutual consent to marry had as its objective the "marital community," which implied far more than mere sexual intercourse. The community of marriage as such possessed only a receptivity and a willing predisposition towards sexual inter-

---

[84] The *consuetudo Ecclesiae Romanae* was contrasted with the *consuetudo universalis Gallicanae Ecclesiae*; see Gregory IX, *Compilatio Decretalium*, c. 3, c.i., 4, 16. This qualification is, however, historically incorrect. The theory of the *consensus* was also—indeed, above all—accepted by the Roman school.

[85] Dictum c. 27, q. 2, c. 34; c. 27, q. 2, c. 35 up to and including 39; c. 32, q. 7; dictum post c. 34, c. 18–26. "Inter copulatos tantum est matrimonium"—see c. 16–17, c. 27, q. 2; dictum ad c. 28, c. 27, q. 2. It should be remembered that contemporary law calls the first *ratum* (*tantum*) and the second *ratum et consummatum*.

course.[86] Like Hugh of St. Victor, Peter Lombard regarded the *unio animorum* as the formal essence of the community of marriage.

Both the decretals of Gratian and the writings of Peter Lombard were accepted as authoritative in the Middle Ages, with the result that the theoretical differences of opinion between the two had important practical consequences. The Italian ecclesiastical courts dissolved marriages (on grounds of sexual non-consummation) which were declared by the Frankish churches to be indissoluble. And finally a definitive solution to the problem was reached by Pope Alexander III who, as Orlando Bandinelli, had previously been known as a distinguished canonist, and later by Innocent III and Gregory IX. These popes personally supported the views of the canonists who took their stand on Gratian's decretals, but they were realistic enough to recognise that the view of the Paris school afforded a clearer criterion and provided an easier solution in many matrimonial lawsuits. The legal security of the validity of a marriage thus made them decide in favour of the Paris school, while retaining the essential element in the teaching of the school of Bologna—namely, that marriage was a true and legally valid sacrament formally and exclusively by virtue of the partners' mutual consent to the marriage, but that the marriage was dissoluble if this sacrament was not consummated in sexual intercourse.[87] This is still the legal practice of the Catholic Church. Although Alexander III initially considered it necessary for a priest, or at least someone holding office, to be present (Gregory IX, *Compilatio Decretalium* [hereafter quoted as *Comp.*], x, c. 4, IV, 3), and advocated the observation of local customs (*Comp.* x, c. 4, XVI, 2), he ultimately regarded only the

---

[86] "Consensus coniugalis societatis" (*IV Sent.*, d. 28, c. 3; see d. 31, c. 1, 3).

[87] There is an immense bibliography on the subject of this important decision. Among the most important books are: J. Freisen, *Geschichte*, pp. 212–5, 910–2; I. Fahrner, *Geschichte der Ehescheidung*, pt. 1, pp. 185–93; Esmein and Génestal, *Le Mariage en droit canonique*, pt. 1, pp. 137–50, pt. 2, pp. 48 ff.; G. Le Bras, "Mariage," *DTC*, pt. IX–2 cols. 2149–62; H. Portmann, *Wesen und Unauflösigkeit der Ehe*.

mutual consent of the partners to the marriage as necessary and sufficient, according to the then current formula: "Ego, N., te recipio in meum—ego, N., te recipio in meam" ("I take thee to be my husband—and I take thee to be my wife"). (*Comp.* 1, c. 4, iv, 6. See also: Hugh of St. Victor, *De sacramentis* ii, 11, 5 [*PL*, 176, 488]; Peter Lombard, *IV Sent.*, d. 27, c. 3.) The symbolism of the unity between Christ and his church was nonetheless situated only in the "becoming one" or the "one flesh," and thus in marital sexual intercourse, although (following the view of Hugh of St. Victor) the *consensus animorum* had, of itself, a mystical significance and was consequently a *sacramentum-signum* (*Comp.* 1, c. 4, 1, 2).

This marked an end to the view which was current among certain canonists: namely, the tendency to regard an intention to marry—in other words, a betrothal—together with sexual intercourse, as a marriage (*Comp.* x, c. 4, v, 3). Alexander completely accepted the consequences of the school of Bologna—with the proviso, however, that the *consensus* was clearly distinguished from the intention of the partners to marry, and that this mutual consent was in itself the formal and legally valid contract of marriage. Thus unity was achieved in the chaotic situation which had hitherto prevailed in ecclesiastical legal practice concerning the dissolution of marriage. Pope Alexander III also gave an explicit indication of the fact that he was conscious of accepting a criterion for this dissolution which was different from that of some of his predecessors.[88]

Alexander's teaching must, however, be seen in its proper perspective. He did not assert that a validly contracted but unconsummated marriage was dissoluble and that a validly contracted and consummated marriage was indissoluble. His thesis was that marriage was in principle essentially indissoluble by virtue of the *consensus;* it could be annulled only by an act of ecclesiastical

[88] ". . . Quamvis alii aliter sentiant et aliter etiam a quibusdam Praedecessoribus nostris est aliquando iudicatum" (c. 3, c. 1, iv, 4; included in c. 3, x, iv, 4).

jurisdiction.[89] The only title by which an unconsummated marriage could be dissolved was thus an ecclesiastical "dispensation." That was why, for example, he refused to dissolve a marriage that had been validly contracted, but not consummated, and had been followed by a second and consummated marriage with a third party.[90] Consummation made a marriage of mutual consent factually and essentially indissoluble in principle, and even the church had no jurisdictional power over this (*Comp.* 1, c. 7, III, 28; see also c. 7, X, III, 32). The pope made only one exception to the impossibility of dissolving an unconsummated marriage— in the case of a virgin taking the veil and making her solemn profession, an unconsummated marriage was *ipso facto* dissolved. And maybe even this was not an exception since the profession was made in the name of the church and could therefore be regarded as an implicit ecclesiastical dispensation (*Comp.* 1, c. 2, III, 28; 1, c. 7, III, 28).[91] Alexander III, who, as the canonist Orlando Bandinelli, had used the term "contract" in the context of marriage, considered this contract to be dissoluble in the case of an unconsummated marriage, but even then only on the grounds of a jurisdictional action on the part of the church declaring it null and void.

The popes who followed Alexander continued along the same lines, although many difficulties remained in connection with the various impediments to marriage. Finally, it should be borne in mind that the principle of indissolubility was not dependent on the fact that the marriage had been contracted *in facie Ecclesiae*

---

[89] See especially I. Fahrner, *Geschichte der Ehescheidung*, pt. 1, pp. 185–193. Fahrner gives a more subtle analysis of this question than J. Freisen, *Geschichte*, pp. 212 ff., 901 ff., and G. Le Bras, "Mariage," *DTC.*, pp. 2158–9.

[90] "Quamvis exinde sit diversa quorundam sententia et non eadem consuetudo Ecclesiae, tutius tamen videtur ut primam habere debent quam secundam, cum a primo *sine iudicio Ecclesiae* separari non debeat, postquam cum ea pari voto et consensu matrimonium contraxit" (*Comp.* 1, c. 5, IV, 4).

[91] This was, however, denied in one of Alexander's decretals: 1, c. 5, IV, 4.

(i.e., solemnised by a priest); or on the fact that local customs had or had not been observed (*Comp.* i, c. 4, vi, 6, 8; ii, c. 4, iii, 1; x, c. 4, iii, 2), although clandestine marriages were strongly condemned once more.[92]

The result of this controversy over the indissolubility-in-principle of the marriage by mutual consent and the indissolubility-in-fact of the consummated marriage by mutual consent—a controversy which had involved the whole of early scholasticism—will be considered in the concluding section of this volume in the light of the biblical data on the subject. Two consequences of this somewhat mitigated theory of the *consensus* must, however, be pointed out here. The consecration of this theory was in fact possible only on the basis of a twofold "formalisation"—of a juridical and abstract view of marriage. The "soul" of the "togetherness" of the married state is undoubtedly the human desire for the living community of marriage, the realisation of the *consensus*. As such this desire is a vital element in the total existential and social reality of marriage; and yet it was "extrapolated" from the full function of married life and placed on a juridical plane by the doctrine of the pure *consensus*. It was, in other words, considered in the abstract, becoming a legitimate and even an inevitable formalisation, but nonetheless an abstraction, by means of which the *consensus* was isolated both from sexual intercourse itself and from the local customs of marriage which were deeply rooted in human society.

As far as the first formalisation—concerning sexual intercourse—is concerned, an attempt was made to make up for its disadvantages by establishing a legal bond between the *consensus* and the existential element of married life—the *consensus*, as the formally indispensable element in the constitution of marriage, did not, it is true, include sexual intercourse, but on the other

---

[92] The Fourth Council of the Lateran, summoned by Innocent III, categorically forbade clandestine marriages: "clandestina coniugia penitus inhibemus, prohibentes etiam, ne quis sacerdos talibus interesse praesumat"; c. 51 (M–SC, pt. 22, p. 1038). They were nonetheless legally valid.

hand it did certainly incorporate the "right to sexual intercourse."[93] It is clear from this that the existential view of marriage was, of its nature, bound to influence the juridical formalisation, even though this might come about in a juridical way. If
the intention is to approach marriage from the point of view of
legal security—and this is, after all, an aspect of the social event
of marriage—then it is necessary to be consistent in juridical
formalisations.

There were disadvantages, too, in connection with the second
formalisation of the *consensus* (that concerning the local customs
of the people): clandestine marriages were still forbidden, but
were considered to be valid marriages by virtue of this *consensus*
theory. The idea of making the validity of the partners' mutual
consent to marry dependent on social factors providing legal
security did not arise in the Middle Ages. The question as to
whether the church could in fact intervene in the natural right
of man to contract a (valid) marriage was to be violently debated
in the Council of Trent. Any attempt to make the *consensus* dependent on extrinsic conditions of validity was felt in the Middle
Ages to be an attack on the inalienable rights of the individual.
Rather than do this, the serious difficulty posed by clandestine
marriages was tolerated. These were merely threatened with
punishment, on the principle that they were possible (i.e., valid)
but not permissible.

The Pseudo-Isidorian reformers had appealed to the feelings
of the people and their taste for involved festivities in connection with local marriage customs with the intention of safeguarding the public nature of marriage. But although it met with
resistance on the part of the people, the idea of the *consensus*
gradually gained ground precisely because of the insistence of
the popes on the Roman conception of the *consensus*. The papal
ratification of this theory brought about a marked devaluation
in the marriage customs of the Frankish, Germanic, and Celtic

93 See, for example, Bonaventure, *In IV Sent.*, d. 28, a un., q. 6; Aquinas,
In IV Sent., d. 28, a. 4.

peoples, at least as far as their original significance was concerned. It is true that they were not affected in principle—according to Hugh of St. Victor, the *consensus* could be given not only by a formal dialogue of mutual consent, but also by an action, an *actio rei*, "as is the custom" (*De sacramentis* II, 11, 5 [*PL*, 176, 488]; see also Peter Lombard, *IV Sent.*, d. 27, a. 3).

In one of the decretals included in Gratian's collection, a distinction (which conflicts with other definitions in the decree) is thus made between the *coniugium ratum* and the *coniugium legitimum*—between valid, and legitimate (and valid), marriages (c. 17, Causa XXVIII, q. 1).[94] A legitimate and valid marriage was a marriage that was contracted not only by the handing over of the bride by the father or guardian and the giving of the dowry (the indigenous legal forms of the marriage contract which gave a sufficiently clear indication of the existence of mutual consent to the marriage), but also by the blessing of a priest. A marriage concluded purely by mutual consent, without these customs and solemnities, was merely *ratum*—valid, but not permitted. From this it is clear that Pope Nicholas' epistle to the Bulgars had little influence on the people even in the West. But when the great medieval popes—Alexander III, Innocent III, and Gregory IX—repeatedy took up their stand in defence of the *consensus* alone, the early French scholastics on the one hand dissociated the marriage contract from its social and historical framework and, on the other, contributed, at least in principle, to a more personal evaluation of marriage.

It should not be forgotten, in connection with this question of indigenous marriage customs, that the customs certainly embodied the mutual consent to the marriage in a living and concrete way, but that this consent was not so much a mutual agreement between the two partners themselves as an agreement between the two families negotiating the handing over of the bride.

---

[94] Many earlier decretals were included in Gratian's decree; what we have here, then, is a decretal that did not defend Gratian's *copula* theory, but the doctrine of the *consensus*.

At this stage in human society, the father's will was (in principle) the will of the children, but the indigenous systems of law
were such that any decision in the matter of mutual consent to
marriage was made on the children. Early scholasticism elaborated the principle that marriage was a personal decision of the
two partners themselves, that it was their mutual consent which
constituted the valid contract of marriage. This was in fact a
formal emancipation of the bride and bridegroom.[95] All the rest
—the parents' consent, the formal proposal of marriage, the betrothal, the dowry, etc., even the priest's solemnisation of the
marriage—was merely something surrounding and enveloping
the partners' mutual consent. There was no formal distinction
between secret and public marriage.

This does not in any sense mean that these theologians opposed
popular customs as such; and it was largely because of the
Pseudo-Isidorian decretals, which they regarded as authentic

[95] It should not be forgotten that, in spite of this theory, there were many
child-marriages in the Middle Ages. Parents who secretly gave their children in marriage were sometimes excommunicated by Alexander III (cf.
Gregory IX, *Comp.* 1, 4, 4). This led to a great deal of casuistry—in connection, for example, with cases of a second marriage publicly contracted
with a third party after the breaking of the first, clandestine, marriage contract. Some held that the church could do nothing else but bless this
second marriage, in view of the fact that she could only act here *in foro
externo*, even though those who were marrying in this way were guilty
before God and were not in conscience permitted to proceed with this second marriage. This problem actively engaged the attention of Hugh of St.
Victor (*De Sacramentis*, II, 11, 6) and Peter Lombard (*IV Sent.*, d. 28).
Aquinas was unable to accept such formalistic solutions, and held that it was
better in such cases, because of the clandestine nature of the first marriage,
"to die excommunicated than to live in marriage with someone who was not
one's own wife" (*In IV Sent.*, d. 38, Expositio textus). Even at the end of the
twelfth century, when the theory of the *consensus* had been consecrated
for a long time, the view was still expressed in a poem that "Inchoat consensus patris, sed copula complet"; see *Textus sacramentorum*, in manu-
script, quoted by E. Dhanis, "Quelques anciennes formules septénaires des
sacrements," *RHE*, 26 (1930), p. 584. This clearly reflects the view of
Alexander III, but still regards the mutual consent to marry in the
Germanic and Frankish sense as a handing over of the bride by the father.

papal documents, that they did not do so. Anselm of Laon was thus able to define marriage between Christians as a *consensus secundum morem patriae* (a mutual consent given according to the customs of the country), and to say that a *decretum Ecclesiae* (in other words, the Pseudo-Isidorian forgeries) insisted on these customs being observed (*FRBE*, pp. 299–300).[96] The early scholastic doctrine of the *consensus* was therefore not a reaction against these customs, but a formalisation of their deepest significance. This formalisation was, in the future, to bring about an inevitable weakening in the meaning of marriages concluded according to the precept of "as many customs as countries," especially when sacramental hylomorphism (the doctrine of matter and form) declared the formalised mutual consent to marriage to be the exclusive essence of the marriage contract. This view also had repercussions on the liturgy of marriage itself. A formal *consensus* dialogue gradually found its way into the liturgical books. The marriage ceremonies had for some time been conducted by a priest; now the priest also asked the two partners for their consent to the marriage. (It is clear, therefore, that this liturgical custom is of relatively recent date in the church.)

Finally, after the formalisation of marriage according to its juridical *consensus* element, the question came almost of its own accord to be asked: Ought marriage not, as a consequence, to be called a contractual agreement? It had never been called this in Roman legislation, but only in the later commentaries. But it was precisely these commentators who urged the twelfth-century canonists of the school of Bologna to adopt the legal term "contract." Both Albert and Aquinas displayed considerable reserve

---

[96] H. Portmann, who wrote an important book on the eleventh- and twelfth-century views of marriage, regarded the following text as characteristic of the early scholastic idea of marriage: ". . . ut igitur sit sensus totius diffinitionis: coniugium est viri et feminae coniunctio legitima, i.e., obligatio inter virum et feminam legitime contracta. Sed quomodo legitime, sic scilicet ut obligatio sit contracta propter Deum et ex pari consensu secundum morem patriae, et inter virum et feminam, quos nec natura nec lex divina prohibet copulari" (*Wesen und Unauflöslichkeit*, pp. 65–6).

in this connection. Albert referred to "a certain contract" (*In IV Sent.*, d. 27, a. 6) because the decretalists had used this term. Aquinas was similarly reserved.[97]

The thirteenth-century Franciscan theologians did not oppose the contract theory to such an extent;[98] and Duns Scotus, as the exponent of this tradition, was later to pass the theory—which had become universal since the end of the thirteenth century—on to the whole of theology as a "consecrated" doctrine: according to him, marriage was a contract, and the object of this contract was furthermore limited to the *ius ad corpus* (the right to each other's body) as a function of the foundation of the family (procreation and education). (*Opus Oxoniense*, d. 6, q. un., n. 8; d. 26, q. 1, 17.) From the fourteenth century onwards the medieval view was systematized—partly in reaction to thirteenth-century teaching—with the juridical formalisation of the *consensus* theory as its point of departure. Thus it was that the classic, traditional treatise on marriage came about as a theological speculation on this juridical extrapolation rather than directly on the reality of marriage. The juridical aspects of marriage were theologically systematized by means of an appeal to Aristotelian categories.

Marriage as a Sacrament

After the controversial development of the idea of marriage as a primarily sexual community, as a spiritual communion which was open to sexual intercourse, and as a social institution for the bringing up of children, the thirteenth century saw the emergence

97 "Fit *ad modum* obligationum in contractibus materialibus"; see *In IV Sent.*, d. 27, q. 1, a. 2, sol. 2; also *In IV Sent.*, d. 31, q. 1, a. 2, ad 2. The phrase "*ad modum*" always points, in Aquinas' teaching on the sacraments, to the analogous character of his words. This was frequently overlooked later. While he calls marriage "*ad modum*" a contract, later commentators were to affirm simply and without nuance that marriage was a contract, a sacrament having *forma et materia*.

98 See, for example, Bonaventure, *In IV Sent.*, d. 28, a. un. q. 3 and q. 5; d. 29, a. 1, q. 3.

of a comparatively subtle view according to which marriage—
as a concrete reality—was all three things. In answer to the question: What makes the community of marriage legally and socially
into a marriage?, the medieval theologians would have said that
it was the partners' mutual consent—their *consensus*, primarily
as a spiritual communion and a desire for an interpersonal relationship (*consensus animorum*), but open to sexual intercourse.
This openness was formulated, at least legally (for this was the
view that was taken), as a "right to sexual intercourse." (How
this primacy of the *consensus animorum* was to be reconciled
with the simultaneous assertion of procreation and bringing up of
children as the primary aim of the community of marriage may,
for the time being, be left on one side, since this problem will be
discussed in a later volume.) On the other hand, in answer to the
question: What makes marriage in the concrete and existential
sense into the biblical "becoming one" or "one flesh"? the
medieval theologians would have said: the human experience of
sexual intercourse.

Running parallel to this controversy were the many attempts
made between the eleventh and thirteenth centuries to reach a
clear understanding of the sacramental nature of marriage. This
whole process was subject to various fluctuations, too, and the
problem is best approached from the point of view of the
church's liturgy.

The marriage liturgy of the church as a point of departure.
The priest's blessing or veiling was not made obligatory during
the period in which the *sacramentum* of marriage was accepted
simply as something experienced—that is, before it became the
subject of speculation. On the contrary, this liturgical celebration
was, as we have seen, reserved for the marriages of the lower
orders of the clergy and for those of certain lay people whose
conduct was beyond reproach. In Rome especially the veiling
formed an integral part of the nuptial mass. In fact, it is from
the development of this liturgical blessing of the bride that we

can see the direction which the Christian idea of marriage as a *sacramentum* took.[99]

The Roman liturgy of marriage, which gradually spread to the whole of the West, was a veiling ceremony (*velatio nuptialis*). Both the bride and the bridegroom were veiled, the bride being completely covered by the veil and the bridegroom partially veiled, so that his head was left uncovered. The oldest texts refer to a *velatio amborum*—a veiling of both the bride and the bridegroom. It is therefore clear that there was no "Christianisation" of the Roman custom of the bridal veil (*flammeum*), which anyway was also worn by the Christian bride before the liturgical ceremony took place.[100] In the words of Paulinus of Nola, "[the bishop], joining the heads of the two under the *pax* of marriage, veils them with his right hand while sanctifying them with a prayer" (*Carmen* xxv, 227–228 [*CSEL*, 30, 245]). Ambrose, in a somewhat older text, was less explicit, but made basically the same affirmation: "the marriage must be sanctified by the priest's veiling and blessing" (*Epist.* 19, 7 [*PL*, 16, 1026]). This does not mean that the bishop placed the *flammeum* on the bride, instead of the bride putting it on herself, since—in another text—Ambrose made a clear distinction between this veil and the *pium velamen*, the veil of piety (*De virginitate*, 5 [*PL*, 16, 286]).

On the other hand, there was a marked tendency in the liturgy and literature of Rome to give a central position to the bride in marriage, and consequently to regard the marriage blessing as a blessing of the bride. The ancient Spanish *Liber Ordinum* pro-

---

[99] De Jong's analysis of the Roman blessing of the bride, even though it requires amplification on certain points (this may be apparent from what I have to say on the subject), is absolutely fundamental in this connection; see J. P. De Jong, "Brautsegen und Jungfrauenweihe. Eine Rekonstruktion des altrömischen Trauungsritus als Basis für theologische Besinnung," *ZKT*, 84 (1962), pp. 300–22.

[100] Like De Jong, Ritzer (who is not quoted by De Jong) in *FRBE* also defends the interpretation that the blessing was of the marriage and not of the bride alone—that is, that the ceremony was a veiling of the bride and the bridegroom, and not simply of the bride (*FRBE*, p. 173). De Jong, however, brings out important shades of meaning in his interpretation.

vides clear evidence—which probably dates from the end of the fourth century—of this transition from a blessing of the marriage to a blessing of the bride.[101] In this book a first blessing, pronounced over the bride and the bridegroom, and thus a blessing of the marriage, is followed by a second blessing pronounced over the bride alone. In the *Leonianum* (*SG*, pp. 139-40 [n. 1105-10]), however, there is no marriage blessing, and only a blessing of the bride; the original marriage blessing appears as an introductory prayer to the blessing proper, which was intended for the bride. The so-called nuptial mass was literally a bridal mass: the sacrifice was offered for the bride alone ("hanc igitur oblationem tibi offerimus pro *famula tua illa*").

An entire theology is contained in this shift of emphasis from the blessing of the marriage itself to that of the bride alone. In the first place, of course, it cannot be denied that the Germanic, Frankish, and Lombardic laws of marriage placed great stress on the legal nature of the handing over of the bride, with the result that the bride was the central figure in the marriage ceremonies in these lands—as was the case, although in a different manner, in ancient Rome. There people were thus able automatically to regard the Roman blessing of marriage or veiling ceremony as equivalent to the "handing over of the bride," since a "clothing" (the *Wette*) also played a part in the *traditio puellae* of the Germanic marriage contract (*FRBE*, especially p. 194).[102] Attention, therefore, was automatically concentrated, in the marriage blessing, on the blessing of the bride. The development of the blessing of the bride, as distinct from that of the marriage, may well have been encouraged by this.[103] In Spain, too, the "handing over of the girl" had been entrusted to the "better hand" (i.e., the priest) long before the tenth century, that is, before this practice was adopted elsewhere. Furthermore, it

101 De Jong, pp. 305 ff. See *Liber Ordinum*, edited by Férotin, pp. 437-8.
102 See also E. Meyer, *Die Einkleidung im deutschen Recht* (Festschrift A. Wach), pt. 2, Leipzig (1913), pp. 38-42.
103 De Jong does not consider this aspect of the question in his study.

would seem that the Pauline idea—expressed in 1 Cor xi. 2–15,
and especially in *vv.* 7–8—also played a part: the man is directly
the "image of God," the woman only indirectly. He is more
directly the representative of Christ, and she of the church. And
so it was not the man, but only the woman, who required the
marriage blessing or veiling.

There were, however, other reasons of a theological nature for
the replacement in Rome of the marriage blessing by a blessing
or veiling of the bride alone. In the *Gelasianum Vetus* (*SG*,
208–210 [n. 1442–1445]), the ancient marriage blessing (the
adesto Domine), which had already been relegated to the position of a mere prologue to the blessing proper—that of the bride
—in the *Leonianum*, is entirely removed from the rite of the
solemnisation of marriage (although it is still to be found as a
collect in the bridal mass). This prologue is replaced in the
Gelasianum Vetus by a new prayer with the bride exclusively in
mind. This new prayer was, it is true, originally a blessing of the
marriage, but in the *Gelasianum Vetus* it has been adapted as a
blessing of the bride.[104] In this *Sacramentarium*, mass too is
offered for the bride alone.

The older marriage blessing is preserved in the *Gregorianum*[105]
as an introduction to the blessing of the bride. This is followed
by the formula of blessing proper, which is more harmoniously
linked to the blessing of the bride—the "Deus, qui in potestate
virtutis tuae"—than is the case in the earlier *sacramentaria*, and
which incorporates Paul's view of the church as the bride of
Christ, with the result that the transition to the blessing of the
bride is quite smooth:

. . . God, who hath sanctified matrimony by such a sublime mystery,
that thou hast represented the mysterious union of Christ and his
church [*sacramentum Christi et Ecclesiae*] in the bond of marriage;

104 De Jong, pp. 310–11.
105 H. Lietzmann, *Das Sacramentarium Gregorianum nach dem Aachener
Urexemplar*, Münster (1921), 110–12, *n.* 200, 1–11.

God, through whom the woman is joined to the man and through whom the contract, ordered by thee from the very beginning, has been endowed with a blessing which is unique in that it was not removed either by the punishment of original sin or by the judgment of the Flood: look favourably upon this thy servant, who is about to enter upon the alliance of marriage: she earnestly prays that she may be strengthened by thy protection; may her marriage be for her a yoke of love and of peace; may she marry faithfully and purely in the Lord. . . .

According to the *Gregorianum*, the veiling was therefore simply an *oratio ad sponsas velandas*—a blessing and a veiling of the bride alone. A theological idea, however, is contained in this. There is a striking similarity between this form of the veiling of a bride and the liturgical veiling of a virgin; it is clear that the *Gregorianum* regarded the blessing of the bride as—so to speak —complementary and equivalent to the dedication of a virgin (the *oratio ad ancillas Dei velandas*), and as such gave it a liturgical form. The same liturgical action—that of veiling to the accompaniment of a prayer—was performed both in the case of the bride of Christ and in the case of the bride of the man. The two were linked by the symbolism of the mystery of the unity between Christ and his church, although a hierarchical distinction was made between them as suggested by St. Paul.

A well-defined view of marriage emerges from the liturgy of the *Gregorianum*. The Pauline idea of the church as the bride of Christ is fundamental to this view. In Scripture this meant that every baptized Christian was a bride of Christ, but from the time of Tertullian there was a noticeable tendency to apply this exclusively to women who took the vow of virginity (the *virgines Deo sacratae*). Women thus dedicated to God were, from the fourth century onwards, generally known as "brides of Christ."[106] This idea was given a liturgical form in the veiling of the virgin. The veil used in this ceremony was the fiery red,

[106] See, for example, T. Camelot, *Virgines Christi*, Paris (n.d.).

ancient Roman *flammeum nuptiale*—in other words, the marriage
veil.[107] This liturgical practice was certainly already known in
Milan round about the year 375 (Ambrose, *De virginibus,* 1, 10,
57 [*PL,* 16, 216]; *Exhort. virginitatis,* 7 [*PL,* 16, 364]).

A distinction is made, in a letter of Pope Siricius (384–399),
between a woman's "life as a virgin" and her public veiling by
the church (*Epist. ad espicopos Gallos* [*PL,* 13, 1182–3]). The
bishop's veiling of a virgin was the church's official recognition
and confirmation of the state of life as a virgin upon which she
had already entered. A woman thus personally committed herself
to the life of a virgin, and the ecclesiastical ceremony of the veiling simply made this an official and public state of life. The veiling made the virgin, in a special way, the direct historical form
in which the church was publicly manifested as the "bride of
Christ." The secular marriage veil was the liturgical form in
which this mystery was expressed.[108] The church saw her characteristic quality as the "bride of Christ" represented in the virgin
dedicated to God.

So much praise was bestowed on the high dignity of the virgin
state that the inevitable reaction was that marriage was completely left out in the cold. Manichean tendencies which were
hostile to marriage, however, caused a necessary reaction against
the underrating of marriage, and this led to the view that the
mystery of the unity between Christ and his church was symbolically represented both by marriage (*sponsa uni viro nupta*)
and by the virgin state (*virgo velata*), each in its own distinctive
way. This view acquired its mature liturgical form in the *Gregorianum.* The idea of "marrying in the Lord" (*nubat in
Christo*) occupied a central position in this liturgy. Only a bride
"without spot or wrinkle," that is, a woman of irreproachable
conduct, was, as we have already seen, deemed worthy to re-

---

107 See R. Schilling, "Le voile de consécration dans l'ancien rite romain,"
Mélanges Mgr. M. Andrieu, Paris (1956), pp. 403–14.
108 "Scio, quod ad imprecationem pontificis flammeum virginale sanctum
operuerit caput" (Jerome, *Epist.* 130, 2 [*PL,* 22, 1107–8]).

ceive the marriage or the bridal blessing (Pope Siricius, *Epist. ad Himerium* [*PL*, 13, 1136–7]).This blessing was forbidden in the case of a second marriage, and this is now—though it was not originally—connected with the fact that the mystery of the unity of Christ and his church is only imperfectly expressed in a second marriage.

Furthermore, at the period in which these *Sacramentaria* originated, the marriage blessing was prescribed only in the case of marriages contracted by members of the clergy (in lower orders), who were themselves in a very special sense in the service of Christ (see above, p. 255; also *FRBE*, p. 175). In the original ceremony of the veiling of both the man and the woman, the man's head was not veiled, since he was, according to Paul, the "head of the wife," and it is to him that the woman was dedicated "in the Lord" by being veiled. Moreover, as I have already said, 1 Cor xi. 2–15 also played a part in this, since the man, who was directly the "image of God,"[109] had no need of a blessing. It was only the "weak woman," the Eve (for this idea clearly played a part too[110]), who had need of a protective blessing. As a condition for the bestowal of the blessing on the bride, it was not only required that the man should be baptized, but also that he himself should have led a blameless life (the early church, however, in fact tolerated more from the man than from the woman!). It was in the wife's loving service of her husband that the church's love for and service of Christ, and thus the bridal love of the virgin dedicated to God, were symbolically represented. For the woman, her husband was the *figura Christi*, and for this reason her marital fidelity to and her service of her hus-

---

[109] See, among other texts, Ambrosiaster, *In Epist. 1 ad Cor.* 11, 3–25 (*PL*, 17, 252–4); *In Epist. ad Col.* 3, 8–11 (*PL*, 17, 460). Ambrosiaster provides one of our main sources of evidence of the Roman liturgy of marriage. His commentary on Paul was also inspired partly by these liturgical practices.

[110] See Ambrosiaster, *In ad Col.* 3, 8–11 (*PL*, 17, 460) and *In Epist. 1 ad Tim.*, 2, 13–15 (*PL*, 17, 494). Here, too, De Jong's exposition has to be corrected to some extent.

band was an indirect service of Christ. Both the veiled virgin
(the woman dedicated in virginity to God) and the veiled bride
(the woman dedicated in purity to her husband as the "image of
Christ") were regarded as serving Christ, each in her own way.
The virgin served Christ directly, the wife indirectly.

The veiling of the bride was given, in the *Gregorianum*
especially, a liturgical form which was consciously in keeping
with the liturgical veiling of the virgin, since the same mystery
of the church was symbolized in both, in the case of the bride's
veiling indirectly and in the case of the veiling of the virgin
directly. Just as a special and publicly recognised place in the
church was assigned to the woman by her dedication as a virgin,
so was the bride's marriage—contracted civilly within the family
—given an ecclesiastical confirmation by the marriage blessing;
the church's solemnisation of her marriage gave it a public status
within the church. The ritual of the dedication of virgins in the
Leonianum, which the editor of the *Gregorianum* had in mind
when he was elaborating the rite of the veiling of the bride, states
that marriage is an honourable status on which the church bestows a blessing, but that the status of virginity directly strives
after the state which marriage symbolizes (the bridal community
of Christ and his church), and does so while by-passing the
symbol.

Here we are face to face with a remarkable fact—the fact that
the theology of marriage and that of virginity were complementary to each other, both have been developed from the same basic
conception of the *sacramentum Christi et Ecclesiae*.[111] The dedication of a virgin was not a sacrament, because virginity was a
direct experience of this mystery. In marriage, on the other hand,
the mystery was experienced existentially between human beings

---

[111] A connection was made between the dedication of virgins and the
marriage blessing *in thalamo* even in those lands in which the Gallican
liturgy was in force, and in which the marriage blessing was originally a
"blessing in the bridal chamber"; see Avitus of Vienne (writing at the end
of the fifth and at the beginning of the sixth century), *Epist. 55* (*MGH–
AA*, VI–2, 84); *thalamus sancti altaris*, as against *benedictio in thalamo*.

and manifested in a form pertaining strictly to this world, so that this human, worldly form was a *sacramentum*—a *figura* or type of the supramundane relationship between Christ and his church. This distinction was, however, not made until the eleventh and twelfth centuries, when the church acknowledged explicitly that there was a difference between the sacramental nature of the dedication of a virgin (the veiling of a virgin as a *sacramentale*) and that of the dedication of a bride (the sacrament of marriage).

We come therefore to this important conclusion: the church's veiling of the bride cannot be explained in the perspective of the pagan religious practice of the ancient Roman *flammeum*, but must be traced back to the veiling of virgins dedicated to God, the *virgines Deo sacratae*,[112] of which marriage was a symbolic representation to be realised in the world. Although it did not constitute an explicit assertion of marriage as a sacrament in the "technical" sense, this was certainly an explicit assertion of its sacramental nature. The Pauline formula, "marriage in the Lord," the wife's dedication to her husband in the Lord, here revealed its final and most profound meaning.

It is clear from this complementary juxtaposition of marriage and virginity that virginity is an exclusively "other-worldly" reality without any secular significance as such, but that marriage is a secular reality, already meaningful in itself, but raised by the church's blessing of the bride or of the marriage itself to the level of a supernaturally meaningful reality. Just as virginity was already a reality because of the person's intention to remain a virgin, and this reality was given an official status within the church by the church's veiling ceremony, so too marriage—by virtue of the partners' mutual consent to marry and the civil ceremonies within the family circle—was already a valid secular marriage, but "confirmed by the church" and thus given an official status within the church by the church's blessing or veiling. The blessing gave an ecclesiastical basis to the partners' mutual consent to the marriage.

[112] De Jong, p. 317.

This insight developed gradually between the fifth and the tenth centuries, and was first expressed in the eleventh and twelfth centuries by the early Italian scholastics. The biblical view of marriage, contained in both the Old and the New Testaments, remained fully in force—namely that marriage had in itself a natural, secular meaning. Virginity, on the other hand, had no such secular meaning, with the result that its supramundane character—its being "not of this world"—was immediately apparent. The "other-worldly" character of marriage was less unambiguous than that of virginity, precisely because marriage also had a secular meaning. It was in the light of the veiling of virgins that the church became explicitly aware of the separately religious, "sacramental" nature of marriage—the discovery of marriage as a sacrament was made in the church in the light of "virginity for the sake of the kingdom of God."

The importance of this genesis will be seen when we come later on to consider marriage and virginity as complementary states of life within the church, and to see how each evokes the other. It is a remarkable fact that whenever virginity has been denied the right to exist within the church, the sacramental nature of marriage has also not been recognised. And so, by way of a long and circuitous historical route, we have reached the point where we are able fully to confirm the statement of the Protestant theologian, Max Thurian: "When the vocation of celibacy is underrated, so is that of marriage."[113]

Marriage as a sacramentum *or sacral symbol.* When the canonists and theologians of the eleventh and twelfth centuries began to devote more systematic attention to the question of marriage, the words of the bridal liturgy, "the *sacramentum* of Christ and his church," were clearly in their minds. Two factors led to speculation about marriage as a *sacramentum*. In the first place, it was in the second half of the eleventh century that the Augustinian concept of the *sacramentum-signum*, the "sign of

[113] M. Thurian, *Marriage and Celibacy*, Naperville, Ill. (Allenson, 1959).

sacred things or events," began to exert an influence on the theology of the West. This concept was introduced into early scholasticism by Berengarius of Tours (1050–1120), and marriage began to be considered as a *sacramentum* from this time onwards.

In the first half of the twelfth century, however, when speculation about the "sacral signs of religion" had already begun, a second factor became increasingly important. This factor was the reaction in the church against the various Manichean tendencies of the Catharist and Albigensian sects which ravaged Christendom, especially in the twelfth century. These heresies condemned marriage as a fundamental evil. The Second Lateran Council of the church, held in 1139, in turn condemned their doctrines.[114] The controversy provided early scholasticism with an urgent reason to undertake a more accurate analysis of the sacred character of marriage. The sermon in which Bernard inveighed against this heretical denigration of marriage shows this well (*Sermo 66*, n. 3–5 [*PL*, 183, 1094]). Initially, it was deemed sufficient to stress the holiness and goodness of marriage (Pseudo-Anselm [Roger of Caen], *De contemptu mundi* [*PL*, 158, 698 ff.]; *De nuptiis consang.* [*PL*, 158, 557]). Later, however, an appeal was made to various patristic texts in which reference is made to *sacramentum* (in the patristic sense). We can say, therefore, that the concrete setting for the increasingly explicit awareness of the sacramental nature of marriage was provided by the situation of emergency which prevailed at this time, which forced the church to become aware of the need to think at a deeper level about the goodness and holiness of marriage. The revived theology of the *sacramentum* as a sacral sign was used by the church as a conceptual instrument in her defence of marriage.

That marriage was, from the eleventh century onwards, called a *sacramentum* meant first and foremost only that marriage contained a reference to the mystery of the unity between Christ and his church. There was far too acute an awareness of the

[114] Canon 23 (DS 718 [DB 367]); see M–SC, pt. 21, 532.

worldly character of marriage in the Middle Ages for this secular reality to be considered as a mystery.

The first question which claimed the attention of the theologians was this: Precisely where was the mystery referred to in the bridal liturgy situated? Thought and discussion about this question went on until the thirteenth century, and although there was considerable fluctuation in the views expressed throughout the course of this speculation, it is possible to distinguish four main trends of thought.

1. When they first began to speculate about the *sacramentum* to which the liturgy of marriage referred (prompted to some extent by the theology of the Carlovingian period), the early schoolmen connected the sacramental nature of marriage with the priest's solemnisation of it, and claimed that it was the priest's blessing which gave marriage its "sacramental" meaning. The early Italian scholastics took the initiative here, and established this connection explicitly. They said that the priestly solemnisation of the marriage was in fact its *sacramentum*, like the blessing of baptismal water (Pseudo-Hildebert, *De ordinatione clericorum* 7 [*PL*, 171, 928]). As a result, a second marriage, which—according to Roman, and later also according to Gallican, practice— might not be solemnised, could not be called a "*sacramentum* of Christ and his church" (Hugh of Amiens, *Contra Haereticos*, III, 4 [*PL*, 192, 1289]). The priestly blessing was seen as a concrete liturgical form of the Genesis marriage blessing which, as a blessing of creation, consecrated marriage as an institution of divine origin. As long as marriage continued to be validly celebrated as a contract made civilly within the family, and—despite the increasing ecclesiastical jurisdiction concerning marriage—was felt to be a human, secular reality in its own right, it is clear that the earliest scholastic attempts to define the sacramental nature of marriage had to be made in the direction of the liturgy with which the church surrounded it.

The idea that marriage was a "sacrament" by virtue of its

solemnisation by the priest was short-lived as a thesis, but it did continue to have a lasting effect. Even as late as the thirteenth century, William of Auvergne was to situate at least the saving power of the "sacrament" in the priest's blessing of the marriage (*Tractatus de sacramento matrimonii*, vi, 9).[115] Even Bonaventure, who saw the sacral sign in the partners' mutual consent to the marriage, maintained that its saving power went back to the liturgy of marriage (*In IV Sent.*, d. 26, a. 2, q. 2, c. and ad 4; see also d. 30, a. un.). Albert, who held that the partners' mutual consent was the essential element in the constitution of marriage, as a secular commission, also situated the saving power of the "sacrament" in the priest's blessing (*In IV Sent.*, d. 1, a. 14). Statements similar to these are to be found in Aquinas (*In IV Sent.*, d. 1, q. 1, a. 3; d. 25, q. 2, a. 1, ad 2; see *SCG* iv, 78, ii–ii, q. 100, a. 2), who nonetheless maintained that the liturgy of marriage was in fact external to the essence of this sacrament and was merely a *sacramentale* (*In IV Sent.*, d. 28, q. 1, a. 3, ad 2, and especially d. 26, q. 2, a. 1, ad 1), with the result that a second marriage, which, as we have seen, was not blessed, had the effect of limiting the sacramental nature of marriage (*In IV Sent.*, d. 42, q. 3, a. 2, ad 2).

Although no very clear picture emerges from all this, it does undoubtedly provide evidence of a certain feeling that the liturgy of marriage, as the celebration of a mystery, did have some part to play in the sacramentalism of marriage. This idea remained influential until the Council of Trent, mainly because of the resolute assertions of Melchior Cano (*De locis theologicis*, viii, c. 5), according to whom the priest was also the minister of this sacrament.

Initially, then, Western thought on this subject took a course which had for a long time also been followed in the East: namely, that liturgically celebrated mystery was in fact the sacrament, and marriage, as a sacrament, was a liturgy. Marriage was regarded in the Eastern Church primarily as an act of the priest, a liturgical

[115] See Le Bras, "Mariage," *DTC*, pt. ix–2, cols. 2209–10.

service or *akolouthia*, in which the faithful—and in particular the bride and bridegroom themselves—were actively involved. In the East, marriage, in itself a secular reality, was drawn into the sphere of divine salvation by the priest's liturgical action. (See Chapter 2 following.)

In the West, however, this tendency was never able to develop beyond this first beginning, mainly on account of the *consensus* theory. The West, with its more "secular" attitude, denied that every sacrament in the church had to be an action done by those holding office within the church. Aquinas was among those who denied this (*In IV Sent.*, d. 28, q. 1, a. 3, ad 2 and ad 3), and Duns Scotus claimed that, since marriage was a contract, it was "immaterial who administered the sacrament"—in his view, for example, the father could be the minister on the occasion of the handing over of the bride (*Opus Oxoniense*, IV, d. 26, q. un., n. 15).[116]

It seems to me that the initial failure to link the sacramental nature of marriage with marriage itself, and the tendency to connect it rather with the liturgy of marriage (which was not deemed to be indispensable to the validity of marriage, even though it was made obligatory for baptized Christians from the eleventh century onwards), is of considerable importance in the history of dogma. The Protestant Reformers were later to assert that the Catholic Church had affirmed the sacramentalism of marriage in an attempt to take over the jurisdictional control of marriage. Their reaction against the acceptance of marriage as a sacrament was essentially not so much a refusal to accept the holiness of marriage as a protest against the Catholic Church's jurisdictional power over marriage, which they regarded primarily as an ordinary human reality to be experienced "in the Lord."

It cannot, however, be historically substantiated that the Catholic recognition of the sacramental nature of marriage in fact functioned as a means to bring marriage under ecclesiastical

---

[116] In the *Reportata Parisiensia*, d. 42, *n.* 24, Scotus said quite simply that the bride and bridegroom administered the sacrament.

authority. A brief review of the whole process of development may help to show this. Beginning with Leo the Great, the church, anxious to ensure the public character of marriage, emphasized the contracting of marriage according to indigenous civil customs. Following these authentic church reactions, the Pseudo-Isidorian reforming movement spread various unauthentic writings abroad, and these reinforced the demand that marriage should be made public by the observation of local customs and the celebration of a public nuptial mass with the marriage blessing or veiling. The idea that the church should herself be able to make conditions for the validity of marriages on the basis of her jurisdictional powers did not, as I have already pointed out, secure a firm foothold in the Middle Ages. The essence of marriage was situated in the *consensus,* and the church did not believe that it was possible for her to enter into this. Although they were not indispensable to the validity of a marriage, the civil and ecclesiastical ceremonies were certainly prescribed. Emphasis had been laid on the public aspect of these ceremonies by the fourth Lateran Council especially.

In the gradual growth of the church's control over the whole of public life, the priest emerged as the one who conducted all the ceremonies of marriage. As a result of this, the ancient civil and family customs were integrated into the liturgy, and the church was thus able to place on record, as it were, that the marriage contract had in fact become an ecclesiastical marriage contract! I stress that she was able to "place this on record," because it is nowhere apparent in the Middle Ages that the church ever had the intention of bringing marriage exclusively under her jurisdictional power. She only aimed to ensure that marriage was celebrated publicly because this public aspect of marriage was necessary to the moral and religious life of her members.

Indeed, the church even went so far as to stress the necessity of contracting marriages according to the civil and family customs of the region. Her insistence on the priest's solemnisation of marriage (the nuptial mass together with the veiling ceremony and the blessing), which did not become obligatory until the eleventh century, naturally meant that the marriage contract became an ecclesiastical affair: but the adoption and incorporation into the church of the whole of the marriage contract with the elements essential to its formal constitution was, so to speak, a spontaneous development running parallel to the increasingly public position of the church in medieval society.

The secular formalities of marriage, which had previously been an element of the marriage ceremony according to the customs of the land, simply passed over into an ecclesiastical contract of marriage from the second half of the eleventh century onwards, especially in the Frankish lands—Brittany and Normandy. This did not lead to the conviction that marriage was a sacrament— this had already been said, although only in connection with the veiling of the bride—but only to a change in the church's view as to precisely where that *sacramentum* (the saving significance of the mystery of the unity of Christ and his church) was situated. The bringing within the church's orbit of the marriage contract led to a second marriage also becoming a church marriage, during which the priest himself heard the mutual consent of the partners, although the blessing was still forbidden in such cases.

On the one hand, this situation confirmed some theologians in their view that the *sacramentum* of marriage was to be found in the liturgical celebration of the veiling (the priest's blessing); on the other, it also led to the development of a new conception —namely, that the *sacramentum* coincided with the marriage itself, and was thus connected both with the *consensus* and with sexual intercourse. This view emerged fully in the twelfth and thirteenth centuries, though at this time there was still much discussion about the problem of the relationship between the *consensus* and sexual intercourse in marriage precisely in connection with the *sacramentum*. For the controversy outlined above had repercussions on the attempts to "place" the *sacramentum*, and posed the question as to whether it was to be found primarily in the *consensus animorum* (the spiritual community of the partners in marriage) or in the *consensus carnis* (the intention to have sexual intercourse, and thus in this marital relationship itself).

2. The *sacramentum* then came to be "placed" in marriage itself as a secular reality soon after the controversy about the theory of the *consensus* and that of the *copula*. But at this period a conflict arose between the biblical view of the "becoming one" in marriage and the pure *consensus* theory. That marriage was a "sacred symbol of the union of Christ with his Church" continued to be generally accepted: Anselm of Laon (†1117) was one of the first to go more deeply into this with the help of the conceptual material of the "sacrament as a sign" that had been elaborated in the meantime; marriage itself was a *sacramentum*, contracted either by the good or by sinners, but only the good had the *res sacramenti*, that which was symbolized by the sign, namely personal involvement in the mystery of the Church (*Sententiae. Tract. de sacr.*).[117] Thus even the marriage of unbaptized persons was a *sacramentum*, although it lacked the symbolized reality. In this Anselm was clearly taking up a position in what was later to become a considerable problem, maintaining that the *sacramentum* (that which symbolized the unity of Christ and his church) was the "one flesh" (marriage consummated in sexual intercourse) (*Enarr. in Mt.* 19 [PL, 162, 1412]). This view, that the sacramental symbolism of marriage had human sexual intercourse as its subject, was accepted by many theologians (Honorius Augustodunensis, *Elucidarium* II, 16 [PL, 172, 1147]). Abelard, on the other hand, with the virgin marriage of Mary and Joseph in mind, situated the *sacramentum* in the *consensus animorum* which symbolized for him Christ's unity with his church (*Sermo in Annuntiatione B.M.V.* [PL, 178, 381–2]).

[117] See F. Bliemetzrieder, *Anselms von Laon systematische Sentenzen*, Münster (1919), (Beiträge zur Geschichte der Philosophie des Mittelalters, XVIII–3), pp. 129–51.

Hugh of St. Victor was the first Western theologian to write a "treatise on marriage,"[118] and he provided a remarkable synthesis precisely in connection with the problem under discussion. Hugh's treatise gives in some ways a very modern impression, though it does not achieve the modern idea of anthropological incarnation.

According to Hugh, every marriage, even the marriage of non-Christians, was a *sacramentum;* but there was a difference between the *sacramentum* of marriage between baptized persons and that of marriage between unbaptized persons. Christian marriage was, in Hugh's view, a sacred and sanctifying event (*De sacramentis,* II, 11, 8 [*PL,* 176, 496]; II, 11, 13 [*PL,* 176, 505]). The marriage of unbaptized persons was certainly a holy marital bond, but it did not bring grace. It was—to use a later term—a "valid but infertile sacrament." This doctrine was in keeping with Hugh's thesis that only the marriage before the fall was instituted as a sacrament. In his *De Beatae Mariae virginitate* (*PL,* 176, 857–76), Hugh considered marriage in the light of God's saving intentions—that is, as God's communion of grace with men, disrupted by sin but restored in a glorious manner by the incarnation of the Word. Connecting this with the idea of election—the idea that not everyone is received into God's grace—Hugh saw marriage as a pregnant and meaningful image of God's elective love ("Divinum sacramentum et profundum mysterium" [col. 863]).

According to Hugh, the conjugal love of human beings chosen by God was to be found in marriage. He saw marriage as a lawful community of man and wife, who bound themselves to each other by their mutual consent (col. 859). Marriage was therefore a "covenant" (col. 863). This covenant was, in Hugh's view, essentially a covenant of love, and at the same time a commission to be fulfilled in becoming spiritually one. He regarded this "be-

118 For special studies of Hugh's view of the sacrament, see W. E. Göszmann, "Die Bedeutung der Liebe in der Eheauffassung Hugos von St. Victor und Wolframs von Eschenbach," *MTZ,* 5 (1954), pp. 205–13.

coming spiritually one" as primary and fundamental in marriage, but care for each other's needs in life (*mutuum adiutorium*) and living together in communion of heart and spirit, though not in sexual intercourse, were also implied in it (cols. 860–1). Interpersonal relationship, including the material cares of daily life, was for Hugh the primary and essential task of marriage. Unity and fidelity were therefore the characteristic attributes of this covenant (col. 859). Marriage was thus defined by Hugh as a community in which perfect purity was possible: the best example of such a virgin marriage was that of Mary and Joseph.

The distinctive feature of Hugh's view of marriage was that God had given to its interpersonal relationship, already meaningful in itself, the task of procreating the human race in and through the physical union of man and wife (cols. 863–4). According to Hugh, this corporeal union was the sacramental form in which the corporeal unity between Christ and his church was manifested (col. 864). This task did not, however, form an indispensable element in the constitution of marriage as such, and for this reason Hugh distinguished between two aspects in the partners' mutual consent to marry: the *consensus coniugalis* (the marriage covenant) and the *consensus coitus* (consent to sexual intercourse) (cols. 858 and 873).

The bond of love (*vinculum caritatis*) was an element in the constitution of marriage as such, and thus also in the constitution of the *sacramentum*. Although sexual intercourse was also a "sacrament of Christ and his church," it did not constitute the marriage. Hugh thus took his stand on the strict doctrine of the *consensus*, not on the mitigated doctrine of Pope Alexander III. Both sexual intercourse and the consensus were based, in Hugh's opinion, on the one marital love. He did not, however, go so far as to synthesize the two elements, for the simple reason that he— like most medieval theologians—was unable to absolve sexual intercourse from all remnants of original sin (col. 872). Hugh categorically denied that a marriage was pointless if there was no *consensus carnis* (cols. 858–60, 865). On the contrary, marriage

derived its profound significance and its holiness from personal
marital community as such (*consensus mentis*); procreation was
only an *officium*, a task entrusted by God to this particular community of persons.[119]

When, however, Hugh applied the already traditional view
that the "sacrament of Christ and his church" was formally
situated in sexual intercourse (the *una caro*) to his theory of the
strict *consensus*, he was compelled to make a distinction. As we
have already seen, Abelard had already made such a distinction,
and the ground had also been prepared by Anselm of Laon. The
distinction, then, between the *sacramentum* (image of Christ and
his church) and the *res sacramenti* (personal involvement of the
faithful in the communion of grace) already existed. The fresh
solution which Hugh provided was that both spiritual married
love and sexual intercourse were *sacramenta*.[120] The first was,
however, a "greater *sacramentum* in respect of God and the
soul," while the second was the "great *sacramentum* in respect of
Christ and his church" (especially cols. 860, 864, 874-5; cf. *De
sacramentis*, XII, 1 [*PL*, 176, 519]). Conjugal love was thus the
sacrament of the spiritual love between God and the soul, and
sexual intercourse was the sacrament of the corporeal union of
Christ and his church. Even without sexual intercourse, however, the image of Christ and his church was to be found in
conjugal love (cols. 875-6). Even in the spiritual communion of
marriage the man's love was typically male, and the woman's
typically female, and—according to Hugh—this was in consequence the case even in a marriage without sexual intercourse
(col. 876).

The above argument is to be found in a study by Hugh of
the virgin marriage of our Lady, but the same basic ideas occur
also in his *De sacramentis christianae fidei* (II, 11 [*PL*, 176, 479-
520]), although many authors have interpreted the teaching in

119 "Coniugium est in foedere dilectionis. Coniugii *officium* est in
generatione prolis," *De B.M.V.*, col. 874.
120 "Igitur amor coniugalis sacramentum est, et sacramentum in coniugi-
bus est commixtio carnis," col. 874.

his *De sacramentis* differently. In common with all medieval theologians, Hugh distinguished between the *ad officium* of marriage (the foundation of the family as a commission) and the *ad remedium* (the curative power attached to marriage by God's love after the fall), but he applied this distinction to marriage only as a *consensus carnis,* and not to the essence of marriage, the covenant of love or *consensus mentis* (col. 481). The reality of which marriage was a symbolic representation had a corporeal dimension, Christ's relationship with his church, as well as a spiritual dimension, God's relationship with the soul.

It is because Hugh wanted to stress the *consensus,* yet without wishing to contradict the traditional proposition—that the "sacrament of Christ and his church" was situated in sexual intercourse—that what he says sometimes sounds uncertain. In his view, the "external sacrament" was the cohabitation of man and wife in marriage, which was the image of "Christ and his church," whereas the "inner sacrament" (*res sacramenti*) was the personal communion with God, of which conjugal love was a "sacramental form." But it is quite clear that he would have preferred to situate the "sacrament of Christ and his church" simply and primarily in the spiritual communion of marriage. Only tradition prevented him from doing so. That is why he said: "as we have called sexual intercourse the *sacramentum* of Christ and his church, so also is married love the sacrament *of the same*" (*sacramentum eiusdem*)—that is, the sacrament of Christ and his church (col. 495).

His view may be thus formulated: marriage as a visible community—the image of the unity between Christ and his church—is the form (*sacramentum*) which conjugal love and the interpersonal relationship of marriage (*res sacramenti*) assume, and this love is in turn the form (*sacramentum*) of God's spiritual relationship with man. But, since this visible community does not of itself include sexual intercourse, even a virgin marriage is the sacrament of the community of Christ and his church. The sanctifying character of marriage (col. 496) is therefore situated in married love as the sacrament of God's love for mankind.

Hugh's doctrine had some influence on scholastic thought, although he was not followed in his suggestion of a distinction between married love and marriage as a commission to found a family.

The fact that so many indefinite assertions concerning the "sacrament of Christ and his church" are to be found in early scholasticism is due to the fluctuations in the controversy about the relationship between the *consensus* and the *copula* in marriage. Although he continued to insist on the strict *consensus* theory, Peter Lombard elaborated this in the direction taken by Pope Alexander III. He did not therefore make a radical distinction, as did Hugh, between the community of marriage and sexual intercourse,[121] but saw a double union in marriage: the primary union of the *copula spiritualis per caritatem* (that is, married love incorporated into Christian charity) and the secondary union of the *copula carnis* (sexual intercourse) (*IV Sent.*, d. 26, c. 6). But, unlike Hugh, he did not refer to "two sacraments," but to one *sacramentum* with complementary aspects: the one image of "Christ and the church" was initiated by married love and consummated in sexual intercourse.

Pope Alexander III, who consecrated the mitgated *consensus* theory, had already—as Orlando Bandinelli—said that consummated marriage contained the image of the mystery of Christ and his church; only consummated marriage was therefore indissoluble, and as such the sacrament of the indissoluble union of the church with Christ.[122] It is clear from this that the canonists were especially interested in the *sacramentum* in the sense of an indissoluble sacral bond, while the theologians were especially interested in the "sign" of the *sacramentum*.

Towards the end of the twelfth century the problem was

---

121 "Pactio coniugalis . . . facit matrimonium . . . in coitu" (*IV Sent.*, d. 27, c. 8). He did, however, distinguish sharply between the "consensus coniugalis societatis" and the "consensus cohabitationis vel carnalis copulae" (d. 28, c. 4).

122 Quoted by Le Bras, col. 2156.

solved, not by the postulation of a double aspect in the "sacramental sign," but in the light of the one significant reality—the mystery of Christ and his church represented in the reality of marriage. Two aspects can be distinguished in this reality: the spiritual communion of love, and the union of sexual intercourse. The relationship between these two aspects was seen, not from the anthropological, but from the jurisprudential point of view. In other words, an unconsummated marriage was really a marriage, but it only became indissoluble in sexual intercourse. Nonetheless, this idea went back to an implicit anthropological view: that "the sacrament is the *consensus* of heart and of body; there are not two sacraments in marriage" (Peter of Poitiers [*PL*, 211, 1257]). And, as if it was his intention once and for all to put an end to the reproach of "medieval rigorism" in sexual matters, Stephen Langton declared, "before sexual intercourse, marriage is the *sacramentum* of the union of Christ with the church militant; in sexual intercourse, it is the *sacramentum* of the unity of Christ with the church triumphant."[123]

It was in this way that the idea developed that marriage was objectively the "*sacramentum* of Christ and his church" and therefore indissoluble. The subjective experience of this objective fact, however, is to be found in conjugal love itself as the form of the communion of grace with God—as the form of charity. The first is lasting; but the second may be lost. Hugh of St. Victor certainly had a true intuition of this, but did not develop it.

Later scholasticism situated the *sacramentum* of marriage according to the view that had by that time become classic: marriage was constituted as marriage by the mutual consent of the partners, the *consensus*, but consummated by sexual intercourse. Bonaventure expressed it thus: if we consider only the element that formally constitutes marriage as marriage (the *esse necessitatis*), then we must also call conjugal love without sexual intercourse a sacrament; but if we consider the full reality of mar-

---

[123] In ms., quoted by Le Bras, col. 2200.

riage (the *esse plenitudinis*), then sexual intercourse forms a truly integral part of this "sacrament of Christ and his church" (*In IV Sent.*, d. 26, a. 2, q. 3).

Aquinas based the indissolubility of marriage on the fact that it is a "sacrament of the indissoluble bond of Christ and his church." (*In I ad Cor.* 7, 1 lect. 1; *In ad Eph.* 5, lect. 10; *In IV Sent.*, d. 26, q. 2, a. 1, ad 3 and ad 4; d. 26, q. 2, a. 2, sol. 2, c.; ad 1 and ad 2; d. 27, q. 1, a. 2, sol. 1, ad 2.) The *consensus* was not the marriage, but did constitute it; the marriage itself was the special community of man and wife, and sexual intercourse was a specific part of marriage (*In IV Sent.*, d. 28, q. un., a. 4; d. 7, q. 1, a. 2). The "sacral sign of Christ and his church" was precisely that specific marital union (*In IV Sent.*, d. 27, q. 1, a. 2, sol. 1, ad 2; d. 27, q. 1, a. 3, sol. 2, ad 1 and a. 2, sol. 1, ad 2). Aquinas was therefore bound to make a certain distinction between the community of marriage before the first sex act and the community after it.

Before the consummation of the first sex act the union of marriage pointed to the communion of grace of the individual with Christ, and this communion could be lost through sin. A marriage that was not consummated could also be dissolved for higher reasons. The community of marriage became formally the sacramental sign of the community of Christ with his church in and through sexual intercourse because it then became indissoluble, and the reality of the union of Christ and his church was indissoluble (*In IV Sent.*, d. 27, q. 1, a. 3, sol. 2, ad 1). Aquinas based this anthropologically on the fact that the power of the one party over the other in marriage was not perfect before sexual intercourse (*In IV Sent.*, d. 27, q. 1, a. 3, sol. 2, and 2). He expressed this relationship in a rather medieval manner (*In IV Sent.*, d. 27, q. 1, a. 4, ad 2 [see ob. 2]).[124] His view amounts to this. The saving sign (and the cause of grace) was not the *consensus* itself, but what this consensus brought about—the com-

---

[124] See also d. 26, q. 2, a. 1, ad 4 in connection with ad 5 and together with the text of Peter Lombard being discussed.

munity of marriage (*res et sacramentum*). The *consensus* was a willing consent to this community of marriage, and—because marriage was a sacrament—also the will to link this community of marriage with the saving communion existing between Christ and his church (*In IV Sent.*, d. 27, q. 1, a. 2, sol. 1, ad 2).

In answer to the question: Is the *consensus* a consent to sexual intercourse in the future? Aquinas replied that a consent to marriage is a consent to *marriage!* In his view, sexual intercourse did not constitute marriage, but was only an integral part of it. Marriage itself, to which the partners gave their mutual consent, he called an "association of man and wife directed towards sexual intercourse and everything connected with it" (*In IV Sent.*, d. 28, a. 4, c). It follows therefore that the object of this consent was more than sexual intercourse alone, but that this was "implied in it."

According to Aquinas, then, the community of marriage itself was essentially and primarily the *coniunctio* (the bond of marriage) as the sphere in which the family was founded. But the direct effect of the *consensus* was the unity of life in marriage and not sexual intercourse, since the unity of marriage could exist without sexual intercourse. On the other hand, the real actuation of this community of marriage was the sex act. The sacramental gift of grace was therefore not directly linked with the sex act, but with the marital bond of love actuated by it (*In IV Sent.*, d. 26, q. 2, a. 4). A specifically human community became a communion of grace through the sacrament by virtue of divine power (*In IV Sent.*, d. 27, q. 1, a. 2, sol. 1, c).

Marriage as a sacrament in the technical sense: one of the seven sacraments. So far we have restricted our attention to the *sacramentum-signum* of marriage—to the fact that marriage was regarded in liturgical tradition and in theological speculation as a symbolic representation of the mystery of Christ and his church. Although we have from time to time looked forward to what was to follow, we have not as yet reached the point where mar-

riage was accepted as a sacrament in the strict sense of the word
—that is, not simply as a sacred sign, but at the same time as a
source of salvation, as an effective sign of grace.

A great deal of discussion followed the adoption in the eleventh century of the Augustinian sacramental concept. It was felt
that some of the "sacred signs" of the Christian religion had a
special meaning. This was, of course, clear in the case of baptism (the initiation rite, along with confirmation) and the eucharist, which were "signs" with the power of grace. A distinction
was made by Durand of Troarn (about 1051) of two aspects, the
sacred symbolism and the sanctifying power, in the *sacramentum*
(*Liber de corpore et sanguine Domini*, 5, 11 [*PL*, 149, 1392]).
Following this, a discussion had developed, between 1120 and
1160 especially, about the strict definition of what a sacrament
was.[125] Although it was still vague and not yet positively asserted, the idea that the term *sacramentum* had to be attributed
in a very special way to the seven "sacred signs" was already
growing in the first half of the twelfth century. It was from this
idea that the distinction between "sacrament" and "sacramental"
developed.

It was shortly before Peter Lombard that the *Septenarium*
(the seven sacraments precisely defined) was explicitly asserted.
Peter Lombard consecrated the *Septenarium* of the sacraments at
about the same time.[126] That this *Septenarium* can be found in
the works of all authors in the second half of the twelfth century, despite the fact that Peter Lombard at this time lacked the
authority that he had later, clearly indicates that it was virtually
present already in the first half of the century.

What is remarkable is that marriage was included among these

---

125 See D. van den Eynde, *Les définitions des sacrements pendant la
première période de la théologie scolastique* (1050–1240), Rome and Louvain
(1950); see also E. Schillebeeckx, *De sacramentele heilseconomie*, pt. 1, pp.
107–82.

126 See E. Dhanis, "Quelques anciennes formules septénaires des sacrements," *RHE*, 26 (1930), pp. 547–608, 916–50; 27 (1931), pp. 5–26; see
also D. van den Eynde, *passim*.

seven important sacraments, even though both the saving significance and saving power were regarded as necessary to the
definition of the sacraments proper, which were seen as forming
the summit of a pyramid of various *sacramenta.* At the time when
the *Septenarium* was explicitly recognised, no saving power was
accorded to marriage. This fact is of importance in the history
of dogma. It is of course certain that the early scholastic idea of
the sacrament as possessing a power of grace cannot have been
the real origin of the *Septenarium.* Yet, despite the fact that the
definition of the sacraments proper could not be applied to marriage, marriage was counted among the seven; and other *sacramenta* to which a power of grace was attributed—for example,
the dedication of virgins and the anointing of kings—were not
included in the *Septenarium.*[127] The idea that sacraments in the
strict sense were those of importance for Christian life contributed directly to the inclusion of marriage among the seven,
despite the fact that marriage was not regarded at this time as
having a power of grace, but only as being a sign of a more
sublime mystery. A disciple of Abelard, Mag. Hermannus, who
denied the power of grace to marriage and who regarded the
"sacrament" as a pure sign, counted marriage among the important spiritual sacraments long before the explicit recognition
of the *Septenarium (Epitome theologiae christianae,* c. 28 [*PL,*
178, 1745]). Even though medieval feeling for the sacred nature
of the number "seven" may have played some part in the fixing
of the number of the sacraments at seven,[128] this still does not

---

[127] A characteristic example is this text by Peter Cantor: "In quolibet
septem sacramentorum confertur cumulus gratiae, excepto coniugio quod
institutum est ad remedium et non ad augmentum (gratiae). In aliis etiam
sacramentis confertur cumulus, ut forte in consecratione virginum, quod
non tamen assero . . . Similiter forte in inunctione regum augmentum
gratiae confertur"; in ms., quoted by Dhanis, p. 928, *n.* 14. See also the
Verbum Abbreviatum: "Sunt etiam spiritualia per quae confertur vel augetur
Spiritus Sancti gratia in aliquo, ut ecclesiastica sacramenta praeter matrimonium, ordines, officia etiam ecclesiastica" (*PL,* 205, 126).

[128] J. de Ghellinck has denied that this idea had any influence; see "A
propos de quelques affirmations du nombre septénaire des sacrements au

explain why marriage was included among the seven and not, for example, the dedication of virgins which, in the view of many writers at the time, certainly satisfied the requirements of a "strict sacrament." The definition of a sacrament as an effective instrument of salvation was in use, as it were, ahead of its time. Awareness in faith of the distinct sacramental meaning of marriage clearly preceded the theological expression of its sacramental significance. If this had not been so, the historical action of the inclusion of marriage among the seven sacraments would be completely inexplicable. This awareness must, however, have had a point of contact somewhere in marriage itself. We must go more deeply into this question.

From the eleventh century onwards, the *sacramentum* of marriage was regarded especially as a *sacramentum-signum*, a sacred sign of a saving reality. Later, the other Augustinian view—that of the *scramentum-vinculum* (the sacrament as a sacral bond)—began to have a marked influence on thought. Anselm of Laon adopted the Augustinian view of the "three values of marriage": children, the *fides pudicitae* (fidelity without adultery), and the *sacramentum* (indissolubility),[129] which was the "sign of the union of Christ with his church." The idea that only consummated marriage—which was usually regarded as the *sacramentum* of the mystery of Christ and his church—was indissoluble in the full sense of the word was important in this connection, since "sacrament" meant above all "indissolubility" for the canonists, and this was also the meaning of the word in Augustine in connection with marriage. In Gratian's Decree, which appeared shortly after 1140, *sacramentum* meant simply "indissolubility" (*Decretum*, Causa XXXII, q. 1, dictum in c. 10) and the "sign of

---

XIIe siècle," *RSR*, 1 (1910), p. 496. His denial is based on the fact that the *Summa Abel* provides a collection of many different "groups of seven," based on the principle "septenarius numerus sacratus est," but that the seven sacraments do not occur in this collection. Only a more complete study of unpublished texts could lead to a true appreciation of this question.

[129] Fragment; see Bliemetzrieder, pp. 112–13; also *Enarr. in Matt.* 19 (PL, 162, 1412).

Christ and his church," on the basis of which the indissolubility of the bond of marriage was established (*Decretum*, Causa xxvii, q. 2, dictum in c. 39). Praepositinus pointed to this double meaning in connection with the three values of marriage: "Marriage is called a *sacramentum* because of the third property of marriage, its indissolubility."[130] Bonaventure and Aquinas also made a clear distinction between these two aspects—marriage was called a "sacrament" and a "sign" above all because of its indissolubility or its "mutual obligation" (Bonaventure, *In IV Sent.*, d. 26, a. 1, q. 2, ad 4; Aquinas *In IV Sent.*, d. 31, q. 1, a. 2, ad 7).

Both before and after the acceptance of the sacrament in the strict sense as an "effective sign of grace," the idea of the sacramental nature of marriage, in the sense of indissolubility, was prevalent. The indissolubility of marriage had been presented by Christ in the radical sense of the word. Paul connected Jesus' *logion* with the mystery of the unity of Christ and his church. The two ideas were brought together first by Augustine and later by the scholastics, leading thus to the view that as a *sacramentum* marriage was authentically and radically indissoluble only because it was a *sacramentum-signum*, a sign of the sacred mystery—*vinculum*, a "sacral bond" already existing. This continued to be true moreover even if any grace at all were denied to this sacrament. This seems to me to be the historical reason for the acceptance of the strictly sacramental nature of marriage in the middle of the twelfth century, despite the reluctance of the same theologians to apply the strict concept of the sacrament as an effective sign of grace to marriage.

But this means then that Jesus' *logion* about the indissolubility of marriage was, from the point of view of the history of dogma, the basis of the scholastic assertion of the truly sacramental nature of marriage and not the scholastic concept of the sacrament itself. From the ecumenical point of view, this historically prompted view seems to me to be of considerable importance. It was only later, when this truly sacramental nature had been

130 Quoted by Le Bras, cols. 2198-99.

recognised, that the inner logic of the assertion would gradually lead to the attribution of the full sacramental concept to marriage.

Marriage as an effective saving sign. There are many different reasons why the specifically Christian meaning of the sacrament as a saving instrument was not assigned to marriage, despite its inclusion among the seven sacraments. Canonists, anxious to prevent simony, were hardly able to accept that the marriage contract, which was accompanied by so many financial transactions between the two families in connection with the arrangement of the dowry, was capable of conferring grace.[131] Theologians had other objections: the gift of grace was a work of God, whereas mutual consent to marriage was a work of man.[132] It is clear too from the reaction of Alexander of Hales that the definition of a secrament instituted by Christ could scarcely be substantiated in the case of an institution that was as old as the world itself (*Glossa in Sent.*, IV, d. 26, c. 1 [ed. Quaracchi, Florence (1957), p. 455 f.]).

The thought which lurked at the back of everyone's mind at this time was: how could marriage, which involves "you know what"(!), be a sacramental source of salvation?[133] It is true that the patristic idea that the marriage in paradise had been undermined by sin, with the result that marriage was significant for Christians only as a "remedy against desire," had inhibited the

[131] See Le Bras, col. 2208. There were, however, more reasons than those given by Le Bras.

[132] Guerric of St. Quentin, in ms., quoted by D. van den Eynde, p. 108, *n.* 2. The *pro et contra* arguments of the great medieval *Summae* also reflect this idea; see, for example, Aquinas, *In IV Sent.*, d. 26, q. 2, a. 3, obj. 2.

[133] Rufinus, *Summa Decretorum*, Causa 32, q. 2 (ca. 1158): "Sciendum est igitur quod Ecclesiae sacramenta singula singulas specialiter gratias continent per significationem et efficiunt per virtutem . . . Solum autem matrimonium, *tametsi inter cetera sacramenta praecipuum sit*, ita rem sacram in sexuum commixtione significat, quod eam *lege turpitudinis impediente* minime operetur; signum est enim Christi et Ecclesiae non effectivum sed dumtaxat repraesentativum"; (Singer, p. 481).

theological expression of the growing awareness in faith of the sacramental meaning of marriage. As a secular reality, marriage was at this period regarded only as the basis for the founding of a family, though in the perspective of conjugal love; as a *sacramentum*, it was seen as a remedy against the evils of sexuality caused by original sin. This idea dominated the whole of early and later scholastic thought, even when marriage had been recognized as an effective instrument of salvation. As a sacrament, marriage was seen to be a remedy for those who were unable to live in continence, and for this reason it had a purely negative significance with regard to grace.[134]

But is it not true to say that Hugh of St. Victor—although the "seven sacraments" were set apart a little later than the period at which he was writing—had attributed a sanctifying power to marriage? This is indeed the case, but his view would appear to have had very little influence on theologians until the beginning of the thirteenth century. This is perfectly understandable. Hugh said that the "truth of the sacrament" was to be found "in the power and the spiritual grace which were gained in and through the sacraments by those who received the sacraments worthily" (*De sacramentis*, II, 11, 8 [PL, 176, 496]). This is the strict definition of the sacraments, and Hugh applied it to the marriage of Christians, maintaining that non-Christians received the "sacrament of marriage" and thus the sacral sign of the mystery of Christ and his church, but not the "spiritual effect"—the inner communion of grace with God in Christ by means of which their conjugal love was included in charity. Hugh's views on the efficacity of the sacrament were not, however, adopted by later theologians. This is not entirely incomprehensible, since Hugh had made too radical a division in marriage, even speaking of "two sacraments." After Hugh, however, greater emphasis was placed on the complementary relationship between the spiritual and marital and the physical and sexual aspects in marriage. But

---

134 Mag. Hermannus, *Epitome* 31: "hoc sacramentum . . . mali remedium est, etsi donum non conferat" (*PL*, 178, 1745).

there was always the opposite tendency—the influential patristic view that marriage was only a "remedy against desire."

But the explicit assertion, maintained for half a century, that marriage was one of the seven sacraments, was unable to obstruct the eventual theological expression of this conviction, and the first half of the thirteenth century witnessed a gradual growth towards clearer expression. Between 1220 and 1245 the Paris School began an exciting reappraisal of theology, the work of the early schoolmen was synthesized, and traditional questions were solved. In connection with marriage, the purely negative expression (that marriage was a means of preventing sin) was made more positive by William of Auxerre, who said that marriage did not confer grace, but, as a remedy against evil, preserved us in God's grace.[135] William of Auvergne was one of the first to speak about an increase of grace, although he did not attribute this gift of grace to marriage as such, but to the priestly liturgy of marriage (*Tractatus de sacramento matrimonii*, 9).[136]

Although he was certainly not the first to do so, Alexander of Hales must be accorded the honour of having to some extent developed the idea of the distinctive power of grace of sacramental marriage. He supported his view by what would seem to be *a priori* reasoning. He accepted that, as a human and secular institution, marriage could not confer grace. But, because Christian awareness of marriage included it among the seven sacraments, it was therefore bound to confer grace, since the mark of the *Septenarium* was the "sign and cause of grace." Reacting against William of Auvergne, he refused to attribute the gift of grace to the priest's solemnisation of marriage, maintaining that the marriage itself conferred grace on those who contracted it worthily. In his view, the increase of grace peculiar to marriage was the *unio spiritualis caritatis*—the spiritual communion of

---

[135] *Summa Aurea:* "Matrimonium per quod conservatur gratia; est enim medicina praeservativa, quia praeservat a lapsu." The text is to be found in D. van den Eynde, p. 108, *n.* 1.

[136] See Le Bras, cols. 2209-10.

love, or, more precisely, following the idea prevalent before Aquinas of the sacraments as effecting salvation, a grace which "disposed" those who received it towards this union of love.[137] Among the many subtle distinctions and restrictions which Alexander introduced here was his claim that this specific grace of marriage was conferred only if the marriage was really an intention to bring up children in marital chastity solely in God's honour.

It is clear that Alexander drew his basic inspiration from Hugh of St. Victor, but simply applied these ideas to marriage, and indeed to marriage with sexual intercourse. It is also clear from the conditions which Alexander felt constrained to lay down that the reality of sex caused him some anxiety. Clearly this was really what prevented the full sacramental definition from being applied to marriage initially. On the other hand, however, medieval chariness of sexual matters was not, as I hope to show in a later volume of this work, so fundamental as in the patristic period—the reaction against Catharism had a liberating influence in the Middle Ages—but was an attitude prompted largely by pastoral concern. (The fact that many theologians, even authors of more recent works, have seen more in this is due to a theological misinterpretation of the medieval idea of "natural wounds" as a result of original sin.)

Bonaventure would seem to have been less enthusiastic about

---

[137] "Alii dicunt quod efficit gratiam quam figurat, non ratione sui, sed ratione benedictionis sacramentalis, quae fit adhibita solemnitate et quoad hoc est sacramentum Novae Legis . . . Praeterea, si hoc haberet tantum ratione benedictionis institutae ab Ecclesia, non esset hoc ex virtute ipsius sacramenti, sed plus faceret ibi sacramentale, quam sacramentum . . . Collata est etiam quaedam sanctificatio a Domino cum interfuit nuptiis et cum in Evangelio instituit sacramentum, ratione cuius potest . . . conferri augmentum gratiae . . . Ideo videtur dicendum . . . quod . . . consensus ille animorum, in fide mutuae continentiae et in non dissensu a generatione filiorum ad cultum Dei praeter omnem causam inhonestam, v. gr. cum solum spirituale movet eos, disponit *ad spiritualem unionem caritatis*, quam Dominus dedit in consentientibus digne . . ." (*Glossa in Sent.*, IV, d. 26, c. 7, ed. Quaracchi, pp. 459–60).

this discovery. He clung to the traditional idea of marriage as a "remedy," but asked how it was possible for marriage to be a remedy if it did not confer any grace.[138] His analysis of this question managed, nonetheless, to transcend the idea of marriage as a "remedy." Marriage had this curative character immediately after the fall, but by virtue of Christ's redemption the sacrament of marriage also conferred "aliquod gratiae donum" (some grace) at least on those who received it with the proper disposition. In other words, it bestowed some grace "on those who were united by mutual consent to marital fidelity in order to beget children in the service of God." The grace of marriage brought about the threefold "good of marriage" (*bonum matrimonii*): the *bonum fidei* (fidelity to one's own husband), the *bonum prolis* (children), and the *bonum sacramenti* (indissolubility of marriage). The grace of marriage was thus a *gartia ad remedium* (remedial grace) (*In IV Sent.*, d. 26, a. 2, q. 2 ad 2). It was a "gratia ad copulam *singularem*, et ad copulam *utilem*, et ad copulam *inseparabilem*" (*In IV Sent.*, d. 26, a. 2, q. 2, concl.).

In contrast to William of Auvergne, and in the tradition of Alexander of Hales, Bonaventure attributed this sacramental gift of grace to marriage not only "on the basis of the church's blessing of the marriage," but also "on the basis of the [in fact liturgical] expression of the *consensus*."[139] This is a clear indication of the emergence of the tendency to make the sacramentalism of marriage coincide with the element in the contract that constituted the marriage itself—the *consensus*.

The movement towards awareness of the full sacramental nature of marriage was completed by Albert and Aquinas. When he was faced with this question, Albert the Great first of all considered the various views that were current at the time and re-

---

138 What would in fact have been sinful without this sacrament (the marriage act) became, as a result of the sacrament, "merely a venial sin or even no sin at all" (*In IV Sent.*, d. 26, a. 2, q. 2, concl.).

139 "Ratione enim expressionis consensus . . . et ratione benedictionis Ecclesiae."

duced them to three: the first was that marriage conferred no grace, but was simply a "sign of a saving reality"; the second view accepted a certain gift of grace, though only in the negative sense, as a *recessus a peccato,* a mitigation of the desire so that this should not exceed the demands of the threefold *bonum matrimonii;* and finally there was the view of "certain experts" who maintained that this grace was also positive, that is, *in ordine ad bonum.* Albert's contemporaries, Alexander and Bonaventure, were among those who shared this view, of which Albert said that it was *"multum probabilis"*—in other words, that it could be defended on very good grounds (Albert, *In IV Sent.,* d. 26, a. 14).[140]

Albert did not express a decided preference for any one of these three views, although it is clear from his work as a whole that he personally fully supported the third. Aquinas clearly preferred this view: if God gave an ability to bring something about—in this case, the *bona matrimonii*—then he also gave the grace without which it was not possible to use this ability in a suitable way (*In IV Sent.,* d. 26, q. 2, a. 3; see also d. 2, q. 1, a. 1, sol. 2). In the *Summa Contra Gentiles,* his starting-point was, with Alexanader, the universal feeling in the church that marriage was an authentic sacrament. If it was in fact a sacrament, then it was not only a sign of saving reality, but it was also obvious (*"credendum est quod"*) that we must accept its saving effect as well (*SCG,* IV, 78). The treatise on marriage is unfortunately missing from Aquinas' unfinished *Summa Theologiae;* but, in his general references to the saving effects of the sacraments, he names the seven without any reservations at all in the case of marriage (*ST,* III, q. 65, a. 1, in connection with III, q. 62, a. 1; see also II–II, q. 100, a. 2, ad 6). Although there was some show of resistance after him,[141] this really marked the end of

---

[140] *Probabilis* does not yet have the present-day sense of "probable," but here means "provable."

[141] J. P. Olivi denied that marriage was a sacrament on an equal footing with the other six, and was later to retract this opinion before the General Chapter of his order. Duns Scotus also had difficulties in connection with

this particular development, and the view was universally accepted by theologians at the time of the Council of Trent. Erasmus called it the "more plausible modern view."[142] It was consecrated by a dogmatic definition at the Council of Trent.

Marriage: Secular Reality and Saving Mystery

For the first eleven centuries marriage was seen—both in Christian experience and in Western theology—above all as a secular reality to be experienced "in the Lord" and meriting special pastoral care in the moral and religious sphere. From the eleventh century, to the middle of the thirteenth, however, awareness of marriage as a sacrament developed to the point where it could be expressed for the first time in theological synthesis. Theological reflection about this twofold historical fact inevitably raised this question: how, in the last analysis, do we explain the relationship between the secular reality and the saving mystery (or sacrament)? It is not my intention to reconstruct the development of this relationship in purely historical terms. In the preceding sections, I have attempted to trace the direction taken by Western theological thought by selecting certain texts—perhaps not always the most typical though in my opinion suffi-

---

this question, but accepted the fully sacramental character of marriage "on the authority of the church": "quia communiter tenet Ecclesia sacramentum matrimonii esse septimum inter ecclesiastica sacramenta, et de sacramentis Ecclesiae non est aliter sentiendum, quam sentit Ecclesia Romana, ideo dici potest, quod contractui matrimoniali annexit Deus sacramentum proprie dictum, saltem pro lege evangelica" (*In IV Sent.*, d. 26, q. unica, n. 13). Scotus' difficulty appears to have been concerned principally with the biblical basis of the sacramentalism of marriage (Eph. v. 22 ff.). Durand of St. Pourçain said, at the beginning of the fourteenth century: "Sentire quod per sacramentum matrimonium non conferatur gratia, non est contra determinationem Ecclesiae, nec contra id quod Romana Ecclesia praedicat et observat" (*In IV Sent.*, d. 26, q. 3). Durand had clearly forgotten the confession of faith made in this connection by the Council of Lyons, which had taken place several decades previously.

142 "Plausibilior recentiorum sententia"; see *"Christiani matrimonii institutio,"* *Opera Omnia,* Basle (1540), pt. 5, p. 519.

ciently illuminating—and certain historical events, and by con-
centrating always on those elements which are important for the
history of dogma.

My reason for this emphasis has been that this historical element forms an essential aspect in our present-day study of the
saving mystery of marriage, since it reveals the continuity of the
faith, which is, after all, historical. Viewing the problem from
the point of view of the history of dogma therefore enables us
to look—with greater sensitivity and with greater theological
justification—both for what is relative in the views of the
church, and for the exact location of what is absolute in them.
The relationship between marriage "as secular reality" and marriage "as sacrament"—the result of this entire analysis—has been
described in a masterly way, although of course a way closely
tied to his own particular situation, by Aquinas. I therefore propose to conclude this study of the growth of thought in the
Western Church concerning marriage in the first thirteen centuries with a summary of Aquinas' views on the subject.

Aquinas distinguished three aspects in the reality of marriage:
first, what he called the *officium naturae,* the "natural datum" of
marriage as a commission for man as creature to perpetuate the
human race; secondly, the *officium civilitatis* of marriage—in
other words, marriage as an "anthropological reality" and as a
civil duty (*In IV Sent.,* d. 26, q. 2, a. 2.)[143] and finally, marriage
as a sacrament. According to Aquinas the "civil aspect" was no
more than the specifically human aspect of marriage as a "natural commission." He did not recognise the modern distinction
between "nature" and "society" elaborated at a later stage. But,
for Aquinas, *officium civilitatis* had, in a marriage contract, the
meaning which is now associated with marriage as a social phe-

---

[143] Aquinas used various expressions to denote this "civil aspect" of
marriage; *officium communitatis* (*In IV Sent.,* d. 34, q. 1, a. 1, ad 4);
officium oeconomicum (*In VIII Ethic.,* 12); *institutio in lege civili* (*In IV
Sent.,* d. 26, q. 2, a. 2); *ordinatum ad bonum politicum* (*SCG,* iv, 78);
oeconomica seu civilis (*ST,* 1, q. 92, a. 1, ad 2; iii, q. 65, a. 1). This clearly
shows also that it was an idea found in all his works.

nomenon. He included in the "civil function" of marriage the mutual love of the partners for each other—a love which embraced both friendship (*amicitia*) and readiness to help each other (*mutuum obsequium*) (*In IV Sent.*, d. 26, q. 2, a. 2), especially in everything connected with the home and the household economy, and also the partners' service of the *civitas*, or civil community.[144]

The "civil aspect" of marriage, then, according to Aquinas, included not only conjugal love, both in the sphere of personal relationship (*amicitia*) and in the material sphere (*oeconomia, mutuum obsequium*), but also the civil, political, and social aspects of the marriage contract and of married life, even though these latter aspects were less prominent. (To judge by Aquinas' quotations, it was Aristotle in particular who made him so aware of this social aspect of marriage.) With this in mind, we ought to revise our traditional ideas about the medieval—and especially the Thomist—views of marriage. Aquinas of course continued to regard the "natural datum"—that is, the basic data of "creatureliness" bound up in man's incarnate and sexual nature: procreation, the foundation of a family, and above all the bringing up of children—as the basic point of departure for the actual institution of marriage and therefore for the theology of marriage. But it was not this that acted as a check on his view of marriage, but, as in the case of Paul, the position of inferiority occupied by the woman in society at the time.

When Aquinas says that, apart from the *officium naturae* (the foundation of the family), the man had no further reason for associating with the woman (*In I ad Cor.* 7, 1, lect. 1, n. 314),[145]

---

144 See the texts listed under note 143 above.

145 See also *ST*, 1, q. 98, a. 2 and q. 92, a. 1. Aristotle also expressed the social datum reflected in the biblical idea that "the woman was taken from the man" (the rib!) by calling the woman "a weaker version of the man," or a "failed man," and this idea was adopted by the medieval writers. Aquinas used, for example, the term *mas occasionatus* (*ST*, 1, q. 92, a. 1, ad 1; *In II Sent.*, d. 20, q. 2, a. 1, ad 1; d. 20, q. 1, a. 1; *In I ad Cor.* 7, 1, lect. 1, n. 316).

we must of course understand this "apart from the foundation of the family" as an integral part of the *officium civilitatis*—and this gives Aquinas' assertion a wider perspective than is usually accorded to it, despite the fact that it is limited by the situation prevailing in his own time. This means that, according to Aquinas, the "civil" or specifically human task of marriage was still directed towards the *officium naturae* (*In IV Sent.*, d. 31, q. 1, a. 2, ad 2; see also *ST*, III, q. 29, a. 2), and that is why we were able to say that his *officium civilitatis* expressed the specifically human aspects of the *officium naturae*. It is also why in the course of many texts, he mentions only two aspects of marriage: the *officium naturae* and the "sacrament"; although many commentators, and many of those who "cite" Aquinas, have lost sight of the fact that he really meant a human *officium naturae*. We should be careful to ensure that the *lacuna* which does exist in the medieval view of marriage as a result of an incomplete anthropological understanding is not rendered even more mistakenly by our own ignorance of what these writers were really saying!

This secular reality of marriage, both as *officium naturae* and as *officium civilitatis*—in other words, both the "natural" and the anthropological and social aspects of marriage—was as a whole raised by Christ to the level of a sacrament. In this context Aquinas explicitly named both aspects (*In IV Sent.*, d. 27, q. 1, a. 2, sol. 1). By thus raising this reality, already naturally present in society and experienced in a specifically human way, to the level of a sacrament, marriage became—according to Aquinas—a "spiritual communion," by which he meant a supernatural and religious communion.[146] Marriage was, in its natural, personal (*amicitia*), and social aspects, the "matter" which, by

---

[146] In the texts quoted, *spiritualis* does not mean "spiritual," but what we would call "supernatural." In *ST*, I–II, q. 110, a. 1, Aquinas calls grace an *esse spirituale* ("spiritual manner of being"). *Spiritus* here goes back to the biblical and Augustinian idea of *pneuma*, and is contrasted with the *sarx*, or *caro* ("flesh")—that is, man insofar as he does not live from God's grace.

virtue of baptism, became a sacrament. A supernatural mystery of salvation was, by divine power, brought about in this reality experienced naturally and in a specifically human way.[147] The human and secular reality of marriage itself thus entered salvation. The sacramental character of marriage did not in any way diminish its secular reality or its *officium civilitatis* in all its dimensions,[148] but only brought these within the sphere of Christian salvation. When Aquinas discussed the "essence of marriage" he always meant the secular quality of marriage as *officium naturae* and as *officium civilitatis*, since that essence had been raised to the level of a sacrament: it had become an effective saving instrument working in the power of "Christ's passion."[149]

According to Aquinas, then, the ordinary, secular reality of marriage with all its personal, social and civil obligations continued without any diminution in the sacrament. It would be difficult to claim that this Thomist view encroaches in any way on the natural structure of creation, or detracts from the rightful authority of the state. Indeed, the competence of the state was, in Aquinas' view, presupposed by the sacramentalism of marriage.[150] He found a further argument in support of this in the fact that marriage was a public contract:

"Since marriage is to some extent concluded in the form of a contract, it is, like other contracts, subject to the arrangement of positive, that is, of civil, laws" (*In IV Sent.*, d. 36, q. 1, a. 5), for "insofar as marriage is an *officium naturae*, it is regulated by the natural law; insofar as it is a sacrament, it is regulated by the divine law; and insofar as it

---

[147] "Mediante materiale fit spiritualis virtute divina"; (*ST*, I–II, q. 110, a. 1). The *materiale* here is marriage as both *officium naturae* and *officium civilitatis*. (See context.)

[148] "Ratio sacramenti est quaedam condicio adveniens matrimonio secundum se considerato" (*In IV Sent.*, d. 31, q. 1, a. 2, ad 7).

[149] This applied, in Aquinas' view to all the sacraments. See, in this connection, *In IV Sent.*, d. 26, q. 2, a. 3, ad 1; d. 26, q. 2, a. 1, ad 3.

[150] Precisely how far the rights of the state extended in connection with marriage as a personal decision is, of course, a question which will have to be investigated.

is an *officium communitatis* [or *civilitatis*], it is regulated by the civil law." *In IV Sent.*, d. 34, q. 1, a. 1, ad 4; *SCG*, IV, 78. The marriage of baptized partners was thus regulated by divine and by civil laws (*SCG*, III, 123).[151]

Aquinas thus recognised both the full secular status of marriage together with all the consequences of this status, while at the same time acknowledging the strictly sacramental character of marriage as a saving instrument through which the mystery of Christ and his church was active in the marriage of baptized partners. Certainly, the situation prevailing at his time made it easier for him to accept this human and religious authenticity. There was, at the period in which he was writing, no "Tridentine legal form" for marriage. Every form of mutual consent to marriage—whether celebrated liturgically in the church, conducted outside the church, or even not a public civil ceremony at all, but clandestine—was, for baptized Christians, both a valid and sacramental marriage. But thanks to his sound theological view of marriage—his belief that its status as a secular reality remained undiminished by its having been raised to the level of a sacrament—Acquinas had, as it were, already formulated in advance the difficulties which might be expected from at least an exclusive application of the "common legal form" of Trent. But, before going into this later development, I propose to give an outline of the completely different development of marriage in the East, where—unlike the West—the sacrament was situated first of all in a liturgical celebration of the mystery.

[151] Elsewhere Aquinas adds that the state should not make any laws which might cut across the authority of the church (*In IV Sent.*, d. 42, q. 2, a. 2).

2

The Conception of Marriage
in the Eastern Churches

The Pauline idea of the church as the bride of Christ exerted an earlier and a greater influence in the East than in the West. The Syrian churches were the first to have a liturgical feast of the church as bride,[1] and this feast was of very early date. To a greater extent too than in the West, the Eastern theology and liturgy of marriage were inspired by the idea of the *henosis*, or communion of Christ with his church, in connection with Eph v. 22–32. The Western view of marriage, moreover, with its typically legal bias—marriage as a contract—played no part in the East, where more emphasis was placed on the mystical meaning of marriage and its spirtuality. Finally, the theologians of the Eastern Church had a less pessimistic view of sex and sexuality than the Western church Fathers and schoolmen. All these factors were bound to lead to marriage taking a different form in the East than it took in the West.

I have already referred to the fact that it was a bishop of the Antiochian church, Ignatius, who was the first to insist that Christian marriages should for preference be contracted with the bishop's permission. I accounted for this by saying that it was due to Ignatius' "episcopalism," and noted that his wish was not

---

[1] See G. Khouri-Sarkis, "La fête de l'Eglise dans l'année liturgique syrienne," *Irn*, 28 (1955), pp. 186 ff.; F. Graffin, "Recherches sur le thème de l'Eglise," *OS*, 3 (1958), pp. 317 ff.

carried out in the West in the first eleven centuries. Initially it aroused no response in the East, either. In both the East and the West the view that marriage was a family affair, with the bride's father playing the chief part, was so deeply engrained in the minds of the people that there was an initial reluctance to relinquish this privilege to the bishop. It is clear from the regulations of the Syrian church of the third century that the parents played the leading part in marriage contracts (Syrian *Didascalia*, c. 22 [*AQOK*, 115, 15–19]). On the other hand, these ecclesiastical regulations also indicate the duty of the bishops to provide for orphans and abandoned children, even in connection with marriage. In this, they assumed the role of the father (*AQOK*, 87, 13–29) in a practice which was not introduced until later in the West.

It is also true that, like Tertullian in the West, Clement of Alexandria in the East saw that the ecclesial character and the holiness of Christian marriage was to be found in baptism.[2] Christian betrothal and marriage were contracted according to family and civil customs, and, as I have already pointed out, the betrothal was effected in the East by means of the *arrha*. As a result, the marriage itself consisted of three elements—the handing over of the bride, the bridal procession, and the ceremonies which took place in the bridegroom's house.

In the first three centuries, then, there were no fundamental differences between the East and the West.

From the fourth to the seventh centuries, however, the following situation obtained in the Greek-Byzantine Church.[3] Two kinds of betrothals were practised under the influence of the Roman law: betrothal without any form of law, and betrothal according to the custom of the *arrha*. The church preferred the latter form of betrothal, since, as a promise to marry, the betrothal was binding, and the *arrha*—especially when it took the form of an "engagement ring"—set a clearer seal on this promise.

---

2 See above, pp. 249–56.
3 See Bibliography, 4.

Indeed, the betrothal already contained the mystery of the church as the bride of Christ, with the result that marriage with a third party after a breach with the betrothed was almost understood as adultery (*FRBE*, p. 71, *n.* 278). Thus, although secular feasts held in connection with betrothals were interpreted in the East as "mystical" and "ecclesial," betrothals were not accompanied by a priestly blessing before the eighth century. But from the eighth century onwards there was a form of blessing on the betrothal, though this was not associated with the civil betrothal within the family until the tenth and eleventh centuries, and was in any case not a Greek-Byzantine rite proper, but a custom borrowed from the heterodox churches of the Syriac rite.

As far as the marriage feast proper is concerned, the blessing of the bride and the bridegroom originally had a private character, as it did in the West. As early as the fourth century the blessing was given when the bishop or the priest visited the family during the marriage feast to congratulate those present.

A liturgical action with prayers and hymns was developed from this occasional blessing towards the end of the fourth century.[4] It is therefore clear that the family and civil ceremonies of marriage were given an ecclesiastical basis in the East at an earlier date than in the West.[5]

In the East, the *stephanōma* (the garlanding of the bride and bridegroom) as the rite which was associated with the essential legal proceedings of the *ekdosis* (handing over of the bride) was of fundamental importance from a very early date. What is remarkable in this connection is that, already in Gregory Nazianzen's time, great value was set upon the fact that the ceremony

[4] John Chrysostom refers to "prayers" and "thanksgiving and hymns" (*In Gen. Hom.*, 48, *n.* 6 [*PG*, 54, 443]).

[5] There were no prayers in connection with the priest's blessing in the oldest liturgical books of the East; see the *Euchologion* of Serapion of Thmuis and the *Constitutiones Apostolorum*, c. 8. Gregory Nazianzen records that psalms were sung at the blessing (*Epist.* 232 [*PG*, 37, 376]). John Chrysostom testifies to a liturgy of marriage that was already formed (*In Gen. Hom.* 48 [*PG*, 54, 433]).

of the garland should be performed, not by the father, but by the bishop (priest).[6] This resulted in the development of a liturgical ceremony which gave its name to the entire liturgical solemnisation of marriage—the *stephanōma*—and which may thus be compared with the veiling in the West. This rite, which had a non-Christian origin, but which was subsequently adopted and assimilated by the Church, was given a theological basis by John Chrysostom (*Hom.* 9, *in* 1 Tim. [*PG*, 62, 546]). In this connection he pointed especially to the Christian victory over evil desires, referring to Paul's allusion to the "garlanded competitors" (1 Cor ix. 25; 2 Tim iv. 8). According to the liturgical historians, we may assume that the priestly ceremony of the garland became an ecclesiastical rite under the influence of Chrysostom's Christian interpretation.

After the garlanding, the bride's and the bridegroom's hands were placed in each other. This was undoubtedly the expression of the *ekdosis* (the handing over of the bride) which was originally carried out by the bride's father. Gregory Nazianzen, however, wrote in one of his epistles that he found it a pity he was unable to attend the marriage of Anysius' daughter, as he would so much have liked to have placed the bride's and the bridegroom's hands in each other, and then the hands of both in God's hands (*Epist.* 193 [*PG*, 37, 316–17]). This presupposes that Gregory, who refused to perform the ceremony of the garland himself, nonetheless conducted the ceremony of the *iunctio dexterarum*. The father's *ekdosis* as expressed in the *iunctio dexterarum* was clearly devalued by the Roman-Byzantine law according to which the partners' mutual consent to marry constituted the essential legal action, with the result that it became

[6] Gregory himself was, however, rather unfavourably disposed towards the carrying out by the clergy of this custom which was so important in the marriage contract (*Epist.* 231 [*PG*, 37, 374]). His attitude may indicate that the garlanding by the priest did not originate in the Greek church, but was an introduction from the Armenian church, and first took place in Cappadocia (*FRBE*, p. 77).

purely incidental whether it was conducted by the father or a priest.

But this development led to the priest's performing a considerable number of other actions apart from the blessing of the marriage. Marriage in the East eventually became a ceremony in which the priest to a very great extent played the central part. This does not mean, however, that marriage was taken over by the Eastern Church everywhere to the same extent. In Alexandria, for example, it was usual, already at the end of the fourth century, to ask the priest to "give" the bride and bridegroom "to each other" (*Bibliotheca Photii* [*PG*, 103, 1261]). (This is reminiscent of the previously recorded fact that, in Egypt, the priest had a basic function in connection with pre-Christian and non-Christian marriage feasts.)

In Cappadocia, on the other hand, at the same period—that is, at the time of Basil the Great—the priest's function was limited to the praying of psalms, although there too the basic legal action —the garlanding and the *iunctio dexterarum*—was gradually taken over by the priest. Whereas in Cappadocia the family and civil practices connected with marriage were brought within the church's orbit, in Constantinople there was a movement to dissociate the priestly blessing from the secular wedding feast. John Chrysostom insisted that the marriage blessing should be given at home, on the eve of the secular marriage (*De verbis illis Apostoli "propter fornicationem"* [*PG*, 51, 211]); this was in order that the priest's solemnization of the marriage might be separated from the more worldly wedding feast, of which the legal action proper of the marriage contract continued to form a part. In the one case, then, secular practices were taken over by the church; in the other, there was a tendency to separate the priest's pastoral accompaniment of the marriage from the secular marriage contract. The liturgical form of the marriage ceremony was influenced by both movements.

The practice of receiving the priest's blessing was strongly urged in the East long before it was recommended in the West, although it is not possible to speak of a commandment of the church in this connection. With one exception (*Responsa canonica*, n. 11, added by the Synod of Trullo [can. 2] to the *Corpus canonicum* [M-SC, pt. 11, 940–1]), the oldest Eastern legal assemblies do not mention the priest's blessing of the marriage, but we can say that the blessing by the priest was understood in the Greek Church, from the time of John Chrysostom onwards, as an "honorary right"—and in the Church of Antioch, Alexandria, and Constantinople, from the fourth century onwards, as an "honorary duty."[7] This was true at least of the first marriage, since in the East too the priest's blessing was not permitted in the case of a second marriage until the eighth century.[8]

Like the Latin Church, then, the Greek-Byzantine Church regarded the priestly marriage blessing as a matter of honour and did not bestow it frequently. It was in any case always denied to second marriages. When the church's liturgy of marriage began to acquire—from the eighth century onwards—an extensive form, the priest's "garlanding" too generally did not take place in the case of a second marriage. Theodore Studites (759–826) simply referred candidates for a second marriage to the civil contract (*Epist.* 1, 50 [PG, 99, 1093]). The acerbity with which Theodore expressed himself on this point is a clear indication that some priests gave their blessing to these marriages (*Epist.* 1, 50 [PG, 99, 1089–96]; 11, 191 [PG, 99, 1581–4])[9]—a practice which in the long run could not be checked.

[7] Chrysostom did not mention a blessing by the priest in his sermon opposing the secular celebration of weddings and advocating a Christian celebration of the marriage contract (*Hom.* 12, *n.* 7 [PG, 62, 389–90]). Elsewhere he urged Christians to call in a priest, because in the priest "Christ himself was invited" to the wedding (*De verbis illis Apostoli "propter fornicationem"* [PG, 51, 210]). Likewise, when still in Antioch he observed that Christians were bound to call upon the priest to bless the marriage (*In Gen. Hom.* 48, *n.* 6 [PG, 54, 443]).

[8] In the East, a special appeal was made in this connection to the Synod of Neocaesarea (314–25), can. 7 (*HCDO*, pt. 1, p. 390).

[9] The emperors, who remarried as many as three times, were of course a strong encouragement for the people (*Epist.* 1, 50 [PG, 99, 1093]).

From the eighth century until the eleventh, the imperial legislature was particularly concerned with the law of marriage. At
this period, the priestly marriage blessing was not only an ecclesiastical but also a civil injunction. Pope Nicholas I, in his
epistle to the Bulgars (who were converted to Christianity by the
Greeks), reacted strongly against the Greek view that the mutual
consent of the partners on its own was insufficient and also that
the various customs associated with marriage, including the
priest's blessing, were subject to an injunction, with the result
that their omission was regarded as a sin. (See p. 273.) In order
to reinforce what he said in his letter to the Bulgars, who were
deeply influenced by the ideas of the Greeks by whom they had
been converted, the Pope referred to a work by Chrysostom
which was not in fact authentic.[10] Nicholas' epistle in any case
shows that the development took a different course in the East
from in the West. This is clear from the Byzantine legislation
under the Syrian dynasty (i.e., from the eighth to the eleventh
centuries). Even though the legislation of Justinian (527–65)
had adopted the Roman practice of the *consensus*, marriage
purely by mutual consent was still regarded in the Byzantine
empire as less "fashionable."

The legislation also afforded scope for betrothal by the *arrha*,
which was in the Eastern blood. In view of the fact that, according to the Codex of Theodosius (III, 5, 1. 2), arrangements involving the *arrha* were not legally valid unless they were confirmed by a written document, two forms of marriage contract
were therefore possible: betrothal by the *arrha*, confirmed in
writing (which was more or less equivalent to a "contracted but
unconsummated marriage"), and marriage by *consensus*. In
practice, betrothal by means of the *arrha* became predominant in
the Byzantine empire.

This accounts for the meaning of the Byzantine legislation from

[10] The text which he quoted was taken from the *Opus imperfectum in
Matt.*, 32, 9 (PG, 56, 802), but it goes back originally to a Greek author
(PLSL, p. 326).

the eighth century onwards. The *Ekloge* of Emperor Leo III (717–41) made explicit provision for two forms of marriage contract. If the normal legal form of marriage contract—that is, betrothal by the *arrha*, confirmed in writing (*Ekloge*, tit. 2, 3 [*IGR*, II, 19])—was not possible because of poverty or for some other good reason, the marriage could be contracted purely by the mutual consent of the bride and bridegroom and their parents, either during the church's liturgy or in the presence of two witnesses (*Ekloge*, tit. 2, 8 [*IGR*, II, 23]). The result of this is that the church's rite of marriage made the marriage legally valid in the eyes of the civil authorities even in the eighth century.

Emperor Basil I of Macedonia (867–86) laid down that the priest should perform the ecclesiastical marriage rite, not in secret, but in public (*Procheiros Nomos*, tit. 4 [*IGR*, II, 128]). Thus the following forms of marriage were recognised as valid: the church's rite of betrothal, the church's rite of marriage, and marriage with written confirmation of the arrangements concerning the *arrha* (*Epanagoge*, tit. 16, 1 [*IGR*, II, 285]).

The legislation of Leo VI (the Wise), 886–912, in this connection is worthy of special attention. A difference had come about in the Byzantine empire between the civil and the ecclesiastical view of betrothal. Since the stipulation of the Synod of Trullo, the church had regarded the breaking of a betrothal by marriage with a third party as adultery. The civil authorities found it difficult to accept this appraisal of betrothal, particularly since such betrothals frequently took place between children who had not attained the legally marriageable age. Leo VI found a solution to this difficulty, which on the one hand violated neither the church's nor the civil point of view, and on the other meant that this difference of opinion no longer had any practical consequences in law. He forbade the giving of a blessing to legally unmarriageable children—that is, to boys of fifteen and to girls of thirteen—either on betrothal or on marriage, but every solemnisation by the priest, including the church's blessing on the betrothal, was regarded by the civil authorities as a legally valid marriage (Novelle 74 [*IGR*, i, pp. 144–5]). This judgment of Solomon thus succeeded in reconciling the civil and the ecclesiastical points of view. A purely civil betrothal was dissoluble; but an ecclesiastical betrothal was legally indissoluble, because it was, in the eyes of the civil law, a valid contract of marriage. The church's rite of betrothal was thus a civil contract of marriage. The view emerges very clearly that the priest's blessing had the value of a legitimate and legally valid constitution of marriage.

One difficulty, however, still remained. The Byzantine Church regarded the purely civil betrothal by the *arrha*, even without the priest's blessing, as an unbreakable bond, whereas the civil legislature considered such a betrothal to be purely secular and thus legally open to annulment.

The Golden Bull (Novelle 24) of Emperor Alexius (1081–1118) completed the development which had already begun. The bull maintained that only a betrothal which had been solemnized by the church was a contract of marriage in the civil sense, but forbade the *arrhatio*—which had since the tenth century become more and more a rite of the church—to children who had not attained the legally marriageable age (the Golden Bull of Emperor Alexius of June 1084 [*IGR*, ii, pp. 305–9]). The consequence of this was that the civil betrothal was reduced to an action without legal form (since the *arrhatio* had been removed from it). And, in view of the fact that a betrothal which had not been blessed by the church was henceforth no longer a betrothal by the *arrha*, it became merely a promise, without binding force, as it had become in the West. In this way the church's and the civil points of view were completely reconciled. By the end of the tenth and the beginning of the eleventh centuries, then, marriage by the church had become, in the Greek-Byzantine legal view, the generally accepted obligatory form of law of the marriage contract. The Greek-Byzantine form of betrothal had furthermore become the practical equivalent of what was known in the West as a *matrimonium initiatum, non consummatum*. All this goes to show how little the Byzantine Church was influenced by the Roman theory of the *consensus*, which had nonetheless been put forward insistently by the codices of Justinian and Theodosius. It is clear that the Byzantine law of marriage developed in a distinctively Eastern direction.

This development was a remarkable one. From the eighth century onwards, exclusively church marriages were regarded as legally valid in the civil sense. What held good for Christians in the West only after the emergence of the Tridentine legal form already applied in the East as early as the eighth century—with the one difference, that in the East the situation was brought about by the secular power, and that an ecclesiastical and a legally valid civil form of marriage continued to exist side by side. From the eleventh century onwards this practice was reinforced by new measures. The local bishop became the officiating minister in the church's rite,[11] and permission was given for the first time for the priest's blessing to be conferred on the marriage of slaves.[12]

In the ninth century this practice was given a theological expression in the Byzantine Church. The Church's rite of marriage, the *stephanōma* (ceremony of the garland), was the element which constituted the marriage as a sacrament, and there was no sacrament without this rite. The priest was the proper minister of this sacrament—it was he who bestowed the blessing and laid the garland on the bride and bridegroom.[13]

In Alexandria the eucharist was already celebrated in connection with the marriage ceremony in the fourth century—in contrast to Rome, where it was not known until the fifth century. At this time mass was probably still celebrated at home.[14] In the

[11] See especially J. Zhisman, *Das Eherecht der orientalischen Kirche*, Vienna (1864), pp. 671 ff., a book which is still important. See also the résumé of what Zhisman says in *FRBE*, pp. 107–08.

[12] Zhisman, pp. 637 ff.

[13] M. Jugie, *Theologiae dogmaticae Graeco-Russicae expositio de sacramentis*, Paris (1930), p. 452.

[14] The first evidence of this is to be found in the patriarchate of Timothy (381–5) in the *Responsa canonica* (*IEG*, pt. 1, p. 632, quoted in

Greek-Byzantine liturgy a *missa praesanctificatorum* was celebrated at marriages—that is, a communion rite. Both in the East and in the West the eucharist was celebrated at the solemnisation of marriages, partly as a reaction against and as a Christian replacement for the pagan practice of pouring libations at the marriage feast. Except for a few liturgical books, there is no evidence of any questioning of the bride and bridegroom in connection with a *consensus* in the Byzantine rite.[15]

The whole development of the Greek-Byzantine practices in connection with marriage was influenced, especially from the beginning of the Syrian dynasty, by the views of the non-Greeks in the East on marriage,[16] and in particular by the ideas prevalent in the Armenian Church, the Nestorian and the Coptic Churches, and among the Syrian Jacobites. It is remarkable that, just as it was a non-Catholic group (the Montanists) which was the first in the West to show a tendency to incorporate marriage into the church, so also in the East the non-Catholic Monophysite and Nestorian national churches were the first to bring marriage within the orbit of the clergy. The Armenian Church was the first in the East to make the coronation rite in marriage an official legal action of the church.[17] What is more, the ecclesiastical form of law was a canonical requirement already in the fifth century (Synod of Sahavipan (447), can. 3 [*CCOF*, fasc. 7, 265, 267, *n*.

FRBE, p. 80, *n*. 314). See also the Synod of Gangra (*M–SC*, pt. 2, p. 1098). The first Synod of Laodicea, can. 58, forbade the celebration of the eucharist at home (*M–SC*, p. 2, p. 578).

[15] See the Greek Byzantine rite of betrothal and marriage in A. Raes, *Le mariage*, pp. 47–68. Since 1595 the Uniate Greek Churches have adopted the Latin rite of the *consensus*. The Ruthenian Slavs also adopted this rite into their rituals in the second half of the seventeenth century, and the Russian Orthodox Church took it over from them; see A. Raes, "Le consentement," *EL*, 47 (1933) and 48 (1934) in the bibliography.

[16] See *FRBE*, pp. 84–100; M. Dauvillier and C. de Clerq, *Le mariage en droit oriental*, Paris (1936).

[17] Already in the patriarchate of Nerses I (ca. 364–73), the marriage garland was blessed by the priest (Faustus of Byzantium, 5, 31 [M. Lauer, *Des Faustos von Byzanz Geschichte der Armenier*, Cologne (1879), p. 183; *FRBE*, p. 86, *n*. 337]). Those whose marriage was blessed in this way did not venture to seek its dissolution.

314]).[18] What is remarkable, too, is that the Armenian rite acknowledged the importance of the *consensus* in marriage, which was moreover heard by the priest.[19] The priest also conducted the marriage ceremony in the Nestorian Churches from a very early date, and these communities regarded betrothal as a true marriage, though it had to be completed by the wedding feast (*FRBE*, pp. 89–94). This was also the case with the Syrian Jacobites (*FRBE*, pp. 95–7).[20] Little is known about the earliest practice among the Coptic Churches concerning marriage, but the priest was certainly involved in the marriage contract in Alexandria as early as the fourth century.[21]

The fact that the Armenian rite of marriage, as performed by the clergy, influenced the Greek-Byzantine Church via Cappadocia can be understood if it is remembered that Armenia was ecclesiastically dependent on the metropolis of Basil the Great at the time of the great Cappadocian Fathers of the church.

In conclusion, then, it is possible to say that marriage was regarded, first by the Monophysite and Nestorian national churches, and later by the Greek-Byzantine Church, as a liturgical celebration of a religious mystery conducted by the priest. This attitude towards marriage was the result of three factors. First, the distinctive significance of betrothal by means of the *arrha* made the contract according to Eastern practice virtually indissoluble. Secondly, the priest had a function in the East which probably went back to the role assumed by the priest in the pagan marriage ceremonies. Thirdly, the Eastern Church had, from the very beginning, a mystical and theological conception of marriage. The secular view of marriage which clearly prevailed in the West

[18] This Synod recognized two rites of marriage: one for first marriages; and one for second marriages, or for the first marriage of Christians whose way of life was not exemplary.

[19] This was already taking place during the patriarchate of Catholicos Sahak (387–439), can. 26 (*CCOF*, fasc. 7, 323, *n.* 387). The Armenian marriage ritual, as it is known to us from eighth- and ninth-century texts, can be found in A. Raes, *Le mariage*, pp. 77–102.

[20] For the present-day Syrian marriage rite see A. Raes, *Le mariage*, pp. 103–34.

[21] For the Coptic marriage rite, see A. Raes, *La mariage*, pp. 23–45.

until the eleventh century (the idea of marriage as a secular
reality to be experienced "in the Lord") was apparently unknown in the East—although there too, and indeed centuries before it took place in the West, the church's liturgy of betrothal
and marriage came about by the church's canonisation of the
ancient family and civil marriage customs.

3

The Post-Tridentine Period

THE TRIDENTINE FORM OF THE MARRIAGE CONTRACT

Before considering the Tridentine legal form concerning marriage, certain statements made by the teaching office of the medieval church should be taken into account. In the official definitions of the Lateran Council (1139), the church excommunicated all those who held in contempt and condemned the "legitimate marital union" (DS 718 [DB 367])—in other words, Catharism, whose adherents were at that time propagating with some violence the view that legitimate marriage should be held in contempt. In an official document issued by a local synod at Verona in 1184, in reaction against these Manichean tendencies, marriage was for the first time called a "sacrament" and placed on the same footing as baptism, the eucharist, and the sacrament of penance (DS 761 [DB 402]). What is remarkable is that this occurred in 1184—that is, before the sacramental nature of marriage had been fully clarified. The church's reaction against Manicheism, together with her view of virginity, contributed to her growing explicit consciousness that marriage was a true sacrament. Furthermore, a consciously anti-Manichean tendency was expressed in the liturgical books which I discussed in connection with the blessing of the bride and the veiling of virgins; before honouring the excellence of virginity, this liturgy safeguarded the mystical meaning of marriage in a clear reaction against its disparagement by the Manichees.[1]

The confession of Faith which Pope Gregory X submitted to the Emperor Michael Palaeologus at the Council of Lyons (1274) expressed belief in the seven sacraments, among which marriage was explicitly named (DS 860 [DB 465]). Marriage was listed in an even more solemn form in the *Decretum pro Armenis* issued by the Council of Florence (1439) among the seven "technical" sacraments which were not only a sign of grace but also *de facto* bestowed grace, by virtue of Christ's passion, on all who received them with a religious disposition (DS 1310 [DB 695]). The Decree also stated that marriage was constituted, at least *regulariter*, by the partners' mutual consent to marry (DS 1327 [DB 702]), so that the idea that the mutual consent to marry of baptized persons was itself sacramental was already implicitly present. (The ecclesiastical legal form prescribed by the Council of Trent did not, of course, exist at the time of the Council of Florence.)

Both early and later scholasticism had already gradually prepared the way for the formation of this assertion that the sacrament of marriage was identical with the marriage contract. Peter Lombard had called the *consensus* the *substantia sacramenti*— all the rest, including the priest's blessing, forming, in his opinion, part of the "ceremonies" of this sacrament (*Sent. IV*, d. 28, c. 2). Albert had said quite simply: "this sacrament consists merely of the contract itself" (*In IV Sent.*, d. 27, a. 6); and Aquinas had observed: "the words expressing the *consensus* of marriage are

[1] The preface in connection with the dedication of virgins in the oldest version of *Leonianum* reads thus: "Although the honourable state of marriage is not impaired by any ban, and although the marriage blessing given in the beginning [i.e., the Genesis blessing on marriage] still remains in force, there are bound to be certain select souls who neglect marriage as it is expressed naturally in the physical union of husband and wife, but who seek with the deepest longing the supernatural reality of which marriage is the sacred symbol, and who therefore do not experience marriage in fact, but aspire rather to that which is symbolized by marriage"; see L. C. Mohlberg, *Sacramentarium Veronense*, Rome (1956), pp. 138-9. Only then does the *Leonianum* go on to the dedication proper.

the *forma* of this sacrament, not the priest's blessing, which is a sacramental" (*In IV Sent.*, d. 1, q. 1, a. 3 ad 5). This marks a complete break with the earliest view of the sacramental character of marriage as elaborated by early Italian scholasticism. It was, however, Duns Scotus who was to draw the final inference from this train of thought and say that this sacrament was not administered by the priest, but by the bride and bridegroom themselves (*Report. Par.* IV, d. 28, q. un., n. 24).

The Reformation compelled the Council of Trent to go thoroughly into the question of marriage. The sacramental nature of marriage was solemnly recognised, the council affirming that it was one of the seven sacraments instituted by Christ (DS 1601 [DB 844])—a sacrament, in other words, in the true and proper sense of the word (DS 1800 [DB 970], the introductory *doctrina;* DS 1801 [DB 971], the condemnatory canon), conferring the grace that it signified (DS 1606, 1608 [DB 849, 851]. The distinctive grace of the sacrament of marriage was generally indicated in the words: the grace of marriage "completes the natural mutual love of the partners in marriage," confirms the indissolubility of the contract of monogamous marriage, and sanctifies the partners (DS 1799 [DB 969]). The council's first draft gave the impression that Eph v. 25–32 was the explicit biblical basis of the sacramental nature of marriage. The council Fathers rejected this preliminary draft, however, and the final text said simply that this Pauline text only suggested (*"innuit"*) the sacramental character of marriage. In addition, the council asserted the monogamous character of marriage (DS 1802 [DB 972]), and the church's right to lay down the impediments that made a marriage invalid (DS 1804 [DB 974]).

The council also condemned the view held by the Reformers that the church erred in regarding a legally valid marriage as indissoluble even in the case of adultery (DS 1805 [DB 975] with canon 7, DS 1807 [DB 977]).[2] In cases of this kind, and in other

---

[2] The church did not in this canon 7 solemnly define in a direct manner the indissolubility of Christian marriage in the case of adultery. There was

cases, the church only recognised the possibility of a "separation of bodies," in other words, a separation "from bed and board" (DS 1808 [DB 978]). The council also declared that a legally valid marriage which had not been consummated in sexual inter-course—i.e., *ratum sed non consummatum*—could be dissolved by the church; this was, however, said in conjunction with the practice of the church that such a marriage (i.e., *non consum-matum*) could be dissolved on entry into a religious order by solemn profession—something which was not accepted by the Reformers (DS 1806 [DB 976]). Finally, canon 10 affirmed the superiority of the state of virginity "for the sake of the kingdom of God" above the married state, and canon 12 established that all matrimonial causes were under the jurisdiction of the ec-clesiastical courts (DS 1810, 1812 [DB 980, 982]). (See pp.

---

no direct condemnation of those who upheld or who practised the in-dissolubility of marriage in such cases, but rather a condemnation of those who asserted that the church erred in this connection in her view. The Greek Church, which permitted or tolerated remarriage in the case of adultery, but—unlike the Reformers—did not maintain that the Roman Church held an erroneous view in this connection, was consequently not formally condemned in canon 7. The immediate reason for the choice of this indirect formulation by the Fathers of the Council of Trent was the fact that, although the church's teaching on this point had been fairly constant, some *auctoritates* in the ancient church and among the medieval theologians and canonists had held a dissentient view. The council Fathers appear to have been fully conversant with the arguments for and against in this mat-ter; see *CT*, pt. 9, 409–10; pt. 3, 578; see also, for the divergent opinions of "Ambrosius (i.e., Ambrosiaster) et alii," pt. 6, 535, 26; see also pt. 3, 578, 7; pt. 9, 420, 21; 680, 18; 721, 4. Moreover, the Council of Trent was also the scene of an attempt on the part of the French bishops, under the leadership of Cardinal de Guise, to reinforce the authority of the church's councils against the supreme power of the Pope in the exercise of judicial authority. This group of bishops insisted that the condemnation of canon 7 contained a condemnation of "Ambrose and others" which could not be permitted. In order to escape from this *impasse*, the condemnation was consciously for-mulated in an indirect manner. See especially P. Fransen, "Echtscheiding na echtbreuk van een der gehuwden," *Bijd*, 14 (1953), pp. 363–87; "Die Formel 'si quis dixerit Ecclesiam errare' auf der 24. Sitzung des Trienter Konzils," *Schk*, 25 (1950), pp. 492–517, 26 (1951), pp. 191–221; "Ehescheidung im Falle vom Ehebruch," *Schk*, 27 (1952), pp. 526–56.

362 ff.). Although all these canons were embellished with an *anathema sit,* none of them contained as such a real doctrine on faith.

The Council of Trent was, however, particularly important in the history of marriage in the church because of its introduction of the so-called "Tridentine legal form" of marriage. I have already said that in the period before Trent, from the tenth and eleventh centuries onwards, the situation had developed to the point where the church in fact exercised complete jurisdictional powers in matrimonial affairs, although no fundamental assertion had been made in this respect. The humanists, however, had discovered that the situation had formerly been quite different and simply stated this fact without making any ideological comments about it.[3] These new historical insights came at a most opportune moment for the Reformers, who availed themselves of the humanists' rediscovery of the "civil marriage" practised in the early church in order to deny the church's power of jurisdiction over marriage, and in the end to deny the sacramental nature of marriage. In reaction to this, the Council of Trent declared: "whoever asserts that matrimonial lawsuits do not come within the province of (the jurisdictional power of) ecclesiastical judges, let him be anathema" (DS 1812 [DB 982]).

Nonetheless, the contents of this canon and of the council's new legislation in connection with marriage need to be interpreted very carefully, and the debates of the council must be taken into consideration. The theologians had been given the task of submitting a report about the Reformers' assertion that matrimonial lawsuits came under the exclusive control of secular judges.[4] One of these theological reports made the traditional distinction between marriage as a contract and marriage as a

[3] See Esmein, pt. 1, p. 50.
[4] A good analysis of the Tridentine decree on marriage can be found in G. Le Bras, "Mariage," *DTC*, pt. IX-2, cols. 2234-47; see also H. Conrad's essay, "Das tridentinische Konzil und die Entwicklung des kirchlichen und weltlichen Eherechts," in G. Schreiber's, *Weltkonzil von Trent*, pt. 1, Freiburg (1951), pp. 297-324.

sacrament. The conclusion was that the church was competent in everything as far as the sacrament was concerned, but not as far as the rest was concerned.[5] If this report and the council debates are compared with the canon that was finally approved, it is clear that the church was in fact only anxious to safeguard her own competence; she did not deny the competence of the worldly powers, which was passionately defended by many of the council Fathers, but simply did not take this into consideration. Various bishops maintained that it was wrong to assert that all matrimonial lawsuits came within the competence of the church (*CT*, pt. 9, pp. 673, 660-1, 663-4). For this reason, twenty-five council Fathers, including three cardinals, continued to the very end to vote against the canon because of its one-sidedness.[6] The purport of the council's definition, then, is that the church had jurisdictional powers in matrimonial affairs, but did not deny the proper jurisdictional powers of the state in marriage. The church aimed simply to safeguard her own jurisdictional powers threatened by the Reformation, and not to provide a treatise on the competence of the church and of the civil authorities in connection with marriage.

Even the Council of Trent, then, did not provide an answer on the matter of principle. Historical circumstances had led to the church acquiring virtually exclusive legal powers in matrimonial affairs. But most of the council Fathers who provided at least the beginning of a vindication in principle of this right seem to have based the jurisdictional powers of the church on the sacramental nature of the marriage contract, and at the same time to have limited them to this. The radical unity of the marriage contract and the sacrament of marriage, despite the formal distinction between the two, was not, however, asserted with such clarity by the council as it was to be asserted later. It is therefore historically incorrect to link the later theory—according to which the church had exclusive competence in matrimonial affairs—in

5 Le Bras, "Mariage"; see also Esmein, pt. 2, Appendix A, pp. 483-9.
6 Le Bras, col. 2241.

any way with the Council of Trent. The opinion of the Fathers of the Council of Trent may be summarized as follows: the state was not denied its purely civil powers of jurisdiction, but no theologian or council Father was able with any certainty to define precisely where these powers were situated.

Another important question was debated at Trent and was settled by a far-reaching decision. This was the introduction of an ecclesiastical legal form as the normally valid form of the marriage contract.[7] The council laid down that a marriage between baptized Christians was henceforth to be regarded as valid only if it had been contracted in the presence of the parish priest (or priest authorized by him) and at least two witnesses. Repeated evidence of an explicit desire for the requirement of the presence of witnesses for the validity of the marriage contract are to be found in a number of theological writings before the opening of the council, but the inviolability of the *consensus* theory had caused many to hesitate about this. Were so-called clandestine marriages, which had hitherto always been accepted as valid, subsequently to be regarded as invalid? The Reformers regarded such marriages as invalid, and this put the council Fathers in a delicate position.

There was moreover the central problem as to whether the church had any real hold over the partners' mutual consent to marriage. This question was answered in two ways by the theologians of the council. The influence of these two theological views is to some extent perceptible in the Tridentine decree *Tametsi*. Some theologians were of the opinion that the church had the power to submit the marriage contract itself to her compulsory legal forms so as to make it valid (". . . et huiusmodi contractus irritos et nullos esse decernit" [the Decree *Tametsi*, DS 1816 (DB 992)]); but others justified the invalidity of marriage without the church's new legal form on the grounds of the *inhabilitatio personarum*, the declaration of the unfitness of the persons (". . . eos Sacra Synodus ad sic contrahendum omnino inhabiles reddit"

[7] See Esmein, pt. 2, pp. 177–89; H. Conrad, pp. 305 ff.

[DS 1816 (DB 992)]). This latter view, of which the Patriarch of Aquila was the originator, was fairly generally accepted, although not without opposition (*CT*, pt. 9, col. 643, 655), and seems to have been the decisive factor in the acceptance of the ecclesiastical legal form as the condition of validity in marriage.

It is, moreover, clear that this condition of validity was not introduced by the Council of Trent as a measure in opposition to a possible civil contract of marriage. Certain historians have claimed[8] that the council was not only reacting against the practice of clandestine marriages, but also against "secular marriage." They do not, however, furnish any proof of this from the proceedings of the council itself. It is undeniable that there were conflicts over marriage between church and state, particularly the municipalities, during the fourteenth century. What is more, local synods of the church had, long before the Council of Trent, pointed to the unlawful character of marriages in which the partners' mutual consent was heard by laymen of noble descent, maintaining that this task was the sole right of the priest.[9]

The ancient custom of the priest's "blessing" of the marriage had for a long time had legal force, although it was not a condi-

---

[8] See, for example, H. Conrad, p. 305.

[9] Laymen, of whatever condition, were forbidden to hear the marriage *consensus* instead of a priest in, for example, canon 5 of the Synod of Treves (1227); (Hartzheim, *Concilia Germanica*, I, pp. 526 ff.). This practice was also forbidden by the Synod of Magdeburg (1370) (Hartzheim, IV, pp. 411 ff.) This was also intended especially as a measure against clandestine marriages, in which the church frequently had no supervision over possible impediments to the marriage. Even in cases where a priest was present at a marriage which did not take place "in front of the entrance to the church" (*in facie Ecclesiae*), such marriages were called clandestine—this emerges clearly from the fourth Lateran Council (1215), can. 51; (*M–SC*, pt. 22, p. 1038). The church's reaction against the Manichean heresies rampant among the Waldensians and the Albigensians also contributed to her insistence on the presence of a priest at Christian marriages. These heretical tendencies attacked not only marriage itself, but also the sacrament of order and the church's jurisdiction. Clear proof of this is provided by Honorius Augustodunensis (*PL*, 192, 1290). A clandestine marriage therefore ran the risk of being suspected of heretical tendencies.

tion of the validity of a marriage.[10] The main purpose of the priest's intervention and of the church's solemnisation of marriage in public (*in facie Ecclesiae*) was to ensure control of the impediments to marriage, something which was also possible in the case of public "secular marriages." From the eleventh and especially the twelfth century onwards, the policy of public solemnisation of marriages by the church, and consequently of the priest's intervention, was pursued even more vigorously.[11] But it must not be forgotten that the church's solemnisation and blessing of marriage had incorporated the "secular" (the civil and family) contract of marriage. In other cases, marriage took place exclusively in the presence of a priest.[12]

The introduction by the Council of Trent of an ecclesiastical legal form, carried out in front of the parish priest and at least two witnesses, as a condition of the validity of marriage was therefore intended solely as a measure against clandestine marriages. This is clear from the *acta* and from the attendant legislation: the council insisted upon the publication of the banns of marriage—a practice which had been observed for centuries—and the registration of contracted marriages in the records of the church. What is more, there was no mention, in the first draft of the new legal form of marriage, of the presence of a priest as a condition of validity—three lay witnesses were at this stage considered to be sufficient (*CT*, pt. 9, p. 640; see also the conciliar debate, pp. 642–80).

10 The Frankish civil marriage legislation also laid down in 802 that marriages should be blessed by a priest (*Capitularia*, miss. gen. of Charlemagne, c. 35).

11 *CIC*, c. 28, x, 4, 1: "ad valvas Ecclesiae"; see also c. 3, x, 4, 3. In 1215, the fourth Lateran Council had expressly laid down that marriages should be celebrated publicly by the church, although this was not a condition of their validity.

12 See, for example, Pseudo-Anselm's statement in this connection: "In some districts, marriages are contracted by the priests' solemnisation (*consecratio*), in other districts, however, without being solemnised" (Bliemetzrieder, ed., *Anselmus von Laon Systematische Sentenzen, Beiträge zur Geschichte der Philosophie des Mittelalters*, pt. 18–3, Münster [1913], p. 140).

In the debate on the draft schema a cardinal proposed that one of the three witnesses should be a priest; only about twenty of the council Fathers adopted this proposal (*CT*, pt. 9, p. 642). What is remarkable, however, is that some of the Fathers suggested that one of the three witnesses should be a public servant (*CT*, pt. 9, p. 656). This is a clear indication of the fact that the ecclesiastical legal form for marriage was in no way intended as a measure against the authority of the state. It was only in the third schema that the presence of the parish priest (or one delegated by him) was proposed as a condition of validity (*CT*, pt. 9, pp. 760–5). In the fourth schema, which was finally approved, it was accepted that the presence of the parish priest (or authorised priest) and two witnesses at least was necessary for a valid marriage (*CT*, pt. 9, pp. 888–90, 966–71).

Lutheranism had also placed clandestine marriages in a slightly different light. In keeping with the ancient Germanic sense of justice, a marriage was invalid according to Luther if it was contracted by anyone subject to parental authority without the consent of the parents. In the Interim of the Diet of Augsburg (1548), Emperor Charles decided that parental consent was a moral duty, but not a necessary condition of validity. The Council of Trent also took this view in the Decree *Tametsi*, against the view of certain French theologians. This marked the end of the long influence of an ancient Germanic view which had played an important part in the West throughout the whole of the Middle Ages.

The Tridentine ecclesiastical legal form was also not intended to give a new liturgical form to the *consensus* of marriage. Dictated by pastoral motives, its purpose was to obviate the dangers of clandestine marriage. The theory of the *consensus* remained intact. Furthermore, according to the later statement of the congregation set up for the purpose of providing an authentic interpretation of the Tridentine decrees, the priest played a passive part in Christian marriage—he was present purely as a "qualified witness." He was a witness to the marriage even if he was present against his will. His purely passive presence alone was sufficient, even if it was the result of force or of chance circumstances. It was not until new abuses, particularly that of the so-called "surprise marriage," caused the appearance of the Decree *Ne Temere* on the 2nd August, 1907 that the priest was required to be *actively* present—in other words, to take an active part in the marriage contract and to hear the *consensus* himself. (*ASS*, 40 [1907], 525.)

The final clause of the Tridentine decree stated that the new form of marriage law would be operative only in those countries in which the decree was officially promulgated. This put the Netherlands, for one, in a delicate position. The decree was promulgated in the Netherlands at the time of the Spanish rule, but the country followed the Reformation once the Spanish rule had come to an end. This led to the question as to whether the marriages of Reformed Christians were in fact valid. Pope Benedict IV stated in his Declaration of 1741 that Protestant marriages and mixed marriages were valid in the Netherlands and in Belgium. In Protestant countries only exclusively Catholic marriages came within the scope of the decree *Tametsi;* whereas, on the other hand, in those countries which had remained Catholic the validity of a purely Protestant or of a mixed marriage was not recognized if the Catholic legal form had not been observed.

In 1907 a new decree, which followed the granting in 1906 of a privilege for mixed marriages in Germany (*ASS*, 39 [1906], 81 ff.),[13] laid down as a requirement for the entire church that all Catholics, even those intending to contract a mixed marriage, were bound to submit to the Catholic legal form of marriage if their marriage was to be considered valid (*ASS*, 40 [1907], 525 ff.). Germany's privilege in this connection ceased with the

[13] According to this privilege, mixed marriages were valid in Germany without the Tridentine legal form. This privilege continued to remain in force, at least for married partners born in Germany, during the period following the appearance of the decree *Ne Temere* until the appearance of the new edition of the Codex.

publication in 1917 of the Codex (can. 1099, par. 1), with the result that, up to the present, every Catholic—even a Catholic entering into a mixed marriage—is bound to submit to the Catholic form of law of the marriage contract (can. 1094). This has given rise to a situation which at present seriously impedes progress towards a solution of the ecumenical problem, especially in Germany.

The Evangelical Church has presented urgent *desiderata* on this point to the Second Vatican Council, in view of the fact that one marriage in four in Germany is a mixed marriage. Professor Schlink of Heidelberg University has even gone so far as to say that, in the view of the Evangelical Church, the success of the Second Vatican Council depends upon its attitude towards mixed marriages. It was impossible at the time to foresee that the decision of the Council of Trent—and the ratification, with certain modifications, of this decision by the decree *Ne Temere* and the present-day canon law (in other words, arrangements which were introduced as measures against clandestine marriages)—would lead, in the changed climate of European thought, to such difficulties both in ecumenical matters and in the matter of modern, democratic loyalty of the state. And the Catholic now no longer wishes to be deemed an outsider in the ecumenical movement or in civil life.

The decree *Ne Temere* (1907) nonetheless simplified the problem within the Catholic Church by enabling marriages to be contracted by any parish priest or bishop competent in his own official district (can. 1094-5). In other words, it was no longer necessary for the prospective partners' own parish priest to be at the marriage. The Council of Trent had, moreover, given no thought to the fact that a competent priest might perhaps not always be available. To correct this omission *Ne Temere* recognized, in addition to the normal ecclesiastical legal form, an "exceptional legal form" for special cases, in which no priest needed to be present, but which still made marriage public, legally valid, sacramental, and ecclesiastical. In a simplified and extended form, this provision was adopted in can. 1096. If the prospective part-ners are unable to approach a parish priest, or another priest, without great difficulty, harm, or disadvantage, then—according to this canon—it is sufficient for the marriage to be contracted before two witnesses. This may, for example, be the case in danger of death, or on the understanding that it can reasonably be established that the priest will not be available for a month. A further decree of 10 March 1928 was revoked by a decree of 25 July 1931 and the "unavailability" of the priest was seen to be not only a physical but also a moral unavailability (*AAS*, 23 [1931], 388).[14]

This exceptional legal form offers considerable possibilities, since there is a clear tendency in the practice of ecclesiastical law to extend its application. This legal form is in fact equivalent to the form of marriage contracted by Christians in the first ten centuries. From the ecclesiological point of view, there is much to be said for a marriage contracted between Catholic partners according to the Tridentine legal form. But whenever this form of law comes into conflict with man's natural rights to a valid marriage, it ought to be possible for marriage to be contracted according to the exceptional form.

If, for example, the church deemed it undesirable to grant a dispensation for a mixed marriage, it should be possible for such a marriage to be contracted according to the exceptional form of law; in this way it would still be a legally valid, sacramental mar-riage. But under present canon law this possibility does not in fact exist. I do not claim that this would be the best solution to the delicate case of mixed marriages, but that it would at least be a very practical solution. By means of it the priority of the natural right of man to a valid marriage would be asserted in any case of conflict between this and the right of the church.

[14] See also the decree of the Congregation of the Sacraments of 24 April 1935 (*AAS*, 28 [1936] pp. 313–14). According to the commission set up for interpreting the code, the exceptional form also applies if the disadvantage is not only to the priest, but also to the prospective partners (decision of 3 May 1945, *AAS*, 37, p. 149).

Finally it should be noted that this exceptional form of law is not the same as the secret marriage or "marriage of conscience" (can. 1104) which is permitted under certain circumstances by the bishop. This is a valid, sacramental marriage, although it is not contracted publicly.

POST-TRIDENTINE SPECULATION ABOUT MARRIAGE AS CONTRACT AND AS SACRAMENT

It is evident from the theological writings that appeared immediately after the Council of Trent that, despite the sacramental character of marriage, its distinctively civic character was also accepted (e.g., Bellarmine, *Disputationes de controversiis christianae fidei*, Prague [1721], especially pt. , p. 727, n. 7; p. 743, n. 6, 9; p. 777, n. 17), and that both aspects formed a single unity, the ordinary secular marriage contract acquiring a deeper meaning because of the sacrament (*Disputationes* c. 6, pt. 3, p. 741, n. 18).[15]

According to Bellarmine, the state, with the general welfare of its members in mind, had full administrative authority over the marriage contract as a secular reality. After making this assertion, however, Bellarmine took a sudden turn in his reasoning, saying that one would perhaps deduce from this that the state may pass marriage laws insofar as marriage is a contract between human beings. This secular contract, however, was for Christians the sacrament itself, with the result that the sacramental or ecclesiastical character of marriage was "dependent on the civil contract" ("ex contractu civili sacramentum Ecclesiae pendet"). In view of the fact that the church had sole jurisdictional power in respect of the *sacramentum*, the church had an exclusive right to lay down conditions of validity. The state

[15] See also c. 21, pt. 3, p. 781, n. 39: "Contractum humanum, qui in sacramento matrimonii praerequiritur."

only had this right if the church accorded it (*Disputationes*, c. 21, pt. 3, p. 781, n. 42–4).

Bellarmine accepted the direct authority of the state over the financial and social aspects of the married state, and the exclusive authority of the church over the purely spiritual aspects of marriage. As far as those aspects of marriage which were both civil and spiritual were concerned, such as impediments to marriage and separations, Bellarmine maintained that the authority of the state was dependent on that of the church (*Disputationes*, c. 21, pt. 3, p. 781, n. 42–4). His position may be stated thus: insofar as marriage is a sacrament, the church has exclusive competence, but this sacrament is the actual contract of marriage itself.

The theologian T. Sanchez took a somewhat different view. Reacting against those authors who asserted that the state had no authority to decide on impediments to the marriage of its Christian subjects, he maintained that the state had an equal right to take such decisions as the pope. The sacramental character of marriage did not constitute an obstacle to this, since the civil contract was the matter of the sacrament, and the state might disregard the sacramental nature of this contract and thus regard it as invalid. The state might disqualify persons from entering into a contract, declaring them incompetent (*inhabiles*), with the result that such a contract was invalid; and in that case there was no matter present for the raising of the marriage to a sacramental level. The pope's power over the sacrament existed only so long as the "human contract" was present. If there was no human contract, there was no sacrament. (*Disputationes de sancto matrimonii sacramento*, Antwerp [1620], lib. 7, disp. 3, n. 2; lib. 3, disp. 4, n. 4).

It is important to bear Sanchez' view in mind. The civil contract constituted the matter for the raising of marriage to the sacramental level, and the state had authority to attach conditions to this contract, provided that these conditions were justified from the point of view of the natural law. Sanchez was not, of

course, familiar with the later problem caused by the civil contract of marriage preceding the church marriage; this necessitated
a revision of the whole situation on account of the ecclesiastical
legal form which was an indispensable condition of validity, since
in such circumstances a civil marriage contracted previously did
not constitute a marriage contract.

Sanchez was also clearly aware that the church was restricted
to the substance of marriage as a sacrament and that she only
had control of the matter of the sacrament, since she did not
make any of the sacraments, but only administered the sacraments
instituted by Christ (*De sacramentis in genere*, disp. 138, c. 5, n.
63–4).[16] This measure of control nonetheless gave the church the
power to limit the authority of the state in matrimonial affairs
by virtue of the supernatural aspect of marriage in the concrete.
He claimed that, in the present Christian order, the pope had
acted thus to set the conditions of validity, which was exclusively
a church matter. This reservation was, however, made only in
respect of Christian princes, who in any case came within the
church's jurisdiction as believers. A statesman who was not a
Christian was not affected by this limitation.

This restriction was important, because it marked the beginning of the idea that the church had no power to deprive the
state of anything that was its natural due. Christians, too, were
therefore bound to obey non-Christian princes insofar as these
enacted just laws concerning the validity of marriage (*Disputationes*, lib. 7, disp. 3, n. 7).[17]

In the middle of the sixteenth century, the leading pro-
tagonist of the view that the sacrament of marriage and the marriage contract were not fully identical was Melchior Cano. He
said that the distinction, although inadequate, was nonetheless
real. Following the early Italian scholastics, he maintained that

16 Billuart was also to accept this view later (*De matrimonio*, disp. 1, a.
5, petes 5).

17 Sanchez did not, of course, know the modern state as a neutral gov-
erning authority without any formal view of life.

the partners' mutual consent to the marriage was the matter of this sacrament and the priest's blessing its form (*De locis theologicis*, VIII, 5, Padua [1762], p. 218), the priest consequently being the minister of the sacrament. Cano's work appeared some years after his death, in 1563, during the Council of Trent. His view was supported by many theologians after the council.[18]

MODERN SECULARISATION AND THE REACTIONS OF THE CHURCH

The really decisive commencement of the process of secularisation in the seventeenth century—the beginnings of which can be traced back to the latter half of the fifteenth century—confronted the Church with a completely new situation. Speculation about marriage ceased to be the exclusive concern of theologians. Scholars of the various new sciences—first of all the humanists and positive theologians, later on the philosophers and encyclopedists, then the evolutionists, and later still the ethnologists and sociologists—began to devote their attention to the subject of marriage.

In the Protestant countries, marriage legislation automatically came under the control of the state, although Protestant theologians and jurists continued to differ about this.[19] The Calvinist theologians declared themselves more clearly in favour of the state's assumption of jurisdictional powers over marriage than the Lutherans. Nonetheless, this Protestant view of marriage did not mean that marriage was secularised. In the Protestant countries marriage still remained within the province of the Christian communities, and there was no suggestion of any real "civil" marriage.

[18] See, for example, Estius, *In IV Sent.*, d. 26; Sylvius, *In Suppl.*, q. 42, a. 1, ql. 1; Toletus, *Instructio sacerdotum*, 7, 2; Tournély, *De matrimonio*, q. 5, a. 2. Most German theologians still supported this theory at the beginning of the nineteenth century.

[19] See especially G. Joyce, pp. 237 ff.

A certain change of emphasis took place also in the Catholic countries. The church maintained her traditional position in Austria, Italy, and Spain, but in sixteenth- and seventeenth-century France there was a confusion of ecclesiastical and secular jurisdiction: royal laws and ordinances were added to canon law; the royal judges were obliged to apply canon laws, and the ecclesiastical judges were similarly obliged to respect the royal laws and ordinances. In this connection, Esmein had good reason to say that the whole of canon and civil law derived its binding force at this time from the sovereign prince, so that the ground was already prepared for civil marriage proper.[20]

This process of secularisation continued throughout the eighteenth century. Everything that was not strictly connected with the sacramental union came within the competence of the secular judges. The Gallican theologians took the old distinction between marriage as a sacrament and marriage as a contract as the basis for their speculation, but with them the distinction became a dangerous division. All that Melchior Cano had said was that the *consensus* of marriage was the matter and the priest's blessing the form of the sacrament. The eighteenth-century theologians, however, said that the *civil* marriage was the matter and the priest's liturgy was the form; and so, according to this view, the state had exclusive competence in the arrangement of civil contracts of marriage and in judging the legal validity of such contracts.[21] The Jansenists went even further. In making an adequate distinction between marriage as a sacrament and marriage as a contract, they no longer maintained that the contract was the matter of the sacrament.

The state also attempted to force the church into a totally dependent position. In Austria, the process of the secularisation of marriage legislation was set in motion in Febronianism, a move-

---

[20] See Esmein, pt. 1, pp. 36–48.

[21] J. Launoy, *De regia in matrimonium potestate*, 1, 4, 3, Cologne (1731), p. 749: "Spiritualis potestas a saeculari pendet quoad naturam civilis contractus matrimonii, cui iam legitime facto divinitus accedit sacramenti ratio."

ment which also had ecumenical aims.[22] In 1781 and 1783 the whole of marriage legislation was made the concern of the state by the Emperor Joseph II, with the result that the establishment of impediments to marriage, the granting of dispensations, and the arrangement of mixed marriages came under the exclusive authority and competence of the state.[23] It cannot, however, be claimed that this was something entirely new, since civil marriage was already possible in the Netherlands from 1580 onwards; and in England similarly we find it in 1653 under Cromwell. There had also been conflicts in Italy between the church and the various states concerning authority in matrimonial affairs. As early as the fourteenth century, too, there had been the famous conflict between Pope John XXII and Ludwig of Bavaria, who had claimed competence in matrimonial matters for himself as emperor. He had been given theological support in his claim by the theories of William of Ockham and Marsilius of Padua.

The measure introduced by Joseph II, however, still enabled marriage to be legally contracted according to the Tridentine legal form. Joseph's brother, Leopold I of Tuscany, took over this legislation, and these Jansenist and Febronianist views were confirmed in 1786 by the Synod of Pistoia. The Synod was condemned by Pope Pius VI (DS 2659 and 2660 [DB 1559 and 1560]). This is the first case in the history of the church of a papal defence—albeit one made in a letter to a bishop—of the proposition that all matrimonial affairs were subject to the exclusive jurisdiction of the church.[24] Pius VI's letter was, of course,

[22] A typical work is *De statu Ecclesiae et legitima potestate Romani Pontificis liber singularis ad reuniendos dissidentes in religione christianos compositus*, published in 1763 and written by Johann Nikolaus von Hontheim, coadjutor of the archbishop of Treves, under the pseudonym "Justinus Febronius." The author was a follower of the Jansenist Van Espen of Louvain.

[23] See G. Joyce, pp. 255–62.

[24] Pius VI's letter to the bishop of Mottola in Naples, 16 September 1788 (Migne, *Theologiae cursus*, pt. 25, p. 694; part of this letter is also included in DS 2598 [DB 1500a]).

neither a dogmatic definition nor, despite the pope's appeal to the Council of Trent, an authentic interpretation of canon 12 of that council. The letter was essentially a papal rebuke of a bishop who had opposed the canonical statement of an archiepiscopal court which moreover possessed full royal authority.

On the other hand, this disciplinary measure with its doctrinal appendix shows that theologians of this period apparently had a different view of marriage from theologians in the past, and even from most theologians at the time of the Council of Trent. Another reason for the radical position taken by Pius VI is clearly his fear lest the increasing secularisation of marriage should lead to a complete loss of its sacred character. What is more, there was at that time no balanced, worked-out theology concerning the relationship between the church and the state. The church simply defended her established position against the state.

Seen as a whole, this process of secularisation was not really a *coup d'état* against the essential authority of the church as principle—it was more a resumption by the state of a right which was strictly its own but which had become, because of historical circumstances, the exclusive right of the church. In the first ten centuries there had been no suggestion that this was the exclusive right of the church, although of course the situation was quite different at that time, by reason of the intermingling of state affairs and church matters. In the eighteenth century, however, the church did not defend the principle of her exclusive right to the jurisdiction of matrimonial affairs, but simply defended a right historically acquired. It must be admitted, however, that the declaration of Pope Pius VI was a first step in the church's assertion in principle that she had full jurisdictional powers over marriage in its totality, and that the distinction between the contract and the sacrament of marriage did not provide any reason for depriving the church of any of her jurisdictional power in matrimonial affairs.

The French Revolution marked the real beginning of the

period of civil marriage proper[25] and of papal reaction to this, expressed in a more positive assent in principle to Pius VI's proposition. The notion of freedom of conscience which has developed in more recent times led to the acceptance of the validity of marriages devoid of any religious content, and to papal reaction to this idea, expressed in the proposition that no valid marriage that was not at the same time a sacrament was possible for baptized Christians. (*Acerbissimum vobiscum* 27 September, 1852, by Pius IX [DB 1640]; the *Syllabus* of Pius IX [DS 2966, 2973 (DB 1766, 1773)]; the encyclical *Arcanum divinae Sapientiae*, by Leo XIII [DS 3145 (DB 1854)].) The church's exclusive jurisdiction in the matrimonial affairs of baptized Christians was based in principle on this. According to Pope Pius IX, the religious element in marriage belonged to its essence. This became statutory by its inclusion in the church's codex (canons 1016 and 1960: "Causae matrimonii inter baptizatos iure proprio et exclusivo ad iudicem ecclesiasticum spectant").

[25] See A. Latreille, "L'Eglise catholique et la laïcité," pp. 59–98. This is a good recent survey of this development, in which marriage is dealt with among other questions.

Conclusion

THE RELATION OF MARRIAGE TO THE CHURCH

The most important features in the development of the idea of marriage may be summarised as follows:

1. For Paul marriage was a "worldly" event to be experienced by Christians "in the Lord." This meant above all that one baptized Christian had to marry another baptized Christian. Marriage between Christians was an image of the mystery of the unity of Christ and his church.

2. For Tertullian and (in the East) for Clement of Alexandria, marriage was "ecclesial" when it was contracted, according to civil and family customs, between baptized Christians. The marriage of two Christians contracted according to civil practices was, in other words, a church marriage.

3. Between the fourth and the eleventh centuries, a marriage liturgy developed in the Western Church. This was not binding on Christians, and it existed alongside and in association with the civil and family contract of marriage. The church stressed the public character of marriage which was evident above all in the civil and the ecclesiastical ceremonies. The ninth century saw the beginning of a tendency to hold these civil ceremonies in the church itself, with the result that these popular practices were gradually taken over by the church and given a liturgical form.

378

4. This tendency was completed in the eleventh and twelfth centuries, by which time so-called "civil marriage" had been completely absorbed into marriage contracted by the church. From this time onward marriage was both validly and legitimately contracted in a marriage liturgy, into which the "civil" ceremonies of marriage had been assimilated. The same period also saw the development of the explicit idea of the sacramental nature of marriage, although initially this was connected only with the priest's blessing of the marriage and not with the partners' mutual consent to the marriage. At this time, then, "church marriage" came to mean not simply a marriage between two baptized Christians, but a marriage between baptized Christians validly and legitimately contracted in and through the marriage liturgy of the church.

This was not the end of this development, however, since the church was at this time clearly of the opinion that she could not intervene in the matter of the *consensus* itself. She could surround it with liturgical rites, but she could not declare a marriage invalid if this mutual consent had been given without the liturgical ceremonies. In this sense, the principle of Roman law adopted by the popes—that a marriage without either civil or ecclesiastical forms of law was nonetheless valid—still remained in force. A clandestine marriage, without any public forms of law, remained a true "church marriage" for baptized Christians: it was valid, and therefore sacramental.

5. The Council of Trent went a stage further. Although it was the sole aim of the council to ensure that Christian marriages were contracted in public, its insistence on the presence of a priest as a condition of the validity of the partners' mutual consent to marry resulted in the marriage contract of baptized Christians being brought—in all normal cases—completely within the church's orbit. It was only in exceptional cases that Tertullian's principle—that the mutual consent of the baptized partners constituted a "valid church marriage"—remained in force. In normal cases, marriage in which the *consensus* of the baptized

partners took place without the presence of a priest was not only not a church marriage, but not a marriage at all. The post-Tridentine theologians discussed the relationship between marriage as a mutual *consensus* and marriage as a sacrament at considerable length in their attempt to come to a clear understanding of the question, but in the long run it was generally accepted that the *consensus* and the sacrament were completely identical.

6. In contrast to the West, in the East the marriage liturgy was made obligatory very early on; between the eighth and the eleventh centuries the state itself virtually made the liturgical celebration of the marriage contract an obligatory condition of validity. This resulted in marriage acquiring a mystical and liturgical significance very early in the East.

7. The final result of this development is that it is impossible for baptized Christians to contract a legally valid marriage which is not at the same time a sacrament. The introduction of the Tridentine legal form has meant that, for a baptized Christian, civil marriage is in fact not a contract of marriage but only a practical arrangement of financial status. Although the state laws clearly intend it to be a contract of marriage, this civil form of marriage is, for a baptized Christian, virtually no more than a pretence of going through the *consensus*, since this is validly accomplished afterwards in the liturgy of the church. This has led in our own time to many serious problems, in connection both with the cause of ecumenism and with the Christian's loyalty as a citizen to the state. These problems will be considered in our further examination of the subject and synthesis in a later volume of this work.

Epilogue

CONCLUSION TO VOLUMES
I AND II

Throughout this book our chief purpose has been to listen to God's word on the subject of marriage, in the form in which this word has come to us throughout history—the claims and statements and experiences of the men with whom God has made a covenant of grace. Because we have listened—or at least attempted to listen—patiently and in active silence, what we have to say in response to this word should be all the more meaningful. Man is all too prone, in conversation, to speak himself— even when his conversation is with God. And when this happens, there is always a serious risk that God will himself fall silent. Of course, it is perfectly possible to say important things about man, his world, and the historical meanings that he has given to marriage and the family, outside the sphere of our dialogue with God. But if we do restrict our speculation to the purely historical aspects of human life, the ultimate significance of these very aspects will escape our attention.

Man is, after all, not a purely earthbound being; nor, for that matter, is he purely a being who stands erect in sovereign freedom—purely a being who, through his observation of the world in which he lives, his technical conquest of it, his comprehension of it in speculative thought, and his aesthetic experience of it, seeks to humanise it in the service of his fellow-men. He is

also a being who, because of the mystery of life and his in-
cipient consciousness of the existence of the living God, can
freely choose, after standing erect in this world, to kneel in order that he may perceive the deepest meaning of this living God
and acknowledge this divine mystery. It is only when we have
begun to listen to God in our dialogue with him—the content
of which is his life and ours—that our answer to what he says
will become a real response, and that the dialogue will cease to
be two entirely disconnected monologues, in which the one partner never understands the other's viewpoint, simply because it
does not interest him.

My aim in this theological analysis has not been to provide a
purely historical reconstruction, with the emphasis on "who
said what" or with an eye to giving every Christian author
whose works have been quoted the recognition that was due to
him. Quotations have been included for the purpose of illustrat-
ing a definite tendency in the history of the church. It is possible
that these movements might have been better and more accurately assessed if other quotations—from the writings of different church Fathers or theologians—had been used. It has,
however, been my constant aim to trace the dogmatic element
in the history of this development, and to see how a human appraisal of the situation and Christian awareness of the actuality of
marriage gradually led to a view that resulted in the word of
God being expressed in dogmatic terms.

When I review the whole theological analysis of these first
two volumes, certain critical moments are at once apparent.

First, there is the principal theme of this book—that marriage
is a secular reality which has entered salvation. But this worldly
quality of marriage as a human commission always closely
linked to the prevailing historical situation is subject to development, since human existence is a reflective existence. And in just
the same way God's offer of salvation to man always follows this
human history, and so assumes certain characteristics which become increasingly clear with the passage of time. The history of

salvation began in the misty dawn of man's existence. The mists were slow to clear because man was at first concerned with living, and only gradually grew into a self-questioning being who was concerned to discover the meaning of his life. This is why it is impossible for the Christian view of man and of human marriage and family life to be a pure datum of revelation; it is more the result of a reflective human existence illuminated by revelation. Our very living as human beings is in itself a view of life and of the world. This view is never contradicted by revelation. It is corrected by revelation where correction is needed, and received by it into a transcendent sphere of life.

The first light shed by divine revelation on the secular reality of marriage resulted in the human realisation that God himself, the utterly transcendent being, was outside the sphere of marriage. Marriage is essentially a reality of the created world which has significance in life here and now, but which loses its inherently secular significance for individual man, and for mankind as a whole, on death and at the end of time. Marriage is a good gift of creation, but one which belongs strictly to this world. It is within marriage that the essential fellowship of man can be fulfilled in the most meaningful and human way.

As a dialogue, marriage has in itself such a deep power of expression that it became the prophetic medium through which the dialectic of the life of the people of God with God was most clearly expressed—the concrete married life of Hosea and Gomer became the prophetic symbol of the historical dialogue of love between God and his people, and this covenant of grace implied a moral message for married life in the concrete. (See Ezekiel.) Because salvation comes to us in a secular, historical form, marriage has—both in its interpersonal and relational aspect, and as the means of founding a family—a subordinate function towards God's activity within the covenant: "I will make of you a great nation." Marriage is intimately connected with the Promise, and therefore always contains a reference to Christ. Every marriage, even civil marriage, is Christian—whether in the full sense, in the pre-Christian sense (marriage as having an orientation towards Christ), in the anonymously Christian sense, or even in the negatively Christian sense (a deliberate denial of this Christian aspect of marriage).

Christ's appearance was a confirmation of the primarily interior significance of marriage which, for the believer, had to be experienced "in the Lord." Salvation in Christ gives an unbreakable solidity to the inner structure of marriage, a quality which can only be experienced within the community of grace with Christ. According to Jesus' *logion* on indissolubility, marriage is a consecration of oneself for the whole of one's life to a fellow human being, one's chosen partner—and, according to Paul's interpretation, doing this just as Christ gave his life for the church. The indissolubility of marriage is connected in the closest possible way with the definitive character of the community of grace with God in Christ, sealed in baptism. On the other hand, the New Testament achieved a second demythologization of marriage arising from its eschatological view of life. The Old Testament vision had already stripped marriage of its pagan religious elements and raised it to the level of a secular "good" of the created world which had to be experienced in the light of faith in Yahweh. The New Testament reinforced the relative value of this good gift of creation in the light of the kingdom of God. The dogmatic link between Genesis (the divine institution of marriage as a good gift of creation, explicitly confirmed by Jesus' *logion*) and Eph v (marriage as the image of the covenant of grace between Christ and his church) is 1 Cor vii (complete abstinence as the eschatological "relativisation" of marriage). The primacy of the kingdom of God, not only with regard to marriage, but actually in marriage, is a biblical fact which no dogmatic consideration of marriage can afford to ignore.

At the same time it is evident, especially in the writings of Paul, not only that social structures are experienced "in the Lord," but also that there is a danger of transforming these social structures into theological realities when they are viewed in an eschatological light. In other words, the biblical ethos of marriage bears clear traces of the prevailing view of the position of woman in society.

It is also clear from the history of the church in the first eleven centuries that marriage was experienced as a secular reality which, because of its moral and religious implications, required special pastoral care. Tertullian in the West and Clement of Alexandria in the East both testify to the fact that marriage contracted civilly within the family by baptized Christians was itself a "church marriage." From the fourth century onwards, a marriage liturgy evolved which existed alongside the civil form of marriage, but which was not made obligatory in the West until the eleventh century, and even then was not regarded as a condition of validity. Up to the eleventh century this liturgical form of marriage remained completely free. It was obligatory only in the case of clergy in lower orders—in other words, in the case of those members of the clergy who were permitted to marry. Not only was this marriage liturgy not obligatory for other Christians; it was reserved for those Christians whose conduct was blameless, and was refused to those who married for the second time. Until the eleventh century, then, marriage was contracted civilly, although it was accompanied by church ceremonies.

From the eleventh century onwards, however, civil marriage—in its native Germanic, Gallic, Longobardic, Gothic, and Celtic forms—was taken over by the church. At this period marriage was contracted *in facie Ecclesiae* (i.e., by the priest at the entrance to the church), and the social elements peculiar to the earlier secular form of marriage contract were incorporated into the liturgical ceremony. In other words, what had previously been secular became liturgical; and what had previously been a civil contract, made within the family circle and supplemented by a priestly ceremony of blessing or veiling, became a single liturgical whole conducted by the priest.

From the eleventh century onwards, too, various circumstances led to the actual transference of jurisdictional power over marriage to the church's sphere. The Pseudo-Isidorian decretals of the ninth century were not the direct cause of this transference, but their "authority" certainly added impetus to it. In order to exercise this power of jurisdiction the church needed to have a precise idea of exactly what constituted marriage as marriage. She was confronted by three systems of law: first, the Roman theory of the *consensus;* secondly, the idea prevalent among the Western European tribes, among whom the marriage contract was seen to be situated above all in the father's handing over of the bride to the matrimonial authority of the bridegroom; and, finally, the view that had existed since the earliest times among all peoples, namely, that marriage was consummated in sexual intercourse.

The church—which had supported the *consensus* theory expressed in the letter of Pope Nicholas I to the Bulgars, but had found it difficult to persuade the Germanic and Frankish tribes in the West to accept this—came eventually, after a long period of controversy, to the point where she herself accepted the view that the partners' mutual consent to marry was the essential element in the constitution of marriage, but that this element could be situated in indigenous practices, in accordance with the principle that there were as many different customs as there were countries. Her adherence to the Roman idea of law, however, led the Church eventually to insist on a "formalised" marriage *consensus,* and this was included, together with other practices, in the liturgy, although this purely formal dialogue had none of the strength of the original indigenous secular forms of the *consensus.*

Finally, sexual intercourse was regarded as the element which ultimately consummated the marriage contract and made it permanently indissoluble. This was the subject of a long controversy which was finally resolved at the end of the twelfth and the beginning of the thirteenth century by Pope Alexander III, whose decision was confirmed by Innocent III and Gregory IX.

A valid but unconsummated marriage was in principle indissoluble (that is to say, it could not dissolve itself), but it could be dissolved by an appeal to the hierarchical power of the keys. A consummated marriage, on the other hand, was absolutely indissoluble.

Does this do violence to the unconditional, absolute nature of Jesus' *logion?* We have already seen how Paul actually formulated this in the light of baptism which he regarded as the basis of the radical indissolubility of marriage. But now an (unconsummated) marriage between two baptized Christians could be dissolved! But it is important to bear in mind that, although Christ declared that marriage was indissoluble, he did not tell us where the element that constituted marriage was situated—what in fact made a marriage a marriage, what made it the reality which he called absolutely indissoluble. This is a problem of anthropology, since it is concerned with a human reality, the essence of which man must try to clarify in its historical context. And this human reality can be approached from various directions—it can be seen as a legal institution within human society and as an existential fact of human life. The Catholic Church took her stand—in her assertion of the indissolubility of marriage, at least—on the existential point of view, maintaining that marriage in the full sense of the word (that is, marriage that came within the authority of the unconditional pronouncement of God's word) was a community of persons which had been entered into by mutual consent and which was consummated in sexual intercourse.

This was also the Jewish view of marriage which Christ had taken as his point of departure. Although I do not deny that, though it was less explicit than that of the church Fathers, the scholastics had a certain antipathy towards sex and sexuality (this is something which will be discussed in a later volume), it is also impossible to dispute that the great medieval popes, on whose pronouncements the church's legal practice in connection with marriage is still based, included sex and sexuality in the "one flesh" of which Christ said that it was indissoluble. This constituted a complete contradiction of the one-sided, spiritual view expressed by Hugh of St. Victor in his theology of marriage. On the other hand, it remained possible for a virgin marriage to be experienced as a fully interpersonal relationship without sexual intercourse.

Nonetheless, the fact that such a union was bound to be constantly threatened by real dissolution robs the assertion that the church regarded virgin marriage as the ideal realisation of marriage as such of all its real force. Such a realisation of marriage is a real possibility in the light of the kingdom of God, and, viewed in this light, it can even be a stronger intrinsic bond than marriage in which sexual intercourse plays a part, as it was in the case of Mary and Joseph. It cannot, however, be regarded as the ideal of married life itself, but only as an indication of the limits set by the kingdom of God around the "ideal marriage" (which is naturally celebrated as a physical union). Sexual intercourse is by definition the expression of a personal decision to serve the kingdom of God in a secular way, not in a directly eschatological way.

This decision—by which man opens himself, through the other person, to the kingdom of God—is irrevocable, since it is in this decision that the mystery of the *henōsis*, or the union of Christ with his church, is completed. Love—the personal decision of the partners to be faithful to each other—is the natural soul of the community of marriage. The doctrine of the *consensus* is, so to speak, only a legal formulation of this decision. Since marriage also has social implications, there must be some legal security as to whether a person is married or unmarried. The marriage contract, made by the partners giving their mutual consent in the presence of witnesses, provides this legal security, but this *consensus* is a formalised juridical moment abstracted from that much richer existential totality of marriage which cannot be "extrapolated" in completely juridical terms. Purely as a juridically abstracted entity—and despite the fact that as such it goes back to the totality of marriage from which it was abstracted—marriage remains dissoluble; and it is right to say that marriage remains dissoluble when this *consensus* is not incarnated in effective sexual intercourse, which is precisely what points to the "formalisation" of the *consensus* as the element that constitutes marriage. And so if it is clear from the concrete community of marriage and marital intercourse that this formal consent to marry is a vital and inspirational moment in a totality which is effective, physical, and existential and which embraces the whole of man, then marriage—as a making concretely present of the mystery of Christ and his church—is indissoluble.

It is abundantly clear from the whole context of Alexander's decision that the ecclesiastical decision in favour of the mitigated theory of the *consensus*—that of the *consensus* as the element that constituted the juridically recognisable state of marriage—was prompted by the practical legal problems raised by contemporary matrimonial lawsuits. What is more, the decision also expresses the conviction that the *consensus* is the real soul of the living community of persons in marriage, and not sexual intercourse in itself (which can, of course, be experienced in many different forms, including non-human forms). Although the word *consensus* may sound juridical—as indeed it is—it is nonetheless clear from the whole of twelfth- and thirteenth-century scholasticism that what is meant is that in marriage man decides to commit himself to sharing the whole of his life with a *consortium vitae*, a partner, and that this decision and lifelong commitment is expressed in the juridical formula. This human commitment is the soul of the sexual relationship in marriage, which thereby becomes the expression of a lasting union of two *persons*—a *human, sexual relationship*.

From this juridical formalisation of the *consensus*—the supporting and at the same time humanising moment of marital living together—there arises a whole series of problems concerning fitness for sexual intercourse (*aptitudo ad copulam*) which is necessarily a prerequisite for the validity of the *consensus*, whereas in contrast, ability to have children (*capacitas genera-tionis*) is not necessarily a prerequisite. But it is precisely these and similar problems at the juridical level, brought about as an inevitable consequence of the initial juridical abstraction, which confirmed the scholastic view that marriage is only authentic and fully consummated in its human incarnation. It must, of course, be admitted that these medieval ideas were less prompted by an anthropological view of the human embodiment of married love than by the primary and virtually exclusive view that marriage was subject to the *officium naturae*—to the task of procreation which God had entrusted exclusively to this particular com-munity of persons.

The theologians of the later period of scholasticism, however, did not always fully appreciate the medieval background which had occasioned this juridical formalisation, with the result that the "treatise on marriage" became a study of the juridically formalised constitution of marriage rather than a dogmatic study of the whole reality of marriage. In this way, the theology of marriage developed into a theology of a juridical abstraction which was legitimate in itself, but which led to the neglect of the study of marriage as an anthropological datum—as what Aquinas called the *officium civilitatis*. The theology of marriage was thus able to help the canonists, but it was of scarcely any help in pastoral matters. The formalisation of the marriage *consensus* also led to many problems in missionary countries. A mutual consent to marriage given according to indigenous customs, at least in-sofar as these are morally justified, is always more valuable from the social and sociological point of view than a "formalized" *consensus* which ignores these morally justified customs, since this frequently results in an emasculation of the social aspects of marriage. The church has, however, always accepted this in principle, in allowing for the possibility of the inclusion of le-gitimate features of popular customs in the sacramental liturgy, despite the rigid form given to it by the Tridentine reforms.

At the same time as this controversy over the relationship between the mutual consent to marriage and sexual intercourse in marriage was taking place—that is, in the eleventh and twelfth centuries—theological expression was being given to the Christian idea of the sacramental nature of marriage. The basis of this development was the liturgy of marriage, in which marriage was called a *sacramentum* or symbolic representation of the mystery of Christ and his church. It was the incorporation of the Pauline text into the liturgy together with Jesus' *logion* concerning the inviolable character of marriage—the liturgy together with the Bible, in other words—which provided the norm for this conscious development, and not the sacramental concept which had in the meantime been formulated in scholastic circles. Although the technical concept of sacrament had initially (i.e., in the middle of the twelfth century) not been regarded as applying to marriage, theologians now explicitly and emphatically maintained that marriage was one of the "seven important *sacramenta*" of the church, even though it did not have the same value as the two fundamental sacraments of baptism and the eucharist.

Initially, there was a tendency, as in the East, to situate the sacramental character of marriage in the liturgical celebration of the mystery of marriage. The medieval theologians of the Western Church, however, eventually came to accept the view that the sacramental nature of marriage, from the purely dogmatic standpoint, coincided with the legally valid contract of marriage between two baptized Christians—even if this contract had been made within the family, and even if the marriage had been clandestine. In this way, marriage as an anthropological reality (what Aquinas called the *officium naturae* and the *officium civilitatis*) entered salvation and its social, cultural, and civil aspects continued undiminished within this sphere.

This reality became the "sacrament" of the mystery of the living communion between Christ and his church, prefigured in "natural" marriage and *de facto* raised to a living sign in the marriage of baptized Christians. Thus an ordinary secular reality was seen to be an effective instrument of salvation in married and family life by virtue of Christ's redemption. The medieval controversies over this led to the view being accepted that this *sacramentum* was the totality of marriage, even though not all its aspects had the same symbolic meaning—married love itself being the sacramental form of the mystery of Christ's unity with his church, and the "one flesh" resulting from the consummation of marriage in sexual union being the sacrament's true subject.

It should, however, be noted that, according to the medieval view, the power of this sacrament to confer grace was due neither to the *consensus* of marriage not to the *copula* as such, but to the *coniugium*—the bond of marriage or the complementary relationship of the partners. This gave rise to a certain difference between the patristic and the scholastic view of the indissolubility of marriage. According to the patristic view, it was not *permissible* for marriage to be dissolved because of the primacy of the *obligatio*—the moral obligation not to disrupt marriage. The medieval theologians, on the other hand, emphasized that it was not *possible* to dissolve a marriage. Both these views, however, came together in the common assertion that remarriage was not permitted after separation.

A radical change was brought about by the Council of Trent, despite the fact that this had not formed part of the original intention of the council Fathers; their sole concern had been to combat that evil of medieval society, the clandestine marriage. The council resolved that the only valid contract of marriage for baptized Christians in the future was one made in the presence of a priest and two witnesses. This led to the old patristic and medieval term "church marriage"—that is, a marriage contracted in virtually any way between two baptized parties—acquiring an entirely new significance. For a marriage to be a legally valid church marriage, it did not necessarily have to be contracted liturgically or in church, but it had to be contracted in the presence of a priest. Any other marriage contracted between two baptized Christians was normally declared null and void, and therefore regarded as concubinage.

The consequences of this conciliar decision in the changed world situation in which the church found herself later on were enormous, from both the humane and the ecumenical points of view. A serious discrepancy developed between the views of the church and of the world as a result of the emergence of civil marriage in the modern secular state. The church was unable to accept this civil marriage, and society felt that Christians did not take their civil duties seriously. The church's jurisdictional monopoly in connection with matrimonial matters became a theological thesis, insisted on by the popes, although not with infallible papal authority. Marriage, which had (up to the eleventh century) always been a secular reality experienced "in the Lord," now seemed to have become an exclusively ecclesiastical affair, and the "natural right" of every human being to be able to contract a (valid) marriage was restricted for baptized Christians—directly in the case of Catholics, and consequently indirectly in the case of non-Catholics too—by a positive injunction of the church, although the original intention of this commandment had been quite different. The church had provided a certain solution to this conflict between the "natural law" and the "positive law of the church" in her "exceptional legal form"; although the application of this exceptional form was confined to certain clearly defined cases.

This situation has led to the growth of a strong desire in the church today for the possibility of extending the application of this exceptional legal form to cover all cases in which the keeping of the "normal" Tridentine legal form is at variance with personal conscience and conviction. If the application of this exceptional legal form were extended, it should be possible for a Catholic partner too to regard a "civil marriage" or a "marriage affirmation" made according to the practice of the Reformed Church as a public and as a sacramental marriage.

This also raises the question of the real meaning of man's personal initiative to marry. To what extent may the church or the state intervene in this personal act? May they intervene so far

as to regard this act of personal initiative as null and void in certain cases, not for reasons based on the natural law, but simply
because one definite form of law and no other has been laid down
for the contract of marriage? And if this is possible, or even
necessary, by virtue of the essentially social character of marriage, ought not this positive form of law, as a *ius positum*, to
give way in certain cases? Or must many borderline cases of marriage still be called "concubinage"? These are some of the problems which are brought about both by concrete human situations
and by conflict between the medieval view—which postulated
that the personal, mutual consent to marriage, as an inviolable
institution, was, at least as far as the form of law was concerned,
not open to the intervention of the church or the state—and the
modern, post-Tridentine view.

What is more, the movement of positive theology would seem
to suggest that there are many subtle gradations in the sacramental character of marriage, and that this sacramental character
does not stand or fall by the liturgy of marriage but is rather
raised to a culminating point in it. For unlike the West, the Eastern Church regarded the liturgical celebration of marriage as the
real sacrament, so that the priest conducted the ceremony and
administered the sacrament, and the faithful—first and foremost
the bride and bridegroom—played an active part in this liturgy so
that God's blessing would be given to the mystery of married
life. This *akolouthia*, or liturgical service, was made obligatory
for baptized Christians centuries before it became obligatory in the
West. It was also, as a result of the legislation passed between
the eighth and the eleventh centuries under the influence of the
emperors of the Syrian dynasty, a condition of the validity of the
marriage contract.

In this conclusion to the first two volumes of this work I have
given prominence to only a few aspects of scriptural and ecclesiastical tradition. What has clearly emerged, however, is that
any dogmatic study of marriage is bound to take two fundamental facts into account: first, that marriage is without quali-

fication a secular reality, fully human and consequently subject to development and evolution; and secondly that this reality has not been somehow "added" to salvation, but has been included in salvation in its total and human dimension—and that this incorporation into God's salvation has not come about (as "liberal" Christians would affirm) simply because the state of being a Christian has to be experienced within the purely worldly sphere, but also and above all because this secular reality, which has been taken up into salvation, has itself become sacramental in the technical sense.

Later on in this work these two basic assertions will be considered in the light of the concrete problems which marriage raises. First, we shall consider what tradition has to tell us about the relationship between the interpersonal aspect of marriage and the founding of a family, and between married love and sexuality. Then we shall direct our attention to the urgent problems of marriage today.

Bibliography

N.B.—Footnotes in the text frequently refer to books listed in this bibliography. If only one work of a particular author is listed here, all that is given in the footnote is the author's name and the page reference of the book listed in this bibliography. If, on the other hand, two or more works by the same author are referred to, the short title is given in the footnote, so that it is clear which of the author's articles or books is meant. Only in cases where a point of detail is commented on does the footnote give the full reference. In cases where a book or an article is quoted or referred to outside the chapter or section in which it is listed in this bibliography, it is given as a full reference in the footnote, in order to avoid confusion.

General

WESTERMARK, E., *Histoire du mariage*, 3 pts., Paris (1934–   ).

1. *MARRIAGE IN THE GRECO-ROMAN AND THE ANCIENT WORLD*

Environmental Studies

CARCOPINO, J. E. J., *Daily Life in Ancient Rome: the people and city at the height of the Empire*, New Haven (1960).

FLACELIÈRE, R., *La vie quotidienne en Grèce au siècle de Périclès*, Paris (1959).

Marriage

CORBETT, E., *The Roman Law of Marriage*, London (1930).
DE COULANGES, FUSTEL, *La cité antique*, Paris (n.d.).
ERDMANN, W., *Die Ehe im alten Griechenland*, Munich (1933).
NIETZOLD, J., *Die Ehe im alten Aegypten zur ptolomäisch-römischen Zeit*, Leipzig (1913).
PAULY and WISSOWA, see especially "confarreatio," "coemptio," "contubernium," "sponsalia," etc. (See PW-*RKA* in list of abbreviations.)
SAMTER, E., *Familienfeste der Griechen und Römer*, Berlin (1901); *Geburt, Hochzeit und Tod*, Berlin (1911).
WAHRMUND, L., *Das Institut der Ehe im Altertum*, Weimar (1933).

2. SECULAR MARRIAGE AMONG THE WESTERN EUROPEAN TRIBES

BRANDELIONE, F., *Saggi sulla storia della celebrazione del matrimonio in Italia*, Milan (1906).
BEYERLE, F., *Die Gesetze der Longobarden*, Weimar (1947).
ECKHARDT, K., *Germanenrechte (Texte und Übersetzungen). Die Gesetze des Karolingerreiches*, Weimar (1934).
HOOPS, J., "Ehe, Verlobung," *Reallexikon der Germanischen Altertumskunde*, 3 pts., Strassburg (1911–16).
NECKEL, G., *Liebe und Ehe bei den vorchristlichen Germanen*, Leipzig and Berlin (1934).
PAPPE, H., *Methodische Strömungen in der ehegeschichtlichen Forschung*, Würzburg (1934).
RODECK, Fr., "Beiträge zur Geschichte des Eherechts deutscher Fürsten bis zur Durchführung des Tridentinums," *MBG*, pt. 26 (1910), pp. 20 ff.
VON SCHERIN, C., *Quellen zur Geschichte der Eheschliessung*, pt. 1, Bonn (1925); *Leges Saxonum und lex Thuringorum*, Hanover and Leipzig (1918).
ZALLINGER, O., *Die Eheschliessung in Nibelungenlied und in der Gudrun*, Vienna (1923); *Die Ringgaben bei der Heirat und das Zusammengeben im Mittelalterlichen Deutschen Recht*, Vienna (1931).
ZEUMER, K., "Geschichte der westgotischen Gesetzgebung," *NAADG*,

23 (1898), pp. 477–516; 24 (1899), pp. 39–122, 517–629; 26 (1901), pp. 91–148.

3. *THE CHURCH'S MARRIAGE LITURGY AND THE*
EARLY AND LATER SCHOLASTIC THEOLOGY
OF MARRIAGE

(in connection with Chapter 1)

ANDRIEU, M., *Les 'Ordines Romani,'* I (Spicil. Lov.), Louvain (1931); *Le Pontifical Romain au moyen-âge,* I, Vatican City (1938).

ANNÉ, L., "La conclusion du mariage dans la tradition et le droit de l'Eglise jusqu'au VIe siècle," *ETL,* 12 (1935), pp. 513–50.

ALVES PEREIRA, B., *La doctrine du mariage selon saint Augustin,* Paris (1930).

BRANDL, L., *Die Sexualethik des hl. Albertus Magnus,* Regensburg (1955).

BIONDI, B., *Il diritto romano cristiano,* Milano, 3 pts. (1954).

LE BRAS, G., "Mariage," *DTC,* pt. IX-2, cols. 2123–317.

BROWE, P., *Beiträge zur Sexualethik des Mittelalters,* Breslau (1932).

BÖHNER, P., "Die natürlichen Werte der Ehe nach dem hl. Bonaventura," *FS,* 24 (1937), pp. 1–17.

BINKOWSKI, J., "Die Ehegüter nach Duns Scotus," *WW,* 7 (1940), pp. 37–56.

CAMPBELL, G., "St Jerome's Attitude towards Marriage and Woman," *AER,* 143 (1960), pp. 310–20, 384–94.

DOOLEY, W., *Marriage according to St. Ambrose,* Washington (1948).

DAUVILLIER, J., *Le mariage dans le droit canonique de l'Eglise depuis le décret de Gratian (1140) jusqu'à la mort de Clément V (1314),* Paris (1933).

DAUDET, P., *Etudes sur l'histoire de la juridiction matrimoniale. Les origines carolingiennes de la compétence exclusive de l'Eglise,* Paris (1933).

DIDIER, J., "Le mariage de la sainte Vierge dans l'histoire de la théologie," *MRS,* 2, (1952), pp. 135–8.

DELHAYE, P., "Le dossier anti-matrimonial de l' 'Adversus Jovinianum' et son influence sur quelques écrits latins du XIIe siècle," *MS,* 13 (1952), pp. 65–86.

D'ERCOLE, G., "Il consenso degli sposi e la perpetuità del matrimonio nel diritto romano e nei Padri della Chiesa," *Studia et documenta historiae iuris*, 5 (1939), pp. 18–75.

ESMEIN, A., and GÉNESTAL, R., *Le mariage en droit canonique*, 2 pts., Paris (1929–35).

FAHRNER, I., *Geschichte der Ehescheidung im kanonischen Recht*, Freiburg i. Br. (1903).

FALK, F., *Die Ehe am Ausgang des Mittelalters*, Freiburg i. Br. (1908).

FOURNIER, P., and LE BRAS, G., *Histoire des collections canoniques en Occident depuis les Fausses Décrétales jusqu'à Gratian*, 2 pts., Paris (1931).

FRANSEN, P., "Ehescheidung bei Ehebruch," *Schk*, 28 (1954), pp. 536–60.

FREISEN, J., *Geschichte des Canonischen Eherechts bis zum Verfall der Glossenliteratur*, Tübingen (1892²).

FRIEDBERG, E., *Ehr und Eheschliessung im Mittelalter*, Berlin (1864); *Das Recht der Eheschliessung in seiner geschichtlichen Entwicklung*, Leipzig (1865).

FUCHS, J., *Die Sexualethik des hl. Thomas von Aquin*, Regensburg (1955).

GAUDEMET, J., "L'Apport de la Patristique latine au Décret de Gratian en matière de mariage," *St G* 2, (1951), pp. 48–81; "L'Eglise et la vie familiale," *L'Eglise dans l'Empire romain (IV-VIe siècle)*, pp. 515–61, ed. G. Le Bras, *Histoire du Droit et des Institutions de l'Eglise en Occident*, 3 pts., Paris (1958).

HINSCHIUS, P., *Decretales ps.-Isidorianae et Capitula Angilramni*, Leipzig (1863).

HUARD, J., "La liturgie nuptiale dans l'Eglise Romaine," *QLP*, 38 (1957), pp. 197–205.

JOYCE, GEORGE H., *Christian Marriage. An Historical and Doctrinal Study*, 2nd ed., New York and London, Sheed and Ward (1948).

JOUNEL, P., "La liturgie romaine du mariage," *MD*, 50 (1957), pp. 38–57.

LADOMERZKY, M., *Augustin, docteur du mariage chrétien*, Rome (1942).

LINDNER, D., *Der "usus matrimonii," Eine Untersuchung über seine sittliche Bewertung in der katholischen Moraltheologie alter und neuer Zeit*, Munich (1929).

MAYAUD, J., *L'indissolubilité du mariage. Étude historico-canonique*, Strasbourg (1952).

MOULARD, A., *Saint Jean Chrysostome. Le défenseur du mariage et l'apôtre de la virginité*, Paris (1923).

MÜLLER, M., *Die Lehre des hl. Augustinus von der Paradiesehe und ihre Auswirkung in der Sexualethik des 12. und 13. Jahrhunderts bis Thomas von Aquin*, Regensburg (1954).

NAZ, F., and LEROUGE, J., *La dispense "super matrimonium ratum et non consummatum,"* Paris (1940).

PETERS, J., *Die Ehe nach der Lehre des hl. Augustinus*, Paderborn (1918).

PORTMANN, H., *Wesen und Unauflösigkeit der Ehe in der kirchlichen Wissenschaft und Gesetzgebung des XI. Jahrhunderts*, Emsdetten (1938).

PREISKER, H., *Christentum und Ehe in den ersten drei Jahrhunderten*, Berlin (1927).

REUTER, A., *S. Aurelii Augustini doctrina de bonis matrimonii*, Rome (1942).

RITZER, K. (see *FRBE* in list of abbreviations).

RONDET, *Introduction à l'étude de la théologie du mariage*, Paris (1960).

SCHAHL, C., *La doctrine des fins du mariage dans la théologie scolastique*, Paris (1948).

SMITH, E., *Papal Enforcement of Mediaeval Marriage Law*, London (1940).

TURMEL, J., *Histoire des dogmes*, pt. 5, Paris (1936), pp. 529–69.

VEIT, A., *Volksfrommes Brauchtum und Kirche im Mittelalter*, Freiburg i. Br. (1936).

VEREECKE, L., "Mariage et sexualité au déclin du Moyen Age," *VS-S*, 57 (1961), pp. 199–225.

WARREN, F., *The Liturgy and Ritual of the Ante-Nicene Church*, London (1912).

ZIEGLER, J., *Die Ehelehre der Pänitential-Summen von 1200–1350*, Regensburg (1956).

4. SECULAR MARRIAGE RITES AND THE LITURGY OF MARRIAGE IN THE EAST

(in connection with Chapter 2)

DALMAIS, J., "La liturgie du mariage dans les Eglises orientales," *MD*, n. 50 (1957), pp. 58–69.

DAUVILLIER, J., and DE CLERCQ, C., *Le mariage en droit canonique oriental*, Paris (1936).

JUGIE, M., "Mariage dans les Eglises Orientales," *DTC*, pt. IX-2, cols. 2317–31.

RAES, A., *Le mariage, sa célébration et sa spiritualité dans les Eglises d'Orient*, Chevetogne (1958); "Le consentement dans les Rites Orientaux," *EL*, 47 (1933), pp. 34–47, 126–40, 249–99, 431–45; 48 (1934), pp. 80–94, 310–18.

ZHISMAN, J., *Das Eherecht der Orientalischen Kirch*, Vienna (1864).

5. THE COUNCIL OF TRENT AND THE PROCESS OF SECULARISATION

(in connection with Chapter 3)

FRANSEN, P., "Ehescheidung im Falle vom Ehebruch," *Schk*, 27 (1952), pp. 526–56; 29 (1954), pp. 536–60; "Echtscheiding na echtbruek van een der gehuwden," *Bijd*, 14 (1953), pp. 363–87.

JEDIN, HUBERT, *Das Konzil von Trient*, Rome (1948) also *A History of the Council of Trent*, Milwaukee (1957).

CASTAN LACOMA, L., "El origen del capitulo 'Tametsi' del Concilio de Trento contro los matrimonios clandestinos," *REDC*, 14 (1959), pp. 613–66.

LATREILLE, A., "L'Eglise et la laïcité," *La laïcité*, Paris (1960), pp. 59–98.

MUELLER, F., *The Inseparability of the Marriage Contract and the Sacrament according to the 17th Century Authors*, Rome (1958).

Index of Sources

Greek Fathers

ATHENAGORAS
Legatio pro christianis, c. 33   244n., 251n.
CHRYSOSTOM
De verbis illis Apostoli "propter fornicationem"   348, 349n.
Epist. 1 ad Cor., 19, 3   283n.
Hom. 9 in 1 Tim.   248n., 346
Hom. 12, n. 7   349n.
Homilia 16, ad populum Antiochenum   244n.
In Gen. Hom., 48, n. 6   346n.
CLEMENT OF ALEXANDRIA
Stromata 4, 20   251
CYRIL OF ALEXANDRIA
Comm. in Johannem, 2, 2   280n.
EPIPHANIUS
Adv. Haer., 51, 30   280n.
GREGORY NAZIANZEN
Epist. 193   347
       231   251, 346n.
       232   346n.
Orat. 40, 18 in S. Baptisma   248n.
IGNATIUS OF ANTIOCH
Ad Polycarpum, 5, 2   245
JOHN DAMASCENE
De fide orthodoxa, 4, 24   280n.
ORIGEN
Comm. in Matt., 14, 16   281
In 1 Cor.   281n.
SERAPION OF THMUIS
Constitutiones Apostolorum, c. 8   346n.
Euchologion   346n.

THEODORE STUDITES
  Epist. I, 50   349
         II, 191   349

                          Latin Fathers

AMBROSE
  De Abraham, 1, 7   281
  De virginibus, 1, 10, 57   308
  De virginitate, 5   304
  Epist. 19 *ad Vigilium*   261*n.*
  Epist. 19, 7   279*n.*, 304
  Exhort. virginitatis, 7   308
AMBROSIASTER
  Comm. in Epist.
    1 *ad Cor.*, 7, 40   251, 252, 261*n.*
            11, 3–25   309*n.*
    ad Col., 3, 8–11   309*n.*
    1 *ad Tim.*, 2, 13–15   309*n.*
            3, 12–13   261
  Liber quaestionum novi et veteris Testamenti   250, 259
AUGUSTINE
  Contra Julianum, 3, 57   285
                   5, 12   285
                   5, 16   285–9
  De bono coniugali, 21   286
                     24   285
                     32   286, 286*n.*
  De coniugiis adulterinis, 2, 5   286
  De consensu evang., II, 1, 1   289
  De nuptiis et conc., I, 11   285
                      I, 11, *n.* 13   285
                      I, 11, 12   282
                      I, 11, 13   289*n.*
  De pecc. originali, 34, 39   285
                     37, 42   285
  Epist. 252   249
         254   249
         255   249
  Sermo 9, 11, 18   242*n.*, 248
        51, 13, 22   242*n.*, 248
        332, 4   248
CYPRIAN
  Epist., 1, 1, 2   249

HIPPOLYTUS
   Philosophoumena, 9, 12, 24   247
ISIDORE OF SEVILLE
   De Eccles. Officiis, 2, 20   265
   Etymol., 9, 7   289
        9, 8, 19   291, 291*n.*
JEROME
   Epist. 130, 2   308*n.*
TERTULLIAN
   Ad uxorem, 2, 2   252f.
        2, 3   242*n.*
        2, 7   280
        2, 8–9   246*n.*
        2, 9   252, 280
   Apologeticum, 6, 4–6   240
        42   244
   De corona, 13   252
   De idol., 16   247*n.*
   De monogamia, 11, 1   246*n.*
   De virginibus velandis, 12, 1   242*n.*, 247
   De pudicitia, 4   246*n.*
ANON.
   Epistola ad Diognetem   245

Theologians

ABELARD
   Sermo in Annuntiatione B.V.M.   319
STEPHANUS AFER
   Vita S. Amatoris de Auxerre   263
ALBERT THE GREAT
   In IV Sent.
      d. 1, q. 1, a. 3   315
      d. 1, q. 1, a. 14   315
      d. 26, a. 14   337
      d. 27, a. 6   302, 359
ALEXANDER OF HALES
   Glossa in Sent.
      IV, d. 26, c. 1   332–5
      IV, d. 26, c. 7   335*n.*
ANSELM OF LAON
   Enarr. in Matt., 19   319, 330*n.*
   Sententiae Tract. de sacramentis   319

PSEUDO-ANSELM (ROGER OF CAEN)
  De contemptu mundi   313
  De nuptiis consang.   313
AQUINAS
  In VII Ethic., 12   339n.
  In II Sent.
    d. 20, q. 1, a. 1   340n.
    d. 20, q. 2, a. 1   340n.
  In IV Sent.
    d. 1, q. 1, a. 3   315
    d. 1, q. 1, a. 3, ad 5   359
    d. 2, q. 1, a. 1, sol. 2   337
    d. 7, q. 1, a. 2   326
    d. 25, q. 2, a. 1 ad 2   315
    d. 26, q. 2, a. 1 ad 1   315
    d. 26, q. 2, a. 1 ad 3 and 4   326
    d. 26, q. 2, a. 1 ad 4 and 5   326n.
    d. 26, q. 2, a. 2   339, 339n.
    d. 26, q. 2, a. 2 ad 1 and 2   326
    d. 26, q. 2, a. 2, sol. 2c   326
    d. 26, q. 2, a. 3   337
    d. 26, q. 2, a. 3 ad 1   342n.
    d. 26, q. 2, a. 3, obj. 2   332
    d. 26, q. 2, a. 3 ad 3   342n.
    d. 26, q. 2, a. 4   327
    d. 27, q. 1, a. 2, sol. 1   341
    d. 27, q. 1, a. 2, sol. 1c   327
    d. 27, q. 1, a. 2, sol. 1 ad 2   326, 327
    d. 27, q. 1, a. 2, sol. 2   302n.
    d. 27, q. 1, a. 3, sol. 2 ad 1   326, 327
    d. 27, q. 1, a. 3, sol. 2 ad 2   327
    d. 27, q. 1, a. 4 ad 2 (see obj. 2)   327, 332
    d. 28, q. un., a. 3 ad 2 and 3   315–7
    d. 28, q. un., a. 4   88n., 326
    d. 28, q. un., a. 4c   327
    d. 31, q. 1, a. 2 ad 2   302n., 341
    d. 31, q. 1, a. 2 ad 7   331, 342n.
    d. 34, q. 1, a. 1 ad 4   339n., 341–3
    d. 36, q. 1, a. 5   341–3
    d. 38   300n.
    d. 42, q. 3, a. 2 ad 2   315
  In 1 ad Cor.
    7, 1, lect. 1   326
    7, 1, lect. 1, *n*. 314   340
    7, 1, lect. 1, *n*. 316   341n.

AQUINAS (*cont.*)
  In ad Eph. 5, lect. 10   326
  Summa Contra Gentiles
    III, 123   342–3
    IV, 78   337, 339*n.*, 342–3
  Summa Theologiae
    I, q. 92, a. 1   340*n.*
    I, q. 92, a. 1 ad 1   340*n.*
    I, q. 92, a. 1 ad 2   339*n.*
    I, q. 98, a. 2   340*n.*
    I–II, q. 110, a. 1   341*n.*
    II–II, q. 100, a. 2 ad 6   337–8
    III, q. 62, a. 1   337
    III, q. 65, a. 1   337, 339*n.*
ARNOBIUS
  Adv. Gentes, 1, 2   244
ATTO OF VERCELLI
  Epist. ad Azonem   276*n.*
AVITUS OF VIENNE
  Epist. 55   263, 310*n.*
BELLARMINE
  Disputationes de controversiis christianae fidei:
    pt. 3, p. 727, *n.* 7   370
    pt. 3, p. 743, *n.* 6, 9   370
    pt. 3, p. 777, *n.* 17   370
    c. 6, pt. 3, p. 741, *n.* 18   370
    c. 21, pt. 3, p. 781, *n.* 39   370
    c. 21, pt. 3, p. 781, *n.* 42–4   371
BERNARD
  Sermo 66, *n.* 3–5   313
BILLUART
  De matrimonio, disp. 1, a. 5, *petes* 5   372*n.*
BONAVENTURE
  In IV Sent.
    d. 26, a. 1, q. 2 ad 4   331
    d. 26, a. 2, q. 2 ad 2   336
    d. 26, a. 2, q. 2 concl.   336, 336*n.*
    d. 26, a. 2, q. c and ad 4   315
    d. 26, a. 2, q. 3   325
    d. 28, a. un., q. 3 and 5   302*n.*
    d. 28, a. un., q. 6   298
    d. 29, a. 1, q. 3   302*n.*
    d. 30, a. un.   315
MELCHIOR CANO
  De locis theologicis, VIII, c. 5   315, 372

PETER CANTOR
   Verbum Abbreviatum   329
CYPRIAN OF TOULON
   Vita sancti Caesarii, I, 59   261
DURAND OF ST. POUCAIN
   In IV Sent., d. 26, q. 3   338n.
DURAND OF TROARN
   Liber de Corpore et Sanguine Domini, 5, 11   328
ERASMUS
   Christiani matrimonii institutio (*Opera Omnia*, Basle)
     pt. 5, p. 519   338
ESTIUS
   In IV Sent., d. 26   373
EUSEBIUS
   Hist. Eccl., 6, 40, 6   248
FAUSTUS OF BYZANTIUM, 5, 31   357n.
MAG. HERMANNUS
   Epitome theologiae christianae, c. 28   329
   Epitome 31   333
PSEUDO-HILDEBERT
   De ordinatione clericorum, 7   314
HINCMAR
   De Divorcio Lotharii et Teutbergae   270, 271n., 275
     Resp. 5   270, 271
     Resp. 11   271n.
     Interr. XIII   289n.
   De nuptiis Stephani et filiae Regimundi comitis   270, 275
     Ep. 22   271, 271n., 289n.
   De raptu   271
   Epist. ad Nicolaum   270
   Epist. 2 ad Nicolaum   271, 271n.
   Opera Hincmari   266
HONORIUS AUGUSTODUNENIS
   Elucidarium II, 16   319
HUGH OF AMIENS
   Contra Haereticos, III, 4   314
HUGH OF ST. VICTOR
   De Beatae Mariae virginitate   320, 322
   De sacramentis christianae fidei   290n.
     II, 11   322
     II, 11, 5   295, 299
     II, 11, 6   300n.
     II, 11, 8   320, 333
     II, 11, 13   320
     XII, 1   322

PSEUDO-ISIDORE
  Decretale Callixti II, c. 16   246*n.*
  Decretum (false decretal attributed to Pope Evaristus)   269, 300
LACTANTIUS
  Epitome 61   285
PETER LOMBARD
  Epitome   290*n.*
  IV Sent.
    d. 26, c. 6   293, 324
    d. 27, a. 3   299
    d. 27, c. 2, 3   293, 295
    d. 27, c. 4   293
    d. 27, c. 7   293
    d. 27, c. 8   324*n.*
    d. 27, c. 9   290*n.*
    d. 28   300*n.*
    d. 28, c. 2   293, 358
    d. 28, c. 3   293, 294*n.*
    d. 28, c. 4   324*n.*
    d. 31, c. 1, 2   293
    d. 31, c. 1, 3   294*n.*
J. LAUNOY
  De regia in matrimonium potestate, I, 4, 3, p. 749   374*n.*
MODESTINUS
  Digesta 32, 2, 1   291*n.*
PAULINUS OF NOLA
  Carmen XXV   261
    227–8   304
POSSIDIUS
  Vita S. Augustini, 27, 4–5   248
REGINO OF PRUMM
  De ecclesiastica disciplina   276*n.*
RUFINUS
  Summa Decretorum, Causa 32, q. 2 (c. 1158)   332*n.*
T. SANCHEZ
  De sacramentis in genere, disp. 138, c. 5, *n.* 63–4   372
  Disputationes de sancto matrimonii sacramento:
    lib. 7, disp. 3, *n.* 2   371
    lib. 3, disp. 4, *n.* 4   371
    lib. 7, disp. 3, *n.* 2   371
    lib. 7, disp. 3, *n.* 7   372
DUNS SCOTUS
  In IV Sent.,
    d. 26, q. un., *n.* 13   337*n.*

DUNS SCOTUS (*cont.*)
  Opus Oxoniense
    d. 6, q. un., *n.* 8   302
    d. 26, q. 1, 17   302
    IV, d. 26, q. un., *n.* 15   316
  Reportata Parisiensia
    d. 42, *n.* 24   316*n.*
    IV, d. 28, q. un., *n.* 24   358
SYLVIUS
  In Suppl., q. 42, a. 1, ql. 1   373
THEODORE OF CANTERBURY
  Canones sancti Theodori   267
TOLETUS
  Instructio sacerdotum, 7, 2   373
TOURNELY
  De Matrimonio, q. 5, a. 2   373
WILLIAM OF AUVERGNE
  Tractatus de sacramento matrimonii, VI, 9   315, 334
WILLIAM OF AUXERRE
  Summa Aurea   334

Councils and Synods

COUNCIL OF CARTHAGE
  Codex can. Ecclesiae Afric.   272*n.*
COUNCIL OF FLORENCE
  Decretum pro Armenis   358–9
LATERAN COUNCIL   357
SECOND LATERAN COUNCIL
  can. 23   313*n.*
FOURTH LATERAN COUNCIL
  can. 51   297*n.*, 364*n.*
COUNCIL OF LYONS
  Confession of Faith of Pope Gregory X   358
COUNCIL OF TRENT   358–63
  can. 7   359
  can. 10, 12   360
    Decree *Tametsi*   363–4
      CT, pt. 3, 578, 7   360
      CT, pt. 6, 535, 26   360
      CT, pt. 9, 409–10   360
      CT, pt. 9, 420, 21   360
      CT, pt. 9, 680, 18   360
      CT, pt. 9, 721, 4   360

COUNCIL OF TRENT (*cont.*)
    CT, pt. 9, col. 643, 655   363
    CT, pt. 9, p. 640; pp. 642–80   365
    CT, pt. 9, p. 642   366
    CT, pt. 9, p. 656   366
    CT, pt. 9, pp. 673, 660–1, 663–4   362
    CT, pt. 9, pp. 760–65   366
    CT, pt. 9, pp. 888–90, 966–71   366
SYNOD OF THE BAVARIAN CHURCH
  can. 12   267
SYNOD OF ELVIRA
  can. 54   244, 262
SYNOD OF GANGRA   354*n.*
SYNOD OF LAODICEA
  can. 1   246
  can. 52   247*n.*
  can. 53   247*n.*
  can. 54   251
  can. 58   251
SYNOD OF MAGDEBURG   364*n.*
SYNOD OR NEOCAESAREA
  can. 7   349*n.*
SYNOD OF ORLEANS   264
SYNOD OF PAVIA   262
  can. 10   262*n.*
SYNOD OF PISTOIA   375
SYNOD OF SAHAVIPAN
  can. 3   354
SYNOD OF TREVES
  can. 5   364*n.*
SYNOD OF TRULLO
  can. 2, *Responsa canonica, n.* 11   351, 353
SYNOD OF VERNEUIL   264*n.*, 267
SYNOD OF VERONA (local)   357

Canon Law Collections

ALEXANDER III   321, 324
  c. 3, C. I, IV, 4   293, 296
  c. 3, X, IV, 4   293, 296
    Codex Iuris Canonici
    can. 1016   377
    can. 1094   368

ALEXANDER III (*cont.*)
    can. 1099, par. I   368
    can. 1960   377
    Constitutio Apostolica   247
    Corpus Iuris Canonici
    can. 3, X, 4, 3   365
    can. 28, X, 4, I   365
    Didascalia Apost.
    can. 17   249n.
    Syrian Didascalia
    can. 22   249, 345
GRATIAN
    Consuetudo Ecclesiae Romanae   293, 293n.
    Decretum Gratiani   270
    Causa XXVII, q. 2, dictum in c. 39   331
    Causa XXXII, q. 1, dictum in c. 10   330
    c. 17, Causa XXVIII, q. 1   299
    dictum c. 27, q. 1, 2, c. 35–39   293, 293n.
    c. 27, q. 2   293, 293n.
    c. 27, q. 2, c. 34   293n.
    ad c. 28   293n.
    c. 32, q. 7   293n.
    post c. 34, c. 18–26   293n.
GREGORY IX
    Compilatio Decretalium
    c. 3, C. I, 4, 16   293n.
    c. 7, X, III, 32   296
    I, 2   295
    I, 4, 4   300n.
    I, c. 2   296
    I, c. 4   295, 297
    I, c. 7   296
    I, c. 5   296n.
    II, c. 4   297
    III, 1   297
    III, 2   297
    III, 28   296
    IV, 3   294
    IV, 4   296n.
    IV, 6   295
    V, 3   296
    VI, 6, 8   297
    X, c. 4   294, 297
    XVI, 2   294

Papal Decrees and Letters

BENEDICT IV
  Declaration · 367
CALLIXTUS
  Decretum (false) 2, 16 · 270
EUTYCHANIUS
  Exhortatio ad presbyteros · 246
EVARISTUS
  Epist. Papae Evaristi, c. 2 · 246
HORMISDAS
  Decretum, 2 · 273
  Decretum, 9, 3 · 255
INNOCENT I
  Epist. ad Vitricium, c. 4–6 · 255*n.*, 262
LEO I
  Epist. ad Rusticum · 263*n.*, 273*n.*
  Epist. 167 *ad Rusticum* · 273
LEO VI (the Wise)
  Novelle 74 · 351–2
LEO XIII
  Arcanum divinae sapientiae · 377
NICHOLAS I
  Epist. ad consulta Bulgarorum, c. 3 · 273*n.*, 350
  Responsum ad Bulgaros, c. 3 · 256, 266, 388
PIUS VI · 375
  Letter to the bishop of Mottola (Naples) · 375
PIUS IX
  Acerbissimum vobiscum · 377
  Syllabus · 377
PIUS X
  Decree *Ne Temere* · 368
    can. 1094–5 · 368
    can. 1096 · 368
  AAS, 39 (1906), 88*ff*. · 367
  AAS, 40 (1907), 525*ff*. · 367–8
PIUS XI
  AAS, 23 (1931), 388 · 368
  AAS, 28 (1936), 313*ff*. · 368
PIUS XII
  AAS, 37 (1945), 149 · 369
SIRICIUS · 255*n.*
  Epist. ad episcopos Gallos · 308–9
  Epist. ad Himerium · 255, 265, 308
    c. 8 · 265
  Epist. 36 · 281*n.*

Miscellaneous Sources

Gregorianum   306–12
Leonianum   306, 310, 358
Liber Ordinum (Spanish)   304, 305*n.*
   Opus imperfectum in Matt. 32, 9   350*n.*
EMPEROR ALEXIUS
  The Golden Bull, *Novelle* 24   352–3
EMPEROR BASIL I
  Epanagoge, tit. 16, 1   351
  Procheiros Nomos, tit. 4   351
EMPEROR JUSTINIAN
  Codex Justiniani
    IX, 4   236
    IX, 32   236
  Digesta
    XVII, 30   291
    XXIII, 2   236
    XXXV, 15   241
EMPEROR LEO III
  Ekloge, tit. 2, 3   351
       tit. 2, 8   351
EMPEROR THEODOSIUS
  Codex Theodosianus, Lib. III, tit. 7, lex 3   241
PATRIARCH CATHOLICOS SAHAK
  can. 26   355*n.*
CHARLEMAGNE
  Capitularia, miss. gen. c. 35   365
AESCHYLUS
  Khoephoroi, 264   236
CICERO
  Topica, 14   242*n.*
DEMOSTHENES
  Kata Neairas, 122   236
  Pros Makartaton, 51   238
PLATO
  Nomoi, 5   237
PLAUTUS
  Mercator, 5, 1, 5   237
SUETONIUS
  De viris illustribus, 5, 29   242*n.*